63

2—

Hist.

THE EVOLUTION OF
ENGLAND

THE EVOLUTION OF
ENGLAND

*A COMMENTARY ON
THE FACTS*

BY

JAMES A. WILLIAMSON

SECOND EDITION

OXFORD
AT THE CLARENDON PRESS

OXFORD UNIVERSITY PRESS
AMEN HOUSE, E.C. 4
London Edinburgh Glasgow New York
Toronto Melbourne Cape Town Bombay
Calcutta Madras
GEOFFREY CUMBERLEGE
PUBLISHER TO THE UNIVERSITY

FIRST PUBLISHED, FEBRUARY 1931
REPRINTED, OCTOBER 1931, 1934
SECOND EDITION, FEBRUARY 1944
REPRINTED, 1945, 1946

PRINTED IN GREAT BRITAIN

PREFACE

THE reader who is not a professed student of history is often shy of text-books which give him an array of dates and details without indicating the relative significance of the events recorded. It is for this reader that the present volume is designed. It is not a text-book, since it omits many things with which a text-book of its size would be obliged to deal. Instead, it selects those transactions which best illuminate the central theme, the development of the English community and of the country it inhabits. For such a purpose, to cite an example, the Wars of the Roses are important because they helped to eliminate the feudal aristocracy and to prepare the ground for Tudor rule and the growth of a national spirit; but the general character of the wars demands our attention rather than the details of the battles.

Throughout the book I have tried to give due prominence to the geographical factors—in the earlier periods, to the physical geography of England as it was, and in the later, to the English consequences of the discovery of the outer world by Europeans. The evolution of a nation cannot be explained on political lines alone. The stage is important as well as the company, and each has its reactions upon the other. Geographic circumstance, economic motive, and political action, are an ever-recurring sequence. Politics, however, are the major interest, not only the politics that are shaped by economic motive, but those also that spring from religious beliefs and the general spirit of the age. To describe and account for movements of the spirit is generally more easy than convincing, but it is at least possible to register their results as shown in laws and institutions and acknowledged principles of conduct.

A commentary of the kind here attempted involves the expression of opinions, and few opinions can hope to please everybody. It is possible to be provocative in discussing the sixteenth century, and almost impossible to avoid it in writing of the twentieth. In dealing with the more recent period the expression of party views is inevitable. The reader will find, I believe, that mine are not drawn exclusively from the tenets of any one party, and I can claim, for the best of reasons, that party allegiance has not affected my version of the modern tendencies of English history.

J. A. WILLIAMSON.

PREFACE TO THE SECOND EDITION

CORRECTIONS for which my thanks are due to a number of critics and correspondents were introduced in reprints of the First edition. In the present edition the last sections have been re-written and the subject-matter continued to the outbreak of the second world war.

J. A. W.

1943

CONTENTS

CONTENTS

LIST OF MAPS

LIST OF SOVEREIGNS IN ENGLAND
FROM EGBERT TO GEORGE VI

802–39	EGBERT	1399–1413	HENRY IV
839–58	ETHELWULF	1413–22	HENRY V
858–60	ETHELBALD	1422–61	HENRY VI
860–66	ETHELBERT	1461–83	EDWARD IV
866–71	ETHELRED I	1483	EDWARD V
871–900	ALFRED	1483–85	RICHARD III
900–25	EDWARD THE ELDER	1485–1509	HENRY VII
925–40	ATHELSTAN	1509–47	HENRY VIII
940–46	EDMUND THE MAGNI-FICENT	1547–53	EDWARD VI
		1553–58	MARY I
946–55	EDRED	1558–1603	ELIZABETH
955–59	EDWY	1603–25	JAMES I
959–75	EDGAR THE PEACEFUL	1625–49	CHARLES I
975–78	EDWARD THE MARTYR	1649–53	THE COMMONWEALTH
978–1013	ETHELRED THE REDE-LESS	1653–58	OLIVER CROMWELL, Lord Protector
1013–14	SWEYN	1658–59	RICHARD CROMWELL, Lord Protector
1014–35	CANUTE		
1035–40	HAROLD I	1659–60	IRREGULAR AUTHORI-TIES
1040–42	HARDICANUTE		
1042–66	EDWARD THE CONFES-SOR	1660–85	CHARLES II
		1685–88	JAMES II
1066	HAROLD II	1689–1702	WILLIAM III (and MARY II to 1694)
1066–87	WILLIAM I		
1087–1100	WILLIAM II		
1100–35	HENRY I	1702–14	ANNE
1135–54	STEPHEN	1714–27	GEORGE I
1154–89	HENRY II	1727–60	GEORGE II
1189–99	RICHARD I	1760–1820	GEORGE III
1199–1216	JOHN	1820–30	GEORGE IV
1216–72	HENRY III	1830–37	WILLIAM IV
1272–1307	EDWARD I	1837–1901	VICTORIA
1307–27	EDWARD II	1901–10	EDWARD VII
1327–77	EDWARD III	1910–36	GEORGE V
1377–99	RICHARD II	1936	EDWARD VIII
		1936–	GEORGE VI

LIST OF BRITISH MINISTRIES
FROM 1721 TO 1940

(The ministries are described by the name of the person generally agreed to have been the leading member.)

1721–42	SIR ROBERT WALPOLE
1742–44	LORD CARTERET
1744–54	HENRY PELHAM
1754–56	DUKE OF NEWCASTLE
1756–57	WILLIAM PITT, THE ELDER (with Duke of Devonshire)
1757–61	WILLIAM PITT, THE ELDER (with Duke of Newcastle)
1762–63	EARL OF BUTE
1763–65	GEORGE GRENVILLE
1765–66	MARQUIS OF ROCKINGHAM
1766–68	WILLIAM PITT, THE ELDER (now Earl of Chatham)
1768–70	DUKE OF GRAFTON
1770–82	LORD NORTH
1782	MARQUIS OF ROCKINGHAM
1782–83	EARL OF SHELBURNE
1783	CHARLES JAMES FOX and LORD NORTH
1783–1801	WILLIAM PITT, THE YOUNGER
1801–04	HENRY ADDINGTON
1804–06	WILLIAM PITT, THE YOUNGER
1806	CHARLES JAMES FOX
1807–09	DUKE OF PORTLAND
1809–12	SPENCER PERCEVAL
1812–27	EARL OF LIVERPOOL
1827	GEORGE CANNING
1827–28	LORD GODERICH
1828–30	DUKE OF WELLINGTON
1830–34	EARL GREY
1834	LORD MELBOURNE
1834–35	SIR ROBERT PEEL
1835–41	LORD MELBOURNE
1841–46	SIR ROBERT PEEL
1846–52	LORD JOHN RUSSELL
1852	EARL OF DERBY
1852–55	EARL OF ABERDEEN
1855–58	LORD PALMERSTON
1858–59	EARL OF DERBY
1859–65	LORD PALMERSTON
1865–66	EARL RUSSELL (formerly Lord J. Russell)
1866–68	EARL OF DERBY
1868	BENJAMIN DISRAELI
1868–74	W. E. GLADSTONE
1874–80	BENJAMIN DISRAELI (from 1876 Earl of Beaconsfield)
1880–85	W. E. GLADSTONE

1885–86	MARQUIS OF SALISBURY
1886	W. E. GLADSTONE
1886–92	MARQUIS OF SALISBURY
1892–94	W. E. GLADSTONE
1894–95	EARL OF ROSEBERY
1895–1902	MARQUIS OF SALISBURY
1902–05	A. J. BALFOUR
1905–08	SIR HENRY CAMPBELL-BANNERMAN
1908–16	H. H. ASQUITH
1916–22	D. LLOYD GEORGE
1922–3	A. BONAR LAW
1923–4	STANLEY BALDWIN
1924	J. RAMSAY MACDONALD
1924–29	STANLEY BALDWIN
1929–31	J. RAMSAY MACDONALD
1931–5	J. RAMSAY MACDONALD
1935–7	STANLEY BALDWIN
1937–40	NEVILLE CHAMBERLAIN
1940–	WINSTON CHURCHILL

I

ROMAN BRITAIN

I. THE LAND OF BRITAIN

IT is not easy for us who know only the modern face of England to form an idea of its aspect in the days when history began. Yet it is needful to do so if we are to understand the meaning of that history, to gain an ordered view of the vast design of which our own lives form but a tiny incident. For the land and its waters are the stage upon which the countless players enact the long drama, its opening scenes dimly visible through the mists of the past, its final movements unknowable behind the curtain of time to come. That the people have moulded the land is obvious enough—they are seen doing it more energetically in our generation than they have ever done before; but that the land has moulded the people is equally true, although it is a truth needing deeper thought for its appreciation.

In a distant pre-historic age the land of Britain was part of the continent of Europe, joined southward to the soil of present France and eastward by a great flat plain to Germany. The Channel was then but a gulf stretching inwards no farther perhaps than the Isle of Wight. The Thames flowed on through the now vanished eastern plain until it met the Rhine, and together they sought the ocean somewhere north of what is now the Dogger Bank. The westward face of the land presented its cliffs to the Atlantic storms as it still does. But few of them can have been the cliffs we see to-day, for waves and frosts have gnawed them unceasingly, and all cliff-coasts have given ground slowly but surely to the sea.

From this beginning—if we like to call it so, for in limitless time we must choose some starting-point—Nature changed Britain into an island. The level sank, the northern sea crept over the plain between Britain and Denmark, and the Channel bored eastwards until its waters met those of the new North Sea in the Straits of Dover. The whole process was so slow that no pre-historic savage in his single lifetime could realize that it was taking place. Yet the final moment, when some terrific tempest burst through the last land-ridge between Britain and the

B

Continent, must have struck the imagination of the men who witnessed it, although they could not have conceived how great a day it was to prove in the history of the world. For the breach was never closed, although for years, perhaps centuries, the pass may have been dry at low water. Then the scouring tides deepened it, and the island was fairly launched upon its ocean.

The new Britain was in general a slightly tilted plane. Its eastern shores shelved gently up from the waters' edge, and the height of the ground rose steadily towards the west and north. This is to speak of broad averages, for in the east the Yorkshire moors and the Kentish Downs formed local exceptions, as did the low lying Cheshire and Lancashire plain and Severn basin in the west. But roughly it is true that Britain presented its most approachable and habitable side to the Continent and not to the Atlantic, and this made easier the transit of many waves of invaders, which came over one after another until naval defence changed the narrow seas from a highway into an obstacle for those who would possess the land. Yet another feature of the making of the island had a significance for its future inhabitants. Its surrounding waters, covering submerged land in the south and east and eroded land in the west, were everywhere comparatively shallow. Fishing on the bottom was thus possible, and all through history it has provided an important food-supply and an occupation which has moulded the character of the coast population. This appears so obvious that we are apt to take it as inevitable; but in many parts of the world the conditions are different, and there are peoples who have lived close to the sea and yet have had little business on its waters.

Since the early history of the island is largely a history of invasions, it will be useful to survey its coasts from the invaders' point of view. The invasion period covers many centuries, a much longer time, in fact, than the period of successful defence in which we now live. But in those early days man had little power to modify the face of Nature, and the changes made by Nature herself were so slow as to be measurable by thousands rather than by hundreds of years. The following description of the coastline may thus be taken as approximately true from the time of the primitive Britons to that of William the Conqueror.

From the Firth of Forth down to Flamborough Head the east coast formed the edge of a firm, undulating country which rose sharply to the heights of the Pennine Chain. Much of this coast was bordered by cliffs, and there can be little doubt that the shoreline has moved inward considerably since the North Sea overflowed the prehistoric plain. In river-mouths and other gaps in the cliffs invaders would have found landing-places. But there were not many such spots, and it must have been easy for the natives to defend them. South of Flamborough Head the level of the land drops almost to that of the sea. Here, on either side of the Humber mouth, was a waterlogged area, great stretches of it covered by high tides but exposed as wet mudbanks at low water. Through the midst of it the Humber estuary pushed its way far inland and then opened out into a vast and dismal swamp, from whose western side the Forest of Elmet ran up to the slopes of the Pennine hills. Until much later times, when the hand of man had effected some improvement, the estuary, the swamp, and the forest formed a barrier to communication between the midlands and the north, a fact which had large consequences to the history of northern England.

South of the Humber the coast of modern Lincolnshire presented the same marshy aspect down to the Wash, where the Humber conditions were repeated on a larger scale. The Wash bit far into the land, merging imperceptibly into the Fens, so that it was hardly possible to decide where sea ended and land began. The Fens, in fact, in their undrained condition, had no definite coastline which could have been drawn upon a map. All that a voyager could have seen as he sailed in from the open sea was that the mudbanks grew more extensive and that some of them rose above the level of all but exceptional floods. The water, he would have found too, became less salt as he pushed inland. At some point where the sea-tides failed it became entirely fresh, since the inner fens were formed by a dozen sluggish rivers flowing out of the firmer ground beyond. Fish and fowl abounded in this vast expanse, but otherwise it had little attraction for the incoming colonist. For the plundering raider it had its good points. The stagnant channels would float his vessels into the heart of the land, and on many an island in the swamps he could form camps in which to rest from fighting and collect his booty undisturbed.

East of the Wash the curve of the Norfolk coast offered firmer landing-places and an area of dry, habitable land behind them.

BRITAIN AT THE DAWN OF HISTORY

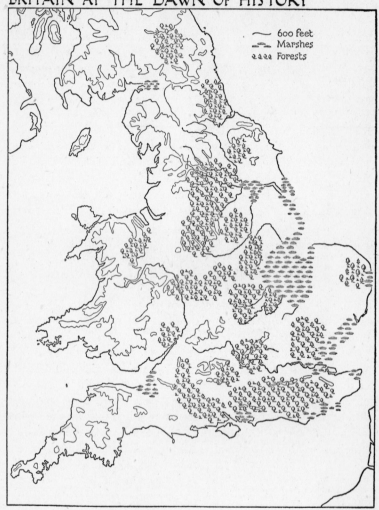

600 feet
Marshes
Forests

Soon, however, the shoreline broke down into another fen region, of which the Broads remain, reduced and regulated by the hand of man, to this day. South of them, the Suffolk shore continued drier and more definite for a space, projecting farther out to sea than it now does. Then, as the Essex coast drew towards the estuary of the Thames, another marsh system began, half land, half water, extending on the northern side of the river right up to the spot where London was destined to arise. South of the Thames, and round the Forelands, there was the same alternation of marsh and cliff; marsh in the Medway estuary, low soft cliffs along Sheppey and north Kent, marsh where the Stour ran up to Canterbury, clear water in the Wantsum between the mainland and the Isle of Thanet, another marsh by Deal, then high cliffs for a few miles on either side of Dover.

Here the east coast ended and the south began, first with over twenty miles of tidal swamps from the cliffs of Folkestone to those of Hastings. Shingle beaches and low islands divided the marshes from the open sea. One such beach has grown ever broader through the centuries until it has become the promontory of Dungeness, a large cape, but comparatively new; Caesar in his day would have looked for it in vain. One such island bore in medieval times the first town named Winchelsea, until town and island were engulfed by the sea in the thirteenth century. Few parts of our coast have undergone greater changes than has this. Westward of this great marsh lay a few miles of cliff, in two clefts of which the successive ports of Hastings were afterwards to arise. The Hastings area was in primeval times a peninsula bordered on either side by inundated marshlands, and connected with the high ground of mid-Sussex by a neck not three miles wide. Another spur of hilly ground formed the site of the present Bexhill, and then the coast broke down into the great tidal swamp of Pevensey Bay, which bit many miles inland behind the ridge of chalk downs that run obliquely into the sea at Beachy Head. The West Sussex coast consisted partly of the cliffs formed by the attacks of the sea upon this ridge and partly of the low plain of Selsey which lay to seaward of the ridge at its Hampshire end.

We have now surveyed the coast from the Forth to the Isle of Wight, the invaders' coast of early history, and have seen that to the external view it presented alternate stretches of defensible cliff-land and indefensible marshland. From the

Wight round westwards to the Clyde the conditions may be more briefly dealt with. On all this half of the coastline cliffs were the rule and fenny tracts the exception. Everywhere the western cliffs have been falling, slowly or quickly according to the hardness of their material, as cliffs always do when the sea laps their bases. The Isle of Wight, for instance, is known to have diminished in size within quite recent centuries. It is evident from maps of the Tudor period that the Solent was a narrower strait then than now, and not long before the Roman occupation the Wight may have been joined to the mainland. The Scilly Islands are likewise the fragments of a former westward extension of Cornwall, the drowned land of Lyonesse of the Arthurian legends. Along the Scottish coast the same forces were at work. The Hebrides represent the remnants of a very ancient mainland, and the tangle of lochs and inner islands are the result of subsidence and ages of assault by the Atlantic storms. All this coast, even as we now see it, is of much older formation than that of the eastern Channel and the North Sea.

The surface of the land has had great influence upon its history; and here again the greatest and most recent changes have been in the east rather than the west. Broadly speaking, in the times when the coastline bore the aspects above described, the eastern half of England was either flat swamp and fen, or undulating ground clothed with forest. Here and there, as on the York and Lincoln Wolds and the Kent and Sussex Downs, there were bare uplands, but in general the hills of eastern England were neither too bleak nor too dry to support a vigorous growth of trees. This was a land which, in all but a few favoured patches, required much pioneering work by colonists who wished to till the soil. But conditions over most of northern Europe were similar or even harder, and those in the western half of Britain were in general far less attractive than in the east. For there, in place of fens and undulating lowlands, were high barren moors and tumbled rocky masses which in Wales and the Pennines reached the dignity of mountains. The lower grounds, of the upper Thames, of Somerset, the Severn basin, and Cheshire, were often swampy or tree-clad as in the east, but it was only in them that really prosperous communities could establish themselves, for the moors and mountains were capable only of sparse and savage habitation. Again it should be repeated that this is to speak of average conditions. Everywhere there were favoured valleys and patches of good soil, but they were small and their occupants isolated by the surrounding wastes. If England became in after days a country of rich pastures and cornlands, it was thanks to the labour of many generations of her people. They shaped the land, and in the process the land shaped them into the men who were fit to subdue the virgin wilds of America and Australia.

Two circumstances need further mention. The woodlands were nearly everywhere to be found, but in places they grew to dense forests, an obstruction both to colonization and military invasion. One such forest lay between the Humber swamps and the Pennine range. Another stretched north-eastwards from the site of London until it reached the edge of the Fens, and the two obstacles together cut off the more open ground of Norfolk from easy communication with the midlands. The greatest forest of all, called by the Saxons the Andreds Weald, lay between the North and South Downs, covering much of West Kent, nearly all of Sussex, and part of Hampshire. This forest was the more impenetrable because it covered some sharply undulating country with steep slopes and swampy bottoms. It isolated the coastal strip of open ground formed by the chalk ridge running into the sea at Beachy Head. Invaders could settle on this open stretch, but they had no possibility of expanding more than a few miles inland. Even as late as the eighteenth century, when the Weald had been largely cleared, the Sussex coast was difficult of access from London during the greater part of the year. The valleys of the English rivers, in the state in which we see them to-day, would offer attractions to incoming pioneers. But in their unimproved condition they generally did not. Most of them were waterlogged swamps, subject to frequent flooding and incapable of cultivation without much preliminary labour. As obstacles to transport they must have been more formidable than now, for bridging and even ferrying were in most places impossible owing to the nature of the banks. The position of early London was mainly determined by the quite exceptional occurrence of patches of firm ground on either side of the stream.

Such was the aspect of primeval Britain in the days when it began to be possessed by inhabitants capable of something more than adapting themselves to the conditions as they found them. To adapt the conditions to human needs meant the transition from savagery to civilization, and with it the story of this book begins

II. THE PEOPLE OF BRITAIN

In the year 1912 some workmen found at Piltdown in Sussex a human skull which is thought to have lain buried in a layer of gravel for a quarter of a million years. The owner of that skull was the earliest man-like inhabitant of this country who has yet been traced. For countless generations his kind dwelt here; although where they originally came from is an unsolved problem. They were the palaeolithic men of pre-history. They held the land, not then an island but the corner of a continent, for a far longer period than any of their successors have done. They lived by hunting wild animals, and there can have been very few of them at any given time, for hunting can support only a sparse population. They made rough flint implements, which have been picked up in thousands, and doubtless many others of bone and wood which have perished by the lapse of time. They used no metals, but they were able to make fire, and some of them scratched drawings upon bones and upon the walls of caves.

There were many successive types of these palaeolithic men, adapted to the changes of climate that followed one another in the geographical evolution of the world. There was a warm time, when fierce tropical beasts ranged the forests with these ancient hunters. There was a cold time, when an ice-cap spread southwards from the Pole, and great glaciers enveloped all but the south of England. There was the time of sea-encroachment, when the northern waters drowned the low eastward plains, and the Channel cut the land-bridge between the Foreland and Cape Grisnez. Through all these vicissitudes palaeolithic man continued, slowly—very slowly—improving his flint implements and growing in skill to make his living out of savage Nature.

After the lapse of many thousands of years we discern a new way of life, whose exponents are styled the neolithic men. Whether they developed here or came in from without is unknown, but somewhere they were evolved out of the palaeolithic stock. Neolithic man was recognizably the father of civilized man, for he had in him the roots of the matter. His mind was moving. Instead of merely suiting himself to the conditions like a beast, killing other beasts and eating plants and wild fruits as he chanced to find them, he began to mould the conditions to suit himself. He made beautifully shaped stone implements, he tamed animals and kept them ready for his use, he wove their wool into clothing, he shaped clay into pots and pans and baked them with fire, and he built himself villages around which he cleared the forest and tilled the fields for corn. It was all very slow, but at least it was movement of the sort which modern men call progress. What language these neolithic men spoke, how many there were of them, how they were governed, and whether they made any noticeable change in the face of the country, are all dark questions to-day. Two things throw a gleam of light upon them. They built those circles of great stones of which Stonehenge is the best-known example, and they buried their dead, or at least the great ones among them, with elaborate care under great mounds of earth. These things indicate a strong religious belief and a tribal or national government able to concentrate the labour of many hands upon a single task. The burials show something more: that the neolithic men were of low stature, the average nearer five feet than six, and that their skulls were very long from front to back in proportion to the breadth across the ears. This neolithic stock, sometimes called the Iberian race, still exists in our islands, although it has been overlaid by subsequent waves of invaders. Its typical characteristics are those of a short, spare man, with swarthy skin, black hair, a long skull, and a harsh voice.

The next settlers in Britain were certainly invaders who came across the new seas surrounding the country. They were of the race called Celtic, which seems to have spread over Germany and France and to have pushed the bulk of the Iberians of those lands westward into Spain. These Celts were tall, fair men with broader skulls than those of the Iberians. The first of them crossed the Channel many centuries before the written history of northern Europe begins. They conquered the Iberians, enslaving some and driving the rest into the mountains of the western half of the island. They owed their victory in part to their superior weapons, for they had discovered the use of bronze, and of it they had fashioned knives, swords, and axes which outclassed even the beautiful stone implements of neolithic man. No doubt they were superior in other ways also, for they had evidently built boats in which they could cross a broad expanse of water; and a craftsman who could fashion a seaworthy boat would make no trouble of building a fair wooden house on the soil which he had won. With building goes much else—tilled fields, flocks and herds, perhaps even some reclamation of marsh land, everything in fact which distinguishes civilization of a sort from the life of the wandering hunter. Neolithic man had begun these things, but there is reason to believe that Celtic man greatly improved them. Boats, again, give a chance for trade to develop with distant peoples, and there is plenty of evidence that the Celts of Britain traded with the peoples of the continent. They had a rich treasure in the tin of the Cornish mines, a metal that was in great demand in the civilized states which were now springing up around the shores of the Mediterranean in the south. In exchange the richer sort of Celt obtained finely woven and brightly coloured fabrics in which to clothe himself, and his taste for personal adornment is shown by the metal pins, beads, bracelets and necklaces which are found in his burial mounds. He even shaved himself with a bronze razor, which implies that he occasionally washed his face. Altogether, the Iberian must have been a savage in comparison with him.

These first Celtic arrivals are known as the Goidels, and their language survives in the Gaelic of the Highlands and the Erse of parts of Ireland. They had in their society a noble class and a priestly class in addition to the mere tillers of the soil. The Goidels were organized in tribes under the headship of chiefs, and there are traces of a system of slavery existing among them. The slaves at first were most likely the conquered Iberians. Afterwards there was some fusion of the races, for later burials show skulls which are neither of the pure long-headed nor of the pure broad-headed type, but a mixture of the two.

Meanwhile, two changes were taking place in continental Europe. A new race of fair people, the Teutons, were arriving from the east and pushing the continental Celts westward across the Rhine, and the use of iron was spreading northwards from the Mediterranean among Celts and Teutons alike. Iron implements were almost as superior to bronze as bronze to stone, and so the swarm of iron-using Celts who were driven to seek new homes across the Channel were able to conquer their bronze-using cousins already in possession of Britain. These newcomers were called Brythons, and they gave our country the name it bore for a thousand years. They spoke a different language from that of the Goidels—Welsh is its modern survival

—and their invasion was followed by the same processs of partial eviction and partial fusion, so that by the time our written history begins with the visits of Julius Caesar the people of Britain were already a well-mixed stock. The Brythons or Britons, as it is more convenient to call them, maintained an active trade with the Continent, supplied Druids to the Celtic priesthood of Gaul and adventurers to fight in the Gallic wars, made coins in imitation of those of Rome, and increased the still scanty extent of cultivated soil. It is possible that it was they who achieved a great engineering work, the reclamation of Romney Marsh from the sea tides, and no doubt they cleared some of the areas of the primeval woodland which covered most of the island. But in general there can have been even yet but little change in the natural conditions of the country, whose transformation was to be the task of long centuries of much more highly organized labour than theirs. It is necessary to avoid exaggeration in either direction. The Britons of Caesar's time were only at the beginning of civilization, but they were far in advance of the blue-painted savages who used to figure as 'Ancient Britons' in the first chapters of our history-books.

III. THE ROMAN EMPIRE

The Roman Empire is a difficult thing to describe, for there is nothing like it in the modern world. Yet without some appreciation of what it really was, it is hardly possible to form just ideas about its province of Roman Britain. First it may be useful to clear the ground by mentioning one thing which it was not. The empire of Rome is often likened to the present British Empire of India, but the notion is wholly false. The Indian Empire is maintained by force, humanely applied, it may be granted, but none the less force. It consists of subject races and a ruling race, of different complexions, languages, religions, standards of conduct and methods of doing business; and the differences extend to such minor matters as social etiquette and preferences in food, drink, and dress. There has never been a general tendency for the one side to give up its own traditions in these things and adopt those of the other. Individuals who have done so have been generally despised by both parties. Still less has there been any approval of intermarriage between the races, and the children of such unions have been treated as aliens

by both. The only point of resemblance between the two
empires lies in a single one of the many effects of their sway
—both have ensured peace in the regions they have covered.
The Pax Britannica and the Pax Romana form a just parallel,
but one that has often been extended beyond its true limits.

The Empire of Rome presented hardly one of the features
above referred to. It originated from the exceptional courage
and energy displayed by the people of a single small state in
a world composed of a multitude of such states. The states were
of two sorts, city states, living partly by agriculture but mainly
by trade and manufacture, and country states, living mainly by
agriculture and much less by trade. At the beginning the difference in these forms of state life arose from geographical circumstances and not from any unlikeness in the race, colour, or
conduct of the peoples concerned. That is the first point to
grasp about the Roman Empire. It extended among peoples
who were for the most part of similar origin and had no colour
barriers to keep them asunder. All round the Mediterranean,
on its African shores as well as its European, there were city
states, of merchants, craftsmen, and owners of the adjoining land,
flourishing independently in the days of Rome's growth from
a village. Interspersed with them were country states, tribes
occupying areas of land, but lacking, perhaps, some essential
geographical advantage for developing into cities. North of the
Mediterranean, in Spain, Gaul, Britain, Germany, and the
Balkan Peninsula, were more country tribes, with here and
there cities or the beginnings of them. It is true that all these
people were not of the same ancestry. But there was no great
difference in their inherited ideas. They were not very conscious
of the difference in their origins, and though they worshipped
their own gods they thought of them as local and not universal
powers. It seemed quite natural for men who wandered into
other states to conform to the religions they found there. Moreover, all this area of the earth had similarities in its natural
conditions. Climates melted into one another, there were few
sharp contrasts in adjoining regions, there were no impassable
obstacles such as deserts, pestilent jungles or unscaleable
mountain ranges, and above all, the same sea washed every
coast. A man might sail from Tyre to Carthage in Africa, and
thence to Carthagena or New Carthage in Spain; from Athens by
Syracuse to Marseilles, and thence through the straits to the

Atlantic and the coasts of northern Gaul and Britain, all in the same ship. And men were doing this when Rome had scarcely been heard of.

In such a world there was born, in the earlier centuries of the thousand years before Christ, a lusty infant destined to grow into the city of Rome. Its inhabitants, at first countrymen living in an overgrown village, were successful in their wars with their neighbours, extended their sway over central Italy, and developed their village into a town and their town into a city. Still the dominion spread, over the plain of Lombardy tenanted by Celtic Gauls in the north, over the island of Sicily in the south. The Sicilian expansion brought on a duel with Carthage, mistress of the trade and sea-power of the western Mediterranean; and in this struggle Rome won. The victory brought with it the Carthaginian possessions in Spain, which became a new province of Rome. Simultaneously Rome was drawn into quarrels in the Levant, and Greece and Asia Minor fell under her sway.

All this rapid expansion caused changes at home. In her early days Rome had cast out her kings and had made herself a republic, governed mainly by the aristocracy, but with certain popular rights established. But the conquests enabled the aristocrats to monopolize power. They seized most of the booty, became fabulously wealthy, introduced hordes of slaves, and extinguished the free peasantry who had been the backbone of the early Roman state. Rights of citizenship were extended to the peoples of the Italian provinces, and the Latin language soon prevailed in them over all other tongues. But the political rights of the commons of Rome could not be extended because the idea of a representative assembly had not been thought of, and the barriers of time and space limited the scope of a democracy in which every citizen had to attend in person and shout for his rights. Consequently the domination of Italy meant the permeation of the whole country by the Roman tongue and law and methods of government, imposed upon peoples mostly of kindred stock to the Romans, but administered always from the fount of authority in the city itself. The Roman culture covered Italy, but the nation living under it was Italian, not Roman.

The distinction is more apparent in the overseas provinces, in Africa, Spain and the Levant. There the peoples were neither Roman nor Italian. They were 'provincials' of diverse races, all welded into unity by the Roman mind. At first all the officials came from Rome; then by degrees the wealthy provincials were admitted to citizenship and office. There was little of the feeling which moderns call patriotism. In the ancient world the rule of the strongest seemed natural to all men, and the provincials were well pleased to be admitted to equality with the people of the strongest city. Their loyalty went sincerely to her who had proved herself a generous conqueror, and when the turmoil settled down there were no narrow regional sentiments. To be a Roman citizen was a more inspiring thing than to be a good African, Spaniard, or Macedonian. When, in the first century before Christ, Julius Caesar conquered Gaul and a mass of Celtic tribes were added to the Empire, they speedily fell under the domination of the Roman idea and became genuine citizens of the Roman state. After a generation or two it would have seemed to a Gaul as ridiculous to seek independence from the Empire as it would now to a Kentishman to seek separation from the kingdom of Great Britain. The armies were developed after the same plan. The heavy-armed infantry of the legions were recruited from the full citizens, although by Caesar's time few legionaries were actual Romans, and probably a minority were Italians; and in addition there were large bodies of provincial 'auxiliaries', horse and foot, who were not fully admitted citizens at all. Such was the Roman Empire when it received its first Emperor in the person of Augustus, an empire dominated by the Roman mind and spirit acting upon men of diverse origins, hardly one per cent. of whom had the true Roman blood in their veins. The Empire was an idea, a habit of thought, established by force, but, once established, needing no more force to maintain it among men to whom no other idea thenceforward made any appeal—a different empire, indeed, from that of British India.

Augustus was the first Emperor, and he attained the office because the time was ripe for some man to do so. Ever since the rapid expansion had set in, the small band of aristocrats who ruled the republic had been splitting into jealous factions, demoralized by the wealth and power they had attained, and ready to cut each other's throats for more. Great officers plundered the provinces they were set to rule, civil wars broke out among the factions, and the whole Roman world cried out, not for liberty, but for order. Caesar saw that the only solution was for a single man to rule. He determined to be that man, but his fellow-aristocrats murdered him as the prize was within his grasp. Then, after more years of bloodshed, his nephew Octavianus (Augustus) struck down all opponents and imposed his sway upon the whole. Nominally the republic continued with himself as its guardian, and the senate still existed. But the senate was in the power of the Emperor, for he commanded the armies, and in effect the republic was no more. The Emperor was a despot who came ere long to be worshipped as a god, one more god among the many who competed for the reverence of easy-going votaries to whom the idea of heresy would scarcely have been intelligible. None but the Jews, and their outgrowth the Christians, had any desire to suffer martyrdom for a religious belief; and they made no great stir in the Roman world until it was already growing old.

Augustus gave the Empire its permanent form of government and very nearly its permanent geographical outline. The frontiers in his day extended from the Straits of Gibraltar along the ocean coasts of Spain and Gaul to the mouth of the Rhine, up the course of the Rhine to near the northern slopes of the Alps, then across eastwards to the upper Danube, and down the banks of that river to the Black Sea. From the eastern end of the Black Sea the line struck southwards so as to include Asia Minor, Syria, and Palestine, and so to the head of the Red Sea. The whole northern coast of Africa under Roman sway completed the encirclement of the Mediterranean. On this African side there was no definite land frontier, for the civilized coastal area melted imperceptibly into the deserts, from whose poor and sparse inhabitants no great danger was to be feared. It was otherwise on the long European land-frontier. There a definite line existed, that of the Rhine and the Danube, with a fortified rampart bridging the gap between their upper waters. And outside the Empire on this side lay the wilds of Germany, peopled by the vigorous Teutonic tribes who were ultimately to break through and ruin all. Augustus made a half-hearted attempt to conquer Germany, and then gave it up. Thereafter, although the province of Dacia was occupied for a period to the north of the Danube, that river and the Rhine became approximately the border of the Roman world, which had to maintain great armies for its defence. The men of later times realized

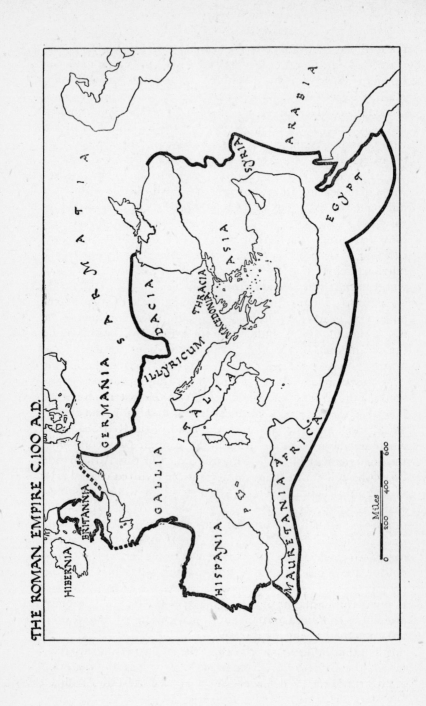

THE ROMAN EMPIRE C.100 A.D.

that Augustus had made a mistake in not persevering in Germany. With the force at his command he could probably have conquered the country. He could then have drawn his frontier from the Black Sea to the Baltic, a line but half as long as that with which he had rested content. Within it he would have had the hardy Teutons as citizens of the Empire instead of its enemies, and the whole would have been immeasurably stronger to resist any new wandering hordes from the East. It was the loss of an army under Varus that decided Augustus to break off the German enterprise. Probably no single battle has had so decisive an influence on the history of the world as the slaughter of Varus and his legions in the depths of the German forest. Had the fight gone otherwise we might be citizens of the Roman Empire to-day.

In other ways Rome was unenterprising. Her citizens produced no great travellers or explorers by land or sea. They showed little curiosity about the outer lands, and never attempted to reconnoitre and estimate the strength of the foes who might fall upon them. They hated and feared the sea, hardly glancing at the ocean and never making full use of their own Mediterranean. The lamentations of Ovid on his passage from Rome to the Black Sea are typical of his countrymen's views. They would have seemed ludicrous to a Venetian of the Middle Ages, who would have had no better ship to carry him than had the tearful poet. To modern European statesmen the command of the Mediterranean has appealed as the decisive factor in commercial and military supremacy. The Roman, enjoying that command, much preferred to move his goods and his soldiers round by land. The Roman culture, in fact, with all its respect for law, its passion for order, and its worship of wealth, killed the spirit of adventure. The ideal was to sit still, guarded by the frontier legions, luxuriously housed and served in some safe city, and there accumulate possessions. Even the legions became sedentary. They stayed for decades and even centuries in one post on the frontier, and the citizens of the Empire became ever more unwilling to serve in them. The soldier's life grew to be despised as fit only for barbarians.

The Roman world, except in its newly conquered provinces, was not divided into a ruling race and subject races, but resembled a well-stirred pudding in which the ingredients were thoroughly mingled. Instead of racial distinctions there were

class distinctions, from the house-slave and the servile cultivator
to the small landowner and the tradesman of the towns, and
upwards through gradations of wealth to the millionaire money-
lender and the senatorial proprietor of vast estates. In the end
it was money that decided everything. Anyone might be a
citizen and anyone might be a senator, provided he could pay
for the position. With money so powerful, trade within the
Empire was brisk, and there was much going to and fro and
permanent transplantation of people in units and in masses.
It has, in fact, been remarked that there were probably more
people who travelled extensively within the Empire than there
are in Europe to-day. The common language and the universal
law favoured this continual motion. A man from one province
was quite at home in another. There has been found in the
north of Britain the gravestone of a citizen who was born in
Syria, who migrated to our island, married a British woman,
and doubtless left a family of mixed parentage. The case was
typical of many.

The Christian Church, when in the fourth century it
gained the ascendancy, was another unifying force, for it added
a common idea of religion to the common ideas of law, language
and literature. From one point of view the Church weakened
the Empire, for it was anti-military; from another, it strengthened it by making Rome and Constantinople the centres of
spiritual as well as political authority. Without the Church the
idea of a united Europe might have perished in the barbarian
invasions, but thanks to the Church it persisted well into the
Middle Ages.

The fall of the Roman Empire came with its division into two
portions, the Eastern and the Western, in the fourth century,
and the destruction of the Western portion in the fifth. That
destruction was a prolonged affair. It began with the enlistment
of Teutonic tribes to reinforce the legions in their defence
against the farther Teutons. The enlisted barbarians had often
a genuine respect for the civilization which employed them,
and they fought manfully on its behalf. But the inevitable
result was decay and disaster. The outer barbarians pressed on
in ever greater strength. The Goths of Alaric and the Huns of
Attila swept through the West, leaving desolation in their
tracks. By the end of the fifth century the Western Empire was
in fragments, all authority was gone, and barbaric kings bore

sway over the former provinces and their tame provincials. Yet the disaster appeared less to the men of the time than it does to us. Empire and Church were still the ideals men strove for, and they appealed strongly to the incoming hordes who destroyed the one and nearly destroyed the other. The victorious Teutons dreamed of settling down as initiates of the only civilization they had ever known. Their chiefs liked to call themselves senators and to yield nominal allegiance to a puppet emperor. And even when the last western emperor was gone they still felt a vague reverence for his surviving colleague at Constantinople. The Roman Empire faded slowly away instead of dying suddenly and definitely, and ere it went it conquered morally those who had conquered it physically. The proud Rome of Augustus lay in ruins, but among them lived on the meeker Rome of the early Popes.

IV. THE ROMAN PROVINCE

Julius Caesar's raids upon Britain in 55 and 54 B. C. were in no sense a Roman conquest of the country. They served, however, to introduce the stay-at-home majority among the Britons of the south to Roman officers and armies. The more adventurous Britons had already made the same acquaintance in the course of trading voyages and service in the wars of Gaul. Equally, the enterprise of Caesar must have brought to Roman notice some problems of which there had been no previous knowledge, those of the swamps and forests of the south country and of the powerful tides of the Straits of Dover. It is evident that the tides were a great puzzle to Caesar, who was familiar only with the tideless waters of the Mediterranean. On both his visits his ignorance lost him some of his ships. He thought he had drawn them safely up the beach, but a spring tide and a sudden gale drove them together and smashed them. The incident illustrates the small size of the Roman vessels, probably no larger than a Hastings fishing-boat of to-day. On his first raid also, he started his cavalry transports from a different port from that of the infantry. The latter were carried up-Channel by the flowing tide, but the cavalry were caught by the ebb and carried far down to westward and never rejoined their general until the campaign was over. It would seem that the Gauls of the sea-coast, who must have known the conditions, kept their secrets to themselves. With a little better luck they might have seen their great conqueror whirled away to his doom in some of the weather which the Straits can exhibit when they choose.

The century after the Caesar incident was a century of preparation for the Romanization of Britain. Gaul became a peaceful province of the Empire, whose officers no doubt made progress in the study of Channel geography. On the Britons the raids had had a steadying influence, and we hear no more of their stirring up trouble in Gaul. There was certainly an active trade between the Celts of the opposite shores of the narrow sea. It is possible that London was already a town or some importance, for its site was the first practicable landing-place on the Thames for those who wished to travel northwards into the midlands, and it was likewise the only crossing-place on the road from Kent into the same region. The southern Britons thus gained contact with Roman luxury, and among many of them a desire to share it must have arisen. It was the magic of Rome that her power and wealth unnerved her less civilized neighbours before her armies advanced to subdue them. British kings in this century naturally wished to preserve their independence, but exiles from their tribes fled over to the continent and intrigued to bring about a Roman invasion. It was only a question of time before the invasion should be tried.

The penetration of the country in advance by Roman ideas accounts for the rapid progress of the conquest when at length the Emperor Claudius undertook it in A.D. 43. Within twenty years the south and the midlands had been subdued and partly Romanized. London, Colchester, and Verulam (near the present St. Albans) had become towns filled with Romans and their slaves, and with a multitude of Britons who had yielded to the new way of life. There were tempting gains for the enterprising in the first generation of the conquest—slave-dealing, estate development, trade in all sorts of novelties and luxuries, carried on among a generous and unwary people, too often to the accompaniment of fraud and oppression. A great many unworthy Romans poured in to share the spoil, and they did so without an army strong enough to protect them from the wrath of the disillusioned natives. In the whole country there were but four legions—say 18,000 regular troops—and about an equal number of auxiliaries. Most of these were on the frontiers of Wales and the North, where fighting was still going on.

Suddenly, in 61, the occupied south-east revolted against the oppressors. The legions were far away, and panic seized the Romanized. They lifted hardly a finger in self-defence, and the rebels slaughtered them by thousands, whilst the three cities disappeared like chaff in the flames. One legion marching south to the rescue was likewise blotted out, but the others at length turned the scale. The revolt perished amid a counter-massacre, and thenceforward there was peace save on the frontiers. But the Romans had learned a lesson besides inflicting one, and their commanders exerted themselves to provide justice and kindly government for the future. Julius Agricola, who ruled from 78 to 86, is famed for his work in this direction. He also gave the province its permanent form by completing the occupation of Wales and the north of England. The Roman armies raided but never subdued Scotland, and they seem not to have entered Ireland at all.

In speaking of the Romanization of the province it is as well to remember that the process transformed the natives only in the midlands and the south. North of the Humber the occupation remained purely military, and the hill-tribes were over-awed rather than civilized. The same is true of Wales, where numerous forts and garrisons testified to the necessity for repressing an independence which had never been rooted out. This persistence of an un-Romanized fringe makes the history and fate of the British province peculiar, for it was precisely this fringe which survived when the civilized centre and south were submerged by Teutonic invasions. Yet the Roman language and institutions did not survive with the fringe, for they had never been properly established in it, and so Wales and the North-West reverted to a purely Celtic manner of life.

The chief activities of the province were a considerable clear-ance of the land for cultivation, the drainage of swamps, the growth of towns, the shaping of large estates around the villas of wealthy landowners, the making of roads in all directions, and the defence of the frontiers by forts and by the Wall between the Solway and the Tyne. The people who carried out these undertakings were for the most part the British natives, but there was also a fairly large influx of Romanized men from the other parts of the Empire. The troops at first were all foreigners, but legionaries and auxiliaries quartered for so many years in the same spot inevitably took wives from among the natives, and their children in time filled the vacant places in the ranks. The Second and Twentieth Legions, for example, came over with the original conquering army and remained in Britain until the end, nearly four centuries later. The highest officials were commonly sent by the Emperor from Rome, but the chiefs of the British tribes seem to have retained some of their dignity and a share in local administration. Their descendants developed gradually into members of the wealthy class which permeated the whole Empire, thoroughly Romanized in their outlook upon life, and devoid of any desire for independent power. London became the especial headquarters of the non-British merchants and financiers. The other towns were filled with traders and craftsmen of native origin.

The religious aspect of the province presented the varied assortment of cults and creeds which prevailed elsewhere in the Empire. Roman, Greek, Celtic, and even Teutonic divinities have left their traces in the altars and inscriptions set up by their votaries. There was toleration for all, and it is likely that most people worshipped in more than one kind of temple. The religion of the ancient world was concerned less with the salvation of the soul after death than with the propitiation of unseen powers which could bestow good or bad fortune during life. Offerings, prayers, and sacrifices were thus observed without any sense of absurdity in diverse shrines, much as the risks in the modern business world are distributed among a variety of insurance companies. The spread of Christianity in the later days of the Empire made some change in this manner of thought, but the original Christian principles were modified to some extent by the ideas which they overcame, and the influence of local cults can be traced in many parts of the Christian world to-day. The growth of Christianity in Britain is a dark subject. It has left few traces among the things which can be excavated by the antiquarian. Only one buried ruin has so far been discovered which may possibly have been a Christian church,[1] and there are only a few known gravestones of Christians. On the other hand, it is evident that Christianity obtained a sufficient hold among the Britons to survive the catastrophe of the Saxon invasions. It seems not to have become common in the island until well on in the fourth century, when the end of Roman civilization was already in sight.

[1] At Silchester.

The geographical plan of Roman Britain is important for the attempt we shall have to make to understand the Teutonic conquest. The largest habitable area was that of the south midlands and the lands on the south bank of the Thames. This approximately square region included the basins of the Severn and the Thames, and the undulating country lying north-west of London. At its north-west corner it pushed up towards the Irish Sea at Chester. Lincoln marked its north-east corner, London its south-east, and a whole group of towns, Gloucester, Cirencester, Bath, and Caerleon, stood at the south-west angle by the head of the Bristol Channel. Separated from the central square were outlying regions. York, in the middle of the north-eastern country beyond the swamps of the Humber, was the military headquarters of the island, the base of the legions that defended the Caledonian frontier. But in all this region civilian settlement was scanty. The remains are those of officers' houses and of the forts which kept the hill-tribes in order. The importance of the Wall from Solway to Tyne has perhaps been exaggerated. It seems to have been designed rather to check small bands of robbers than for defence against serious invasion. For that purpose the field troops were the real safeguard, and the Wall itself was unsuitable as a military line of defence. Norfolk and Suffolk formed another outlying region, cut off like an island from the central mass by the Fens and the forests north-east of London. Kent in the same way resembled a peninsula, bordered by the Andreds Weald and joined to the central square by the high ground of the North Downs. The Isle of Wight and the South Downs of Sussex formed yet other isolated regions. In the west the mountains of Wales and Cumberland and the moorlands of Devon were obstacles to close settlement by those who followed the Roman way of life.

The Picts beyond the Wall were always troublesome, but in the third century other enemies appeared. These were the Saxon pirates from the shores of Germany which Augustus had failed to conquer. To meet their assaults a new scheme of defence became necessary, and the outworks of eastern Britain had to be garrisoned with troops and ships of war. The northern outwork, that of York, could look after itself. It was already full of soldiers for the defence of the Wall. In the East Anglian, Kentish, and Sussex outworks a system of coast fortresses was established from which long ships could sally upon the invaders

ROMAN BRITAIN

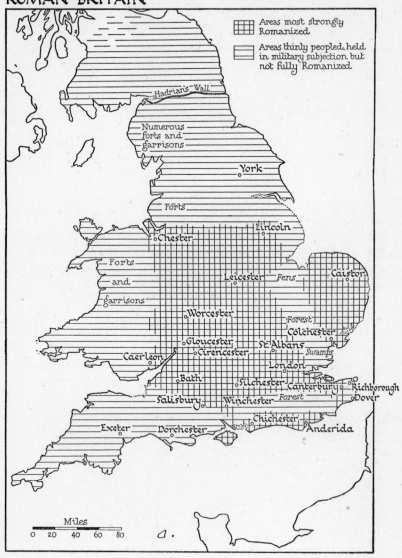

Areas most strongly Romanized

Areas thinly peopled, held in military subjection but not fully Romanized

Hadrian's Wall

Numerous forts and garrisons

York

Forts

Chester

Lincoln

Forts

and

garrisons

Leicester

Fens

Caistor

Worcester

Forest

Colchester

Caerleon

Gloucester

Cirencester

St Albans

Swamps

London

Bath

Silchester

Canterbury

Richborough

Salisbury

Winchester

Forest

Dover

Exeter

Dorchester

Chichester

Anderida

Miles

0   20   40   60   80

by sea, and troops could bring them to action if they ventured
to land. The officer in command of the whole was known as the
Count of the Saxon Shore. So long as the Empire held together,
this scheme of defence appears to have been fairly successful;
and even when the Roman power was cracking, the worst
enemies were not at first the Saxons, but the Picts and Scots of
the north. Yet the Teutons had caught a glimpse of a country
worth fighting for, and after two centuries their descendants
found that 'the day' had come.

A final remark may conclude this glance at Roman Britain.
The occupation lasted four hundred years, a very long time
when compared with the rapid rush of modern history, and yet
not long enough to leave permanent effects upon the country.
The Roman roads, the fabric of the Wall, a number of buried
towns and villas, a vast collection of coins and potsherds, are the
remains of those four centuries of ancient civilization. But of
enduring effects upon our own lives, things which we should
lack or should do differently had the legions never crossed the
Channel—not one. We owe, indeed, a mighty debt to Rome,
but it is a debt incurred by our Saxon and English forefathers
when the Empire itself was dead, but when its mind and its
spirit, its law and its literature, still went marching on, as indeed
they march on to-day.

II

THE SAXON SETTLEMENT

(From the Fifth Century to Alfred)

I. THE TEUTONIC PEOPLES

THERE are a great many matters in the early history of most nations upon which positive statements cannot fairly be made. Knowledge is imperfect. The surviving facts are few, and sometimes seem to contradict one another, and there are frequent gaps in the record which have to be bridged by guesswork. It is often safer to say that our explanations are probable than that they are certain. The Anglo-Saxon invasion of England is an example. Different authorities have taken widely different views of it, and the following sketch of its occurrences has been written, and should be read, with caution.

One clear fact about the invaders is that they were Teutons. They belonged to that group of peoples which had arrived in Germany from some easterly region during the unrecorded centuries before the empire of Rome began to spread beyond the bounds of Italy. The languages of the Teutons show that in the remote past they had had some kinship with the Celts, the Romans, and the Greeks, and even with that ancient people who went into India and there spoke and wrote the tongue called Sanskrit. To this whole series of races the common description of Aryan or Indo-European has been applied, and it is believed that they all originated somewhere in central Asia and migrated in successive swarms at widely separated periods. Thus the Greeks and Romans represent an early Indo-European movement which penetrated westwards and southwards into Europe until it came to rest in the peninsulas jutting into the Mediterranean. The Celts, divided into many tribes, filled central Europe and Gaul and Britain. The Teutons came later, took the places of the Celts in Germany, and were stopped there for several centuries by the Roman power. All these Indo-European immigrants into western Europe had to dispute possession with the more ancient peoples whom they found there, and for the most part they did not exterminate those peoples but ultimately became intermingled with them. An example of this is the mixture of Celts and Iberians in our own country. The

Teutons, with whom we are now concerned, remained for a long time in Germany. By their defeat of Varus they escaped conquest by Rome, but it is evident that they were ill at ease among themselves. Their tribes moved hither and thither. The weaker ones sometimes disappeared, conquered and scattered by others. The Romans when they peered into the turmoil saw new Teuton nations emerging, the product of amalgamations effected by conquering chiefs. Germany, during the whole Roman period, was a simmering cauldron. At length it boiled over in the fourth and fifth centuries and submerged the Empire itself. It should be remembered, however, that it was not the whole Teutonic race that burst over the frontiers. The greater part of it remained in its old home to be the ancestors of the Germans of to-day.

The Teutonic peoples with whom our country is chiefly concerned were those of the northern coast of Germany. As coast people their habits of life were different from those of the forest tribes of the interior. As northern people they were remote from the rich Roman provinces of the continent, and so they were not so easily moved by the temptation to form themselves into marching armies and invade the Empire over its Rhine and Danube frontiers. These coastal Teutons were untouched by Roman civilization and the Christian religion. They were satisfied with their own gods and priests and methods of government. It never occurred to them, as it did to their cousins the Franks and the Goths, to attempt to prop up the tottering institutions of the Empire and to play at being Romans themselves. That is one of the reasons why the Anglo-Saxon conquest of Britain was a very different thing from the Frankish conquest of Gaul or the Gothic conquests of Italy and Spain.

What happened on the continent was briefly this. The eastern half of the Roman Empire with its capital at Constantinople was cruelly raided time after time, but it was strong enough to beat off or absorb its assailants. As the map shows, the Eastern Empire was partly in Europe and partly in Asia and northern Africa, and the non-European provinces remained unscathed until the rise of the Mahometan conquerors in the seventh century. The Eastern Empire was therefore strong enough to survive in its original Roman form, and it continued as a refuge of learning, art, and industry for a thousand years after the disasters of the fifth century.

The Western Empire, on the other hand, disappeared. In the fifth century it was penetrated in all directions by Frankish, Gothic, Burgundian, and Vandal armies. These men liked to think of themselves as members of the Empire, but very soon their rough handling destroyed it. By the end of the century there was not even a pretence of a central authority. Sovereignty was divided between half-a-dozen independent kingdoms, and the farce of appointing a Western emperor was given up in 476. But two general facts should be noted. The Teutons who invaded by land were Christians before they moved, or became Christians in the course of their invasions. Their numbers also were small in comparison with the population of the provinces they conquered. If we add to this their respect for Roman learning and institutions it is easy to understand that sooner or later they ceased to exist as Teutons, and the original stocks of the western provinces emerged from the tide of invasion with their language and religion preserved. In Gaul the Frankish and Burgundian conquerors gave up their own languages and customs and intermingled with the provincials. The ultimate result was the French nation and the French language, the former mainly of Celtic blood and the latter a specialized branch of the Latin tongue. In Italy and Spain the Ostrogoths and Visigoths governed their subjects, but did not merge with them. They lost their early prowess and their numbers diminished, and both branches of the Gothic nation were overthrown by invading armies and vanished in broken fragments from the face of Europe. Their function had been to destroy the Western Empire as a political fabric. But having done so, they left its inhabitants and language intact and ready for new forms of government.

Everywhere the continental provinces of Western Europe survived the invasions. Only the emperor was gone. Christianity, the Roman cities, some memory of Roman law, and the Roman tongue remained. But civilization tottered. Too much of what was left consisted of mere shells and forms with the life drained out of them. Western Europe entered a dark age of several centuries' duration, in which life was brutal, justice a memory, and comfort unknown. And yet the tradition of better things was never lost. Through all the misery and degradation of unpunished crimes, of savage local wars, of Norse and Saracen invasions, it shone as a distant light to beckon Europe upwards. By the eleventh century the worst was over, civilization and a decent life began again to be possible, and the Dark Age gave place to the Middle Age. Western Europe had kept continuity with the Roman Empire from which it sprang.

In our own island the story was different, and here we must return to our own Teuton invaders. They are generally enumerated as the Jutes, the Angles, and the Saxons, and they came from the Danish peninsula and the German coasts about its base. The Jutes were evidently a distinct body from the others, with laws and customs of their own which rendered Kent, their chief region of settlement, a peculiar community down to modern times. It is not so certain that the Angles and the Saxons were different nations. There is some ground for believing that they were one people, who called themselves Angles and were called Saxons by their enemies. It is not easy to distinguish any differences in their laws and methods of allotting land, and if their language developed into different dialects that was probably explained by local circumstances after their arrival in this country. In addition there were among the invaders some Frisians from what is now the Dutch coast, but they were not sufficiently numerous to form a separate community in England. All these people were pagans to whom Christianity made no appeal. They were skilled in seamanship and in tilling the soil. They were utterly illiterate and untouched by the glamour of Roman civilization. Their numbers were probably outgrowing the resources of their own country. What they saw in Roman Britain was not a superior society of which they might aspire to become members, but first, a desirable store of riches to be sacked, and second, a more pleasant land and climate than their own, where they might with advantage make their habitation. When once they should move in earnest, a much rougher game was in prospect than that played by the Franks and Goths on the Continent.

II. INVASION AND DESOLATION

Throughout the fourth century the Saxon pirates made plundering expeditions to the British coast, but the defences were sufficient to prevent serious damage. There was no Teutonic settlement in the island during this century. The Saxons indeed were not as yet the most formidable enemies of the province.

That distinction belonged to the Picts and the Scots, the former of whom were the ancient inhabitants of Caledonia whom Rome had never subdued, and the latter a Celtic people who were moving over from Ireland into western Scotland. These invaders broke through the northern defences by land and raided the western coasts by sea. The Wall and the forts and the frontier armies ought to have been a sufficient defence, but they were not. The latter part of the fourth century was a time of anarchy and revolution in the Western Empire, and various adventurers drew off the defenders of Britain to back their ambitious strokes upon the Continent. The protection of the province was thus fatally weakened, and in about 380, by one account, the Wall ceased to be held against the Picts. Then, early in the fifth century, the Goths burst over the Rhine into Gaul, and one of their hosts entered Italy itself. The imperial power became a shadow, and the communications between Rome and its British province were cut, never to be restored. That is the real meaning of what is called 'the departure of the Romans'. There was at the last no conscious striking of the flag, no visible exodus of marching legions. There was only an interruption of contact with Rome. Everyone must have regarded it as merely a temporary misfortune, and only after the lapse of many years was it recognized as final.

There were, and there had long been, no Romans to depart. The people, the troops, and the officials in Britain were provincials, chiefly Celtic, no doubt, but mixed with strains from all parts of the Empire. There may have been hardly a man of Roman blood among them. These people were fully permeated with the Roman culture only in the midlands and the south. In the north and west they were still Celtic in speech and tribal in their customs, and it is quite likely that these unsubdued borderers took part with the Picts in ravaging the settled area.

For a generation after the severance from Rome we must picture the wealthy middle and south of Britain as frequently attacked, raided, and weakened by the Picts and Scots, yet retaining its appearance of a Roman province. The cities seem to have held out even if country villas were plundered, and local leaders took office and carried on the administration on the Roman system. The Teutonic pirates had been sharing in the attack, but had not yet done so in sufficient weight to render it decisive. Then, some time before the middle of the fifth century, the conditions changed. The Teutons began to appear in greater numbers, and the defence collapsed. At the same time we cease to hear of the Picts and Scots. Of their withdrawal there is no satisfactory explanation. The stock tradition asserts that the British provincials employed the Teutons to drive them out of the country, but it is hard to imagine how any regular arrangement can have been possible in the confusion. However, the bare fact is clear that the next stage consisted of a heavy and successful onslaught by the Teutonic nations.

Of what then took place there are conflicting versions. It must be repeated that we have no eye-witness's account that really tells us anything. All we can see is that about 450 a Roman province plunged into a fog of war and that about 600 there emerged something that was not in the least like a Roman province, something utterly different from a Roman province in language, religion, government, industry, military organization, and everything by which we describe a human community. In that century-and-a-half of lost history one picture vanished from the canvas and another took its place. It is a fascinating mystery.

The historians of the nineteenth century produced a reasoned story of those hundred and fifty years. They told how various Teutonic armies under named leaders landed at specified places and at given dates, and carried out a steady, piecemeal conquest of the country; how the British resisted continuously and gave ground inch by inch; and how the invaders consolidated each position as they won it and dug themselves in with their own system of landholding and agriculture whilst the fight was still raging on the moving frontier a few miles ahead. The whole effect is like that of trench warfare in 1914–18, a creeping advance at an average rate of some two or three miles a year. It is not in the least likely to have taken place in fact. Savage, undisciplined fighters, subsisting on their own local tillage, could not possibly have carried on war in that fashion. The authority for it all is the Anglo-Saxon Chronicle, which certainly does tell a story that can be read in this way, although it can be read in another way as well. The Chronicle was the work of Saxon scribes, but it was written centuries after the time of the Saxon conquest. Its stories were folk memories, carried down from generation to generation in poetic songs roared out at feasts and camp-fires, and in genealogies composed to prove

the high descent of Saxon kings. Such tales may have a
foundation of a few facts, distorted by the mists through which
they are dimly seen. But they are not history. They are what
a credulous people accepted as their history in default of the
true record which they had never preserved. We can make a
nearer approach to the truth by methods they never dreamed of.

A more recent school has rejected this version and has substituted another, which is a still greater strain upon our belief,
because it conflicts with facts that really are established. It
amounts to this, that in the country at large there was no
Anglo-Saxon conquest at all, but only a settlement on the
south-east coasts, a settlement of a few pirates who never
penetrated far inland and added no appreciable element to the
national stock. By this theory, we English of to-day are not of
Teutonic descent but are sprung in the main from the people
of a Roman province, as the modern French, Italians, and
Spaniards undoubtedly are; the Roman towns survived, as on
the continent, and the people in them, and most of their ways
of life; and there has been continuity with the Roman Empire.
This will not do. It has some solid realities to overcome. The
Teutonic language prevailed over the greater part of England
when history began again after the lost period. The religion of
the people was pagan. Their laws, government, land-system,
and military system were Teutonic. They themselves believed
that they were Anglo-Saxons, the children of invaders, and not
Celtic Britons, the children of the Roman Empire. These things
are hard to explain away, and the attempt to do it is uncon-
vincing.

From the researches and criticisms of other recent workers
we may construct a more credible theory of what took place.
And there is no harm in doing so, provided we admit that it is
largely unproved and liable to be upset by the emergence of
new facts. It would seem that rather before the middle of the
fifth century a great combination of Teutonic war-bands fell
upon the province and fairly burst through the coast defences.
Having done so, they rapidly penetrated the whole country up
to the western hills. They took and plundered city after city and
the luxurious country villas by the score. They slaughtered,
enslaved, or drove off the inhabitants until the survivors made a
stand in the wild, poor country of the west which the pirates had
no great incentive to attack. This great series of raids probably

submerged the whole south and midlands in the course of a very few years. It did not mark a permanent advance of the Teutons, for the tide ebbed as rapidly as it had flowed. Its importance is that it destroyed utterly and for ever the Roman life of the province. The towns and villas were blackened ruins, their inhabitants for the most part dead. The stock-in-trade of industry and the implements of agriculture were destroyed or carried off. The grain stores and flocks and herds were recklessly consumed by the invaders. In a word, the roots of civilization were torn up. The evidence for this is not in the Saxon Chronicle; it is in the revelations of the spade. Site after site of Roman towns and villas has been excavated in recent years, and their indications point to one conclusion: sudden disaster by fire and sword not later than the middle of the fifth century. There were, no doubt, survivors, but there must also have been much slaughter. How extensive it was we may judge from another circumstance. The Latin tongue, the language of the wealthy towns, died out. The few poor refugees became merged in the unromanized Celtic tribes of the mountains, and Welsh is the speech of their descendants to this day.[1]

Such, and so rapid, may have been the end of Roman Britain, a grimmer fate than was experienced by any other province of the Western Empire. This, however, was hardly the beginning of Saxon England. The savage hordes who did these things were plundering pirates, not industrious colonists. Having stolen all there was to steal, having reduced the land to a smouldering wilderness, having gorged themselves on the crops and the livestock, it is not likely that they changed suddenly into peaceful tillers of the soil. It is more probable that when they felt the pinch of the famine they had made most of them withdrew overseas to the homes whence they had come.

Then the way was clear for the true Anglo-Saxon conquest of England, the steady infiltration year after year of working colonists, bringing their wives and children and their stock for agriculture. Then began that creeping advance narrated by the Chronicle, the advance of settlement across a wasted land. These colonists would yet have skirmishes to fight, for we can imagine bands of Britons still haunting the forests, living as

[1] Another Celtic language, Cornish, survived in the south-west of England until the eighteenth century; and some of the British refugees crossed the Channel and imposed their national name upon Brittany.

wandering hunters where their fathers had lived as peasants or craftsmen; and we can imagine also a few favoured spots that had escaped the fury of the great raids. There are indications indeed that Roman London did not fall in the general sack, but was abandoned at some later date. But in the main the incoming colonists must have filled a vacuum, and their slow advance was a consequence of their scanty numbers. For they could not have come in thousands as the pirate bands had done. Great crowds cannot suddenly establish themselves on a new soil if they are to live from the outset by their own labour. They must have come by families and villages, a score here, a hundred there. Only when the pioneers were well rooted could the settlements expand. We have a parallel to suggest what the process was like. For the rude Teuton from Denmark to bring his family and household goods across the North Sea must have been quite as difficult an undertaking as it was for the Englishman of the Stuart period to transport himself across the Atlantic. In that Stuart period the colonization of New England was pushed vigorously after the pioneer voyage of the *Mayflower* in 1620; and after eighty years of effort New England contained less than 100,000 inhabitants. That gives us some measure of the Anglo-Saxon advance.

The above seems the explanation that best agrees with the few facts ascertainable about the fall of Roman Britain and the rise of Saxon England.

III. THE SAXON COLONIZATION

The Anglo-Saxon colonies began on the coastline of the eastern half of England and worked their way slowly inland. The earliest colonists were undoubtedly Jutes, who occupied first Thanet and then Kent not long after the middle of the fifth century. By their own traditions, they had some fighting with the Britons before their possession was secure. We cannot tell on what scale this fighting really was. It may have been quite petty skirmishing between scanty bodies of colonists and remnants of the Celts who clung to the ruins of what had been a strongly Romanized area. Kent was for purposes of settlement a peninsula with its neck joining central England in the neighbourhood of London. All its western border was closed to expansion by the wet forests of the Weald and the barren lands of Surrey. Elsewhere the Jutes landed in the Isle of Wight and the region round Southampton Water. But here their settlements were overlaid or conquered by subsequent arrivals of Saxons, and their peculiar laws and customs did not survive as they did in Kent. The open country of the South Downs was another isolated area shut in to the northward by the great forest. It was seized by Saxons, who speedily reached the limits of their expansion and settled down as the small and backward kingdom of Sussex. Other Saxons took the northern bank of the Thames estuary and founded the kingdom of Essex. North of them appeared Angles (if they were really a distinct people) in the geographical outwork of East Anglia. A few more Angles settled on the high inner parts of what is now Lincoln-shire. They are named the Lindiswaras in early records, and it was long before they expanded into the great kingdom of Mercia. Angles in greater strength occupied the dry coastlines and open country north of the Humber estuary. From their scattered settlements arose the kingdom of Northumbria. Some time after the founding of these early establishments a stream of newcomers poured into the midland square and founded Mercia, whilst another stream took the coastline west of the Isle of Wight and pressed northwards to the Thames and west-wards towards Devon and Somerset. These last-named settle-ments grew into the kingdom of Wessex.

There were three great waterways into the heart of England from the east coast—the Humber and its contributing rivers, the Wash and its feeders, and the Thames. The raiding pirates who destroyed Britain may have used the first two, but it would seem that the colonists did not imitate them until after the coastlines were occupied. The explanation may be that the good lands to which they led were too deep in the interior, too close to the Britons of the western heights. Security was essential to a struggling agricultural community, and security was best obtained in the east. Only later, when the colonists had grown more numerous, were they ready to engage in a fighting ad-vance. As for the Thames, the indications are that in the early stages it was closed to the invaders—in other words, that Roman London held out. That it did ultimately fall is fairly certain. The obliteration of the Roman street-plan and the reconstruc-tion of the city on a new one are grounds for assuming that there was a considerable gap between the life of Roman London and that of the later Saxon London. But the date of the desertion is one of the vital facts that have been lost. We may infer, however, that Roman London survived the general sacking of the province. Had it been taken at the outset, the colonists would have passed up the Thames and settled on its banks, and we should expect to find communities astride of the river. Actually the Thames does not flow through counties, but divides them. It is therefore probable that the river basin was not approached from its mouth, but from the north and the south by two independent movements, by Mercians from the midlands and by West Saxons from the south coast. Here again there is no certainty, but only a theory. There may have been early settlements common to both banks, and subsequent wars may have separated them. Some have even surmised that Wessex was entered by people who came up the Thames, in spite of the Chronicle's statement that the kingdom began on the south coast. But the Thames theory does not seem very probable.

Little as we know of the events of the Saxon colonization, it is possible to be more certain about the nature of the communities it produced. From the seventh century onwards, when the mists of the pioneering days begin to clear away, we have a variety of details about the new kingdoms.

The social order is worth consideration, for it was the germ from which all subsequent English life developed, and some of its peculiarities persisted almost to our own time. The unit of settlement was the kindred, the large family or group of families which came over the sea, perhaps in the same ship, broke the soil at some chosen spot, and worked in common at the agricultural tasks which would have been less easy for single individuals. The ordinary free man among the Teutons had to belong to a recognized kindred if he was to enjoy and preserve his liberty. Above the free men were a noble class, who held their rank not by promotion but by their descent from heroic or godlike ancestors. The nobles were undoubtedly of higher estimation than the free men, but the extent of their privileges, whether they tilled their own lands or whether they lived entirely by the labour of slaves, are all unknown. Slaves certainly existed, the property of nobles and free men alike Some were prisoners of war, others were offenders degraded from their free kindred for crime, others were members of kindreds broken up by misfortune. These unhappy people were regarded as agricultural stock like the cattle, and had no more right to justice than the animals had. If they behaved badly their owner was held responsible, and he took his own means of disciplining them.

The territory occupied by a kindred was the township (which does not mean a town). Its visible evidences in the landscape were the houses of the families grouped in a little village and surrounded by the great fields in which the crops were grown. The fields were common in one sense, that is, that the ploughing and some other operations were carried out by the common efforts of the whole community. But for the care and ownership of the crops they were split up into little private properties where each family reaped the fruits of its own labour. These separate properties were not fenced off, and all grew the same crop at the same time, so that the village cornland was of the open type and not intersected by permanent boundaries as in modern England. The same part-common and part-private principle applied to the meadow land where the hay was grown. The pasture land was entirely common, and upon it all the village animals grazed together. So also was the marsh, moor, or woodland which surrounded the fields—the waste of the township, whose produce was the property of any who cared to gather it.

It is fairly evident that in the days of the foundation these kindreds gave themselves plenty of room, and that many miles of waste might separate one village from another. For since there was little or no trade each community had to be self-sufficing. Each needed some good soil, a water supply, and a woodland in which to feed swine and to cut fuel and building material, and these advantages were not always found in combination. It is evident also that the natural features determined the size of the communities, and that some could grow larger than others. The expansion of the whole colony was due partly to the arrival of fresh immigrants from overseas and partly to the increase of population in established townships. When a cultivated area became overcrowded some of its members would swarm off to other ground and begin a new township. This process is commemorated by the large number of instances in which place-names are duplicated and distinguished by adjectives like New and Old, East and West, Upper and Lower, and the like. It is not known how long the movement from Germany continued in any given kingdom. A whole tribe may have come over in a few years and expanded subsequently by its own multiplication and swarming off, or the immigration may have been steady for a century. The Saxon Chronicle tells us a good deal about the first arrivals, but nothing about the last.

As the colonies took root they had to build up a system of law and government, and in these matters they copied the institutions of their ancient homes across the North Sea. The township was the smallest unit, and, isolated as it often was, it must have regulated its own local affairs, but no record has been found of any formal township 'moot' or assembly. The next larger unit was the hundred, which certainly had its moot. What the hundred actually signified is not clear. It may have been originally a hundred free families—many more than would be found in the average township, which might contain no more than a dozen. But when the hundred is first clearly visible in Saxon records, long after the pioneer stage, it means a fixed area of land, remaining unaltered in spite of any growth of population; and the hundreds are of varying sizes. The hundred moot was a court which took account of serious crimes, and arranged taxation and military service and similar matters with the king. In the little kingdoms of the east, such as Kent, Sussex, and Essex, the hundred was the largest subdivision of the whole nation. Over all was the king. He was chosen from one of the noble kindreds, although not by any strict rule of hereditary succession, for it was essential that he should be a grown man of good ability.

The king was the general in war and the judge in peace of the whole nation. To assist him he had his council or witan. How this body was composed is not clearly known, but there is little foundation for the old idea that it was democratically elected like a modern parliament. The whole thing may very likely have lain in the king's discretion, without any fixed rules. But the witan had some recognized powers. It could depose a bad king, its consent was necessary to the making of new laws, and it chose a new sovereign when the throne was vacant. A new class of nobles, the thegns, also became important as the kingdoms grew. From the outset the Teutonic kings maintained a bodyguard or war-band of men whose trade was fighting and who were excused other duties. For their support the king allotted them townships in which the free men had to yield them some dues besides working for themselves. When kingdoms were successful in war there were conquered territories to be bestowed on these fighting thegns, some of whom became rich and powerful. Their existence, as may be seen, involved that of unfree or semi-free townships, and this was one of the germs of feudalism, of the baronial manor and its serfs. But in early days it is evident that the township of free men was much the more usual type.

As colonization spread across England, three kingdoms, Northumbria, Mercia, and Wessex, overshadowed the rest in power and size. The reasons for this are partly geographical and partly political. The minor kingdoms, East Anglia, Essex, Kent, and Sussex, soon found their expansion blocked. The natural limitations of Kent have already been mentioned; it was a peninsula, almost an island. So also was Sussex, to the north of whose coastal strip lay a forest requiring vast clearing and draining operations before its soil could be tilled. Essex was bordered on its western frontier by another great forest stretching north-eastward from London. East Anglia was closed to westward growth by the Wash and the great fens.

Northumbria differed from these in that its westward expansion was checked not so much by natural obstacles as by the power of the Britons entrenched in their western mountains. This contact with the Britons prevented the kingdom from stagnating, and when both sides had settled down on a stable frontier and had accepted a common Christianity there was some fusion of the Celtic and Teuton races. The result was that in the seventh century Northumbria displayed remarkable warlike energy, piety, and learning, and became for a time the most advanced state in England.

Mercia and Wessex had the same experience. Both had large territories into which to expand, and each found a line of fusion with the Celts, so that their western borders were peopled by a mixed stock. Each in turn had a period of supremacy, Mercia in the eighth century, and Wessex from that time until the end of Saxon England.

Little is known about the making of Mercia, although it was a much larger area than the earlier kingdoms. Its history must have been exciting, but it is almost all lost. The Wessex record is more fully preserved. It is evident that the West Saxon kings bestowed large estates of conquered territory upon their thegns, who were able in return to bring numerous fighting men to the field. Wessex therefore displayed a social order less simple than that of Kent. There were townships of free men of the primitive type. There were the properties owned by the thegns and inhabited by men who were not entirely free. And besides these, there were lands still held by Britons who had made their peace with the new government, and whose agricultural customs were of Celtic type, perhaps quite different from those of the co-operative township. The mixture of the lively Celt and the solid Teuton produced a stock from which was to arise a succession of talented men throughout the course of English history. In Wessex also there is first seen a new unit of land and administration, the shire. The shire grouped the hundreds, just as the hundred grouped the townships. The shire moots were intermediate between the hundred moot and the king's court or witan; and the ealdormen, who governed the shires and commanded their forces, formed the highest rank among the thegns.

One more point will complete this sketch of the Saxon colonization. Both Mercia and Wessex, by reason of their large size and their military organization, were able to react to the eastward as soon as they had reached their limits in the west. Their kings were conquerors who throve by war, because it yielded them lands with which to endow their fighting men. They could therefore demand the submission of the little closed-in kingdoms of the east. Essex and East Anglia became subordinate to Mercia, and Sussex and Kent to Wessex. The vassal kings were in time replaced by ealdormen as their kingdoms sank to the status of shires. By the time Saxon England was fully grown it had thus taken shape as three chief kingdoms, Northumbria, Mercia, and Wessex, divided respectively by the Humber and the Thames.

IV. THE CONVERSION: SAXON ENGLAND IN ITS PRIME

Just after the eastern kingdoms were well established, but before Wessex and Mercia had reached their full size, the Christian religion came into Saxon England. The beginning of the conversion is marked by a definite date, 597, when Augustine and his monks from Rome landed in Kent. With that event history recommences in England after a gap of a hundred and fifty years. It is a significant fact that the missionaries found the Anglo-Saxons devoted to their pagan gods. There was not a trace of Christianity among them. That is a silent testimony to the zone of desolation that divided the Saxons from the Christian Celts of the western uplands, and it supports the theory of the wholesale devastation of the Roman province before colonization began. The missionaries spread rapidly northwards. Then they were driven out of Northumbria by a heathen reaction, and that kingdom was afterwards converted by a Celtic missionary movement which started from Ireland and came into Northumbria through lowland Scotland. In the south the Roman monks were more successful, and in the course of seventy years the whole country was converted. In Northumbria, as has been remarked, this seventh century produced a fine period of good order and civilization. The Celtic influence was prominent in it because the kingdom had reached the limits of its expansion and settled down in civil contact with the Britons. Wessex and Mercia, on the other hand, were still engaged in their wars of conquest with the Celts, and had not yet reached the stage of fusion with them. The eastern kingdoms were, by reason of their position, wholly Teutonic.

The seventh century witnessed the parcelling out of England into bishoprics and the establishment of monasteries as centres of Christian influence. In the eighth century the system of parishes began to take shape. In general the parish coincided with the township of freemen or with the military estate of the thegn, but this was not always so, and there were many local variations that have left their mark on England to this day. The parish priest and his village church have had an immense influence in shaping the national character, a deeper and more enduring effect than that of the monasteries or even of the cathedrals, whose bishops have always been somewhat aloof from the mass of the people. No medieval bishop, not even Anselm or Becket, moulded the national outlook so powerfully as did John Wycliffe, the parish priest.

The conversion had profound effects upon Saxon England. They may be considered under two heads, political and moral, and it will be convenient to take the political first. The bishops came over from the Continent endued with a learning that rendered them fit counsellors for kings, and many of them stepped at once into that position. So there arose the ecclesiastical influence in the government of the English state, an influence that was to flourish for a thousand years. In theory it survives to this day, for the senior bishops are still members of the House of Lords, although for the last four centuries no great minister of state has been drawn from their ranks.

This was not the only political result of the conversion. It is established that the Church bore its part in the development of feudalism. The clergy needed wealth to support them in their work, and they found the converted kings very ready to endow them. Direct money grants from the state were not feasible, for in the early days there was hardly any coined money. But all the king's subjects were obliged to pay him dues in services and goods; that was their duty as free men of the realm. The churchmen were therefore not slow to suggest to their royal friends that these rights could be transferred. The king might set aside a territory and direct its free men to pay their dues to the bishop or the abbot instead of to the Crown. And this practice, together with that by which the king provided for his fighting thegns, began the process of degrading the free men into bondmen, the process of feudalization which reached its zenith in the two centuries after the Norman Conquest. Probably no one in the early days foresaw what was coming. The thing was not a deliberate attack upon liberty. Yet there can be no doubt that services owed to a monastery or a nobleman were a different thing from services owed to the king. To pay the king taxes in kind or to serve him in battle was no derogation from freedom, but to yield the same things to a fellow-subject was to submit to a class distinction which had far-reaching possibilities. Insensibly the village communities ceased to be considered as the owners of the soil. Their overlord became the owner, and the villagers as well as their land became his possessions. It was the transition from the free township to the feudal manor. In the early days of the conversion all this was in the far future, but its seed was planted, and the growth was destined to be forced by the calamities of the Danish invasions and the Norman Conquest.

On the moral side the influence of the Church was good, yet the good was not unmixed with evil. It brought an improvement in conduct and a lessened callousness in the taking of life, a greater regard for order and decency, a general advance in civilization. The Christian doctrine held up an ideal of piety and good works unknown to the savage cult of Thor and Woden. The effects were seen in a few saintly lives that must have had an immense influence upon the rest. But upon many crude minds the new doctrines bore less desirable results. The Church taught that penance must be done for sin, and the Saxon law was already based upon the principle of payment to atone for crime. So it became easy for Saxon kings to make excessive grants to the Church for the good of their souls. The motive was really selfish, and it weakened the community by removing large areas from liability to national services and so increasing the burden on the remainder. Early in the eighth century the abuse was flagrant, and so good a churchman as the Venerable Bede protested against it. Moved by the same motives of spurious piety rich men founded excessive numbers of monasteries and convents. At first their inmates practised a hard ascetic life. But in time many of these houses lost their ideal and degenerated into sloth and worldliness. Well-born people retired into them with their servants and their luxuries, and lived securely under the cloak of the Church without having to exhibit the courage and manliness demanded by the rough life outside. In some instances the Church uplifted the barbarian, in others it degraded him. And for that loss of virile tone there was a bitter penalty in store.

It is not within the scope of this book to describe in detail the history of the Saxon kingdoms. We have glanced at the process of their development, and must now take a survey of the extent it had reached by the beginning of the ninth century, when the storm of the Danish invasions burst upon the country. It has been shown that the earlier settlements of the south-east were founded essentially as colonies in a wasted land and that their expansion was limited by geographical obstacles. Northumbria had a somewhat greater scope and spread across the country from the east coast to the edge of the mountain area held by the Britons. The Mercians and the West Saxons had more extensive opportunities, and they grasped them much more rapidly. They planted some free settlements of the earlier colonist type, but they also conquered British areas and absorbed their inhabitants instead of expelling them. Thus the military element appears more prominent in these kingdoms in contact with the

Britons. The feudal thegns were powerful in them, and their kings were fighting generals rather than the peaceful judges of a working community. The three kingdoms with frontiers open to the west thus grew much more powerful than the little closed kingdoms of the east. Each of the three in turn achieved a sort of supremacy over the whole island.

Northumbria, the first to fill its own possible territory, was the first to attain overlordship. That was in the seventh century, and it did not last long. Northumbria was too small for the burden it had shouldered. There were hostile Mercians to the southward, Britons in the west, and Picts in the north beyond the frontier fortress of Edwin's Burgh. Incessant battle wore down the kingdom's strength, and the end came in 685 when the Northumbrian monarch and all his army were trapped and massacred at Nectansmere far up in Pictland beyond the Forth.

The eighth century was that of Mercian supremacy, which declined after the death of Offa in 794. Then, in the early ninth century, Wessex took the lead under Egbert, who founded a line of talented kings. They were the effective kings of England when the Danish inroads began, and it was to their ability that the country owed its salvation.

By the ninth century Saxon England was loosely united into a single state, with a supreme king and a number of subject kings whose rank was not much above that of the ealdormen in charge of the Wessex shires. The Church was organized in bishoprics, and the system of parishes was well developed; and in addition to this clerical body in close touch with the people, there were the religious houses whose chief useful function was to foster such learning as existed. The Anglo-Saxon population were still in the main free men, owing allegiance to none but the king, and carrying on a practical self-government in the moots of the hundred and the shire. But already there was a beginning of feudalism in the estates allotted to the Church and the thegns. The thegns and the superior churchmen now constituted the noble class, a nobility of office rather than of birth. The area covered by this state did not quite coincide with that of modern England. In the north it extended up the east coast to Edinburgh, but in the west it did not effectively include Cumberland and Westmoreland (which, with south-western Scotland, formed the Celtic unit of Strathclyde), and in the south-west the Celtic province of West Wales (Cornwall and part of Devon) was still unconquered. Wales proper, then as now, was definitely a separate country.

The employment of this population was almost wholly in agriculture. There was indeed some rudimentary trade along the coasts, and overseas with Ireland, France, and the Low Countries. There must also have been some fishing. But in the main the Saxons were tillers of the soil. Virtually nothing is known of the towns, if any existed worthy of the name. The record even of London is a blank in the early Saxon period. All that we can tell is that there was a very slow emergence of a new town life, but that by the time of Egbert it had not become prominent. This is a fact worth noting in view of events that were shortly to take place. Naval defence was not required until the onset of the Danes, for all the fighting was in civil wars. For military defence every free man was bound to serve in the fyrd or national levy, and in addition the thegns and their retainers formed a smaller but more efficient band of troops. Such was the England, free, semi-civilized, agricultural, not organized for determined fighting, upon which the Danish war-clouds were about to burst.

V. THE DANISH INVASION AND SETTLEMENT

It should be understood that there was a Danish invasion of robber bands, followed by a partial settlement, in the ninth century, and another Danish invasion, of kings leading regular forces and effecting a political conquest, in the late tenth and early eleventh centuries. The two inroads were different both in process and in results. The earlier, with which this section is concerned, was only partially successful, but left a permanent mark on the country. The later was for a time completely successful, but its effects soon faded away.

To understand the plan of the movement we must look across the North Sea. The expansion of the Scandinavian vikings— Norsemen, Danes, and Swedes—began in the eighth century. The reasons for it are obscure, but the fact is clear that there was a great outflow of people in several directions from the Scandinavian homelands. One stream flowed westwards across the cold northern seas to Iceland and Greenland, and even touched North America. Part of this stream branched southwards and covered the Shetlands and Orkneys, and then

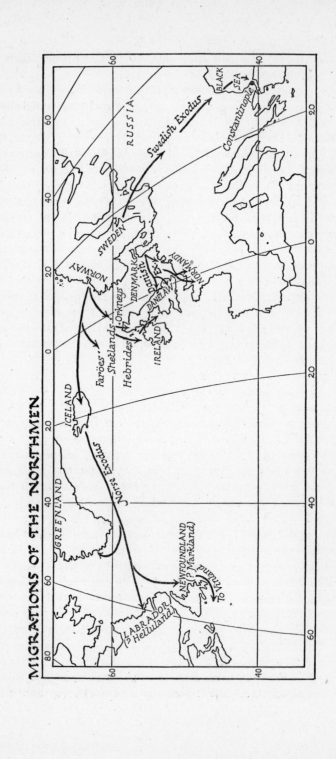

MIGRATIONS OF THE NORTHMEN

reached the mainland of northern Scotland, where the county name of Sutherland shows that its invaders came from the north. The same movement came down into the Hebrides and then to the Irish Sea, to the Isle of Man and the coasts of Ireland and western England. The adventurers to all these regions sailed originally from the Norwegian fjords and are commonly known as Norsemen. Another outflow, chiefly of Swedes, went south-eastwards into Russia and down to the Black Sea. Some of its pioneers penetrated the Eastern Empire and took service as the Emperor's Varangian guard at Constantinople. But the majority settled in Russia as overlords of the Slavonic tribes. They gave their name to the country; for the Russ originally meant, not the native Slav, but the incoming Scandinavian. Our own country was most powerfully affected by a third exodus, principally from Denmark, but with Norsemen and others intermingled. These Danes sailed south-westwards along the coasts of northern Germany and down to the Narrow Seas between England and the Low Countries. There they attacked eastern and southern England and also northern France, the empire of the Franks established by Charlemagne. The Danes, it will be noticed, sprang from the same region that had sent forth the Jutes and Angles four centuries earlier. What had been happening over there in those long centuries we do not clearly know. Perhaps the Danes were in the main descendants of the earlier stock; perhaps they had come in from the north and displaced it. The tearful descriptions by Christian Britons in the fifth century, and by Christian Saxons in the ninth, give the impression that both sets of raiders acted in the same unchristian manner, and they were evidently the same kind of people.

In viewing the whole Scandinavian outbreak we may discern two chief motives, plunder and colonization. In the islands of the northern seas the Norsemen were primarily settlers, for those lands were empty or contained only poor savages possessing nothing worth stealing. Iceland and Greenland, the Shetlands, Orkneys, and Hebrides, were essentially Norse colonies from the outset, and they are a wonderful testimony to the energy of the little nation bred in the fjords and valleys of the Norwegian coast. The Norsemen and Danes who sailed south to the Irish Sea and the shores of the English Channel were, on the other hand, plunderers first and settlers by an afterthought. Like the early Anglo-Saxons, they came to sack a civilized land, and only when they had stolen all they could get did they think of occupying its soil.

They sailed in long open vessels of shallow draught, driven by sail and oar. No modern seamen would venture in such craft on such voyages as they made in the savage northern seas. And as navigators they were equally wonderful, keeping their course without compass, chart, or sextant, divining their position like the seabirds by the signs of Nature. It was no life for weaklings either in body or mind. Only the strong survived, brave, cunning and pitiless, to bite like a blast of white flame into the softened Anglo-Saxons and Franco-Gauls.

Why were these men, of similar blood and speech to the Saxons of England, so utterly different in instinct and character? The answer is that though heredity counts for much, environment counts for more. The way of life shapes the people who live it. We may see this in nations as in individuals. The English stocks in North America and Australia are of different character from the English stock at home. If three brothers are born on a farm, and one goes to sea, another to work in a city, whilst the third stays on the land, by the time they grow old they will have less in common with one another than with strangers of their own several callings. This is a vital fact in the evolution of a people, and it has its bearing upon imperial federations and leagues of nations. There is a limit to the unity attainable by such means. It must at best be a unity without uniformity, based upon a sentiment needing deep roots.

Danish raids on the coast began before the end of the eighth century, and continued with increasing severity through the first half of the ninth. Every summer there was sack and slaughter, but always the robbers went home when the season ended. Monasteries were their especial prey, for such buildings were often stored with wealth; and before long it was not the coast alone which suffered, but many a region in the heart of England. The vikings were alert and adaptable. They advanced up the rivers in their great boats, the heaviest of which would float in water in which a man might wade, left them with a guard at some marsh-encircled island, and landed to seek their prey. Often they took horse and rode far inland. Their movements were so rapid that the force of the countryside could seldom gather on them before they were gone, leaving a trail of blood and ashes in their wake. When they were caught there was a fight, in which skill would often vanquish numbers—on the one side a ring of tough warriors, standing shoulder to shoulder, hewing with keen axes 'over the linden' of their shields, a tactical unit with some long-tried tactician in command; on the other a mob of peasantry whose normal life was the tilling of the soil, half-armed and undisciplined, commanded by some good thegn who had perhaps seen war in the English style, but whose ideal was peace and ease. It needed large numbers to redress the disparity. Sometimes the numbers were sufficient, and a pirate band went hewing and swearing to Valhalla. More often professional skill prevailed, and some shire or hundred was left short of ploughmen until the children grew up. Oversea in the fjords there were merry winters of feasting and drinking and boasting, gold and jewels to dice with, and warriors' labour in fashioning weapons and long ships for the summer's campaign.

So it went on for half a century, in England and France, more obscurely in Ireland, sometimes even down the shores of Spain and round into the Mediterranean. There are three names on the map of modern Europe—Berlikum in Friesland, Burling Gap in Sussex, and the Burlengas, islets off the coast of Portugal—which suggest an epic to the imaginative mind, the Odyssey of some Burling's fleet from Denmark. In 851 things in this country took a new turn. The independent bands united in a 'great army' (it is the Saxon chronicler's phrase), and soon afterwards the Danes wintered in England. The great army had no need to slip away with its booty. It could defy any force the weakened kingdom could turn out against it. For a generation the great army struck north and south and west. Northumbria went down and out before it, Northumbria and East Anglia and Essex and half of Mercia. The Dane could sing of his conquering chiefs; the Christian Saxon could only celebrate his martyrs, St. Elphege at Rochester, St. Edmund at Bury, and hundreds of nameless monks and nuns. It must all have been very similar to that lost fifth century when the Saxon's forefathers had done the like work in the Roman province. Two circumstances averted a like ending. The Saxon peasant was a different victim from the Roman provincial; and Saxon Wessex produced a man. On the first head it may be recalled that the life and culture of Britain, its Roman religion and its Latin tongue, had resided in its cities. When they had gone, all

E

had gone but a horde of fugitives who forgot the imperial tradition and reverted to their Celtic life in the Welsh mountains. As against this, the Anglo-Saxon was no town-dweller. His fields were his home. War swept over them, but if there were any survivors they returned to the plough. There was nothing else to do. And it was easier for them to revive a ravaged township than it had been for the provincials to reconstitute the trade and industry of a gutted city. The township would live of its own; the Roman city depended on a whole ordered province. As for the second factor that saved England, and without which even the first would not long have availed—the man was Alfred.

They were a wonderful family, that house of Egbert, which took the lead in English life for two and a half centuries—a longer time than that from George I to George V. King after king showed high talents, rising sometimes to genius, lived stormily but fruitfully, and died young or middle-aged. That was their tragedy, a constitutional unsoundness that cut them off, generation after generation, in what should have been their prime. But frail as they were in body, they had souls of fire. All through the ninth century, and for more than half the tenth, they first saved and then mended the broken Saxon state. And then the type changed. After many a short-lived hero they bred two long-lived fools, and Saxon England ceased to be.

Alfred, the greatest of them all, came to the throne in 871 as a boy of sixteen, just as the great army was thrusting into the heart of Wessex. The war swayed to and fro until after seven terrible years it seemed as if all was lost. The thegns and rustics had fought gallantly, but man for man they were no match for their grim invaders, the select survivors of hard winters in the northland, of the fury of the northern seas, of marching and fighting on every shore of Europe. By 878 Wessex had collapsed. Her king still lived, but no man knew where. Victory relaxed the wolfish vigilance of the Dane. Alfred saw his chance, and from his hiding-place sent round a word for one last rally; and at Ethandune and Chippenham the miracle was accomplished. Beaten in the field and hemmed in within a starving camp, the great army surrendered to its conqueror. Its field force, that is to say, surrendered, but all eastern England was by this time full of Danes who had retired from active service and settled on the land. It was to be many a year before Wessex could think of reducing them. And so the Treaty of Wedmore, pledged after the surrender of Chippenham, provided that the active host should receive baptism and withdraw north-east of Watling Street or, approximately, of the line from London to Chester. We need not moralize on the baptism. To the converts it was primarily a symbol of defeat, whereby every superstitious man of them carried on his forehead until death the brand of civilization, none the less real because invisible. A lesser man than Alfred would have waited until hunger drove them from their camp and would then have cut them down like the wolves they were; after which a new host would have come to seek vengeance. His practical genius seized the chance of establishing a moral ascendancy that proved decisive. For not a Dane then in England ever gave trouble again. They settled down in their Danelaw and gave no aid to the new bands that afterwards appeared from overseas.

Alfred had thus saved half of England, with the possibility, which his successors fulfilled, of recovering the other half. He knew well that that was not the end, that the north had yet its vikings to send forth. He used the breathing-space to organize his territory for a better defence. He had Wessex, with its sub-kingdoms of Kent and Sussex, and half of Mercia. He had also a shadowy lordship over northern Northumbria, although the southern part of that kingdom fell within the Danelaw. Wessex was already cut into shires, each with its ealdorman to lead it in war. Mercia had also been shired in the days of its greatness, but the system had collapsed in the war, and Alfred began it again on new lines. To every shire he appointed one or more burhs or strong camps, their earthen ramparts and staked parapets to be repaired and defended by the neighbouring countrymen. These became the towns of later England. And so we find the midland counties to-day, which Alfred and his sons delimited as they built the burhs, taking their names from the county towns, whilst the southern counties, which ante-dated the burh system, have names dissimilar to those of their capitals. Alfred also reorganized the fyrd and enabled it to stay longer in the field by a regulation that only half the men of a district should serve at one time, whilst the others tended the crops. He created numbers of new thegns and required that their followers should be equipped with helmets and mail-coats. And, not content with all this, he built a navy, a bold enterprise when we consider his rustic antecedents and the prestige of the Danes at sea. It was genius again that prompted that stroke, so obvious to us with our history, so extraordinary to country-men who had never read a treatise on sea power nor ever thought of fighting otherwise than on land. And without an exceptional driving spirit Alfred's navy must have proved a ludicrous failure instead of the success it turned out to be.

The record of Alfred's proceedings throws light upon another matter, the condition of the Church in the ninth century. It is evident that the clergy had not made steady progress from the days of the conversion. Most of them were illiterate, and the king had to call in Welshmen and Franks to initiate a revival of learning. He attempted also to restore the monasteries to their proper status and to prevent them from being used as hostels for wealthy people who meant to live a worldly life. He was not permanently successful, for we find half a century later that Archbishop Dunstan had to do the same thing. In secular education Alfred did good work. He founded a school for boys and induced some even of his adult followers to copy his example of regular study. He certainly left English learning on a higher plane than that on which he found it, and the tradition he created never wholly died out.

The first Danish invaders, as we have seen, were stabilized in the Danelaw. There is no clue to their numbers, but the inference is that they were a minority among a subject popula-tion of Saxons; for in time Saxon England absorbed them. She was also in their turn to absorb the Normans, another conquering minority. These immigrants certainly affected the development of England by modifying national character and introducing new institutions and ways of thought, but it was after all Eng-land's development and not theirs. They themselves were assimilated, digested, in the process. There was therefore no break and recommencement like that produced by the Saxon conquest of the Roman province. In the regions once covered by the Danelaw we can trace a distinct set of place-names with terminations such as -by, -thorpe, -thwaite, and -ness, which may indicate some considerable settlements. The Danes also substituted wapentakes and carucates for hundreds and hides of land, and preferred to group units in multiples of six and twelve instead of the fives and tens favoured by the Saxons. On a broad view of English history it is possible also to discern a difference of communal character between the east and the west, but this may be due to geographical factors and to the presence in the western parts of a Celtic infusion which was lacking in the east. It cannot be clearly attributed to the Danish element. The Anglo-Saxon language undoubtedly prevailed over that of the invaders.

In another respect the Danes did contribute an enduring influence to the national evolution. From their time forwards a trade existed between eastern England and the lands across the North Sea. Hitherto the Saxons had looked southwards to the empire of the Franks, and beyond that to Rome as the fountain of culture. The Scandinavian adventurers were not all vikings. Some were merchants who ventured far with their wares. And when they opened this eastern window of England they placed her on a trade route which led not merely to their own Baltic lands but southwards from them to the Black Sea and the Eastern Empire, where Constantinople was an emporium of trade with the Asiatics of the Levant. The effects were small at first, but they were lasting; and right down to the Tudor period, and even later, the chief part of our foreign trade issued from the east-coast ports and was directed across the North Sea. This laid us open to German influences, whose results will be noted in their place.

A final word must be said about Scandinavian expansion. When Alfred checked the ravagers of England they turned their efforts to easier prey. They found it in northern France, where in the closing years of Alfred's reign they established a second Danelaw in Normandy. Twelve years after his death the treaty of Clair-sur-Epte (912) stabilized this settlement. The Scandinavians of Normandy, like those of England, quickly suited themselves to their new surroundings, relinquished their native tongue, and adopted that of the French. But they were imposing themselves upon a Celtic rather than a Teutonic population, and the fusion produced a distinct type which long remained a separate nationality and keeps some of its characteristics to this day. The Normans of William the Conqueror were not by any means Frenchmen, although some Frenchmen came to England in their train.

III

THE FEUDAL AGE

(*From Alfred to Henry III*)

I. THE WARS, THE CHURCH, AND THE RISE OF FEUDALISM

WE have already noted the germs of feudalism in the allotment of lands, with the services of their inhabitants, to the Church on the one hand, and to the military caste of the thegns on the other. It may be well to define the sense in which the word feudalism is to be used. It means the holding of land on condition of services rendered to a superior.

At first sight it might appear that rendering personal services was not essentially different from the modern system of rendering money payments, for money will buy service, and so is in a sense equivalent to it. But there was in practice a great difference. Personal services could not be saved up and accumulated like money; they had to be rendered at regular intervals and could never be massed into a capital sum which would pay off the whole debt at a stroke. It followed therefore that the man bound to render service could never terminate the obligation save by flight. He was bound for life; he was not free. And by a custom which hardened before its worst implications were realized, his children were bound after him and were born into the obligation of service. Again, while in modern times one man's money is as good as another's, the same could not be said of service. Consequently the feudal superior had an interest in the quality of his subordinates and developed a right to interfere in the details of their lives. He tried to prevent them from entering into legal relationships, by marriage or otherwise, with other superiors, whereby his claims on them or their offspring might be endangered. This is only one aspect of a process which rendered the majority of the English people unfree in an objectionable sense of the word. Feudal obligations, when the system extended, bound almost everyone. But in practice they were of two sorts, the military service of the nobles and gentry, honourable and well rewarded with rights over others, and the menial and economic services of the common people to these superiors. The military status was desirable and sought after. If one man wished to retire from it another was ready to step into his place, and it therefore involved no practical loss of freedom. The economic services, on the other hand, were not so beneficial to those who owed them, there were no volunteers to fill a vacant place, and there was thus no practical possibility of getting away from the obligation. These economic servants were the real unfree. The two classes came to be distinguished as lords and villeins.

To understand how this system developed from its immature beginnings, it will be necessary first to glance at the outline of our history from the death of Alfred to the Norman Conquest, a period of just over one-and-a-half centuries. Alfred's victory of 878 was not the end of his military efforts. In the last decade of the century new bands of raiders came from overseas and were beaten off. The king died in 900, and his successors devoted themselves to the reconquest of the Danelaw. By 940 they had accomplished the task, and the whole of England was one kingdom, with a northern frontier that included southern Scotland and reached to the foot of the Highlands. There followed about forty years of peace and prosperity under short-lived but able kings of the Wessex line, with one long-lived genius, Archbishop Dunstan, permeating the whole period. This was undoubtedly the golden age of Saxon England. Learning and trade and agriculture flourished, Dunstan disciplined the Church, and the monarchy was strong to protect its subjects. There were disturbances in Northumbria during the early years, but in the end even that turbulent province was reduced to order, whilst the rest of England vented its spirits in purely political disputes which scarcely broke the general peace. Then in 978 the house of Wessex failed, for the first time, to produce a man. Ethelred the Unready, or more correctly the Redeless, 'lacking in common sense', began a disastrous reign of nearly forty years, the longest then on record, and at once it was seen how much England had owed to the ability of his predecessors.

The Danes had more than once tried to renew the invasions earlier in the century, but had long given up the project as hopeless. Now they seemed to divine at once that their chance had come. The new king was at first a minor, and speedily grew up to be an incompetent man. He was not a dullard. He had considerable intelligence, but it was marred by a defect of character, lack of discernment or tact or truthfulness, which resulted always in wrong decisions and foolish acts. No man could trust him, and his want of moral principle invariably called forth the worst instead of the best in those who owed him fealty. The Danish raids began at once—raids only for some dozen years, and then a serious effort at the conquest of the realm as its weakness became more apparent. The Scandinavian homelands had by this time been consolidated into strong kingdoms. The kings saw that their adventurous subjects had found a promising undertaking, and so they followed the example in their own persons. With the opening of the eleventh century the wars thus took the form of invasions by the whole force of an organized state. Sweyn of Denmark fought campaign after campaign on English soil. At length, aided by treachery and despair among Ethelred's subjects, he drove the wretched king fairly out of England, to die in exile in Normandy. But Sweyn died also in the moment of victory, and the manner of his death had its influence upon the future. He had been a brute of the worst type, a slayer of the defenceless, and in particular a scourge to men of religion. At length, as he passed bullying through the wasted land, he fell suddenly from his horse and died screaming on the road. Men said that he had seen a vision in the air and that divine wrath had slain him. The example was not lost upon his followers, and his son Canute adopted a different way of life.

Canute had been a viking like the rest of them, and in his first year of kingship he displayed all the viking courage in a series of pitched battles with Edmund Ironside, the young son of Ethelred. Edmund might have been a second Alfred but that the impartial stroke of death removed him too, and in 1016 Canute was left undisputed king. At that critical juncture Canute ceased to be a viking and saved England by becoming in effect an Englishman. It was a momentous conversion, whose result was that the Danish conquest, complete though it was, left a smaller mark upon the country than the half-successful invasion of Alfred's time. For Canute ruled as an English king, in the best tradition of the Wessex line. He checked violence, worked for a peaceful settlement, patronized learning and industry, supported the Church whilst not allowing it to become luxurious, and healed the wounds of thirty years of warfare. He was not King of England alone, although he made it his headquarters. His empire comprised all the Scandinavian homelands and conquests except Normandy. It was a maritime empire with the North Sea as its medium of communications. Five hundred years later such an empire might have been permanent. But in the eleventh century shipping and navigation were not sufficiently advanced. Communication was too difficult, and Canute's empire fell apart after his death in 1035. For seven years two more Danish kings ruled England in turn, and then the line failed.

The English Witan bethought them of Edward, a son of Ethelred brought up in Normandy. They called him to the throne, to reign for twenty-four years as Edward the Confessor. His rule was as ill-omened as that of his father, but in a different sense. He was an unworldly pietist who might have done good work as the head of a monastery. As King of England he failed from lack of sympathy with his task. He had grown to manhood as a foreigner. There was much in England to displease him, and he was quicker to see the faults than the merits of his new subjects. He was more at ease with Normans, churchmen and laymen alike, and he did not disguise the preference. His reign saw a steady permeation of England by Norman influence and the preparation for the invasion that speedily followed his death.

All this is the background of the rise of feudalism. In the century-and-a-half from Alfred to the Confessor a great change took place in the structure of society. In the first place, the small thegns who lorded it over a manor or two ceased to be the highest rank in the nobility. The necessities of leadership in war and of administration in peace led, as we have seen, to the shiring of the country and the creation of ealdormen (later called earls) to command the thegnhood of the shires. A further development occurred amid the last great struggles with the Danes. Shires were grouped into larger units, and the great earldoms of Wessex, Mercia, East Anglia, and Northumbria became holdings for a handful of families forming a supernobility. These greater earls were each as strong as the king. Tradition and a habit of thought alone preserved the royal power, and there were signs of a time to come when the Crown would sink into feebleness and the earls would be sovereigns of independent states. That condition did come to pass on the continent. In the England of Edward the Confessor it was well on the way, and its accomplishment was prevented only by the Norman Conquest of 1066. Its onset did much to establish English feudalism, for great nobles competing for power desired above all things to increase the numbers of their own dependents, and grasped every opportunity of turning free men into vassals within their jurisdiction.

There were reasons why the free men could not resist the process. In the old Saxon society a man had looked to his kindred for justice and protection. He inherited membership in a band of free associates who preserved order amongst themselves. The kindred was an excellent arrangement for pioneer colonists planting their settlements in a new country. But after the occupation was complete it began to decay. In a settled society men migrated as individuals and not in groups, and when they moved they lost touch with their kindred. The first Danish invasions, those of the ninth century, broke up what was left of the system, for they made England a cauldron whose contents could not settle down in the same order as before. Afterwards, in the golden tenth century, the courts of the hundred and the shire administered the law over all the inhabitants within their areas. Had the peace continued, it might have become possible for a free man to live independent and unattached as he does in England to-day. But the new calamities of Ethelred's time destroyed civil order once more. Might alone could secure right, and the weak had to find protectors and pay their price. So there arose the practice of commendation whereby the free man commended himself to a strong superior, promised service in return for justice, and became a feudal vassal no longer free.

Taxation also worked in the same direction. Ethelred raised enormous 'danegelds' to finance his defences or buy off his enemies. His successors continued to levy geld as a regular practice. Assessment was made upon all lands, and the administration must have been unbelievably pure if the more powerful did not escape with a lighter burden than that of their small neighbours. Payment was in cash. A raided township or a bad harvest spelt inability to pay; and once more the poor free man had to bow his head beneath the yoke and do homage to some lord who would answer for his liabilities. Feudalism was the child of rapine and injustice, born in all fully settled lands whose people lived solely by the cultivation of the soil. Socially, it was an evil, but it may be confessed that it was a necessary evil. In an age of constant war and invasion it provided the only alternative to anarchy; for the technique of administration was then so rudimentary that even a moderate-sized realm like England was too large to be governed from one centre in times of trouble. Not until the age of the Tudors did that become possible, and they had a mechanism of the state immeasurably superior to that of the Saxons. In one aspect feudalism was socially advantageous, for it separated the functions of the fighter and the worker. The ancient Saxon fyrd or levy of all the free men seems at first sight an attractive method of defence, but in practice it must have produced a great deal of famine and distress by withdrawing hands from the fields. Under feudalism the villein ploughed but did not fight, and the military vassals maintained professional soldiers who made war with greater efficiency. There is no clear dividing line between the two military systems. The one decayed whilst the other grew stronger. But the fyrd was never abolished. It was occasionally called out after the Norman Conquest, and in the form of compulsory service in the militia it survived into the nineteenth century.

The Church was a great promoter of feudalism. Bishoprics and abbeys were endowed from the days of the conversion with the services which the free men properly owed to the king. As has been shown,[1] the process involved a fallacy in reasoning which the political thought of the time was unable to penetrate. The king as a public officer rightly claimed the service of his subjects, but it was too often the king as a private individual who transferred that service to a monastery for the good of his own particular soul. The Church did of course perform work of public importance and to that extent was justly endowed, but the scale of its rewards was excessive and tended to become more so. For what the Church got it kept. The military noble might die without heirs or might forfeit his fief to the king for misconduct. But though the abbot was mortal his abbey was not. It was a legal abstraction which never died, even if the Danes left not one stone of its building upon another or one monk with his skull uncloven. The abbey as a holder of land survived all such accidents with its title unaffected; and, relinquishing nothing, it added steadily. Thus the Church piled manor upon manor through the centuries, sometimes by public grant, sometimes by private benefaction, sometimes by forgery of title-deeds; and the descendants of the free Teutonic

[1] See above, p. 42.

kindreds became its feudal villeins, as tightly bound as those who
had fallen to the fighting barons.

It is one of the essentials of European societies that they are
never uniform. At no time in the history of any of them is it
possible to say, 'such and such was the system, and there were
no exceptions'. That undoubtedly is the chief secret of European
expansion over the world, for uniformity in a people is no sign
of vigour, it is a presage of death. Feudalism itself showed
infinite local varieties. Some of the old free men lingered until
it had reached its zenith and had begun to produce new free
men in the course of its decay. And throughout there was a
growing element of the national life which refused to fit itself
into the feudal system in any permanent manner. That element
was contained in the towns. The Anglo-Saxon pioneers were
no town-dwellers. They saw the cities of the Roman province,
and they plundered, burned, and passed on. But inevitably
their grandsons came back again to repair the broken walls.
Trade began as soon as agriculture was established. Trade
implied markets in the country and seaports on the coast—
towns or their rudiments. Towns were beginning to grow by
the time of Alfred, on breaks in the coastline, on river-fords, on
defiles where the Roman roads still threaded swamps and
forests, round minsters and abbeys, round market-places policed
(at a price) by businesslike thegns. London was early re-
occupied—if it had ever been quite deserted—as the natural
gate of entry for foreign produce. Fishermen of the coast turned
merchants and ventured over the narrow seas. Sheer Danish
plundering must have been a stimulus, for it needed depots for
the exchange of its spoil. Alfred saw a military value in the
towns as bulwarks against the flood of invasion. He established
new ones purely as fortified camps to be garrisoned by the
neighbouring countrymen, and they in time resided permanently
and became townsmen. In the later Danish wars towns were an
important feature in the military landscape, and the tenth-
century conquest of the Danelaw swayed to and fro round the
ramparts of the famous 'five burghs'—Nottingham, Stamford,
and their neighbours.

Now feudalism was a system based upon the land, and it was
at its ease only in an agricultural society. Many of the town-
dwellers were cultivators of the fields outside their walls, and
therefore the early towns were feudalized, owing service to some

lord as if they had been normal manors. Craftsmen also might be villeins so long as they worked only for the local demand, but when they began to manufacture in excess of it they entered into relations with the merchant; and he was never a unit of the feudal system. The merchant was of necessity a migrant, not bound to the soil. He neither gave nor received personal services, but bartered or traded for cash. Feudal law very soon recognized that the merchant was an exceptional person whom it could not grip, and gradually the 'law merchant', an affair of the merchants among themselves, came into being. Merchants organized themselves in guilds and brotherhoods, craftsmen followed the example, and then the towns they haunted began to draw apart from the land system, to bargain for exemption from their feudal services, and to secure charters of privilege which made them accountable solely to the king. The craft and merchant guilds were like the ancient kindreds in a new and flexible form—kindreds not of blood but of interests. The times afforded only two forms of society whereby the common man could live in security, the kindred of equals, or bond-service to a fighting protector. Military feudalism killed the old peasant kindreds, which were too weak for defence. The new craft and merchant kindreds could survive by virtue of the town walls that guarded them. They throve and expanded until they overshadowed feudalism.

A very interesting combination of feudalism and the merchant union is to be seen in the development of the Navy. Alfred built a fleet of royal ships, their crews paid out of the national revenue. The great Saxon kings of the tenth century maintained this navy, and even the feckless Ethelred was able on occasion to concentrate respectable fleets against the Danes, although he seldom had the wit to use them efficiently. These squadrons contained hired merchantmen as well as king's ships, for the seaports were growing busier. Canute carried on the system of a paid fleet, with the *buscarles* as a service of regular sea-soldiers to man it. Under Edward the Confessor, the second of the two incompetents of the Saxon house, the plan broke down. In 1052 Godwin, the great half-Danish Earl of Wessex, was in revolt against his sovereign. He returned suddenly from exile, raised the seamen and shipping of his Wessex coast (which included Sussex and Kent), and sailed into the Thames at the head of such a force that the poor king could make no resistance.

Godwin was restored to all his dignities, and it was perhaps the manner of his triumph which caused a change in naval policy. The Navy was feudalized. The five chief ports of Sussex and Kent secured trading privileges, in return for which they were bound to supply ships and men for fifteen days' service a year without payment. Medieval tradition asserted that the Confessor established this Cinque Ports system. The truth about its origin is unknown, but it took root and expanded. The original five were Hastings, Romney, Hythe, Dover, and Sandwich. To them were added in the twelfth century the 'ancient towns' (in reality thriving upstarts) of Rye and Winchelsea; and in course of time over thirty minor havens joined the confederation as 'limbs' of the predominant seven. Thus the ports grew strong and rich as privileged merchant unions with nothing feudal about them except their service to the king. And that, it will be noticed, was of the honourable fighting kind, and not the menial duty of villeins. Quite suitably the freemen of these towns became known as the Barons of the Cinque Ports, at a time when the word *baron* was losing its original significance of 'man' and assuming that of 'nobleman'.[1]

The population of England at the close of the Saxon period has been estimated at about two millions. The total is arrived at by the application of a certain amount of guesswork to the incomplete data in Domesday Book. But, even admitting the uncertainty, there are considerations which preclude belief in any higher figure. We know that in Tudor times the numbers were not more than double the above estimate, and meanwhile there had been a great change in the English landscape, a growth of towns and their industries, a clearing of forests for tillage, and a conversion of vast scrubby wastes into sheep pasture. On this reasoning it is hard to believe that the much less improved surface of Saxon England could have supported

[1] It was shown by the late Dr. J. H. Round that the Confessor's charter to the Ports cannot be proved to have existed, and that the earliest demonstrable general charter was that of Henry II. Nevertheless the arrangement could have existed without a general charter. The word 'Cinque' proves an early foundation; for after the rise of Winchelsea and Rye the number was not five but seven. It is probable that the system began with separate bargains with the different ports in the late Saxon period, but it is almost certain that Edward the Confessor's charter creating the close confederation of later times is mythical. See 'The Cinque Ports', by F. W. Brooks, in *Mariner's Mirror*, April, 1929.

more than two millions, even allowing that their standard of comfort was lower. It is true that in the prime of feudalism, just before the Black Death of the fourteenth century, the population rose as high or higher than under the Tudors. But most of the surface improvement had then been made, and the great feudal magnates were more efficient managers of estates than their Saxon predecessors, or than the small gentry and yeomen who succeeded them. They had a greater power over labour, and wealth sufficient to enable them to take long views and work for ultimate rather than immediate returns. It is easy to see how the land was more productive under them than it was before or after.

In ancestry this eleventh-century population was predominantly Teutonic or, to use a more fashionable term, Nordic.[1] There is a school which disputes this Teutonic origin, but it has not proved its case. The weight of the evidence points to the supersession of the Celtic by the Teutonic nationality in the east and centre of England. In the west there was, by the same testimony, a fusion, and a Celtic element remained. But it can have been nowhere predominant save in Cornwall and on the Welsh border, and perhaps in the Cumbrian mountains. In the east the Danes superimposed a later Teutonic element upon the original one. Their actual numbers are not approximately known, but it is unlikely that they equalled those of their Saxon vassals. They were, however, a ruling caste, and they left permanent traces in language and customs. By the eleventh century the older Danes of Alfred's Danelaw were in sentiment Englishmen, and the newcomers who settled with Canute were comparatively a handful who were dispersed over the whole country. For effective purposes fusion was complete before the Norman invasion.

[1] The two terms are not strictly parallel. Teutonic is a racial description and is here used to include Scandinavian as well as North German. Nordic means a physical type—tall, blue-eyed, fair-haired and complexioned, and long-skulled—and it applied to the Celtic as well as the Teutonic peoples. Together with the Iberian and Alpine types it is present in varying proportions in the composition of most European peoples. It is true to say that the Nordic type was more marked than the other two among the Teutonic stocks, but physical fusion took place in remote prehistory before the national groups can be distinguished. The original Celts were largely Nordic, but in the British Isles they early became crossed with the Iberian stock, and in France with the Alpine in addition.

Scotland was still a melting-pot for diverse elements, the Picts of the north and centre, the Norsemen of the islands and parts of the coast, the Scots of the south-west, the Britons of the western border with England, and the Angles of the south-east. A crucial event was the redrawing of the border in the tenth century so as to exclude from the English realm the northern part of ancient Northumbria from the Tweed up to Edinburgh. Round this English element transferred to Scotland the Lowlands were in time to crystallize, and in the process its language prevailed, whilst a modified feudalism also spread northwards across the border. But fusion was stayed at the edge of the Grampians, and many hundred years were to elapse before there was any real union between Lowlands and Highlands. In the late seventeenth century they were still mutually hostile countries, and Macaulay has pointed out the absurdity of Sir Walter Scott's patriotic fervour over the victory of Killiecrankie, where in reality it was the poet's own Lowland kindred who fled before warriors of a different breed and tongue.

The history of Saxon England covers a period of six hundred years, a longer time than that which separates us now from the Battle of Crecy. For generation after generation the same families occupied the same soil, following the ways of their forefathers, changing those ways so slowly that few men can have been conscious of any change at all. There lies the snare of a rapid historical rush over the ground such as we have attempted here. To us all appears dynamic and unresting. To those of the old time all must have seemed static, they and their society locked immutably to the enduring earth. Hardly one of the great movements we have witnessed—the rise of the monarchy, the welding of the people, the growth of feudalism—can have been even dimly apparent to the ordinary man, whose vision of history went no further back than his grandfather's memories. Violent storms swept the surface of the nation, but the solid depths beneath remained unaltered save by changes of an almost geological slowness. So was laid a foundation of inherited custom and outlook which has formed the basis of all the structures superposed in later times. It is the starting-point of the evolution of England.

II. THE NORMAN CONQUEST

We are sometimes tempted to view the Saxon period as a mere introduction and the Norman Conquest as the true beginning of English history. But that is an exaggeration. As a political event the Conquest was of the first importance, for it involved the ruin of all the ruling class in Saxon England and the transference of their power and possessions to foreign adventurers. It caused also the introduction of new elements into the national language, the strengthening of the Church, and the modification of law and institutions, although some of these things might have been effected if peaceful development had been uninterrupted. But in the evolution of the nation the Conquest was an important stage which yet fell short of a new beginning. Duke William and his knights overcame King Harold and his thegns, and the losing party, some thousands in number, were very effectively ground into powder and returned to the soil from which they had sprung. Nevertheless the great body of instincts, habits, traditions, and folk-memory that constituted the English nationality continued. 'Norman England' consisted of some two million Anglo-Saxons and perhaps twenty thousand Norman and French soldiers and clerics, and in course of time the greater element absorbed the less. Even the predominance of the French language, which appears so complete in the written records, was in fact superficial. There could never have been a time when one person in twenty spoke or understood it.

The Norse and Danish settlement in France had been stabilized a generation later than the Danelaw in England when, in 912, Charles the Simple, the Carolingian king, had recognized Rolf as Duke of Normandy. William, who held the fief one hundred and fifty years later, was the sixth duke in the succession. During that period the Normans changed out of recognition. Their vigorous intellect and character adapted themselves to the new medium of French society even more rapidly than the earlier Franks had adapted themselves to the Gallo-Roman culture of the Gaul which they had conquered. But whereas the Franks had lost themselves in the provincial mass, the Normans dominated even whilst they changed. By 1066 they were French-speaking, patrons of learning, supporters of the Church, builders in stone, and fighters on horseback in the new knightly style as yet unpractised in England.

F

To all these pursuits they brought a zest and efficiency, a brilliance of thought and a hardness of decision, which marked them off from the other communities of France in a very definite fashion. Perhaps it was a happy accident of numbers. The Norman settlers, it would seem, were sufficiently numerous not to lose their identity amid the subject-people of their province, and yet not so numerous that a large proportion of them were left unprovided for in the distribution of the spoil. They comprised no class of mean whites, and preserved the self-confidence of a ruling race.

After all allowance is made for their own merits, we must remember that they owed much to France. Normandy was incomparably more brilliant than the Danelaw. That may not prove that Carolingian France was more civilized than Saxon England, for it is often the element of contrast in the partners of a marriage that accounts for the high qualities of the off-spring. Vikings and tenth-century Frenchmen were both good types of mankind, and they were in strong contrast to one another; Danes and Saxons were much more alike. The factor of language will serve as an illustration of the point. Language in those days was more instinctive, more closely interwoven with the inmost habits of thought of its speakers, than it is now. As a man was, so he spoke; and as he spoke, so he became. The Normans, with all their inherited memory of the fjords and the seas, of pine forests and snowfields, of heroic raids, baresark fights against odds, and the savage old virtues of the northern twilight, learned to speak and think in the tongue of France, the modernized Latin that told of the sun-scorched plain and the dusty highway, of vineyards and cornfields, of cities and bishops and emperors, of the craftsmanship of stone and the subtlety of books. These things entered through the tongue into the Norman brain and enriched it with a double inheritance.

We need not dwell on the technical reasons for the English adventure of 1066. Edward the Confessor died in January, and the Witan elected Harold, Earl of Wessex, the son of Godwin, to the vacant throne. Duke William had already marked that throne as his, and his Norman barons, and still more his Norman churchmen, thirsted to set their ruling hands upon English earldoms, manors, sees, and abbeys. They despised the solid conservative English, too sleepy in their isolation; out of date in their Church, whose priests were mostly illiterate; out of date in their feudalism, which lacked the hard legal definitions whereby the chivalry of France kept villeins in their place; out of date in their armies, which rode to the field, but dismounted to fight surrounded by a rabble of tramping peasants who possessed no weapons but bludgeons and sickles tied to poles. The clear-sighted Norman mingled no pity with his contempt. He saw a great enterprise and he answered its call. And when good fortune made the struggle infinitely shorter and easier than he could have dared to hope, he exploited his triumph with unsparing severity.

William was a gambler, or he would not have pitted Normandy against England across a Channel that was strategically as wide then as the Atlantic is now. He had to leave much to chance, but he left nothing to chance that he could in any way provide for. He understood the value of diplomacy in cloaking the true nature of a war of aggression, and he advertised through Christendom the justice of his claims. He denounced the enormity of Harold's breach of an oath taken on the holiest of relics. He thus induced the continental Church to take up his cause and bless it as a crusade against the infidel. He collected the shipping of his Norman coast, and perhaps hired more from elsewhere. Certainly he set every shipwright to work turning out new transports with feverish haste. He prepared for a long war. Feudal law gave him the right to call out all his Norman chivalry. But the periods of service for which they were bound were not enough for an enterprise of which no man could calculate the end. He did not therefore employ the feudal levy, but gathered an army of mercenaries who served for pay or for the hope of plunder. The Norman nobles for the most part sent their sons or brothers to represent them, and picked adventurers were welcomed from every neighbouring province. Their followers were trained soldiers, for the numbers transportable were limited, and one can guess that every useless hand was weeded out. This expeditionary force, from 4,000 to 12,000 strong,[1] was concentrated in the estuary of the Dives as the summer of 1066 drew on.

[1] After weighing the circumstantial evidence, my own preference is for the lower figure, but I give the higher in deference to some of the modern authorities. It should be regarded as an outside possibility. There is no contemporary evidence of any value. The Norman chroniclers talk of 60,000 men and from 700 to 3,000 ships. The Norman coastline was com-

Harold also made his preparations. He was one of the best commanders Saxon England produced, a general who practised strategy besides leading in the fight. History, read and written backwards, has always underestimated him. Had some nameless bowman's arrow flown three inches wide Harold's statue might stand by Alfred's as that of another hero-king who saved the nation from disaster. On such an accident does reputation hang. Harold played a faultless opening in this year 1066, and it was not his fault that death robbed him and England of its fruits. He had two distinct invasions to guard against—William and the Normans from across the Channel, and his own brother Tostig, his mortal enemy, with allies from across the North Sea. Tostig had been banished from England after richly deserving it. He tried first for aid in Flanders, and then betook himself to Norway, where he found in King Harold Hardraada, the last of the vikings, an adventurer who would play his game. These two, Tostig the Anglo-Dane, bitter, viperish, and fearless, and Hardraada the Norseman, six feet six of baresark bone and muscle with the native Norse cunning superadded, prepared that summer to land in northern England no less assiduously than Duke William to land in the south. Had there been no native army the rival invaders would have met somewhere on English soil and fought to the death there. It was an elemental situation, as of leopard and wolf each stalking the same prey, and a prey that had teeth and claws as good as theirs. English Harold had thus to divide his forces. To guard the north he left Edwin and Morcar, Earls of Mercia and Northumbria, whilst he himself took post in his own Wessex, ready to give or summon aid in accordance with which invasion should begin first. His navy was inadequate to watch both coasts. He left the North Sea to the enemy and concentrated his ships at the Isle of Wight, whence a westerly wind, that most to be expected, would enable them to strike along the coast fronting his Norman opponent. But the fleets of those days were not capable of a waiting game. Victualling for long periods needed a technique that had yet to be invented, and money for wages was probably lacking. In the end the ships dispersed to their home ports before

parable to that of the Cinque Ports, and they were able to produce 57 ships between them for the King's service. William's shipbuilding could not produce the vast numbers indicated. Shipwrights cannot be improvised out of untrained peasants.

either invasion was launched, and sea-power played no part in the defence.

The Norsemen landed first—in the Humber at the end of August. Against them Harold's generalship succeeded. Properly managed, the odds were against any invader. His force was bound to be small, for no great army could be transported in one mass across the sea. For parallel reasons the army that met him would also be small, for the resources of government were too rudimentary to provide for the feeding of anything like the whole strength of England at one spot. The first clash might therefore be between equal forces. If the invader were beaten, that was the end of it; his remnants would be swept forthwith into the sea. But if he won, that was not the end of it, but only the beginning. For he would have beaten only the first of a number of armies which England could produce one after another, and which he would have to fight in turn. And the odds were that sooner or later he would meet with the defeat which would decide the whole venture. So it fell out in the first of the two campaigns of 1066. Tostig and Hardraada beat the northern Earls at Fulford, near York, and so won the first round. Harold from the south, having yet seen nothing of Duke William, started to the rescue. His little army picked up the wrecks of Edwin and Morcar and fought the second round with the Norsemen at Stamford Bridge. Here the tide of battle flowed the other way, Tostig and Hardraada and the best of their men were killed, and the survivors were glad to take ship and sail home. The Norse invasion was ended. Harold's merit had been speedy action. He had brought the second English army on the scene before there had been time for any second Norse army to arrive. It sounds simple, but Ethelred the Redeless had never found it so.

Meanwhile what had William been doing, and what did he mean to do? With his fleet and army all ready, he had waited some weeks at the mouth of the Dives. The chroniclers say it was because the winds were unfavourable, but it may be that the English fleet at the Isle of Wight made the risk of crossing too great. When this fleet had dispersed, William moved. The medieval chroniclers give not the slightest inkling of his plan, and modern historians write as if he had none—surely an injustice to a great statesman and soldier. Geography supplies the missing clue—the geography of the Sussex coast nine hundred

THE CINQUE PORTS

The seven head ports are underlined

Margate
Ramsgate
Fordwich
Bekesbourne
Sandwich
KENT
Deal
Kingsdown
Dover
Appledore
Folkestone
Tenterden
Hythe
SUSSEX
Rye
Romney
Lydd
Winchelsea
Hastings
Seaford
Pevensey
Beachy Head

THE HASTINGS DISTRICT IN 1066

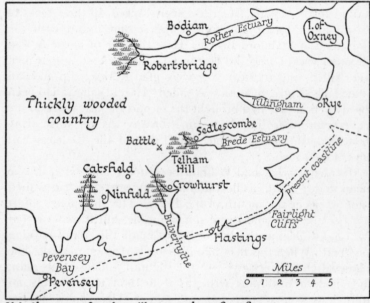

Bodiam
Rother Estuary
I. of Oxney
Robertsbridge
Thickly wooded country
Tillingham
Rye
Sedlescombe
Battle ×
Brede Estuary
Telham Hill
Present coastline
Catsfield
Ninfield
Crowhurst
Bulverhythe
Fairlight Cliffs
Hastings
Pevensey Bay
Pevensey
Miles
0 1 2 3 4 5

Note, the names of modern villages are shown for reference years ago, so utterly different from that of to-day. The map shows the conditions. The town of Hastings stood on the seaward edge of a jagged and hilly peninsula. To the west lay the tidal basin of Bulverhythe, prolonged inland by the swampy course of the little river Asten flowing from Battle. To the east and north ran another long tidal inlet, filled with water at high tide, an oozing quagmire at low, more than half a mile wide throughout. This was the estuary of the Brede, a stream which also rose near Battle. The Brede swamp and the Bulverhythe swamp made Hastings a peninsula, and the neck was the ridge of high ground which runs north-west from Hastings town through Battle to the main mass of Sussex. But for the full story we must look farther inland still. North of Battle was terrible country for an invading army, and especially for an army of mounted knights. It was the great Andreds Weald of Sussex, the Anderida Silva of Roman days, a tangle of forest and thicket spread over short steep slopes divided by swampy bottoms and a myriad of streams and brooks. There were no ordnance maps. A man's map was in his own brain, and nothing but years of journeying and hunting in such a country could put it there. Harold, we may suppose, knew this country, for it was his own. William did not know it, and had no intention of fighting his way to London through it. And yet he deliberately landed near Hastings. He could only have done so with a different purpose in mind.

We follow William's proceedings, which reveal that purpose. In the middle of September he sailed from the Dives, but he did not get across the Channel. Probably the wind changed in mid-course, blew hard from the west, and made it impossible to reach his objective. However that may have been, he fetched up at St. Valery on the Somme estuary, east of his starting-point, but on the wrong side of the sea. He had some ships wrecked and many men drowned in this unlucky venture. A fortnight later the Channel weather was kind, and he sailed safely over to Sussex at the end of September. He landed on the shore of Pevensey Bay, the great spreading basin that is now dried up like Bulverhythe and turned into sheep pasture. Thence he struck eastwards, round the head of Bulverhythe, and down into the Hastings peninsula. He captured the town (a fair-sized place which supplied 400 fighting men to the Cinque Ports fleet), made it his headquarters, and fortified it with an earthwork and a wooden palisade. And there he sat tight, although Harold was far away in Yorkshire and a Sussex thegn was galloping night and day to bear him the news. William saw something in Hastings which modern students, looking at modern Sussex, do not see. This peninsula was a strong place, well-nigh impregnable, guarded on all sides by sea and swamp, approachable only by the narrow neck that runs out at its Battle corner. There William with his little army could hold out in face of a greater Saxon army, and in the meantime, since the Saxons had not appeared, he sent out parties far and wide to forage and ravage and advertise to southern England that its new king had arrived.

William, with his ancestral viking lore, knew all about this invading game. He knew that in fair fight he would have to win battle after battle before England was his, and that one battle well lost would be his ruin. But a Norman was more than a viking; he was a politician too. Politics promised something better than a wild dash through the Weald to London. The Confessor's reign had left England demoralized, full of schemers and self-seekers to whom a revolution promised pickings. Harold was indeed a man, but his time had been too short. He was an earl's son, not a king's son, and his fellow earls were disloyal in their hearts. They and many another could argue that he was no less a usurper than the Norman. Then there was the Church. The Saxon Church was conscious of slackness, and its moral authority was low. The continental Church had pronounced Harold an outlaw and blessed his opponent, who enjoyed the prestige of a reforming mission. Therefore, all these things considered, there can be little doubt that William chose Hastings not as a base for a military advance, but as a fortified bridge-head from which to overlook his enemy's kingdom, to stir up disloyalty and revolt, and to entice every unscrupulous traitor to come and join him. He might perhaps spend the winter in this fashion, safely ensconced in his peninsula, and in the spring of 1067 he might take the field with half England already his, with Edwin and Morcar, shufflers both as they afterwards proved themselves, even attacking Harold in the rear. It is all supposition, but it explains the facts, and the fact of that landing at Hastings needs explanation.

Things did not turn out in that way, for Harold was a general. When the weary rider clattered into York and told what he had seen at Pevensey, the English king rose at once to the crisis. He searched faces perhaps, and caught Edwin or Morcar covering a crafty smirk. The whole thing flashed upon him. That Norman camp was a wasps' nest that he must stop at once, even if he could not smoke it out. He mounted and rode south with his personal guard, leaving the others to follow as they could. He spent a few days in London gathering men; then south again through the Weald and down to the gate of the peninsula. That was his post until England could gather at his back. On Battle hill, where the Abbey stands now,[1] he drew up his men—how many of them, nobody knows, probably a mere four or five thousand, like those of the Norman.

As one goes seawards from Battle Abbey to Hastings the road dips into a deep valley and then climbs a higher slope over against the Saxon position. This is Telham Hill, and here the Norman army took post to hold the entrance to the peninsula. William and his knights were quartered in Hastings, but at early dawn on the morning after Harold's appearance—the morning of 14 October—they hastened up to the front. There stood the Saxons across the valley, and the standard of the Fighting Man waving over them showed that Harold himself was present. Harold had come to fight the first battle against these new invaders. If he won it he would tumble the Normans into the sea as he had the Norsemen. If he lost, he could fight again—England could produce half-a-dozen such armies as he now commanded. For William the alternatives were losing all or winning something, but probably not all. Nevertheless he judged it best to fight. These Saxons facing him were an advanced guard. Behind them lay all England slowly getting into motion, and even now there might be reinforcements coming south through the thickets of the Weald. If he stayed on Telham Hill, Harold would also wait and grow stronger. So William attacked without delay, three hours after daylight on that October morning. The Saxons had appeared only in the previous evening, and he had not taken long to make up his mind.

The battle raged with varying fortune all day. To modern

---

[1] There was no abbey and no village in 1066. Most likely the place had no name. Some moderns attempt to prove it was called Senlac; others with unseemly heat have denied it. It does not much matter what it was called. It has been Battle ever since.

eyes these armies were mobs without any drill or discipline or training in combined action. They could have had no more skill in manoeuvre than a mob has, and so we must picture the proceedings as alternate long pauses whilst the Norman chiefs shuffled their crowd slowly forward down one slope, across the valley, and up the other slope; and sharp clashes of fighting on the crest of the Saxon position followed by a recoil swifter but less orderly than the advance. This occurred time and again, and Harold was content. He would try no premature counter-stroke with the disadvantage of mob-movement on his side. But the less experienced of his men, peasants who may never have fought before, grew restive; and when towards evening a Norman attack showed obvious faint-heartedness and rolled back without an effort, these Saxons thought that all was over but the plundering and burst headlong down hill in pursuit. At the bottom, all in disorder, they were duly massacred by the Norman horse whom William had waiting for them. The Saxon position was now more thinly held, and the next attack was a real one. But still Harold had a chance. The lost men were his worst, and his best had stood steady in their ranks. Both sides had lost heavily, and the English dead could be replaced whilst the Norman could not. And then at dusk came the disaster. A dropping arrow struck Harold through the eye, his housecarles looked for a moment behind them, and a rush of knights burst in and killed him. His brothers Gyrth and Leofwine fell too, and as the light failed the house of Godwin was no more. A small band fought on even after that, and withdrew in the darkness as the weary Normans fell to sleep on the hill. Next day William found that against all expectation he was already King of England. It was not the killing of a few thousand Saxons that had made him so. It was the simultaneous extinction of Harold and his two able brothers. After them there was no one left to bring on the second and third and fourth English armies which might have answered the Fulford of Hastings with another Stamford Bridge.

As soon as he realized this gift of fortune William made new plans. There was no need to stay in Hastings. England was his to take. London was a strong city and full of men, but over them was no king, nothing but a mere Witan, a gang of politi-cians who were thinking rather what to say than what to do. Edwin and Morcar could have called out the midlands and the north, but in their minds the news of Hastings aroused the calculation not of 'How shall we beat the invader?' but of 'How much will he give us?'—a question to which in due time the answer proved disappointing. William grasped the situation and set out for London. Straight through the Weald it was sixty miles. But he did not go through the Weald. There might yet be hardy patriots lurking there who would give mail-clad riders a terrible time in the bogs and thickets. He turned eastward along the coast by Romney and Hythe to Dover, and thence only did he take the long road to the Thames by the crest of the open chalk downs, where a knight had a fair chance to kill a peasant.

The events that followed proved Hastings to have been a decisive battle, a unique battle in the history of those days, because by itself it gave decisive success to an invasion. The reason, as has been said, was that Harold and his brothers were all killed. What that entailed was shown by the story of the next four years. There was fighting spirit left in England, and it broke out in western, northern, and East Anglian revolts, movements which, if organized, might have driven the Norman army out of the country. But there was no leader combining ability with the rank necessary to secure him recognition, and the revolts were all put down. William was accepted by the Witan and duly crowned on Christmas day, little more than two months after Hastings, and thereafter his position was never seriously shaken.

We have devoted more space to the campaign of 1066 than will commonly be available for military affairs in this book, partly because the geographical factor is interesting and has not in the past been adequately recognized, and still more because the unexpected swiftness of the result had an enormous effect upon the future development of England. Had William won success only at the end of the long war he had in prospect when he started from St. Valery, he would have been obliged in the course of it to make terms with the greater part of the Saxon thegnhood. They would have retained their estates, and their ideas of feudal organization would have survived with much less modification than was actually the case. William would probably have reigned like Canute, as an able foreigner adapting himself to English institutions, with a limited number of his Normans sharing power with a Saxon majority; and the whole effect would have worn off after a generation or two. It is plain that many of the Saxons expected such an outcome and would have been content with it, for the revolts between 1067 and 1071 were the local outbreaks of minorities, and within two years of Hastings there were Saxons fighting under William's banner against their fellow-countrymen.

The history of the Conqueror's reign supplied a bitter disillusionment. William exploited his triumph unsparingly. He confiscated lands on the slightest excuse, not only the lands of those who fought against him, but often, it would seem, of those who merely refrained from supporting his throne. When, after twenty years, the Domesday Survey was drawn up in 1086, the Saxon earls had vanished and the thegnhood had almost ceased to exist. In their place stood a Norman nobility and knighthood possessed of almost every fief and manor in the country. So also with the Church. The parish priesthood, of the social status of villeins, may have remained Saxon, but the bishoprics and abbeys were in the hands of foreigners, not only from Normandy, but from France and Italy as well. A small body of outsiders thus became the ruling class, and although in time their stock was absorbed into the English nationality their work in remoulding English institutions was permanent.

By this process of wiping the slate the way was cleared for the establishment of a new and different kind of feudalism. Anglo-Saxon feudalism had grown up haphazard and without any uniformity. The Church fiefs often owed no service to the Crown. Many of the thegns owed none, save the general obligation of all free men. In many parts of the country there were still great numbers of free, lordless peasants. It had been largely a matter of chance, for pre-Conquest feudalism had been far less a conscious creation by the king than an effect of misfortune in the Danish raids compelling poor men to seek the protection of rich. William made feudalism a system. To all his new grants he attached the condition of military service. The grantee was obliged to place so many knights and their retinues at the king's disposal in the field. The baron thus enfeoffed might make his own bargain with his knights, and they in turn with other knights subordinate to themselves, until several grades of tenancy came into being. The Norman-French love of consistency was a spur to these arrangements, and the foreign lawyers were ready with a maxim that the king was the supreme and universal landowner, and that every acre in the country was held directly or at one or more removes from him. This conflicted with the Saxon free man's old idea of absolute ownership by the occupants, which had now to give way to the dictum: *Nulle terre sans seigneur*. The change was not completed in the Norman period. It extended to the baronage and the gentry and the majority of the peasants, but Domesday shows that in 1086 there were still free men of the minor sort, especially in East Anglia. In the twelfth and thirteenth centuries nearly all peasants became villeins, unable to quit their manors and bound to render strict service to their lords; but at the same time the townsmen were being emancipated, and the example was to spread to the peasants in the fourteenth century.

Land-grants in reward for military service were the essence of continental feudalism. On the continent they led to a dangerous weakening of royal authority, since the great tenants might employ their strength against the king. In England this danger also existed, but in a smaller degree. Two things helped to check it: first, that the greatest landowners received a multitude of manors scattered over the country, from which they could not easily concentrate their knights for rebellious purposes; and second, that William emphasized the principle that a man's first duty was to obey the king rather than his immediate over-lord. The dispersal of the fiefs has been considered as a subtle device on the part of the Conqueror, but it may have arisen naturally from the fact that the Saxon confiscations were spread over several years; a Norman chief may have secured a Wessex estate after Hastings and then have claimed a share of the midlands and the north as those regions were dealt with in their turn. Domesday merely records the result and not the process. In the time of Edward the Confessor, its entries run, so-and-so (a Saxon) held this manor; now (1086) such-and-such a man (nearly always a Norman) has it. The principle of direct loyalty to the king was steadily enforced, and summed-up in the famous Oath of Salisbury, wherein sub-tenants, as well as tenants-in-chief, did homage to William. The ceremonial no doubt made the theory familiar, but it would have been of little value without the king's severity in punishing rebels.

In Church affairs the Conquest bore fruits as important as in any others. It was a time when reformers all over Europe were seeking to purge religious life of the abuses which had invaded it. In the tenth century the famous monastery of Cluny in France began a new system of discipline intended to abolish worldliness and sloth, and revive the ideal of a pious and laborious life. The movement spread throughout the eleventh century and culminated in 1073, when Hildebrand became Pope as Gregory VII. His policy was that temporal princes could not be trusted to control religion, since they were always tempted to make appointments for reasons of state rather than of piety. Discipline, therefore, must be in the hands of the Pope, whose authority was to permeate all kingdoms. William agreed that the English Church must be purified, and worked zealously with his archbishop Lanfranc to that end. But he held that since the bishoprics and abbeys owed him feudal service he must have the deciding voice in naming their holders. This investiture question, as it was called, afterwards produced a long contest between the Crown and the Papacy, but in William's time the discussion remained friendly owing to the king's genuine keenness for reform and his no less positive determination to be the chief reformer. Gregory therefore left effective control in his hands. The king on his side removed the clergy from the jurisdiction of the ordinary courts, and gave them a legal system of their own. The result was a real transformation of the Church. The Saxon ecclesiastics, who had been undeniably slack, gave way to foreigners with a better tradition. A period of fine stone building set in—the Norman style—both in cathedrals and smaller churches. The abbeys grew for a time more efficient as centres of religion and learning. The parish clergy, hitherto illiterate peasants, were better instructed, and the special nature of their office was made more evident by the fact that they were forbidden to marry. At a time when Latin Europe was awaking vividly to the things of the mind the Conquest opened the way for the new culture to enter England.

The administration of justice, too, evolved in new directions. The early Saxon system had been that of the king's court or witan, the shire court or moot, and the hundred moot; and the primitive ideal of punishment had been that the offender must pay compensation to the person he had wronged. When, in Danish times, there was a decay of freedom, the weak had been obliged to commend themselves to the strong in order to secure redress, and the patron naturally claimed a share of the fine

due to his dependent. Norman feudalism pushed this principle
further. The vassal was the lord's man—in the lower ranks
indeed, his thing, his possession. To the lord therefore it
pertained to keep order among his living chattels. Again, the
sword of justice was no burden to its wielder, but a source of
profit. Criminals were not expensively maintained in gaol.
They met with summary punishment, corporal or financial.
Rival authorities were known to dispute keenly for the privilege
of hanging a felon, for his goods were confiscated to pay the
costs of the ceremony. Therefore, it was a much-prized right
for every lord of land from the king downwards to hold his
court, and all his dependents were bound to attend, to render
'suit of court', under penalty of fines for absence. To the king's
court, or Curia Regis, came the tenants-in-chief. To the manor
court, held generally by the lord's steward, came all the rustic
villeins of the estate. In theory, judgement was pronounced by
the voices of all the suitors present, but the fines went always
into the coffers of the lord. This feudal system of justice never
ousted the rival system of the shire and hundred moots. The
two existed side by side on terms which must have presented
infinite variations of detail. At the top, of course, the Curia
Regis supplanted the Witan, a change rather of name than of
thing. But the king was as fully alive as his barons to the profits
of the minor justice, and the shire moots survived as the county
courts under officers of the king's appointment. Gradually they
encroached upon the feudal jurisdictions and abolished them.
But this change was not complete until the much later time
when all villeins had become free men and so had passed
naturally from the scope of one court to that of its rival. In
this right of administering justice the towns participated. When
a town secured a charter of privilege its most valued item was
often that of the holding of a court by the mayor.

Finally, a word must be said about the means whereby this
new feudal fabric was knit together. The king's own personality
counted for much, but the king could not be everywhere. He
needed eyes, ears, and tongues to represent him far and wide.
His great vassals were not perfect instruments for the purpose,
for they had private interests of their own. So we find in the
Norman period a service growing important which had been
only rudimentary before, a service of trained officials, not
fighting barons but lawyers or men of education drawn from

the ranks of the clergy. For the most part their names have perished, but we can discern the importance of their works. They were the nerves of the new kingdom. The Domesday Survey reveals a surprising energy and system among these unknown civil servants. It is the work of many hands, busily extracting the truth in the teeth of local opposition in every district simultaneously, and in its surviving form it represents a boiling-down of the resulting information by highly skilled editors. These men kept the state together and made it ever more efficient. They acted also as a bridge over a bad time like the reign of Stephen, so that when order was restored the methods of the past could be resumed and developed. We must bear them in mind as an ever-present background of feudal government.

The Norman Conquest, therefore, while it did not originate English feudalism, gave it a new form. The form included elements borrowed from the continent, and yet it was not entirely continental. The difference was that the king was stronger here than abroad. And as the system differed, so the reaction of the people to it differed. It is not in the nature of European man to live indefinitely within a structure of stone and steel, however well devised. The craving for freedom urges him to patient undermining or to wild revolutionary revolt. In Latin Europe the cities, with traditions reaching back to the Roman Empire, were the pioneers of liberty, whilst the peasants remained for long centuries in chains. In England the peasantry, who never altogether lost the memory of the kindred and the moot and equal rights, pressed much earlier for emancipation. No sooner was the system perfected than it began rapidly to decay. In the fourteenth century the life was ebbing out of it; in the fifteenth it was gone. The English villager became the yeoman-farmer or the free craftsman or labourer. And since the peasants formed the great majority, the effect was national. Town and country developed together without the contrasts seen in France and Italy. The knight of the Conquest, who regarded his serfs as cattle, became in time the English gentleman bound to his dependents by very different ties. English liberty passed, like that of other lands, through the night of feudalism, but it entered later and emerged earlier.

III. THE FEUDAL STATE

The Norman Conquest broke down the isolation of the English and made them more truly partners in the world of Christendom than they had been before. In the Danish centuries men had peered across the North Sea towards the cold lands whence came the axe-men and the traders in the snakelike ships. By comparison it was England that had been the land of sun and softness, of security and the grace of life, and all without had been harsh as the east wind that brought the foe. But the Normans opened wide the other gate which had stood half closed before. Statesmen, churchmen, merchants, and scholars began to pass to and fro on the road to the south, and England found that her sunshine had been but a twilight to the glow that bathed the lands of the Latins and the shores of their Mediterranean Sea.

It was a strange world, this Christendom of the feudal age, and not so large by half as the Europe of to-day. Jutting into the Atlantic lay the great peninsula that had once been the Roman province of Spain. Two-thirds of it now owned the sway of the Saracens, Mahometans who had come from the east along the coast of Africa four centuries before. They were mild conquerors, who cared for art and science and ruled as justly as any Christian power. But the Christians had no love for them and kept no truce with them. In the mountainous north the European held firm against the Asiatic, and in the twelfth century the reconquest spread over southwards, winning valley after valley of the rivers that cut the Peninsula from east to west. One date may serve to clarify the process. In 1147, eighty years after Hastings, the Christians took Lisbon, and the kingdom of Portugal was born. There were English crusaders in the host, and a Winchelsea monk became the first bishop of the conquered city. As for Spain, when it drove back the Moors it did so not as one kingdom but as four, and it was several centuries before they were united. France was nominally one kingdom, in the sense that it had only one king. But the French king had little power outside his royal domain, and the great duchies and counties from Flanders south to Aquitaine were almost independent states. The Count of Flanders was a very powerful prince because his territory, with a frontage on the North Sea and an inland waterway by the Rhine into the heart of Europe, was already growing rich by trade and manufacture. East of France lay the Holy Roman Empire, which was both more and less than modern Germany. It did not include any large part of the Baltic coasts, but it stretched southward over the Alps and northern Italy almost as far as Rome. It was this diversity of climates and peoples that prevented the Empire from ever being welded into a nation. In the German part the great princes were almost independent powers, and in the Italian south the cities such as Milan and Florence aspired to the same position. Beyond Germany were the half-civilized Christian states of Hungary and Poland which looked for their religion to Rome. In the south-east the Greek or Byzantine Empire, with an independent church, stretched over the Bosphorus into Asia Minor. Eastward still were lands of which few western men could tell, Mahometan kingdoms and empires to the shores of the Indian Ocean, and the vast dim plains and steppes of the Slavs, for ever changing their frontiers, in what is now Russia. Beyond them again lay central Asia and the mysterious farthest East, which had sent forth swarms of conquerors in the past, and were to do so again in the future. Twelfth-century Christendom lay under a menace of which it could not exactly discern the nature.

It was an age of war, war on the petty scale between kings and feudal magnates, war on the great scale between Europe and Asia. From Russia and Livonia in the north-east, round by the Volga and the Don to the Black Sea, the Caspian and the Caucasus, southward through Syria to Egypt, and thence westward along Africa into Spain, Christendom was ringed about by Heathenesse. The grand crusades for the recovery of Jerusalem began in 1096. They attracted kings and princes of the first rank, but though these warriors took the city they held it for less than a century. But any war against the infidel was a crusade, and crusading went on all round the vast perimeter. A Scottish Earl Douglas died fighting the Mahometan in Spain; the French King St. Louis led a force to Egypt; Poles and Hungarians smote eastwards against the semi-heathen Slavs; and of Chaucer's knight we read, 'In Lettow had he ridden and in Ruce,' in Lithuania and Russia, that is, with the crusading order of the Teutonic Knights.

In the Spanish west, Asia was driven back. In the east she took the offensive. Central Asia sent forth two hordes that almost overwhelmed Christendom. The first were the Turks, fierce tribesmen who took service with the cultured Saracens, mastered their employers, and adopted their religion. Seljuk Turks under Saladin retook Jerusalem. Ottoman Turks swept over the Bosphorus into Europe, and in later days pushed their conquests up to the frontiers of the Holy Roman Empire. The Turkish advance was comparatively slow. More terrific was a second manifestation of Asiatic might, the outpouring of the Mongols from the barren plains to the north of China. These Mongols under their emperor, Genghiz Khan, were without exaggeration the most wonderful fighting men the world has seen. From a breeding-ground so arid and desolate they could not have been very numerous. Yet in one generation they conquered China with its settled government and teeming cities, struck down the Moslems of Persia and the nearer East, trampled over the Slavs of Russia, and poured triumphant into central Europe. Whilst the Great Khan was giving law to China his generals were routing the feudal hosts of Germany upon the Danube. It was all done without elaborate armament or novel engines of war. The bow and the horse were the Mongol weapons, and the secret of their use lay in discipline and self-denial and brains. Napoleon's marshals were blundering amateurs compared with the princes trained by Genghiz Khan. In 1241 it seemed as though the last hour of Christendom had struck, and panic spread even to Flanders, France, and England. But the Mongol chiefs were content with Asia (which for them included Russia). They had seen the west and enjoyed its conquest, and then they withdrew as swiftly as they had come. In Asia their sway lasted for three generations, with peace and order from the Caucasus to the China Sea. They were not Mahometans, and they had fought the Christians without rancour. So mild were their manners that Europe had hopes of converting them, and the first men of our race to describe the mysteries of high Asia were friars sent into Mongolia in the wake of the retreating horde.

Christendom had failed to stop the Turk and had made scarcely an effort to stem the Mongol rush. Oblivious, save for a moment, of these elemental forces on the horizon, the men of Europe battled over their local problems, developed slowly from fiefs into states, and hammered one another into rudiments of the nations that rule our modern world. It was not

CHRISTENDOM IN THE THIRTEENTH CENTURY

ICELAND

SCANDINAVIAN

KINGDOMS

SCOTLAND

IRELAND

ENGLAND

TEUTONIC
KNIGHTS

SLAVONIC
PEOPLES
under Mongol
Overlordship

MONGOL EMPIRE
stretching to China

Flanders

POLAND

HOLY
ROMAN
EMPIRE

ROMAN
CONVERTS

FRANCE

GREEK CONVERTS

HUNGARY

Venice

Genoa

SPANISH
KINGDOMS

PORTUGAL

SOUTHERN
SLAVS

Rome

KINGDOM
OF
SICILY

EASTERN
EMPIRE

Constantinople

ADVANCING

Saracen Remnant

MOORISH STATES

TURKISH

POWER

Alexandria
EGYPT

Miles
0   200   400   600

that they had any idea of progress. The word would have meant nothing to them. They looked backward, not forward; and the past, that golden imperial past whose cities and palaces lay in ruins around them, furnished a twofold ideal, of civil order to restrain crime, and of religious discipline to combat sin. They called it the Holy Roman Empire. They had proclaimed it first in the year 800, when Charlemagne the Frank went to Rome to be crowned by Leo the Pope. Charlemagne's empire included all western Christendom except the British Isles, and in his time the ideal prevailed. The Emperor wielded the physical power, and the Pope the moral power. Charlemagne's grandsons broke the unity. They partitioned the heritage in 843, and after many vicissitudes the arrangement came to be that described earlier in this section; the Empire meant Germany and northern Italy, and France was a separate kingdom. The other kingdoms which emerged after Charlemagne's time were also independent of the Empire: Portugal and the Spanish states in the west, Sicily in the south, Hungary and Poland in the east; whilst England and Scotland remained unattached, and Denmark, Norway, and Sweden represented the spread of Christianity, but not of the Empire, in the north. The ideal of the Holy Roman Empire had failed in that the temporal power had not expanded with the spiritual. Nevertheless there persisted through the Middle Ages a feeling that the Emperor was different from other princes, and that Christendom ought to recognize a central authority. Men saw it as the only deliverance from the wars that local interests were constantly stirring up.

On the spiritual side the ideal was more successful. The authority of Rome did permeate the whole of western Christendom. In the bad times after Charlemagne's death there was great slackness in the Church, but in the late tenth century a revival set in. The strict rule of the monastery of Cluny was copied throughout Europe, and the Popes were chosen from men who were at once pious, learned, and able. One consequence was perhaps unexpected. The balance between Emperor and Pope was upset, and instead of working in harmony they quarrelled. The difficulty was created by feudalism. The Emperors (and other sovereigns) regarded the lands of abbeys and bishoprics as military holdings bound to do the usual service, and so they claimed the right to choose the holders.

The Popes as they grew stronger claimed that their interest must prevail, and that none but the Church must appoint her own officers. It was called the Investiture Contest, and it raged for two centuries and more. In the Empire the Church prevailed and the imperial power was shattered. In the outer kingdoms it was on the whole the kings that won, and their victory did much to prepare the way for the system of independent states which modern Europe exhibits. But though these monarchs asserted their right to control appointments they had no thought of splitting up the Church. Most of them, like William the Conqueror in England, supported the spiritual authority with vigour, and the doctrine and practice of Rome were universally obeyed. The Reformation lay unforeseen in the future.

In different places and at different times these debated theories had more or less effect in accordance with the personal abilities of the Popes or sovereigns who bore rule. But there was something permanent and almost universal, a common factor throughout Christendom; and that was feudalism as it bore upon the ordinary man. Everywhere the peasant was unfree, bound to his birthplace, compelled to till his lord's domain and to yield tolls and dues from the scanty produce of his own little strip in the common field. Untravelled and unlettered, without imagination, with senses mostly run to appetites, the serf lived his life on a narrow scale. It has been said that the average villager never saw more than three hundred different people in the course of his existence—no more than one may see now in ten minutes in a city street. The changing seasons found him always at work, his ploughing, sowing, harvesting, ditching, and wood-cutting all done with a maximum of fatigue and a minimum of tools, with an instinctive skill that the pampered modern man has lost. The Church was his friend when it gave him holy days and a ceremony to entertain him, and above all when it taught him of an easeful heaven where he would do nothing but stroll and sing. It was too often his tyrant when it demanded his toil and his dues like any baron, and extorted them with a skill that the baron might envy. Sometimes a gaily dressed company would come to the manor-house, sometimes a pilgrim would pause to talk as he tramped by from the unknown, sometimes a pedlar would arouse cupidity with an opened pack. These were days to be remembered. More often the unusual was terrible. A drowned harvest, stock driven off by plundering soldiers, a pestilence blowing over in an unseen poison-cloud from the strange lands a few miles off, these things spelt slow death by hunger to those who escaped the quicker fate, an animal's death as the fit close to an animal's life. Yet the European at his lowest had always in him something that transcended the animal. On a festival he could find some brightly coloured rag in which to deck himself, ale or wine wherewith to loose his imprisoned soul. Sometimes he would break forth hopeless and reckless against his tyrants, and die manfully rather than live any longer as a beast. Sometimes a mighty emotion would seize him, as when he forsook all and marched off in his thousands to fall in the First Crusade. These were flames that soon fell cold, but they were a promise of brighter days to come. Such was the lot of the majority in feudal Christendom, three-fourths at least of its whole population.

There was as yet very little consciousness of nationality. Men did not classify themselves as Frenchmen, Dutchmen, and Germans, but as peasants, churchmen, and knights. Peasants were much the same everywhere, with local differences only in the crops they raised and the barbarous dialects they spoke. Even more were the churchmen a universal class, with a common language in Latin and a uniform occupation in the duties of religion. Bishops, abbots, and monks were often on the move, interchangeable from one country to another. William the Conqueror's Archbishop of Canterbury was Lanfranc, an Italian. In the next century an Englishman was Pope at Rome. French and Flemish clerics permeated all Europe. In the thirteenth century the new orders of the friars were formed, and their avowed object was to travel ceaselessly, preaching and ministering to the poor wherever they went. This constant circulation made the Church stronger, not weaker, in every land of the West. Its individuals moved to and fro, but its fabric stood firm and immovable, based upon the property it had everywhere acquired. In the eleventh century began the age of the great stone buildings, the glory of the Middle Ages, the visible sign of the Church's solid strength. The Gothic cathedrals were the work of laymen as much as of churchmen. Feudal magnates allotted the land and the funds, peasants hewed out the stone from the quarries, lay architects drew the plans, and humbly-born artists carved the decorations, tuned the bells and designed the coloured windows. All lived closer to the earth of this world and gave far more thought to the pains and pleasures of the next than men do now. The branches interlacing over forest glades and the tense flames roaring upwards from the blacksmith's forge gave them the models for their vaults and traceries in wood and stone. The miracles of the saints inspired their gorgeous windows, and the scowls and leers of devils are portrayed with a wealth of skill in their minor carvings. The churches and their burial-grounds spoke always of the day of judgement when knight and villein would gather in a common throng.

The scholars were a wing of the great army of churchmen, and they too were international. There were few books by which they might learn the wisdom of a sage in another land; they had to go to him and hear him speak. Bishops and abbots indeed might travel by proxy and have their parchment volumes copied by the labour of their monks. But the poor scholar tramped and starved. He was nearly always in minor orders, a churchman in law if a layman in fact, and his gown and his Latin were a passport through every Christian land. Some went farther, into the realms of the Saracens in Spain and the East, where they learned things that Europe had forgotten since the fall of Rome. It was the Saracens and not the men of the West who had kept alive the learning of the past—the science of Aristotle, the medicine of Galen, the geography of Ptolemy the Alexandrian. Whilst the rude minstrels of the West were celebrating the glory of action in the Song of Roland, all trumpet-calls and hot red blood and clash of steel, the Persian poet Omar was contemplating the futility of effort in such lines as these:

> The moving finger writes, and having writ,
> Moves on, nor all thy piety and wit,
> Can lure it back to cancel half a line,
> Nor all thy tears wash out a word of it.

Those two poems, written in the same generation, were written in different worlds. The energy of Europe, the wisdom of the East, the scholars were to wed them and bring to birth a stranger world of which they little dreamed. At places where a wise man taught, others would gather to him, and so began the universities, at Paris, at Oxford, in Italy, in Spain, back-waters in the moving stream, rich gardens where the questing

bees could add new flavours to their store. The scholar of
fortune is the counterpart of the soldier of fortune in the shaping
of the medieval world.

Another migrant class were the merchants. The early
merchant was of necessity a traveller. He had no posts and
telegraphs by which to control a distant trade from a central
office. He had to buy in person in one market and sell in person
in another. Like the churchman and the scholar, he was a man
without a country, and when he learned to combine forces with
others of his kind he did so, often enough, in unions like the
Hanseatic League, strong companies which even employed
fleets and ambassadors, but yet were flowing to and fro in a
variety of states under different territorial princes. Merchant
brotherhoods were like the churches of trade, with fixed guilds
in every centre and moving individuals circulating between
them. They evolved a practice of trade that may be compared
with the institutions of religion, a system of banking, book-keeping, bills of exchange, insurances, that gradually became
common to all the European world. Geographical facts determined their trade-routes. Unimproved Nature made transport
difficult on most lines and easy on only a few. Thus the commerce of medieval Christendom flowed in a few great arteries
and not in a network of veins as now. The greatest of these
arteries was from the Flemish delta up the Rhine, over the
passes of the eastern Alps, and thence into the north Italian
plain. On and near this route arose the chief cities of the age.
The merchants, as we have seen, were outside feudalism, which
was a system of holding the soil. They and the churchmen and
the scholars built up the towns of Christendom, and as the
peasants sunk ever into deeper bondage the townsmen grew
free and self-governing. They, with their wealth and their walls,
were the natural allies of a king hard pressed by his turbulent
barons. Where the towns were strong, feudalism decayed earliest
and national states first took shape. Where the towns were
feeble, freedom lagged and feudal disorder reigned unchecked.
The extreme example is Poland, which remained a tyrannous
anarchy until the eighteenth century.

Finally, we must picture this Christendom as a great peninsula, jutting from the mass of Asia, and washed on three sides by
the sea. From the Black Sea round in a circle to the Baltic there
were everywhere coasts and ports. The seamen formed another

moving swarm, kneading and leavening the stationary mass. And yet the seamen were never, like the other wanderers, an international class. They had a strong sense of country and violent methods of expressing it. The law-merchant and the ritual of the Church became universal. The seamen of every coast and nation were particular. They had their special ships and rig, their separate sea-languages, their exclusive knowledge of the perils of their native shores, and a contempt for the methods of others. Common ideas spread slowly among them, particularly in the northern seas, where charts and instruments were unknown long after they were adopted in the Mediterranean. With their nationalism went freedom. They had no feudal lords and knew little of land governments, and the landsmen on their side were content to leave them alone. And yet there were contacts, of intermarriage, of villein boys running off to sea, of successful captains settling down on shore. The sea influence worked surely if slowly, and the lands with a large sea-population were generally lands of early freedom.

A static, dull majority tied to the soil, a moving upper crust of wits and enterprise, such was the Christendom of which England became a full member after the Conquest. We have now to follow her fortunes in that society and to see how she gradually drew apart again in the guise of a nation, something different from the 'folk' of the Saxon centuries. The difference is not easy to define, although it is real enough. We may say that the Anglo-Saxons had been a people, with common employments, customs, language, and ways of thought. But they had shown little patriotism, no devotion to an ideal or an ambition, little shame at being ruled by a foreign conqueror like Canute, so long as he treated them well. There were exceptions, but in general their leaders had been content to be local magnates and had not thought of themselves as workers for an English state. In these things the Saxons, like all the rest of Christendom, fell short of nationality. The heathen Norsemen had been more a nation than they. But in the time to come the English slowly acquired the national point of view, which means pride in one's own people, a consciousness that it differs from others, a determination to make it differ for the better, above all a hatred of any foreign control. When that change should be accomplished the Middle Ages would be finished in England, and her modern history would begin.

IV. KING VERSUS MAGNATES

We have sketched the settlement made by William after his conquest, and his establishment of the new feudalism of military service, which he built upon the old feudalism of labour and taxation. The success of such a government depended wholly upon the personal character of the king, for his power, if he had the strength to use it, was absolute. The Conqueror was a good king, as even the conquered admitted. He was generally just, although he did unjust things in the heat of passion. But he had a strong sense of order and the paramount interest of the state, which was what England most needed. In his time, as hardly ever before, the country was a unit, and all had to look to the central authority. His newly enriched barons did not think as he did, and they revolted more than once. Their ideal was that of the continent, of independent magnates and a figure-head for king. William had crushed that notion in Normandy in his early years, but the barons thought to revive it in England on account of the king's difficulties with a newly-conquered people. They found to their disgust that the people preferred the king. With the people's aid he easily mastered them. He then showed that he would be master in government as well as in fight, for he deprived the chief culprits of their fiefs without any compunction. His view was that a barony or earldom was held on condition of loyal service, and was not an absolute possession. What the people thought of it all is shown by the Saxon chronicler's summing up of the reign: 'A man might go through his realm with his bosom full of gold unhurt.'

Under William Rufus the system continued, but in a degraded form. The second Norman was as strong-handed as his father, but a selfish, unjust man. He, too, would stand no nonsense from his barons, but he treated them unfairly, and no doubt they passed on the oppression to their vassals. The great Lanfranc, the Conqueror's wisest counsellor, died early in the new reign. The next archbishop was Anselm, an unworldly scholar who described himself as a poor sheep yoked to a violent young bull. If Rufus expected sheepish conduct he was disappointed, for Anselm showed surprising courage and obstinacy. He asserted the highest claims of the Church, and opened the contest for supremacy which the Conqueror and Lanfranc had tactfully suppressed. The quarrel was still undecided when Rufus died in the New Forest. How he died is a mystery, whether by accident, or conspiracy, or by the arrow of some down-trodden serf who saw a chance of vengeance and took it. But on a summer day in 1100 the Red King was found dead, and his younger brother Henry spurred hard to Winchester, seized the royal treasury, and with it the crown.

Henry I was the flower of Norman kingship, a hard, efficient rule that was better in that iron age than any weak kindliness. Justice, not liberty, was the country's cry, for liberty in those times could never be for all. It meant the liberty of the strong to oppress the weak. Henry, like his father, had a taste for order—one might call it a passion for order but that he was a passionless man, a cold intellect embodied in a tireless frame. He had no conquest to make; he could begin where his father left off. And so, after the Rufus interlude, the Norman kingship evolved into a new stage.

There were two quarrels to settle before Henry I could get to his task of perfecting the government machine. He had not by right of birth the best claim to the throne, for his eldest brother Robert was living. Right of birth was not, however, the sole test of a royal claim, although it counted for something. The Conqueror had disregarded it in leaving his English crown to his second son William and only the duchy of Normandy to the eldest son Robert. Robert was on his way back from the First Crusade when Rufus died, and so Henry was able to gain possession of England without a struggle. In 1101 Robert challenged the succession and invaded England, but only to negotiate instead of fighting and to withdraw to Normandy on promise of a money payment. The peace was soon broken, and in 1106 Henry claimed Normandy, defeated and captured Robert at Tenchebrai, and kept him a prisoner for the rest of his life. The English who served Henry at Tenchebrai regarded it as a revenge for Hastings, and held that the victory meant an English conquest of Normandy. That they could do so, forty years after Hastings, shows that already they thought of Henry as an English king and not a foreign usurper. He had made himself popular by marrying a Saxon princess.

The other quarrel was with Archbishop Anselm. He had asserted the right of the Church to check the sinful courses of Rufus, and now it might have been expected that he would work cordially with such a king as Henry. Instead, he raised the investiture question which had already torn the Empire in twain. He refused to do homage for his lands, and he refused to consecrate the persons chosen by the king as bishops and abbots. The king's position was that a prelate, as a holder of land, was a baron and must swear allegiance to the sovereign; and further, that no such appointments must be made without the king's approval. After years of wordy warfare Henry won his point in 1107. It was then agreed that the king should choose new bishops, that they should do homage for their lands, and only then should they be consecrated by their seniors in the Church.

That has been the normal English practice ever since. It was a decision that had an immense effect upon the country's destiny. It was imitated in the other kingdoms that were then slowly taking shape, and its consequence was that everywhere the king could be really master in his realm. It thus became possible for true national states to be evolved, independent because governed from within their own borders. The Church remained as a spiritual force permeating all Christendom, but it did not become a governing power ruling Europe as a single unit, as might possibly have happened had the contrary decision been taken. There were, it is true, reversals of the decision in after times, but they did not permanently succeed. In England the power and wealth of the Church continued very great, but it was as a powerful subject and not as an equal that incorporated religion stood in its relation to the Crown. Even that status was destined one day to become intolerable to the sovereign and his lay subjects.

From the date of the investiture settlement Henry I ruled for nearly thirty years without serious challenge. At his coronation he had issued a charter in which he promised justice to the Church and the barons, the king's immediate feudal subjects, in the stoppage of the abuses they had suffered from William II. He promised more also, that these magnates in turn should be made to mete out the same justice to their inferiors. This justice was the key-note of the reign, and Henry was dubbed by his subjects the Lion of Justice. When in later years he imposed exactions he did so by law, which was the same for all, and not by caprice which singled out a few; every man at least knew how he stood. In establishing this justice the king had absolute authority. It was his will that things should be

SOME CONSTITUTIONAL DEVELOPMENTS

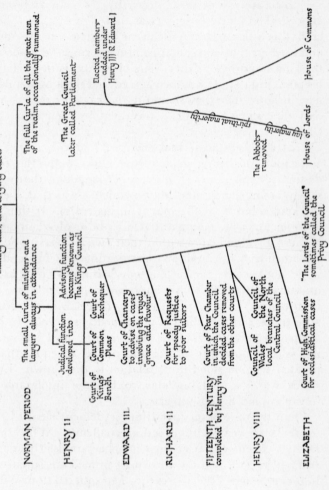

The Curia Regis
to advise the King in deciding disputes
making laws, and levying taxes

**The full Curia of all the great men
of the realm, occasionally summoned**

**The Great Council
later called Parliament**

Elected members
added under
Henry III & Edward I

House of Commons

spiritual majority

lay majority

The Abbots
removed

House of Lords

House of Lords

NORMAN PERIOD

**The small Curia of ministers and
lawyers always in attendance**

HENRY II

Judicial function
developed into

Advisory function
became known as
The King's Council

Court of
King's
Bench

Court of
Common
Pleas

Court of
Exchequer

EDWARD III

Court of Chancery
to advise on cases
involving the royal
"grace and favour"

RICHARD II

Court of Requests
for speedy justice
to poor suitors

FIFTEENTH CENTURY
completed by Henry VII

Court of Star Chamber
in which the Council
decided cases removed
from the other courts

HENRY VIII

Council of
Wales

Council of
the North
local branches of the
Central Council

"The Lords of the Council"
sometimes called the
Privy Council

ELIZABETH

Court of High Commission
for ecclesiastical cases

done in an orderly fashion, but there was no power to compel him. Rufus had willed to be unjust and disorderly, and none had been able to prevent him. The king's decisions were generally pronounced in the presence of his barons. The meeting was called the *Curia Regis*, the King's Court. To it he summoned as many as he chose, and attendance was compulsory. They met, not to press their views upon the king, not in any way to dictate as a Parliament might do, but simply to hear his will. Of course he needed expert advisers and ministers to attend to details, but they were of his choosing. *Curia* is a word of vague meaning. Sometimes it stands for a full assembly of the barons, sometimes for a little committee of the royal instruments. Obviously the latter was more frequently in session. The essential was that the king was there and his word decisive. The *Curia* made laws, levied taxes, tried disputes. In just the same way each baron ruled his vassals, each knightly holder of a manor his villeins—but these jurisdictions existed at the pleasure of the king. Justice was profitable, for the penalties were fines and forfeitures. In a fully feudal system all local justice would have been done in the local lords' courts. The Saxon system had been different; for its shire moots had met under the king's officer, the sheriff. That system had not been abolished at the Conquest, but the lords had encroached upon it. Henry I strengthened the shire courts and pocketed the fines accruing. It was, had any one known it, the beginning of a steady process whereby the king's national law was to supersede local feudal law. We shall meet with its later stages.

For a third of a century Henry I gave peace to England, and then in 1135 he died. He intended his daughter Matilda to succeed to the throne, but his nephew Stephen seized it. For nearly twenty years Stephen reigned but did not govern. The Matilda faction raised revolts, and the barons used the opportunity to make themselves independent of the Crown. The Church seized all the privileges, and more, that Anselm had failed to win from Henry I. Law and justice collapsed. The land was full of mercenary soldiers from abroad, of robber knights and barons, and of castles erected for private purposes without any licence from the state. It all turned upon the personal character of Stephen, a 'good fellow' but no disciplinarian. 'He was a mild man, and soft, and good, and did no justice,' said the Saxon chronicler with the simple directness found nowadays only in small boys' essays. When Stephen died in 1154 all except the robber barons were ready to welcome any rough master who knew his own mind.

They found one in Henry II, son of Matilda and the Count of Anjou, a young man of twenty-one who was already a warrior and statesman of experience. To the courage and energy of his Norman ancestors Henry added a wild passionate temper that made him terrible to his enemies if it sometimes led him to great mistakes. Injustice he certainly did to the few, but to the people at large his reign was a continuation of that of Henry I, his grandfather, a picking-up of the threads of order after twenty years of anarchy. In a few months he routed the mercenaries and packed them off across the sea, destroyed the private castles, and reduced the barons to discipline. For the next few years foreign business held him, for he had great fiefs in France, Normandy derived from his grandfather, Anjou and Maine from his father, and Aquitaine from his wife Eleanor, the heiress of that vast region. Then he tackled the Church, which had got out of hand under Stephen. Henry made his friend Thomas Becket Archbishop of Canterbury in the hope that they would work together for reform. But Becket put the Church first and the state second. The idea of a religious authority, standing above all kings and unifying all Christendom, fascinated him. He lived for it and died for it. Although as Englishmen we must be glad he failed (for had he won our England would not exist), we can yet admire him as a martyr to the faith he held.

He was no sooner consecrated than he was at odds with the king. The real question was whether the Church should rule the state or the state the Church. The ground on which it was fought out was not so much the old one of investitures as a new one of legal jurisdiction. Becket's claim was that no man in holy orders, even of the minor sort which included many who were really laymen, was subject to the king's courts. Henry's claim was that the king's justice must cover all alike. In the Constitutions of Clarendon (1164) Henry formulated his law. Accused clerks might be tried first before the bishop's court, but if guilty they must be given over to the king's justice for sentence. No one was to appeal to the Pope without the king's permission. No bishop might excommunicate any subject of the king without his consent. Investitures were to be continued as by the ruling of Henry I. In sum, the king was to be master in his realm. There is no doubt that it was reasonable and in the best interest of the realm. But the Church had grown so strong, in England and in all Europe, that it regarded the Constitutions as an outrage. Becket resisted, consented, withdrew his consent, fled overseas, stirred up endless trouble, came back again, and was brutally murdered in his own Canterbury cathedral. The sentimental populace, whose enemy he had really been, at once made him a saint and a martyr, and the Church officially followed suit. Jewels and gold were heaped upon his tomb, miracles performed there, and pilgrims trudged and rode from every shire, 'the holy blissful martyr for to seek, that hath them holpen when that they were sick'.

Henry's violent words had caused the murder, but he expressed horror and contrition when the thing was done. Quite probably he was sincere. To slay a bishop at his altar was beyond the limit of the hardiest free-thinking of those days, and it was doubly base in a king whose watchword was the law. He performed a degrading penance and then came to terms with the Pope's legates. Appeals to the Pope were to be allowed. Clerks accused of felony (that is, an offence ordinarily punishable by death) were to be tried and sentenced by the bishop, whose office forbade him to inflict the death penalty. But treason, from the national standpoint the most important felony, was excepted and remained in the king's courts. So did all minor offences, and also all civil suits involving rights to property. On investitures and all other matters the rules of Henry I, reinforced at Clarendon, were to hold good. The Church had saved something, but the king had won more. The benefit of clergy, the right of any educated scoundrel to save his neck by doing a bishop's penance, remained a scandal for centuries. But the Crown had still the appointment of bishops and abbots and could punish them for treason. Its hold was substantially intact.

During all these years of strife Henry had been steadily improving the methods of his government, whittling away bit by bit the powers and duties of the feudal magnates, and transferring them to trained civil servants, appointed or dismissed on their merits at the pleasure of the king. In this he was continuing the work begun by Henry I; and this evolution of the mechanism of the state is one of the most important lines of progress towards true nationality. Freedom from outside control, as we have seen, was another; but it would not have profited much without organized self-control such as pure feudalism could never yield.

Henry I, when calling out a feudal army, had sometimes allowed the clergy to pay money instead of sending knights. Henry II extended the plan to his lay vassals when he wanted a force to serve in France. All paid the tax (called scutage, or shield-money), and the king hired mercenaries to fight. It was more satisfactory for overseas work, for which the short-service feudal host was unsuitable. At the same time the old Saxon idea of the fyrd, or general levy for home defence, was not allowed to die out. The fyrd of the northern counties had done a fine piece of work in Stephen's reign when it routed a Scotch invasion at the Battle of the Standard. With this service in view Henry II enacted in 1181 the Assize of Arms, whereby every free man was required to keep weapons suitable to his rank or property.

The *Curia Regis* had hitherto advised the king on making laws, had supervised taxation, and had tried important cases. Sometimes it had been a great gathering and sometimes a very small one. Under Henry II it began to branch like a living tree. Certain of the regular members specialized in trying suits in which the Crown was involved, others in trying suits between subjects, others again in conducting financial business. Hence arose in time the great courts of King's Bench, Common Pleas, and Exchequer. They were not quite distinct in Henry's time, but the germs are there. In another aspect the official members of the *Curia* advised the king on general policy. They were always with him as a permanent council, the King's Council, distinct from the full *Curia* or Great Council of all the barons, which met only on special occasions. We shall find at a later date other courts, like those of Chancery and the Star Chamber, branching from this advisory side of the *Curia*. Still more important was the extension of authority from the *Curia* to places where the king could not be in person. Judges were sent out from the central court to travel round the country as itinerant justices. Like the parent *Curia* they had a threefold duty, to supervise the sheriffs and local magnates, to try cases which would otherwise have come to Westminster, and to watch the collection of taxes. The king's eyes and lips were being multiplied. The itinerant justices needed local evidence to work upon, and so they employed the jury. They did not invent the jury. No one did; it grew. It can be traced back to the Domesday inquiry and earlier. But it now became a regular institution. The jury were at first witnesses, respectable men who could swear to facts for the information of the judge. Later on they became the judges of fact themselves, hearing other witnesses and giving a verdict.

All this activity produced a national law to supersede the variable local laws of the lords' courts. Decisions were collected and recorded, and principles drawn from them—the Common Law of England, enforced and added to by generations of judges, in addition to the law enacted in statutes. The Common Law lies at the back of many of our national habits and ways of thought. This active twelfth century saw the rise of the lawyers as a specialized profession, a second learned profession to rival that of the clergy. We moderns are sometimes tempted to gibe at the lawyer as an expensive luxury. To understand his necessity we should look back to the haphazard violence he slowly suppressed—crimes unpunished, or the wrong persons punished, the property of the weak seized by the strong, the whole people demoralized by waste and injustice. It was the common state of affairs before these legal-minded kings took it in hand. If the same chronicler had commented on Henry II as on Stephen he would have reversed the terms of his judgement after this fashion: 'He was not a mild man, nor soft, nor good, but he did justice.'

Henry's justice was so strongly knit that after his death the machine worked for ten years without a king. That was the real position in the so-called reign of Richard I (1189-99). He spent his time in crusading, in captivity, in fighting in France, but not in governing England. The trained officials of Henry II carried on their work, and the country was little the worse except in the money it had to find for Richard's hobbies. One result was unlooked-for. In the absence of the king the system continued without the introduction of any new features such as Henry II had constantly added. It became a fixed state of affairs in men's minds. Consequently when the Crown again sought to make changes (and often bad ones), there was a quite novel resistance on the part of the barons. The sword of justice had become two-edged. The Henries had wielded it against unruly subjects. After their time law-abiding subjects used it to smite an unjust king. The idea of constitutional rule was born, which means rule in accordance with some fixed principles, and not with the mere whim of the ruler. If we look into European history we find that this is generally the outcome of absolute rule. It creates a system from which the ruler himself cannot escape, and so he becomes no longer absolute.

The idea of constitutional right runs strongly through the reign of John (1199–1216). He could be as active and daring as Henry II, but he was variable. Sometimes he would fight like a tiger, and at others he would do nothing whilst his enemies advanced. He certainly did not suffer from the foolish generosity which had made Stephen a failure; he was utterly selfish and pitiless. It was a defect in his intellect that he could never understand that there were certain things which even a despot must not do. Henry II had made humble atonement for the murder of Becket, which was only in part his fault. John murdered his nephew Arthur by deliberate policy and never attempted any show of regret. The same attitude appeared in numberless breaches of his word and betrayals of his own friends. He was an able man, but not quite sane, one who would in our day be classed as an habitual criminal.

It was John's misfortune to be matched against two able and sane competitors for power, Philip Augustus, King of France, and Pope Innocent III. Philip invaded his French provinces and stripped him of Normandy, Anjou, Maine, and Brittany, leaving only a part of the southern heritage of Aquitaine. John made a poor resistance, and his Norman vassals welcomed the change of allegiance, for in France as in England the beginnings of a national sentiment can be discerned. Hard upon this disgrace, in 1205, there occurred a vacancy in the archbishopric of Canterbury. The established rule was for the king to choose the new prelate and for the Church to consecrate him. But Innocent III, more than any other Pope, was determined to achieve the ambition of the Church to rule Christendom over the heads of kings and princes. He saw his chance in England in the hatred existing between John and his magnates. He annulled the King's choice and appointed, as archbishop, Stephen Langton, an Englishman then living at Rome. The bond between king and people was already cracked, and the Pope thrust in a wedge. It shows John's ability and the strength of the government founded by Henry II that for years the King kept up a successful resistance. He refused to admit Langton. The Pope replied with an interdict of all religious services in the realm, in those days a dreadful blow at the whole people. The King seized all Church property. The Pope excommunicated him, a sentence of everlasting punishment against him and his supporters alike. John carried on unconcerned, with campaigns in Wales and Ireland and Scotland, and a remorseless levying of taxes by the mechanism of Henry II. The barons were not stirred to revolt by the interdict or the excommunication. They must have seen that in the Canterbury quarrel the King was in the right. If only he had acted decently in other matters he would have been triumphant as a patriot sovereign. But he had no sense of justice. He taxed and confiscated and put to death beyond the limits of the law set by wiser kings. When he summoned the full *Curia*, or Great Council as it now was called, the barons criticized and refused his demands. Lacking their good-will he hired foreign mercenaries with his ill-got wealth. The reign of law was turning into a reign of terror.

Innocent watched patiently until the time was ripe. In 1213 he declared John deposed and commissioned the French king to invade England and carry out the sentence. The Pope had judged correctly. With his barons behind him John would have been invincible, but they had had enough of him and were ready to stand aside. The mercenaries also were mostly French vassals, and their loyalty was doubtful. John saw that the game was up, and saved his crown by submitting to the Pope. He accepted Langton and did homage to Innocent, formally yielding the whole realm of England as a papal fief and receiving it back as the Pope's man. John had no sense of shame and regarded this only as a clever move which he could repudiate when the times should alter. For the moment it succeeded. The great Pope became his friend and protector, cancelled interdict and excommunication, and called off the invasion. The Church, ordering kings like pieces on a chess-board, was nearer at that moment to universal rule than ever before or since. A little later Innocent died, and the moment passed.

Deprived of foreign aid, John's barons had to think of defending themselves, and now they had a man of wits to lead them in the person of Stephen Langton. John made some vague

promise of reform, which from him meant nothing, and set
about recovering his French losses from Philip Augustus. But
his barons would not follow, and his allies were beaten by Philip
at Bouvines in 1214. John returned to find his magnates at
length determined on reform. After various manœuvres they
brought him to terms at Runnymede in 1215, and forced him to
proclaim the Great Charter. Magna Carta is justly renowned
in English history, but not because it inaugurated any new
system of government. It contained very few provisions that
were new. It was mainly a statement of ancient customs, which
it described as rights. What was new was the firm definition of
right, and its statement by subjects against the King. These
principles of government had been created of their own pleasure
by the great sovereigns of the past, and now they were taken
up by subjects and hardened into a constitution whereby future
kings were to be bound. There was nothing in Magna Carta of
which Henry I or Henry II could not have approved except
this, that if the King departed from it the barons had the right
to force him back. The Crown had created Law, and henceforth the Law was to bind Crown and vassals alike. It was
Stephen Langton's brain that put this doctrine into the clear,
hard phrases that have been quoted through the centuries and
form the political background of every English mind: 'No free
man shall be taken or imprisoned . . . or anyways destroyed; nor
will we go upon him, nor will we send upon him, unless by the
lawful judgement of his peers, or by the law of the land'; 'To
none will we sell, to none will we deny or delay, right or justice';
'No unaccustomed tax shall be imposed unless by the common
council of the realm'. There has been a tendency to give these
things a wider meaning than that intended by their authors.
The barons were not claiming these privileges for all. The vast
majority of the people were excluded, for they were not free men
but serfs; and it was their own property, including these serfs,
that the barons were seeking to make safe in their own keeping.
But the men of Runnymede had built more greatly than they
knew, and had established principles that were to be applied
in ways they little dreamed of.

For John it was a bitter hour. He had been beaten by those
whom he despised. He believed the advantage of force had
been but momentary, and he turned at once to redress it. Again
he called in the mercenaries, gave the Charter to the winds, and

passed raging and ravaging through the land. The barons exercised the right of resistance and offered the crown to Louis, the son of the French king. An endless war was in prospect when John died suddenly in 1216, leaving his battered inheritance to his son Henry, a boy nine years old.

With French invaders, masterless mercenaries, and disunited barons all in the field, the situation was ripe for a recurrence of the atrocities of Stephen's reign. But the new respect for law and order prevented the worst. Such things were no longer done, and the few who hankered after them were forcibly discouraged by the majority. The barons rallied to the throne, expelled the French prince (rather ungratefully) and then the mercenaries, and tided over the years of Henry's minority with less scandal than might have been expected. The Church and the rising class of the merchants and citizens had an interest in order. The people, bereft of a ruler, were showing some capacity for self-control.

The effective rule of Henry III began in 1227. He was one of the well-meaning men who did no justice. With the administrative system as it had now developed, this would have mattered less but for another defect in the King's character. He had absolutely no financial sense, no grasp of the relation between ambitions and means, between expenditure and income. He was magnificently generous, but at his people's expense. His warm family affections caused him to endow swarms of foreign nobles, kinsmen of his mother and his wife. His piety admitted swarms of foreign churchmen to English benefices and poured English money into the coffers of Rome. His unpractical ambitions led to schemes of French conquest for which he lacked the generalship, and to the acceptance of foreign thrones, to be won with English money, for his brother and son. They never were won, although the money was spent.

There is reason to believe that the population and wealth of England were growing rapidly in this thirteenth century. Trade was increasing, the cloth manufacture was beginning, great feudal magnates were studying estate-management and reclaiming swamps and wastes. In 1246 an enraptured Pope exclaimed: 'Verily, England is our garden of delights; verily it is an unexhausted well; where much abounds, much may be extorted!' The drain continued for thirty years before it produced an explosion. But all the time disgust was growing. It

is safer to fleece a poor man than a rich; and the very fact that
the English were growing rich added to their fury against these
foreign parasites who battened on them. The feeling did much
to consolidate the nation. Barons, knights, citizens, and native
clergy were being bled alike, and they began to reduce themselves to the common denominator of Englishmen. The common interest bridged the gaps of origin and class, and the
leaders of the revolt were barons, all of French ancestry and
some of French birth, who nevertheless cried 'England for the
English'.

The engine of resistance was the Great Council of the realm,
the amplified form of the *Curia Regis*. The King had to consult
it for his excessive money requirements, and the barons who
composed it gradually hardened into a united party to insist
on redress of grievances. As a court of law and a constitutional
mouthpiece it was more important than as a granter of taxes.
In 1246 it began to be called a Parliament, a meeting for discussion. In 1254 its barons were reinforced by four knights
elected from every shire court to voice the interests of the lesser
landowners. This elective device was no new invention—like
the jury it grew, and from the seed of the jury. If sworn representatives of each neighbourhood could meet the King's
travelling judges, as we have seen under Henry II, it was but
a natural step to bring them all to Westminster to meet the
King; and this had already been done twice under John. Again,
there was no reason why any important class should not be thus
represented. The townsmen were growing important, and it
was a natural step to bring their men to the national Parliament
as well—a step that was shortly taken. It was not the principle
of representation that was new in the revolt against Henry III,
but the work of the representatives that was more prominent.
It has been well said that nothing constitutional is ever new; by
the time it grows constitutional it is already old. One must not
take the aphorism too literally, but it is a good working rule.

In 1258 a Parliament of barons met at Oxford. It was tired
of promises that were always broken, and took the governing
power out of the King's hands. By the Provisions of Oxford a
committee of the barons was appointed to manage the national
business. There were no elected representatives in the Oxford
Parliament, but the managing committee it produced ordered
the election of local committees to inquire into abuses in every

shire. Private ambitions soon split the baronial party, and in 1261 the King repudiated the Provisions. He obtained from the Pope an absolution from his oath, and from Louis IX of France an arbitration that declared the barons in the wrong. This produced civil war in earnest. The barons under Simon de Montfort, a foreigner by birth but English by interest, beat the King at Lewes in 1264, and captured him and his son. Earl Simon summoned a new Parliament in 1265. It comprised the barons, the knights of the shire, and two representatives from each town or city that favoured the cause. It did nothing beyond establishing this precedent. Simon's overbearing ways soon offended his supporters—he was an early example of the dictator—; Prince Edward, the King's son, escaped and headed the malcontents; and Earl Simon was killed at Evesham in 1265.

But the cause of reform was not dead. It had found a new leader in Prince Edward himself. The old King Henry virtually retired from active business. His son, strong-willed, sensible, a hater of waste, a lover of system, took control. The barons' committee of management disappeared, for there was no more need for it. Its authors had been reformers, not revolutionaries, and they were content with the ancient form of rule in good hands. By 1270 the machine of state was in such good order that Edward could allow himself a holiday. He went on the last of the crusades in the Holy Land, and Henry III died in peace in 1272 before his son's return. The reign had witnessed a constitutional advance and an advance towards real nationality, yet it is likely that no one at the time realized the fact. Parliament to them did not mean what it means to us, neither did England; but they had been building both.

IV

THE DECLINE OF FEUDALISM

(*From Edward I to the Wars of the Roses*)

I. THE KINGDOM AND ITS PARLIAMENT

IN the reign of Edward I we may say that the people of England became in some respects a nation, although they had far to go before nationality should be fully achieved. The process was accomplished, save in one important particular, in the two centuries that will be covered in this chapter, from the accession of Edward I in 1272 to that of Henry VII in 1485. By the latter date the national state was complete except that the Church remained to be brought more strictly under the control of law and Crown. That reform was postponed for half-a-century still.

The boundaries of the English realm in 1272 were very nearly what they are to-day, although political divisions within those boundaries were different. In the north the Scottish border followed its present line. The present county of Durham was ruled by the bishop as a fief under his full control, without interference by the King's officers. The bishopric also comprised the district called Norhamshire, which filled the angle between the Tweed and the sea-coast and was traversed by the easiest road for invaders between England and Scotland. The justification of the bishop's exceptional liberties lay in his responsibility for the defence of the border. On the Welsh side also there were similar arrangements. Wales, even before the Norman Conquest, had been vaguely subject to the English Crown, although for practical purposes its princes were independent. But before the end of the thirteenth century the Principality of Wales had shrunk to two small areas. The more northerly consisted of Anglesea and the mountainous region of Snowdon, and the more southerly of a district covered by the present Cardiganshire. Here only did Welsh independence persist. All the rest of what is now Wales had been split into the border fiefs of the various Lords Marchers, nobles who held of the English Crown on much the same terms as the Bishop of Durham. Their office was to defend the marches as a barrier against incursions into England proper. An English earldom, that of Chester, had the same palatine status, and its forces were specially charged to watch the strong Snowdon principality. In the Welsh marches, therefore, the extreme military type of feudalism persisted long after the King's administration had reduced feudal privilege in the remainder of the realm. There were as yet no Welsh shires, with all the law and government that term implies. There were only the principalities and the military fiefs. The latter still gave strength to the most turbulent section of the English baronage.

The baronage as a whole had shown under Henry III that it was the strongest class in the community. But its tone had changed in the two centuries since the Conquest. Its typical members were no longer ruffianly oppressors of a conquered people. They had indeed achieved a more perfect legal grip upon the peasantry; villeinage was more widespread in the thirteenth century than in the eleventh. But the best of the magnates regarded themselves as benevolent despots, with a responsibility to their subjects and a pride in the prosperity of their estates. Their powers, moreover, had been made subject to the national administration and strictly defined by law. There had also been much subinfeudation, the division of great holdings among vassals of knightly rank. These smaller landholders were becoming a powerful class, with their constitutional engine in the shire court which brought them into direct relation with the Crown. The election of knights of the shire to sit with the great barons in Parliament is a testimony to their importance. The shire courts were a civilizing agency. Their members were responsible for many things and had to understand something of law and the national methods of administration. When the shire courts were required to elect members to Parliament they seldom chose the same men twice in succession. It was an onerous duty that was taken by turns, and consequently a very large number of individuals had the experience once in their lives of travelling to Westminster and meeting their fellows from other counties. The public-spirited country gentleman was in course of evolution.

By the end of the thirteenth century the free peasant of the Saxon tradition was almost extinct. The manorial system included almost every rustic not of gentle birth or clerical status. At the same time the lot of the villein was improving. He shared perhaps in the generally increasing wealth of the country. He was certainly less subject to arbitrary oppression. Manorial rights and duties, like all others, tended to become hardened by custom and to attain the force of law. In the fourteenth century it became usual to preserve written records of manorial affairs, of transactions in the manor court, of fines and penalties. These records served both sides as precedents, and whilst they were witness to the lord's rights they were witness also to the villein's small liberties. In the fourteenth century there set in a process of emancipation that will be more fully dealt with on a later page. The culmination of villeinage was followed by its speedy decline.

The greatest social development was in the multiplication of towns and of the industries they sheltered. London has always been the greatest of English towns. It combined the advantages of an inland centre and a seaport. The tides of the Thames estuary enabled sea-going ships to work up and down with fair regularity. To the westward the city had river navigation up to Oxford. To the northward it had a network of tracks and highways, to the southward a bridge and a good road to Dover and the continent. It was inevitably the centre of merchandise and finance. It early acquired rights of self-government under mayors elected by the citizens. Its neighbour of Westminster became similarly the centre of the King's administration, the place of the highest justice, and the gathering-point of national assemblies. Other towns achieved local liberties by means of charters which made them independent of feudal jurisdiction. The nature of the privileges varied. It might be the right to hold a court, to hold and control a market, to trade free of tolls in part or all of the realm, to pay a fixed sum as a composition for taxation, or to enjoy a combination of such boons. Everywhere a local patriotism was produced, ready to contribute to a national patriotism at a future stage. With the exception of London the towns were small in area, and their physical growth was checked by two factors. The chartered rights extended only to the limits originally defined; and those limits were enclosed by the town walls which clearly marked them. The town population was therefore closely packed and the conditions insanitary. Both physically and morally there was a much clearer division between town and country than now. The medieval town was a sharply-outlined feature in the landscape, not a shapeless sprawling mass. Its buildings extended upwards rather than outwards. It might be at least a thing of beauty to the sight, even if noxious to the other senses.

In town and country alike the Church bulked large. The cathedral dominated its city and the parish church its village. The abbeys were fairer buildings than the manor-houses of the country gentlemen. In the thirteenth century the friars arose as new orders of religion active both within and without the towns, and soon they, too, had their stone-built houses and churches. Clerics of all classes, from the bishops and mitred abbots to the monks, friars, parish priests, scholars, and the dubious lower grades that sheltered under the immunities of the Church, pervaded all streets and highways and all haunts of lay society from the King's court to the slum. To the landless younger son of gentle birth the monastery offered a path to high promotion. To the villein or town apprentice the carefree life of the tramping friar or student was an object-lesson in the independence a very little learning could confer. The Church was a great solvent of the rigid castes of the feudal age.

The population of England and Wales, about two millions at the Norman Conquest, is estimated to have exceeded four millions by the middle of the fourteenth century. Population depends primarily upon the available foodstuffs. A given area of country will support very scanty numbers of people if they live solely by hunting wild animals, rather more if they keep flocks and herds, more still if they cultivate the soil. If they manufacture largely, and so have the wherewithal to buy food from without, there is scarcely a limit to their multiplication. Trade accounted for only a small part of the increased means of subsistence in fourteenth-century England, for it was trade in the luxuries of the few rather than the necessities of the many. We must ascribe the increased numbers and greater comfort of the population to a fuller use of the soil. The area of waste land had been reduced, although it was still large as compared with that in modern times. The reclamation of waste was facilitated by the concentration of great properties in the hands of the magnates of Church and state, for wealthy proprietors could afford an outlay that might bear no fruit for many years. An example may be cited. The great triangle of Romney Marsh with its points at Appledore, Hythe and Romney, had been reclaimed from the sea in Roman times. After the fall of the

Roman province some eight hundred years elapsed before any further reclamation in this region was undertaken. Then, in the twelfth and thirteenth centuries, the work began anew under the direction of the monks of Canterbury, who had been granted the rights over the marshes. The 'inning' or embankment of the tide-swept mud-flats was pushed vigorously westwards towards Rye, and large new pastures were thus created for sheep and cattle. Such work was everywhere going on in the medieval period. Rivers were embanked and their swamped basins turned into dry ground, forests were cleared, and even the barren moorlands of the north were attacked by flocks of sheep which gradually destroyed the scrubby alder shoots and enabled good grass to grow and support even more sheep.

The mid-fourteenth century witnessed the culmination of this medieval progress. It was suddenly checked by the Black Death of 1349–50. The plague swept across Asia from the Far East to the Mahometan Levant, thence it was carried by trading vessels to Italy, and from there it spread into France and, finally, England. Exact figures are unknown, but it is reckoned to have killed from one-third to a half of the people. There was no rapid recovery. The medieval land-system was already being sapped by social changes, such as the emancipation of the serfs and the splitting-up of large properties. The Black Death quickened these changes, the number of small freemen increased, and the wealth of the great was reduced. Many areas were depopulated by the plague and reverted to waste; embanking, marling, and similar work were not maintained; and former cultivated lands were converted to sheep pastures employing fewer men. Medieval efficiency and medieval servitude declined together, and the freer England that arose supported a reduced population. It is computed that at the close of the fourteenth century the numbers were about two-and-a-half millions, a hundred years later three millions, and that the pre-1350 figure of four millions and more was not again reached until the reign of Elizabeth.

The men of old time had no notion of statistics, and the crippling disaster of the Black Death was soon forgotten. The smaller society that survived was freer to evolve in new directions, and in one respect the late fourteenth century was a brilliant period in English life. The English language began to emerge as the tongue of all classes of society. Hitherto Latin had been the language of religion, of the law, and of state documents. French had been spoken by the barons and the gentry and written by the poets who supplied chivalry with its romance. The Saxon dialects had sunk after 1066 to be the jargon of serfs and villeins. Yet these had always been in the majority, and their tongue survived in altered form. By the fourteenth century it had simplified its grammar and enriched itself with French and Latin words, and it had also made some steps towards uniformity throughout the land. Then there occurred an upward thrust. The gentry, who had spoken French but had reckoned themselves Englishmen under Henry III, began to speak English under Edward III. French, displaced in social life, invaded official spheres and itself displaced Latin as the language of statutes and parliamentary records. But lawyers and officials still clung to Latin for many purposes, not the Latin of ancient Rome, but a strange clipped shorthand which had the merit of occupying little space on costly parchments. The Church kept to a purer, more literary Latin for its services, but even the loftiest bishop needed English for converse with his peers, and in John Wycliffe there appeared a new type of churchman who translated the scriptures and wrote tracts in his mother tongue. The new English soon found other writers of genius to stabilize and adorn it. Chaucer's poems are the English of a man of rank who moved in the society of courts. William Langland's *Vision of Piers Plowman* is the ruder script of a rustic critic of his time. Bishop Adam de Moleyns' *Libelle of English Policy* is a serious treatise on trade and sea power. Other authors there were, less known to fame. There was this of novelty about them: they were observers and thinkers, not mere entertainers like the minstrels of the past. Hard thinking had hitherto been restricted to religion and the law and to a few works on natural science. The new England was growing conscious of social problems and of economic changes to be faced. It no longer accepted the feudal world as ordained and immutable. Ere the fourteenth century was out the very serfs were asking questions that probed to the roots of society. 'When Adam delved and Evë span, who was then a gentleman?' chanted the peasant rebels of 1381. From such a quarter it was an alarming proposition.

The English military system changed rapidly in the fourteenth century. The essence of the feudal tenure had been armed service in payment for the grant of land. The traditional period of such service was generally sufficient for local defence against invasions, whether of the borders or the coast, but it was too short for aggressive campaigns overseas. We have seen that for this purpose actual service had been commuted to the payment of scutage, and with the money the Crown had hired foreign mercenaries for its wars. A variant of this plan had been the calling out of a fraction only of the feudal force for a longer period, the expenses being defrayed by those who stayed at home. Side by side with this system the old Saxon obligation of every free man to serve in the fyrd had been maintained, and it was often contended by the Crown that this service could be demanded overseas. In the thirteenth century, when the numbers of free men had diminished, the obligation was extended to the villeins, and it proved ultimately to be a factor in their enfranchisement.

Edward I used the feudal force in his wars, and had often considerable trouble in compelling the barons to follow him. He therefore adopted in addition the system of commissions of array, whereby a trusted leader would undertake the duty of raising a force with the King's money for its wages. The men might join voluntarily, or they might be pressed under the fyrd obligation. These commissions of array provided the armies used in the great French wars of the fourteenth and fifteenth centuries. The men so raised often served for years, lost touch with their manor and its villein services, and became professional soldiers. From the payment of wages by the King it was an easy step to a contract by which the captain of the band received a fixed sum and paid the men himself. They became his men, his armed retainers, and when their own king had no further use for them they still kept together, since they had no other means of livelihood. They took service with any other power which could pay them, or they lived by the plunder of the country in which they found themselves. These bands of regular soldiers were the scourge of France so long as the Hundred Years War endured. Some went farther afield, into Spain or Germany, and one famous captain, Sir John Hawkwood, achieved a great name in Italy. After 1450, when France drove them out, they returned to be the scourge of England. The country was full of fighting-men who had forgotten how to plough. Their knightly captains had no thought but of war,

and there were barons of rank and wealth ready to gather them
into armies. Hence came the Wars of the Roses which plagued
England for thirty years until the disorderly elements cancelled
one another out.

With the long-service soldier there developed an extraordinary skill at arms. The bow became the national weapon
and was used as no other nation could use it. The continent
had long produced its shortbowmen and its crossbowmen.
England adopted the longbow, a weapon of greater force and
accuracy than the shortbow and of far greater rate of fire than
the crossbow. The honour of the new invention is attributed
to the Welsh, who used it against Edward I. He was always
ready to profit by experience, and enlisted Welsh archers against
the Scots; and at Falkirk the victory was won by the showers of
arrows that broke the solid array of Scottish spearmen and
allowed the charging knights to scatter them. Half a century
later the longbow had become universal in England. Every one
practised its use from childhood and attained a sureness of eye
and a strength of arm that no foreigner ever learned. The
making of bows, arrows, and strings became skilled crafts, for
the marksman who would win his village competition needed
the best material. The social effects were enormous. The
skilled bowman was a man of worship, were he never so humbly
born. He could quit his villein servitude and march off to
freedom and plunder in France. There he learned at Crécy and
Agincourt that he could look the mailclad knight in the face.
The bowman, in fact, brought feudal chivalry down with a
crash, for he dismounted the knight. It was found useless for
cavalry to charge well-posted archers, since it never reached
them; armour might save the rider, but it could not cover the
horse. In the fifteenth century fighting on foot became the rule.
The archer wore no armour but a steel cap. The man-at-arms
encased himself in ever thicker plate until he grew arrow-proof.
Thus the hand-gun or arquebus came in to exploit the new
gunpowder invented in the thirteenth century. The arquebus
was slow to load, but it would kill. By the sixteenth century it
was supreme, and the bow declined. Long before that time the
heavy gun had proved able to batter walls into ruin and so to
take towns and castles that had been almost impregnable before.
Guns were used in siege-work early in the fourteenth century.
Unlike the longbow they were not an English monopoly,

I

Artillery flourished in France and Italy, and even the Turks made play with it. In 1456 the Turkish cannon broke the walls of Constantinople which had withstood assault for a thousand years. With the decline of the bow the English military reputation underwent a long eclipse. But something remained, a national tradition of good shooting that has persisted through all changes of weapons, carried on by the sailors of Drake to those of Nelson, to the musketeers of Minden and Waterloo, the Yankee marksmen of Bunker's Hill, and the riflemen of Mons and Ypres.

English ships of war became important during the medieval conflicts. About the time of the Norman Conquest, as has been mentioned on an earlier page, the Crown had made a bargain for sea service with the Cinque Ports. The contract was of the feudal type modified to suit a maritime force. Instead of land the Barons of the Cinque Ports were given immunity from tolls, and the right to hold courts; and instead of knights and their retinues they gave the King ships and their crews. From 1066 to 1204 English kings dominated the north coast of France and suffered little risk of invasion from that quarter. The work of the Cinque Ports fleet during that period was chiefly to transport the kings and their armies across the Channel. The loss of Normandy made invasion possible. The Cinque Ports remained faithful to John in spite of his villainies, but he found it necessary to supplement their force with some royal ships specially built for him. The truth was that ships in general were growing larger, but that the Cinque Ports could not keep pace because their harbours were all shallow and could not float the new type of vessel. John and his successors therefore kept their royal ships at Southampton or in the Thames. They drew also upon the tonnage of the new western ports like Exeter, Fowey, and Bristol, and the eastern ports like London, Yarmouth, and Boston, which were rising into prominence with the growth of trade. In spite of this the Cinque Ports were prominent all through the thirteenth century. In the loose time of Henry III they behaved almost as a sovereign power, and made war and peace with the French on their own account in contempt of the national government. Edward I reduced them to order and used their ships to blockade the Welsh coast in his wars with Llewellyn. In 1287, Winchelsea, which was then the richest of the Ports and stood on a low-lying island, was wiped out by the hand of Nature. A great storm washed away both town and island, and Edward rebuilt the place farther inland on the hill where it now stands. Edward I, like John, employed also some regular ships of his own.

By the fourteenth century the great days of the Cinque Ports were over. Their havens were steadily silting up, and their little ships were outclassed by giants of two and three hundred tons built elsewhere. These big vessels were known as cogs. They were broad and roomy, able to carry many fighting men, and driven by a single great sail set on a mast amidships. For warlike purposes they had platforms or castles fitted at bow and stern, from which archers and slingers could shoot down on the enemy's deck. Foreign trade was increasing, and the merchants owned many of these ships. By the common law the King could impress them for his service, although he was supposed to pay for them. With fleets of this sort, drawn from every harbour in the realm, Edward III won the great battle of Sluys in 1340 and blockaded Calais into surrender in 1347. So successful was he that he could dispense with a regular navy. But in the end he overworked his mercantile marine. He continually impressed the ships and neglected to pay for them. Merchants were ruined and shipbuilding ceased. In his closing years the French revived their navy and made an alliance with Castile, which was growing strong at sea. Frenchmen and Spaniards overwhelmed the enfeebled English, dominated the Channel, and invaded our southern coasts. Their raids completed the ruin of English sea-power by destroying the ports from which it sprang. It was a sad ending to the reign of a king who in his great days had styled himself Lord of the Sea.

The English were deeply ashamed of the humiliation. Under Richard II they sought to revive their sea-power by means of a Navigation Act and other measures to encourage trade. But it was a time of bad government, and no revival took place until the brief reign of Henry V (1413–22). He in a few years created a mighty Royal Navy, with vessels of a size unheard-of before. With them he held the Channel and conquered northern France. The effort died with him. His son Henry VI, who succeeded as an infant and never became a man although he lived to be fifty, was in the hands of bad counsellors. They sold off the Royal Navy to save expense, lost France, and lost also a great part of England's trade for lack of protection. Not until the Tudor period did the navy become a strong and permanent factor in the national defence. In the fifteenth century, when English fortunes were so low, a great change occurred in European shipping. The medieval cog, with its single sail, gave place to the three-masted ship with courses and topsails, a lateen mizen, and a spritsail. Such vessels could keep the sea and make head against adverse weather as the cog could not. With them the crossing of the Atlantic and the voyage to India became possible. They were a factor in the expansion of Europe, and of England, over the world. The Latin seamen of the Mediterranean made other inventions in the Middle Ages, the magnetic compass, the portolan chart with an accurate tracing of coastlines, the astrolabe and the quadrant for taking latitudes. These things spread very slowly into English use. They were not fully adopted when the great age of discovery set in with Henry the Navigator (of Portugal) and Columbus, the Genoese who worked for Spain.

The mechanism of the state developed rapidly in the thirteenth and fourteenth centuries. We have seen how the *Curia Regis* of the Norman kings had branched into three distinct functions, judicial in the Courts of King's Bench and Common Pleas, financial in the Exchequer, and political in the King's Council. The Council, besides being a political body, had also to help in judging cases too important for the regular courts to meddle with. The Crown never gave up its function as the supreme law-giver, and its natural adviser in these matters was the Lord Chancellor, the head of the legal profession. From his work there developed under Edward III the Court of Chancery, which dealt with cases not covered by the ordinary law, but pertaining to the King's 'grace and favour'. The Chancery did good work in securing justice among the great, especially in matters of land and property. Richard II established yet another branch of the Council's jurisdiction in the Court of Requests, which was specially designed to give justice to poor suitors who could not afford the ordinary law. Apart from all this there were still matters that the King's Council had to settle, things that affected the safety of the throne and could not be left even to the Chancellor's Court. The Council therefore continued to act as judges as well as advisers to the King, and when they were sitting in this capacity they became known as the Star Chamber. Like the others, the Star Chamber became in the fifteenth century a regular court, but unlike them it always refused to be bound by any laws or rules. It decided as it thought expedient. It was a useful engine of government in troubled times, although it had in it the seeds of tyranny.

In local government there were likewise new developments. The sheriff had long been the King's officer in every shire. He presided at the shire court, did justice, collected taxes, and saw to the election of knights and burgesses to Parliament. Henry II had introduced the itinerant justices to supervise and reinforce this work. Edward I improved them into justices of assize, to travel round fixed circuits at regular intervals, as they still do, and try the offenders presented by the sheriff. Shortly afterwards the sheriff's duties were again encroached upon and split up by the appointment of justices of the peace. These were chosen in large numbers for each county, from the ranks of the local gentry. Their functions were those of police and magistrates combined, to proclaim and enforce the law, arrest evildoers, and commit them for trial at the assizes. It was an excellent move to make men of substance the King's officers in their spare time, a move in the direction of training the people in self-government. In the fourteenth century the justices of the peace were a young institution and not very notable. In after times they grew to be the backbone of the state, preservers of its liberties, and its defenders against revolution.

It would be a mistake to suppose that all these devices meant that England was orderly, peaceful, and well governed. They meant just the contrary. If things had been going well there would have been no need of alterations. The whole medieval period was a struggle between crime and justice, in which crime progressively got the upper hand. Shocking things happened even under a strong king like Edward I. Under his successors the moral condition of the country decayed. New laws, new courts, judges, magistrates were introduced to restore order, but more often than not they failed. The Hundred Years War was partly responsible. By draining the King's wealth it made him weak. By enriching unworthy persons, as war always does, it placed bad men in high office. By accustoming all men to violence it made crime seem natural. It must be remembered that there was none of our modern discipline in these medieval armies, among either officers or men. What they wanted they stole, and if resisted they murdered. Inevitably they brought these manners home with them. Hence the unavailing cry for order and the futile methods of restoring it as the fourteenth century merged into the fifteenth. The creation of new organs of the state availed little at the time, but it was of excellent augury for happier days to come.

The greatest of all these achievements was Parliament. We have seen that under Henry III there were two distinct bodies, each called Parliament. One was the meeting of the great barons alone, formerly the Great Council, the other the experimental addition of burgesses and knights of the shire to the barons. Edward I continued to call both kinds of assembly, for he held very strongly that it was the best means of getting the people to act together and to behave as a nation. The meetings of barons only were at first more numerous. In them the King explained his policy, dispensed the higher justice, and passed important laws. The chief reason for calling in the knights and burgesses was to secure from them grants of extra taxes for the King's wars. People were more ready to pay when their representatives could explain to them why the demand was necessary. But the full Parliament always had another business, that of presenting petitions to the King for justice and reform. At first the petitions were those relating to individual wrongs; next they might be petitions affecting groups of people, the members of some special class or the inhabitants of some particular town; and finally petitions grew common on matters that covered the whole realm. These requests were humbly presented to the King. If he thought fit to refuse them he answered courteously 'Le Roy s'avisera'—the King will consider it, which meant 'No'. If he granted them, the phrase was 'Le Roy le veult'—it is the King's will, and the petition became the law of the land. This method of legislation by petition became general in the Parliaments of the fourteenth century.

In the later years of Edward I the two kinds of Parliament fused into one body. The greater barons, the bishops, and some of the abbots were summoned by separate writs from the Crown. The knights of the shire and the burgesses were summoned by general writs directed to the sheriff of each shire, and the sheriffs thus became the officers in charge of the elections. The knights of the shire were chosen by the suitors at the shire court, in other words, the landowners of the county. The burgesses were picked in various ways which differed in the several towns.

The essential thing was that the town should send its two men, and the central government did not care how they were elected. It generally ended in a small group of the leading townsmen choosing two of their number for what was an unpopular duty, and the poorer people were well content to have nothing to do with it. Sometimes the corporation named the members, sometimes the limited class of freemen of the borough, and in a very few instances all the householders had a vote; but there was never any idea of allowing a voice to the mere labourers and apprentices, who generally boarded in their masters' houses. These loose methods of election gradually hardened into fixed local customs and remained unaltered until the great Reform Act of 1832.

The early Parliaments had no division into houses. The debating was done by the lords and prelates, who alone constituted the Parliament in the original sense of the term. The knights and burgesses were called in only to stand and hear the decisions about their petitions, or to consent to the grant of taxes. Their individual members had no right to make themselves heard; their Speaker alone could answer in the name of all. The ceremony still persists at the opening or dismissal of Parliament—the King on the throne, the Lords seated, the Commons standing, all in the same chamber—; that is still Parliament in the strict meaning of the word. But from the outset the Commons had preliminary meetings amongst themselves to talk over the taxes and petitions and instruct their Speaker what to say. So arose gradually the House of Commons, at first a non-Parliamentary meeting, whose debates were destined to become the most important part of the whole business. The lower clergy, the parish priests, the friars, and the miscellaneous array of 'clerks', were not represented in the Commons. They clung to the privilege of being a class apart, and when they had to pay taxes they preferred to grant them in their own Convocations at Canterbury and York.

The growing importance of the Commons arose out of the wars of Edward III, the struggle with France which was destined to last for a hundred years and more. The Crown was forced to ask for ever more money, and the Commons consented only on condition of their petitions being granted. When the war went badly in the later years of Edward III the Commons grew very assertive. They insisted upon unpopular ministers being dismissed and others appointed, and upon the setting up of committees to watch the spending of their money and to make sure that it did not go into dishonest men's pockets. They began also the practice of impeaching powerful evildoers, that is, of bringing evidence against them and enforcing their trial by the Lords. These were good principles, but they seldom worked well in practice owing to the general corruption of the times. They continued to be tried, and the Commons' privileges grew in the fifteenth century until everything dissolved in the chaos of the Wars of the Roses. The importance of it all is that, although Parliament was a failure in the fifteenth century, its precedents were remembered in later times and revived in a solid form that has become an essential part of English life.

II. THE FIRST AGE OF ENGLISH EXPANSION

The purpose of this section is to review the attempts of the kings and people of England in the Middle Ages to expand their rule beyond the bounds of England itself. The word 'rule' is used advisedly, for that was the essence of our medieval expansion. It was not colonization, which means the overflow of the people themselves into new homes outside their borders. There are indeed a few hints of colonization to be noted, but they were exceptional. The process was in the main an attempt to dominate other peoples, not to displace them. It has therefore very little in common with the foundation of the oversea colonies and dominions of modern times. The reason why there was little colonization in the Middle Ages is fairly evident. England itself had no surplus population. When its numbers increased they could find room in the towns with their growing trade or in the waste lands of the countryside that were waiting to be reclaimed. Medieval England had also no religious dissensions so serious that the minority found it impossible to live in the same land with the majority and were therefore obliged to emigrate. The Lollards indeed were persecuted, but it never occurred to them to take this means of escape, as it did in a later age to the Puritans and the Quakers. What we have now to deal with is the political conquest of Wales, the same thing partially achieved in Ireland, and the same again attempted, but altogether failing to succeed, in Scotland and France. The general result was indeed failure, but the attempt had its permanent effects upon England. The wars helped to weaken the monarchy, to liberate the villeins, to develop Parliament, and to unify the nation. They caused enormous loss and suffering, but they did in the long run produce some good consequences.

We have already mentioned the encroachment of the Lords of the Marches upon the independent tribes in Wales. The thing had been done piecemeal, but it had gone so far that by the accession of Edward I the fiefs of the Marchers occupied more of the country than did the free territory of the Welsh princes. The subjects of these Marcher lords were in the main Welsh, although some Englishmen filtered in with the conquerors. The English element founded the small towns of Wales, where the English language prevailed from an early date.

Edward I was a king who took wide and long views. He saw that the island which contained English, Welsh, and Scots was a geographical unity, the natural home of a united kingdom. United, it would be invincible, for the medieval seas were hard to cross. He was imbued also with the idea that England as he was shaping it was a better governed country than most, and that to extend its laws to Wales could be nothing but a benefit to the Welsh. He therefore seized the opportunity of a conquest. The conduct of Llewellyn, the Welsh prince, offered the excuse. Llewellyn was technically the vassal of Edward. He resented this nominal yoke and refused to do homage. Edward was strict about such obligations, as strict to himself as to others, for he punctually did his own homage to the King of France for his provinces in Aquitaine. From 1277 to 1283 he carried out the conquest of the Principality. The Welsh taught him some military lessons, including the usefulness of the longbow and the uselessness of armoured horsemen in wild country. But in the end strength prevailed. Great castles were built to hold down the country valley by valley, and the English shire system with its laws was in some districts introduced. Llewellyn was killed in action in 1282, and his brother David was taken and executed in the following year. With that the resistance came to an end.

Sentiment and romance have sometimes deplored the conquest. In fact it was good and necessary for both peoples. To the Welsh it gave ultimately a peace that as tribesmen they had never long enjoyed. To England it gave excuse to clip the wings of the Marcher lords, who had claimed excessive privileges on the score of their military services. With Wales no longer a danger the western borders of England could also be reduced to the national law. Edward I showed respect for Welsh sentiment by keeping the core of the Principality intact. Parts of the Welsh law were retained, and the King's son was made Prince of Wales. Two hundred years afterwards a Welsh soldier became the ancestor of an English royal house, and Welshmen and Englishmen alike could look to the Tudors as their natural sovereigns. It was by the Tudor Henry VIII that the settlement and civilization of Wales were completed.

There is scarcely any event in Ireland of importance to the history of the British Isles until a century after the Norman Conquest. Of Ireland we must give a sketch of a condition of affairs rather than a story of events. The country was never conquered by the Romans, although it was affected by one great movement of the later Roman Empire, the spread of Christianity. In some way the Celtic tribes became Christian, and in the sixth and seventh centuries they supported monasteries where learning flourished and whence missionaries came eastwards to convert the heathen English and Scots. It is possible to look back to this as the golden age of Ireland mainly because so little is known about it. But when the country comes within the ken of history it exhibits a condition of chronic anarchy and warfare between petty chiefs and their tribes. One often hears modern Irishmen boasting their descent from the old Irish kings; and they may well do so, for there were times when almost every man in the country was a king, or claimed to be. The fall of Rome left Ireland unaffected, as did also the rise of the Anglo-Saxons in England. The viking Norsemen made settlements on the coasts, the origins of the seaport towns such as Dublin, Wexford, and Waterford. They did not penetrate far inland, and a serious attempt at conquest was defeated by the Irish at the great battle of Clontarf in 1014—whilst Canute was ruling England. Celtic Ireland then gave an example of that faculty it has constantly displayed ever since, the ability to absorb incoming stocks and turn them into Irishmen. The Norsemen disappeared in this way, becoming indistinguishable from the mass, and leaving the seaports as their only memorials. With these the English ports of Bristol and Chester very early carried on a trade in hides, fish, and slaves.

Under Henry II the connexion grew closer. The Irish Church had hitherto been separate from the Church of Rome, with many practices which Rome, had it been greatly interested, would have declared heretical. Henry therefore had no difficulty in obtaining the Pope's permission to conquer Ireland. The licence remained dormant until 1169, when the barons of the Welsh marches led an expedition across St. George's Channel. It was an Irish chief who suggested the movement. He had been turned out by a stronger neighbour, and he enlisted the support of the Earl of Pembroke, commonly called Strongbow. The expeditionary force, of Norman leaders and Welsh troops, gained a footing in the country. Henry himself went over in 1171 and exacted homage from Irish and Normans alike. The Normans established themselves in fiefs that were really independent, whilst the greater part of the land remained under its ancient tribal system. The essential difference between tribalism and feudalism was that the latter recognized individual rights to land and was suited to agriculture, whilst under the former the tribe owned an area in common and used it for pasturing their flocks and herds. As for the English system of law and government, it was established only in the Pale or district surrounding Dublin, and even there it was generally more a theory than a fact.

With this state of affairs the English Crown had to be content for the rest of the medieval period. The King styled himself Lord of Ireland, but had very little lordship to show for it. The Church became Roman, and the people have ever since been devoted adherents of that faith. The Norman barons, like their Norse predecessors, became Irish, 'more Irish than the Irish themselves', as a chronicler put it. A handful of English merchants gained a footing in the ports, where they set up civic corporations after the English model. An assembly sometimes met at Dublin under the name of the Irish Parliament, but it had little power and its decisions were disregarded. The so-called conquest was utterly futile and harmful. If it had been effective it might have made a strong, well-governed Irish province with results so different from the reality as to be unimaginable to us. If it had been completely foiled by the Irish it might have left a strong, independent Irish kingdom, provided that some vigorous ruling family had come forward to complete the work. As it was, the unfulfilled English claim produced a mere chaos that lasted for centuries, so that disorder became natural, and even when the strong Tudor monarchy felt fit to tackle the problem it failed to overcome it and did quite as much harm as good. The whole thing was a tragedy of blind forces, for which no king or people can be blamed. Leaders and subjects acted on the demands of the moment, and when occasionally some far-seeing statesman did arise he lacked the power to do what he saw was right.

The English attempt to dominate Scotland ended in a complete military failure which in the long process of history has produced happier results to both countries than has the partial English success in Ireland. The Scots, in modern times the most clearly defined and united nationality in the world, were formed from a mixture of diverse stocks—the Picts who had fought with Roman Britain, the Celtic Britons of Strathclyde who escaped the Anglo-Saxon conquest, the Angles of the east coast from Berwick up to Edinburgh and beyond, the Celtic Scots who came over from Ireland, and the Norsemen who settled in Sutherland and Caithness and the Hebrides. All these ingredients were important, and the Angles were especially so because they gave their language and many of their customs to the whole of Lowland Scotland. If the border had been drawn for reasons of racial origin it would be a line running almost north and south, from a point near Edinburgh to one near Lancaster, and it would have included in England the east coast up to the Forth and in Scotland the west coast down to the Mersey. Drawn as it was from the Tweed to the Solway it left an Anglo-Saxon element in Scotland and a Celtic element in England, and the speech of the former prevailed in the kingdom which contained it.

The relationship between the border peoples of the two countries led to a good deal of intermarriage between leading families and to the possession by some of them of property on either side of the line. This in its turn paved the way for the spread of feudal ideas of land-tenure, law, and warfare into the Lowlands, but not into the Highlands, where the Celtic tribal customs survived for many centuries. The early Scottish kings bore effective rule only in the Lowlands, where they were manifestly weaker than their English brethren. In the two hundred years after the Norman Conquest they sometimes acknowledged and sometimes denied a vague overlordship by the English Crown. So long as it was no more than a form it aroused little resentment in Scotland, for peoples which had not yet become nations were content with the substance of freedom and not very indignant at the ceremony of feudal homage. It was a shadowy theory throughout Christendom that every ruler owed allegiance somewhere, except the Emperor and the Pope. The Scottish Church, it should be noted, acknowledged no parallel subordination to the English archbishops of Canterbury or York. It looked to Rome direct, and therefore when England attempted to turn the nominal vassalage into a real one the Scottish clergy were foremost in resistance.

That attempt was begun by Edward I. He was possessed by an idea that has, more than any other, led European kings and nations into aggressions upon their neighbours—the idea of 'the natural frontier', or in other words, of geographical facts alone as the determinants of national limits. That idea makes the Frenchman regard the Rhine as his natural frontier—it is so neat and clean-cut; and therefore the fact that the people on both banks of the Rhine are Germans has been disregarded, and unlimited war from the sixteenth century to the twentieth has ensued. With Edward I the idea took an even neater and more cleanly cut form. He was the greatest prince in an island, and therefore the whole island was his natural territory, to the elimination of frontiers altogether. His mind had also another marked feature, that of insistence upon extreme legal rights. Had he been a smaller man we might almost call his a pettifogging mind. He was careful to perform his legal duties to others and insistent that others should to him, but he always liked to be the sole judge of what the duties amounted to. These doctrines led him into the course of action that changed the Lowland Scots from a people into a nation.

In 1290 the Scottish throne was a prize for many competitors. Four years earlier King Alexander III had ridden his horse over a cliff on a dark night and left a granddaughter in Norway as his sole descendant. The Maid of Norway never reached Scotland—she died on the way in 1290. A score and more of barons claimed the succession, alleging all kinds of feudal rules, reasonable and unreasonable, in their own behalf. Arbitration by some outside authority was the only solution, and the Scottish nobility called upon Edward to decide. Apart from his possible right as overlord of Scotland he was already their sovereign as King of England, for most of them held estates in both countries. In 1292 he gave judgement in favour of John Balliol, who certainly had the strongest claim and was as much an English noble as a Scot. So also was Robert Bruce, his most likely competitor. John Balliol assumed the crown and did homage for it as Edward's vassal. Had things stopped at that there would have been no grievance. But Edward's feudal right had been fully acknowledged and he meant to exercise it. He did so by summoning the parties in Scottish disputes to appear before him at Westminster, which was thus to be made the head-quarters of justice for the whole island. Balliol submitted to his patron, but the Scottish nobles revolted. The right of justice was profitable, and it carried with it most other rights. The Scots found themselves incorporated in Edward's realm, and they broke forth without delay. They met in a parliament of their own, abolished appeals to England, and made an alliance with Philip IV of France. In all this they carried the feeble Balliol with them, and he therefore became in spite of himself a rebel against Edward I. The English king was shocked at these proceedings. His own Gascon vassals had carried appeals against him to his overlord the King of France. It was a legal right, and he had not denied it. To the Scots he would apply the same justice as he himself was bound by.

He declared that Balliol had forfeited the Scottish throne for disobedience, marched into Scotland, and took possession of the chief towns and castles without difficulty. He required the nobles to do homage to himself as King, and most of them did so, fearing for their property in England. English affairs and a French war then called Edward south. He left Earl Warrenne as governor under the impression that Scotland was settled. It was not. In 1297 some rebels of minor rank took the field under a knight named William Wallace, and one by one the greater barons joined them. The movement, fed by genuine patriotism, grew formidable. Warrenne despised the enemy and sent his men to attack them across a single narrow bridge over the Forth near Stirling. Wallace allowed half the English to cross and then massacred them before the others could arrive. The news aroused all Scotland, and within a few weeks the victors were raiding northern England.

Edward disengaged himself from his French war and turned on Wallace. At Falkirk in 1298 he revenged himself for Stirling

Bridge. The longbowmen broke the Scottish ranks, and the mounted knights scattered the fragments. Wallace from ruler of Scotland became a hunted outlaw, and after many daring exploits he was taken and executed. Scotland gave a sullen submission, but it took many sieges and a permanent English garrison to extort it. In the last year of Edward's life Robert Bruce, grandson of the claimant of 1292, raised a new revolt, murdered a rival claimant, and had himself crowned king. In spite of the fact that his crime had been committed in a church the clergy supported him and the whole country rose. Edward had to face a new war of conquest. He was determined as ever, but his health was gone. He died in sight of the border in 1307.

Edward II, notwithstanding his father's dying wish, did nothing for several years. Then, when all Scotland but Stirling Castle had been lost, he collected an imposing host to recover it. He marched to relieve Stirling in 1314, and Bruce with a smaller force interposed to cover the siege. The resulting Battle of Bannockburn was Falkirk with the result reversed. The same elements were present, Scottish spearmen and English knights and archers. But Bruce was a general and Edward II was not. Bruce dug pitfalls in front of his spearmen and detailed a small body of mounted men to attack the archers. His position also was cunningly chosen behind the swampy bed of the Bannock Burn. The fighting occupied two days. On the first Edward failed to penetrate the Scottish position, and then played into Bruce's hands by leading his army into ground cramped between the Bannock and the Forth. On the second Bruce seized the opportunity and counter-attacked. Edward's great host was so crowded that the majority had no chance to fight. Only a few of his archers got to the front, and they were charged by the Scottish horse. His knights encountered unbroken ranks of spearmen and failed to pierce them. Confusion developed into panic. Thousands who had not been in action fled, whilst those who had were killed or taken. The attempt to absorb Scotland was ended. Scottish wars persisted for two-and-a-half centuries to come, and battles were won by the English. But Bruce and Bannockburn had made Scotland a nation whose spirit was unbreakable, and union was at length achieved by other means.

Out of it all came the alliance between Scots and French, a genuine kinship of spirit as well as of arms. It lasted as long as the Anglo-Scottish wars, and was broken only by the Reformation of the sixteenth century, which set Scotland on a new path very different from that of France.

The last, greatest, and most disastrous effort of our medieval expansion was the hundred years' attempt to conquer France. From 1066 the English kings had held fiefs in France as vassals of the French crown. Henry II had added to them, John had lost much, and Henry III more. Edward I was so strict in his feudal allegiance that he allowed the crafty Philip IV to trick him out of territories which he had much ado to regain. All this had been mere feudal tenure without much idea of national dominance. Edward III changed the whole aspect of affairs by laying claim to the crown of France. At the same time he changed the method of the French wars by employing long-service English armies instead of the feudal levies of his own French estates. The so-called Hundred Years War from 1337 to 1453 was therefore a national struggle instead of a series of feudal quarrels.

Its fortunes swayed to and fro in accordance with the characters of those in command. The side that had wise leaders rose, the side that had foolish ones fell. Only for a brief moment, when John, Duke of Bedford, faced Joan of Arc, was there equal ability on both sides. The details must be read in other books than this. Here we can take no more than a bird's-eye view. The interest of trade and the desire for political dominance seem to have filled equal places in inspiring Edward III's claim to the French crown. English trade with Flanders was suffering because the Count of Flanders was hostile. The Count was a vassal of the French crown. If therefore Edward could pose as the rightful holder of that crown, he could give the Flemish citizens a lawful excuse for disobeying their Count, which they greatly desired to do. Edward also, as a sovereign prince, was beginning to feel the humiliation of being a vassal for the Duchy of Aquitaine. That status had seemed quite natural to the kings of the thirteenth century, but in the fourteenth feudal ideas were decaying, and vassalage was becoming an indignity. So he claimed the sovereignty, and his whole people, exulting in the strength and unity that Edward I had given them, backed him with enthusiasm. Through all the disasters of the long contest there was never any public outcry against the war. Hatred arose only against statesmen who failed to win it, and long after success was hopeless and the statesmen knew as much, it was the people who insisted doggedly upon going on. The war was popular because it was waged on foreign soil and the fighters were nearly all volunteers. Taxes were high, but individuals got good plunder, and the gains were more dazzling than the losses. Above all, the glory of some brilliant feats of arms appealed to the romantic spirit of a youthful nation. In many ways the Hundred Years War is unique in English history. Never since has a war, once started, been looked upon as anything but a misfortune to be ended as soon as possible.

Edward III in his best days was a good soldier. His victory at Sluys gave him the command of the sea and kept the foe off English soil. Crécy paved the way for the capture of Calais in 1347. After that his son the Black Prince took up the command. At Poitiers he won against odds a harder fight than Crécy, and fed the national pride by bringing home the captive King of France and untold plunder for all his troops from baron to bowman. Thereafter fortune turned. Edward grew old and silly, and the Prince fell sick. John of Gaunt, the King's younger son, a man good at politics but at nothing else, mismanaged the war. The French produced an able king in Charles V and a general of genius in Bertrand du Guesclin. The English lost ground in France and lost also the command of the sea. The reign ended in 1377 with glory smirched, the southern counties ravaged, and popular resentment rising— not against the war but against John of Gaunt. He, by the way, is the only one of Shakespeare's historical portraits who is untrue to history. 'Time-honoured Lancaster', who uttered the soul-stirring rhapsody on 'this earth, this realm, this England', was the last man to whom the poet should have given the honour of his noble passage. He was a selfish politician, incapable of the patriotism put into his mouth.

Under Richard II and Henry IV the war smouldered, with petty expeditions into France and sea raids by both sides against their opponents' Channel ports. With Henry V (1413–22) it blazed up to its highest intensity. All was in his favour —his own martial genius and the fighting spirit of a new generation of Englishmen on the one side, and on the other France with an imbecile king (Charles VI) and a nobility fighting amongst themselves. Henry won the greatest victory of the war at Agincourt, where he gained the worship of his archers by giving and taking hard blows among them in the front line. He then systematically captured every town and castle of northern France, and died, still in early prime, as the acknowledged heir of the feeble Charles VI.

Again fortune turned, slowly but irrevocably. Henry V left Henry VI to succeed him, an infant nine months old, who grew up to be almost as incapable as Charles VI. Two dukes governed during the minority, Humphrey of Gloucester at home, John of Bedford overseas. Gloucester, miscalled 'the good Duke Humphrey', was another John of Gaunt. Bedford was a sound soldier who kept the cause alive for a time. But France changed also. Joan of Arc called forth patriotism and showed how battles could be won. The disinherited Dauphin claimed the crown as Charles VII, an unlovely character but no fool. Bedford died, and the French factions made up their quarrel. Paris was lost by the English, but they long clung to Normandy and Aquitaine amid alternations of truce and petty warfare. Then in three years all collapsed. A French invasion cleared Normandy with a rush in 1450, and in 1453 Sir John Talbot, Earl of Shrewsbury, the last of Henry V's veterans, lost Aquitaine and his own life at the Battle of Chatillon. The Hundred Years War was over. Under cover of all its crimes and bloodshed two things had taken firm shape—the nations of England and France—and one thing had grown ripe to perish— the feudal baronage of the English realm.

III. THE LIBERATION OF THE VILLEIN

It should not be forgotten that the 'free men' whose rights were defined in Magna Carta and whose interests were represented in Parliament were, until the late fourteenth century, a minority of the population. The majority were unfree or villeins. Their distinguishing mark was that they might not leave their manor, that they owed labour services in the cultivation of the demesne or lord's share of the land, and that the lord had various other rights over them, such as that of levying a fine for his consent to their marriage, or of inheriting part of their possessions at their death. The system of villeinage was probably most nearly per- fect in the reign of Henry III, by which time most of the free peasants who still existed after the Norman Conquest had been brought within its scope. But no sooner was the system completed than it began to decay, and the class of free labourers grew noticeable. Men became free in various ways. Sometimes they were made so by their masters as an act of charity, a thing preached but not conspicuously practised by the Church;—or perhaps it would be clearer to say that the wandering, un-propertied friars preached emancipation, whilst the static, land-owning monks practised villeinage. Sometimes the villein prospered, saved, and bought his liberty. More often he simply took it by running away. If a man's life became intolerable on his manor, he might exchange it for a short and merry career as an outlaw in the woods and wastes that intersected all the settled districts. There he might kill deer and rob travellers on the understanding that, once proclaimed beyond the law, any one might put an arrow through him at sight. A proportion of these fugitives sought the towns, where by traditionary custom they were safe from recapture after a year and a day. Others tramped to parts of the country where they were un-known, and took service as labourers for wages on the land. Even in the strictest days of feudalism there must have been so many unattached persons—merchants and lawyers and their servants, pedlars, clerks, pilgrims, and soldiers—that a wander-ing bondman could hope to escape notice.

Villein service meant part-time work for the lord and part-time cultivation of the villein's own holding. On every manor there were certain tasks that were continuous and therefore best performed by paid workers. The swineherd, shepherd, and cow-herd are examples. A certain amount of emancipation was therefore in the lord's own interest. The compulsory villein-labour was often unwillingly and slackly done and needed a deal of supervision. Many lords were therefore ready to commute it for a money payment. This alone did not make the villein a free man. He was still bound to his manor and subject to the lord's rights over marriage and inheritance. He was compelled to attend the manor court and seek justice in that court alone, even if his grievance was against the lord who held the court. No villein might carry his case to the free man's court of the shire. But the villein of commuted service had taken the first step to freedom, for he was paying a rent for his land and could not be deprived of it so long as he paid. The rents became fixed and unalterable, and as prices rose the bargain turned to the advantage of the holder. It was no longer his interest to run away, but he became a more substantial, self-respecting man who developed a strong resentment against the humiliating rights to which he was still subject.

Emancipation on the lines above indicated went on in a growing stream through the first half of the fourteenth century, and on many manors the lord's demesne was cultivated by free labourers paid from the proceeds of the villeins' rents. Then came the catastrophe of the Black Death. The total population was heavily reduced, although there were as many manors as before. However many lords died there were others to step into their shoes, but for the workers swept away there were often no substitutes to be found. There was a shortage of hands for the demesne work, and the free labourers demanded much higher wages, sixpence or eight pence a day in place of the former twopence or threepence. Villein services became more valuable to those who could demand them, and there was a tendency to go back upon the bargains of commutation and insist upon the personal labour. This movement broke down. The villeins formed unions to defend their rights, and against common resistance the lords could not prevail. In another direction they tried to bring the free labourers to heel. For a generation after 1350 the Parliaments passed Statutes of Labourers which sought to limit the wages to rates customary before the Black Death. These statutes were all futile. The labourers had the whip hand and disregarded the legal rates. It was better to pay a man his own price for getting in the harvest than to put him in prison while the harvest rotted on the ground.

It was at bottom all a matter of public opinion. If the peasantry had been docile and the resisters a minority, the law could have been enforced on the day-labourer and the bonds of the villeins could have been tightened. But in the late fourteenth century, in the England of Langland and Froissart and Chaucer's Tales, a spirit of disorderly freedom was abroad. Discipline had slackened in all orders of society. Great lords wrangled for power round the deathbed of Edward III. Money-making merchants were pushing into politics. The Church had grown greedy and lost its moral ascendancy; even an easy-going conservative like Chaucer could hold up most of its members to contempt. The people at large were talking of their rights and listening to orators like John Ball, who stumped the country preaching socialism. Feudalism was dying, root and branch.

The Hundred Years War was quickening the end. It was not a feudal war but a war of professional soldiers, and one in which the English common man had achieved a peculiar eminence with his longbow. If you set a man to slay his betters in heaps on one side of the Channel you must expect him to show a certain disrespect for them on the other.

So, for thirty years after the Black Death, the social contest swayed to and fro, theoretical restriction lost ground to practical emancipation, and the habit of accepting servitude died out. The commons of England, although illiterate, were intelligent and able to think nationally. A definite revolutionary organization underlay the Peasants' Revolt of 1381. It has been shown that there was a head-quarters of secret plotters, who sent out instructions to the shires with the object of raising a simultaneous rebellion all over the country. Actually the risings were not simultaneous, for quarrels over the poll-tax raised Kent and Essex before the proper moment. For some the motive was social, the abolition of villeinage. For others it was political, hatred of John of Gaunt and the corrupt ministers of state, and shame at the reverses of the French war for which the ministers were held to blame. Thus, while villeins formed the bulk of the country rebels, the populace of London, who were free but detested Gaunt, joined them. In most shires the gentry were attacked by their labourers for the economic grievance, but in one or two places they came forward as leaders of the revolt, evidently moved by the political reason. In spite of John Ball and the extremists there was no general desire to overthrow the social order. The villeins wanted freedom from servitude, but were willing to pay rent to the landowners. They all professed loyalty to the King, and in a moment of crisis they accepted him as their natural leader.

In the midsummer days of 1381 the risings began in the counties nearest London. The peasants refused to pay the poll-tax, hunted its collectors, murdered unpopular landlords, and burnt the manorial rolls and title-deeds which contained the record of the villein services. Thousands marched on London, to which they were admitted by the poorer citizens and a party among the aldermen who hated the government. The combined mob destroyed the Savoy, John of Gaunt's beautiful palace in the Strand. Its owner, luckily for himself, was absent in Scotland, but his servants and known supporters were sought out and killed. The same fate befell Simon Sudbury, Archbishop of Canterbury. As archbishop he had imprisoned John Ball, but his chief offence was that as Lord Chancellor he had been head of a corrupt government which had raised heavy taxes and failed to win the war with them. The boy-king Richard II displayed a cool courage which saved the situation. He rode personally into the ranks of the rebels and disarmed them by fair promises. Any of his ministers attempting such a course would have been torn to pieces, for no man trusted their word. For the King all had a touching loyalty, pathetic because he proved unworthy of it. He guaranteed their two demands, pardon for the rebellion, and the commutation of all villein services for a rent of fourpence an acre. With parchment charters to this effect the majority dispersed to their homes, A hooligan element, however, remained about London in hopes of loot, and committed a massacre of the Flemish merchants who dwelt by the riverside. No sooner were the King's ministers in the saddle again than they treated this as an excuse for revoking his promises. They proclaimed every rebel equally guilty, cancelled the charters of pardon and emancipation, and sent forth military columns with sword and rope through every shire. Richard made no protest. He accompanied the Chief Justice on a tour of vengeance and encouraged the slaughter of his subjects. He had shown pluck, but no kingly humanity and not even common sense. He had missed the golden opportunity of gaining the support of his people against the powerful ruling clique whom he and they hated in common.

The great rising had therefore failed to end villeinage at a stroke. For the moment it had checked the movement to freedom. The Parliaments of the following years, in which the villeins were not represented, met in no mood for concessions. Yet while in theory servitude was maintained, in practice it withered rapidly. The bloodshed of 1381 was a thing that the dullest could never forget. A rampart of corpses of lord and peasant lay between the past and the future. Owners of manors were glad to exchange for rents the services of these sullen curs, who had been whipped but had shown what they could do when roused. The peasants on their side had learnt their strength. They had been beaten by guile and not in fair fight, and they never forgot how first they had hunted knight and prior through the woods and had drawn them forth to rustic court-martial and execution. Through the following century right after right became obsolete, and by its end villeinage was over in England. The manor remained the agricultural unit, but it was not the feudal manor. The villeins became perpetual tenants at a fixed rent, able to sell and depart at will, free to plead in the King's courts. The lords cultivated their desmesne by paid labour, or turned it into sheep pasture which needed few hands to produce the most profitable harvest of the new time, the wool-clip for the rising cloth manufacture. In the hundred years after the Black Death England achieved freedom. It did not at the same time learn how to bridle it by discipline. To many a quiet industrious soul the servitude of the rich thirteenth century would have seemed preferable to the riotous contempt for rule of the fifteenth. More blood was to flow in the Wars of the Roses before liberty and order could think of existing together.

IV. THE GROWTH OF TRADE

A backward-looking man under Richard II might see all his world collapsing about him and fail to notice that in the ruins new structures were taking shape. Among them were personal liberty, expanding foreign trade, and new views of religion and the Church. The second of these claims our attention now.

In a perfect feudal system, such as was never attained, there would have been little room for trade or the persons engaged in it. The theoretical manor was a self-supporting unit producing all its own foodstuffs, clothing, and building materials, and producing them in such nicely adjusted proportions that there was never a surplus and never a shortage. Such a manor never existed in fact. Money always did exist, and money implies exchange of goods. In an ideal manor it would have been as useless as it was to Robinson Crusoe on his island. Differences in soil and situation were so great, even in a small country like England, that some parts produced one commodity in excess and others another, and exchange of the surplus always went on. Accidents of weather or the action of foes caused one district to enjoy a good harvest and another to suffer famine. Nature refused to recognize feudalism by distributing fisheries, forests, and mines with an even hand. Scores of such factors might be enumerated. All of them combined to foster internal trade, with its servants in the guise of merchants, teamsters, porters, and boatmen, and its instruments in markets, towns, guilds, and regulations, all outside the scope of the feudal idea of land-holding for personal service. The same factors operated to create trade between the peoples of Christendom. Some had wine, others corn, others salt or wool or fish in excess of their own wants, and commerce resulted. Nay more, there was never a time, even in the darkest age of barbarism, when intercourse did not link continents, when Europeans, Asiatics, and even Africans did not find meeting-points for the exchange of their wares. Commerce is much older than history, but although it has never died out it has had its ups and downs. The rich commerce of the Roman Empire wilted in the dark age of the decline and fall, recovered in the Middle Ages, prospered vigorously in the fourteenth and fifteenth centuries, and helped to amass the capital and stimulate the enterprise which have made our modern world.

The change from medieval to modern society has been defined as the change from status to contract. The meaning of that wise saw may be illustrated in this way. The medieval man said, 'I am your man, your vassal, and because of that I am bound to render you such and such services as long as I live, and so are my children after me;' whereas the modern man says, 'I am your equal, and I will render you such services as long as you pay me, or I choose to do so, and no longer.' It is the economic aspect of the political contest we have noted between order and liberty. But there has been little of the pendulum-swing about it. There has been rather a steady decay of status and increase of contract. The growth of trade has done more than anything else to produce the result.

The main lines of Europe's medieval trade were dictated by her geography. Europe is a peninsula with a long sea-coast on her southern side and another to the north. The southern coast, looking on the Mediterranean and the Black Sea, was important because the countries that bordered it were various in their products, and across the water lay Africa or Asia with peculiar wares of their own. The northern coast, washed by the Atlantic, the North Sea, and the Baltic, had also a variety of climates from Spain to Sweden, although it lacked a farther shore until Europe found America. The north coast and the south were almost in different worlds and had many things to exchange with one another. By the connecting Straits of

Gibraltar it was a long way round, but there was a short cut across the European peninsula by the valley of the Rhine and thence over the passes of the eastern Alps and down into the northern plain of Italy. There were other cross-routes as well—through France to Marseilles, through Germany to the Danube, through Poland to the Black Sea—and the long sea route by the Straits never ceased to be used. But the central Rhine route was so busy that a line of great cities sprang up along its course, from those of Flanders in the delta to those of western Germany north of the Alps, and those of Italy at the southern terminus. The Flemish cities were collectors and distributors of goods for northern Europe, and the Italian cities for southern, and these last were able to draw the trade of Asia through the Black Sea and the Levant. Along the northern coast of the European peninsula there throve also the seaports of the Hanseatic League, some in Germany and some in Poland. Cologne on the Rhine was a member of the League and so also was Riga on the Baltic. Between the two were some seventy members, large or small. The League had contact with Asia through the Polish and Russian plains, but it found its greatest wealth in the Baltic corn and timber and furs, and in the fisheries of the North Sea. Its merchants, known in England as the Easterlings, were the grand carriers of northern Europe, with a regular service of ships plying between all the ports of this long coastline.

England lay on the edge of the medieval trading system, but she had effective contact with it. London looked across the narrow sea to the Flanders towns, and the Straits of Dover were a bottle-neck for the traffic from east to west, which was often a temptation to the unscrupulous mariners of the Cinque Ports. England had products of her own wherewith to buy foreign luxuries. The tin of Cornwall was an ingredient for the making of bronze, the lead of Derbyshire roofed the great churches of all Christendom, Sussex had an iron industry to supply ploughshares and weapons. Hides were produced everywhere in England and many were obtained from Ireland, which was predominantly a cattle country. Above all, England pastured huge flocks of sheep, and their wool had a peculiar quality not found in that of other lands. It was absolutely essential for the weaving of the best kinds of cloth, and the merchants came to buy it from the manufacturing cities of Flanders and even from distant Italy. Wool was the wealth of

medieval England, and of modern England also until the age
of the industrial revolution produced other industries to
surpass it.

Little is known about the trade of the late Saxon period save
that it must have been considerable. That there was much
money in the country is shown by the enormous Danegelds levied
by Ethelred to buy off his tormentors. Some of these Saxon
coins have been found in western Asia, whither they passed
by way of trade from the vikings of the Baltic to the Greeks
of Constantinople, and thence to the Moslems of Syria. In the
first century after the Norman Conquest foreign merchants
came freely to England, Flemings, Frenchmen, and Germans
from Cologne, whilst the ports that were to join in the Hanseatic
League were taking the place of the older viking venturers to
the eastward. In the thirteenth century the League was consolidated. It had fleets and wealth and was strong enough to
wring great concessions from English kings such as Henry III.
It possessed a great *kontor* or fortified head-quarters in London
(the site is now covered by Cannon Street Station), and it had
other houses at Boston and King's Lynn. These German
Easterlings had often greater weight with the Crown than had
its own subjects, and they established a stranglehold on the
North Sea trade. In the wake of the Conqueror came the Jews
as traders and financiers. They grew so unpopular, not altogether by their own fault, that Edward I banished them all
in 1290. Into their places came the bankers of Italy, whose
memory survives in Lombard Street. They lent money to the
Crown, and were repaid by licences to export wool. They
collected also the taxes due to the Pope and transmitted them
in the form of thousands of woolsacks. Merchants of Genoa,
Venice, Pisa, and Ragusa joined in the wool trade. They
brought a knowledge of book-keeping and banking, of Arabic
numerals, insurance, and bills of exchange, and they came in
ships of a size never seen in the north before. A carrack was a
huge Genoese merchantman, an argosy was an 'Aragozy' or
Ragusan; and Venice began in 1317 a regular service of liners
to England and Flanders, great vessels driven by sails and oars
and known as the Flanders Galleys. Conservative as they were,
the English seamen began to realize that improvement could be
made in their native cogs and nefs. Spaniards and Portuguese
and Gascons from Bordeaux crowded into English ports with

their wines and fruits, all seeking English wool or the cloth into which it had been made.

Most of this business was not so much English trade as trade with England. The native merchant had but a minor share in it. Our kings, even Edward I and Edward III, had not grasped the idea that commerce could add to national strength. They thought only of levying taxes on merchants, and it was often easier to mulct the foreigner than the Englishman. Consequently they gave foreign traders an undue share of encouragement. Nevertheless the oldest of English trading corporations did take shape in the thirteenth century. It was a body known as the Merchants of the Staple. It received a monopoly of exporting wool, hides, tin, and lead to northern Europe. These were raw materials difficult to obtain out of England, and thus the Crown was able to levy high duties on their export. To collect these duties it was useful to make the trade flow through a definite channel or staple market. After Edward III had captured Calais the Staple was fixed at that town, and thither only might the wools be exported. But Spaniards, Portuguese, and Italians were still allowed to buy wool direct without dealing with the Company. The Staple at Calais thus became the mart for buyers from the north of Europe.

With the English wool the foreign artisans made expensive cloth, finely and smoothly finished and dyed in brilliant colours. It was freely imported into England for the costume of the rich. At the same time the English peasant was making for his own wear a very different kind of cloth, shaggy, unbleached, and undyed, rank with the natural grease of the wool. It must have been an irritating fabric to skins unprotected by linen undergarments, but for the poor the only alternative was a yet more offensive dress of leather. This rough cloth industry went on in the villeins' hovels throughout the land, for the raw material was abundant. Soon after the Conquest two developments became prominent. Cloth finishing—the fulling, bleaching, shearing, and dyeing of the rough article—became the business of the rising towns and their craftsmen; and the unfinished or half-finished product began to be exported to the Netherlands to serve as raw material for the more skilful Flemish workers. For centuries the English clothmakers produced inferior stuff, and it was not until the Tudor period that they began to hold their own. The import of fine foreign cloth and the export of cheap English cloth therefore went on side by side until the English improved their processes and the export alone prevailed. The growth of the cloth export is the key to English trade-expansion and is a large factor in the founding of the overseas empire. Whilst it was establishing itself in the late medieval period the standard of comfort in Europe was rising, and whole classes of people were buying good cloth who before had used homespun or none. English wealth rose concurrently, the people became a community of sheep-graziers and clothiers, the merchants who handled the stuff amassed fortunes, and, not content with European markets, sought others beyond the oceans. The whole forms the economic basis of the rise of England to the rank of a great power. The senior officer of the British Empire after the King is the Lord Chancellor, and his seat of office is the woolsack. The symbolism is true to the facts.

At first the cloth export was largely in the hands of the foreigners who came to England with their own ships. But the English had always a share, and in the fourteenth century they increased it. The Hundred Years War brought rich merchants into politics. They had their spokesmen in Parliament and even among the ministers of the Crown. English traders in foreign parts needed to combine to secure fair treatment. Hence arose under Henry IV a national association of cloth exporters, a super-guild combining the energies of the local guilds in the various seaports. The King, who as Duke of Hereford had been banished by Richard II, had passed some part of his exile in the Baltic lands of the Teutonic Knights and the Hanseatic League. He had studied the conditions of trade, and soon after gaining the throne he issued a charter which combined all the English merchants doing business with Germany and the Baltic into one company. This was in 1404, and the body was afterwards known as the Eastland Company. In 1407 he made a similar grant for the benefit of the men trading in the Low Countries. They were called the Merchants Adventurers. The two companies had very different fortunes. The Eastland men after a brief period of vigour were overcome by their German rivals of the Hanseatic League. For the greater part of the fifteenth century little is heard of them, and it was not until the Tudor period that their importance revived. The Merchants Adventurers, on the other hand, throve from the outset. They carried English cloth into the Netherlands, where they sold it at their marts in Bruges and Antwerp. They were constituted as a regulated company, a different thing from a modern trading body. Every member carried on his own business for his own profit or loss. But they obeyed common rules on prices and dates and places of sale, and they negotiated as one body for common privileges. They elected one of themselves as governor and others as his assistants. The governor resided at the overseas mart to supervise the business there. One such governor was William Caxton, who learned the art of printing during his term of office in the Low Countries.

Most of the seaports, from Newcastle round the coast to Exeter and Bristol, had their local associations of merchant venturers subject, so far as the Flanders cloth trade was concerned, to the great head-quarters overseas. Those who carried on the wine trade with Bordeaux did not form a general company, chiefly because Bordeaux was an English port until the loss of Aquitaine in 1453. The merchants who dealt with Spain and Portugal combined to elect consuls in Seville and Lisbon, but they seem to have had no charters from the Crown until 1530, when Henry VIII incorporated them. These men of the western seas were always more individual in their methods than those who worked eastwards, a characteristic which became very prominent in the great days of Drake and Hawkins.

England, as we have seen, exported raw materials and cloth, and imported mainly luxuries. But there was one import that became a necessity as the high agriculture of the great days of feudalism declined. This was the import of fish. Herrings were caught in vast quantities in the Baltic and shipped westwards by the Hanseatic League. For some mysterious reason the fish changed their habitat to the North Sea. It was a serious blow to the League, for the Flemings and English could then share in the catch. Almost as important was the cod fishery on the coast of Iceland. English, Scots, Danes, and Germans competed in that remote region, and there was wild work there, wholesale battles, massacres, and kidnapping of the poor inhabitants. The salted stockfish became a staple article of English food, and the long, stormy voyage was a training for the mariners who would one day sail the North Atlantic to America.

The attitude of English governments towards trade is interesting. Merchants as a class had their rights recognized in Magna

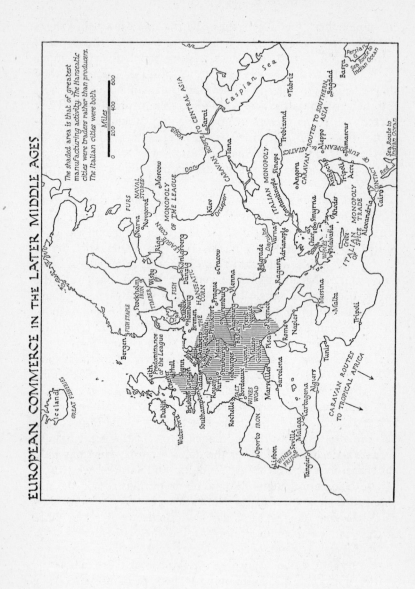

EUROPEAN COMMERCE IN THE LATER MIDDLE AGES

The shaded area is that of greatest
manufacturing activity. The Hanseatic
cities were traders rather than producers.
The Italian cities were both.

Miles
0   200   400   600

Carta. Under Henry III the Hanseatic League grew strong in England. Edward I made the customs a definite tax. English merchants had their rates fixed as the great custom, which thenceforward continued unchanged. Foreign merchants obtained some privileges from the King and agreed in return to pay an additional duty called the petty custom. Edward III with his costly wars needed higher taxes, but he did not increase these customs. Instead he obtained from Parliament the grant of a separate duty called the subsidy. This was not permanent like the customs, but was renewed from time to time. It became usual for the King to have it granted for his life in the opening Parliament of his reign. The subsidy was sometimes known as tonnage and poundage (tonnage on wines, poundage on other goods), and under that name it gave rise to a famous dispute in the time of Charles I. Edward III has been called the 'Father of English Commerce', but in reality he was more of a step-father, and his merchants suffered severely from some of his measures. In treating of the navy we have seen how he ruined the traders by impressing their ships and neglecting to pay for them.

Under Richard II the merchant friends of John of Gaunt were influential, and for the first time we see a mercantile policy adopted by the government. A mercantile policy means a deliberate attempt to make the country richer by regulating its trade. Mercantilism had a long career. It began in a feeble fashion under Richard II and lasted until England became a free-trade country in the middle of the nineteenth century— nearly five hundred years. Mercantilism is still pursued by most foreign states, and there are signs of its revival in our own. We must therefore note some facts about its origin. The first and crudest attempt to increase the national wealth was made by an act of 1381 which forbade any one to take gold or silver out of England, since the practice would entail 'the destruction of the realm'. In 1382 there was passed the first Navigation Act in English history. It ordered that English merchants must use none but English ships. This was a useful principle, for naval defence rested upon the merchant vessels far more than upon the King's ships. At the moment we had lost command of the sea and our coasts were being raided by Frenchmen and Spaniards. The act was therefore an attempt to revive the mercantile marine. It failed because it was too sweeping.

There were not enough English ships to carry the trade, and the new rule could not be put into force. Very soon it fell into oblivion. This early Navigation Act achieved nothing, but it shows the lines on which men were thinking. In 1392 another piece of mercantile legislation was passed. It forbade foreigners to sell their goods by retail in England. They must dispose of them wholesale at the ports of entry and allow native traders the profit of distributing the wares throughout the country.

Henry IV, as we have seen, did something for trade by chartering the regulated companies. This was another aspect of mercantilism, which regards commerce as a competition in which disciplined team-work is essential to success. 'A well-ordered trade' was a phrase often on the lips of English statesmen, and Napoleon, a great mercantilist, expressed the same idea when he said that commerce could be 'manœuvred like a regiment'. Henry V's contribution was the building of a fighting navy which inspired respect abroad and saved English merchants from oppression. With the seas made safe trade could flourish.

In the long unhappy reign of Henry VI (1422–61) English commerce fell on bad days. To neglect the navy has always been the mark of a bad government in England. That of Henry VI was the worst of all, for it sold off all the fine ships of Henry V and left the country without defence. The consequences were seen at once. French raids on the coast began again. The Hanseatic League grew aggressive. It bullied the English merchants out of its own ports and magnified its privileges in theirs. It permitted its seamen to indulge in unchecked piracy in the North Sea. It even took to interfering in our politics. The invasion of England by Edward of York in 1471 was promoted by the League, and his victory was a revolution fomented by a foreign power. In reward he had to grant the Easterlings greater privileges than they had ever had before. All this resulted from the lack of a strong navy. Returning to Henry VI, we find that he yielded to a Danish demand that Englishmen must not frequent the Iceland fishery. He passed an act to prohibit his subjects from going there. Many of them disregarded it, and the consequence was a long maritime war with the Danes in the northern seas. The Merchants Adventurers had to submit to hard treatment in the Netherlands and complained that their government gave them no support.

As early as 1436 these disasters gave rise to an essay on sea power and mercantile regulation by an English thinker, who is believed to have been Adam de Moleyns, Bishop of Chichester. He called it *The Libelle of English Policy* and wrote it in English verse so that its doctrines might be the more easily remembered by unlearned men. The double refrain of the *Libelle*[1] is, strengthen the navy and encourage trade: 'Cherish merchandise, keep the Admiralty, That we be masters of the Narrow Sea.' In four lines he sums up the mercantile doctrine:

> For if merchánts were cherished to their speed,
> We were not like to fail in any need.
> If they be rich, then in prosperity
> Shall be our land, lordës and commonalty.

Fifty years were to pass before these maxims were to be put into serious practice. Henry VI was a hopeless king. Edward IV and Richard III did a little for their own subjects but more for their rivals. Not until Henry VII began a new age with the victory of Bosworth did mercantilism come into its own.

V. THE CHURCH AND THE LOLLARDS

In the fourteenth century the position of the Church changed for the worse. Its wealth continued as great as ever, but its moral authority fell very far from the standard set in the great days when Innocent III had made John his vassal. For the greater part of the century the Popes stood almost in that relation to the kings of France, for the papal court resided not at Rome but at Avignon, where French influence was strong. The papal power was often used for purely political ends. A feeling therefore grew up in fourteenth-century England that religious issues were hollow and not worth fighting for. The question of investitures or appointments to bishoprics affords an example. In earlier times this had been desperately contested between Crown and Papacy. It now became a matter of easygoing compromise. Edward III did not seriously resist the Pope's right of appointment, and the Pope avoided quarrel by appointing the men whom the King desired. In the background were the revenues collected by the papal agents in England. Relations being good, the Crown allowed this money to leave

---

[1] 'Libelle' means a little book, not a libel in the modern sense of the word.

the country, but it could always have checked the flow had it chosen so to do.

Parliament, it is true, was hostile to papal influence and desired, like Henry II, to keep the control of the English Church in England. In 1351 it passed the Statute of Provisors, which declared papal appointments illegal and punishable by the imprisonment of those who accepted them. In 1353 it enacted the more famous Statute of Praemunire, which outlawed the persons and confiscated the goods of any who should take to foreign (i.e. papal) courts matters that ought to be tried before the King's courts. Both these measures were amplified and re-enacted in subsequent years, but neither was seriously enforced. The Crown preferred to keep them in reserve and share the spoils with Avignon. Nevertheless the law remained in a dormant state, to be awakened on a distant day by Henry VIII. Only after two centuries did 'the penalties of praemunire' become a phrase of terrible meaning and an engine of destruction to the papal power in England.

The bishops of the late fourteenth century were often men who served the King in matters of state. Simon Sudbury, who was murdered by the rebels of 1381, was Lord Chancellor as well as Archbishop of Canterbury. William of Wykeham, Bishop of Winchester, was also Lord Chancellor, and rose to office by his financial ability. There were others of the same stamp. Many were good servants of the state, but few were conspicuous for piety or service to religion. Among the abbots and cathedral dignitaries there were many foreigners whose intrusion was allowed because the Pope obliged the Crown in the promotion of the bishops. The regular clergy, that is the monks, were satisfied with the arrangement, since their worldly superiors were not severe disciplinarians. The seculars or parish priests suffered badly. Their bishops, who ought to have championed their interests, were absorbed in politics, and many a country priest was reduced to beggary by the appropriation of most of his proper stipend to some monastery or cathedral stall. A few fine characters were rendered more saintly by privation. Chaucer's 'poor parson' stands for their type: 'Christes love and his Apostles twelve, he taught, and first he followed it himself.' But many were degraded to theft and sharp practice, or neglected their parishes and picked up a living by layman's work. Those who kept their ideals often turned to revolutionary doctrines, as did John Ball, the most notable of the priests who took part in the revolt of 1381.

The Church as a whole lost the respect of the people, but it did not lose its power over them. Its courts were as busy as ever in summoning moral offenders and punishing them by fines and penances. It had jurisdiction over wills and inheritance, and was accused of selling its justice. It was active in claiming its tithes from laymen, who felt a grievance in having to support a clergy whose lives were as worldly as their own. Among Chaucer's portraits the poor parson stands alone as an admirable character. His prioress is an elegant fine lady, charming but useless. His monk is a hunting man, more devoted to sport than to prayer. His friar tells pious lies to gain money from the credulous. In one tale a blackmailing summoner is carried off by the devil in the very act. We can believe Chaucer the more readily since he was no red-hot reformer with a one-sided view. He was a contented, humorous man of the world, who enjoyed his life and accepted things as they were. Although there must have been exceptions to all his statements they probably strike a general average of truth.

Among the laymen and the parish priests there were many who demanded reform. The laymen sought it in Parliament, but the alliance between the Church and the Crown checkmated their efforts. The priests appealed to the poor and succeeded only in stirring up discontent. Among them there was one man of dogged character and original mind who stood in a class by himself. He was John Wycliffe, Yorkshireman, Oxford scholar, and rector of Lutterworth. Wycliffe's indignation was stirred by the worldly lives and excessive wealth of the clergy and by the devotion of bishops to affairs of state instead of to their proper duties. In the closing years of Edward III, when the country was feeling the pressure of taxation, he recommended the confiscation of Church property and its distribution among poor gentlemen, who would take better care of the peasantry and increase the military strength of the nation. The proposal would have been sound, but for the certainty that the poor gentlemen would have received little and the great lords nearly all. The unscrupulous John of Gaunt evidently thought so, for he took up the plan with zest and made himself Wycliffe's protector. When the Bishop of London called Wycliffe to account, Gaunt attended the court at his side and the proceedings broke up in disorder.

Wycliffe had been saved by a bad man, but was not ready to become his instrument. He went back to Oxford, where he evolved further startling doctrines. By 1380 he was denying transubstantiation and asserting that confession to priests and prayers to saints were unnecessary. He went on to advocate the abolition of the Pope's office, of monasteries, and of much else, leaving little of the vast array of clerics but the parish priests. They were to be properly paid and to devote themselves to preaching the godly life rather than to elaborate ceremonies. John of Gaunt, who had been attracted by the hope of plunder, was disgusted. He tried in vain to persuade Wycliffe from his daring course, and then cast him off. The reformer was driven from Oxford, where many had agreed with him, and retired to his parish of Lutterworth in Leicestershire. There he spent his last years in two activities. He wrote unceasingly: Latin arguments to convert the learned, English tracts for the simple, and translations of the scriptures into the English tongue. He also trained and instructed disciples who were to spread his doctrines through the countryside. When he died, on the last day of 1384, his 'poor priests' were journeying far and wide, and the new religion of the Lollards was established. It has continued under other names to this day.

The Lollards survived, but they did not triumph. The Peasants' Revolt of 1381 alarmed the rich lords and convinced them that they and the Church must stand together. Until the time of Henry VIII the governing classes would never listen to any plan of confiscation. It might spread further than they liked. Wycliffe had had no hand in the Revolt. John Ball the revolutionary priest was not one of his men. The Lutterworth rector was a man of peace—one of those fighting men of peace who crop up in almost every age of English history. But the Revolt made the great men distrust Lollardism, and it spread chiefly among the peasants, the town craftsmen, and some of the country gentlemen. After its founder's death few of its preachers were learned and many were barely able to read. Books were a difficulty, for as yet there was no printing, and the bishops were active in tracking down and destroying all manuscript copies of the reformer's works. In 1401 (under Henry IV) the Statute *De Heretico Comburendo* enabled the

Church to burn Lollards, a penalty hardly known in England before. Burnings were numerous, chiefly of poor men who refused to abjure their faith. Henry V made an example of one man of the better sort, Sir John Oldcastle, although he was hanged as a rebel before being burnt as a heretic. All through the fifteenth century the martyrdom continued. Lollardism was driven underground but never stamped out. In the early sixteenth century, just before Luther's Reformation began in Germany, it was as active as ever. Apart from its religious merits it was an element working for freedom, and possibly on a larger scale than we know. The only records we possess are those of the executions, and we cannot tell what proportion they bore to the adherents of the faith. But the fact is clear that when Henry VIII took in hand to reform the Church his people in the main supported him, and for that some of the credit is Wycliffe's. Great men's popular labels are often misleading, but Wycliffe's title of 'The Morning Star of the Reformation' is well deserved.

In European history Lollardism is also important. Richard II married a Bohemian princess. Some of her attendants were converted to Wycliffe's doctrines and carried his books to Bohemia. There they inspired John Huss and his followers, whose struggles and sufferings prepared the way for Martin Luther's victory.

VI. THE SUICIDE OF THE FEUDAL BARONAGE

The emergence of the House of Commons as a power in Parliament made little difference to the supremacy of the governing class in England. The King, the bishops, and the great lords controlled the administration, and when a commoner became a minister of the Crown, it was because he was the servant of one of these interests and not because he enjoyed popular support.

This governing class steadily deteriorated in its average character, as one may see by comparing the twelfth and thirteenth centuries on the one hand with the fourteenth and fifteenth on the other. The former period yielded kings of first-class merit in Henry I, Henry II, and Edward I, and churchmen of high ideals in Anselm, Becket, and Langton, whilst its baronage sometimes produced leaders able to place the interest of the state above that of faction. But in the fourteenth century Edward II was a complete failure, Edward III began passably well, but grew demoralized long before his death, and Richard II, whilst emitting flashes of courage and ability, was so puffed up with conceit and so lacking in self-control that to his subjects he appeared a very bad king indeed. The fifteenth century produced before 1485 only one king with a real sense of duty to his people, Henry V. And his view of duty was narrow—to repress Lollardism and to attain military glory. To the latter he devoted his reign of nine years, ministering with unsparing energy to the pride of England, the humiliation of France, and the future misery of both. Few of our kings have been so intent upon their mission, and few have so misspent their genius. The other four sovereigns of this age hardly reached a decent average of kingship—Henry IV, of solid talents but selfish at heart and not of stainless honour; Henry VI, a good-natured simpleton, with periodical fits of insanity; Edward IV and Richard III, thoroughly unprincipled men, able but base, whose talents served only to degrade their people by the example of successful villainy. It was the same with the bishops, politicians all, few of them patriots, none of them saints, hardly any caring for the spiritual as apart from the material interests of the Church.

To the Crown and the Church the nobles looked for examples of conduct, and from such exemplars they got little good. The baronage of these two centuries may be allowed one virtue, that of readiness to stake their lives in battle or conspiracy. Their courage was high indeed, but all their other qualities were low, and thus the use to which they put their virtue rendered it something near a vice. Of mercy, justice, public spirit, religious zeal, faithfulness, the instances are few and far between. The ideals of chivalry were more talked about than ever, more often celebrated in books and monuments, and ever more rarely practised. Froissart in the fourteenth century, Malory in the fifteenth, wrote deathless prose about them. But Froissart was in his life a parasite of the great, a seeker of snug places. As for Sir Thomas Malory, it has lately been suggested that he was a common bully and disturber of the peace, who composed the epic of the Round Table whilst in gaol for his misdeeds. The romance of chivalry gilded a reality of crime, just as the delicate perpendicular churches were reared by artistic worldlings.

Intellects were vigorous; souls slept. Yet we must never forget that whilst the Middle Age was rotting from the top, a new worthiness was springing obscurely in the ruins. The Lollard peasant could die for his belief, there were fine men amongst the country gentlemen and simple knights of the wars, there were honest citizens who devoted their wealth to charity and civic works. The change from medieval to modern England was not the end of an old order followed by the beginning of a new, but rather the growth of a new within the husk of the old.

The long French war had much to answer for. It accustomed noblemen to live in the midst of armed followers, to strike rather than reason, and to view bloodshed with unconcern. Even the wealthiest could hardly afford to keep an army in private pay, but the lack was supplied by the custom of livery. This meant that a magnate would secure the support of all the lesser gentry of his region, who would wear his livery or coat of arms and turn out for him when called upon. Their service had to be paid for, and thus appeared the corresponding custom of maintenance. The great lord 'maintained' the cause of his adherent through thick and thin. In any trial for violent crime, in any suit for the possession of land, the court would be invaded by an armed band wearing the same device as the defendant, and perhaps by another with the badge mounted by the plaintiff. Judge and jury had to pocket their honour and side with the strongest, and justice became a farce. Livery and maintenance corrupted Parliament also. The county magnate compelled the county sessions to elect his nominees as knights of the shire. The great lords rode to Westminster at the head of their retainers, and the Commons debated beneath the shadow of the sword.

From the time of Richard II political bloodshed became common. A defeated faction was brought to trial, often on flimsy charges, judgement was swift, and execution instant. Sometimes the murder was undisguised. Richard set the example by killing his own uncle the Duke of Gloucester without the pretence of a trial. When Henry IV deposed Richard in 1399 there was a slaughter of the ministers of state, and the fallen King himself quickly died in Pontefract Castle, undoubtedly murdered. The common people copied their betters. Certain lords conspired against Henry IV, were betrayed, and took to flight. The country folk surrounded them and killed them out of hand without troubling to secure them for the King's justice.

So it went on throughout the Lancastrian period—plot, rebellion, betrayal, and the axe to close the incident. An illiterate people had long memories. No one ever forgot that the first Lancastrian had gained the throne by revolution and murder. Few were restrained by conscience from arguing that by revolution and murder the Lancastrian dynasty might fitly end. And so it did end when the poor meek Henry VI paid the penalty for his grandfather's crime.

Henry V might have stayed the rot. He was a master whom none could withstand. He had it in him to be another Edward I. But he produced only a semblance of peace at home by leading off his gentlemen to kill abroad. He ruined his own health by hard campaigning and died at the age of thirty-four. For a dozen years his brother John, Duke of Bedford, carried on the French effort. At Verneuil he won another Agincourt, but at Orleans Joan of Arc turned the scale, and thenceforward the English cause declined. The burning of Joan was typical of the fifteenth century. It is true that the court which tried her was composed wholly of French clergy, and that the French King whom she crowned lifted not a finger to save her. But Bedford stood in the background, and by his orders the sentence was carried out. He burned a gallant woman because he thought it would have a good moral effect. And he was in character the best of the Lancastrian house.

After Bedford's death the feeble Henry VI was declared of age to rule in person. He never did rule. Instead he looked on whilst France was lost and the barons drew apart into the factions that were to fight the Wars of the Roses. The English people, imbued with the belief that none could beat them in fair war, could only conclude that they were betrayed and that it was time to change the government.

In 1450, when the last shreds of Normandy were being lost, the chief minister of the Crown was William de la Pole, Duke of Suffolk, and the most prominent critic of the government was Richard, Duke of York, who would have a good claim to the throne if Henry VI should die childless. Suffolk was the descendant of a merchant who had prospered in the fourteenth century. York was a member of the royal Plantagenet stock of which the House of Lancaster was a branch. The disaster in Normandy was generally blamed upon Suffolk. He had been incapable, greedy, and not above suspicion of murdering his opponents.

He had bought a truce with France by surrendering the province of Maine and marrying the King to a French wife, Margaret of Anjou. He was now accused of deliberate treachery. The Commons impeached him on a variety of charges, some probable, some foolish. Henry, prompted by his wife, stayed the trial and attempted to save the Duke by banishing him for five years. It was useless. The doomed man was stopped on the high seas and beheaded by persons who were never brought to book. They were certainly adherents of the Duke of York, but he was away in Ireland and therefore personally innocent. It was one more political crime in a long series, but it marked a new level in the rising anarchy of the times. For Suffolk was a royal favourite and under the royal protection, and had nevertheless been done to death on board a ship of the King's own navy. The servants of the Crown were forgetting their allegiance.

Not a month afterwards there arose a new peasants' revolt in Sussex and Kent. It was not due to villeins' grievances, but to indignation at the national disasters. Its leader was a mysterious person who called himself Jack Cade or John Mortimer or, more significantly, John Amend-all. Who he really was remains unknown. He had military experience and was certainly no peasant. Cade and his rebels routed the royal forces at Sevenoaks and entered London. There they executed unpopular officials, pillaged some rich houses, and made the mistake of withdrawing to billets in Southwark for the night. The mayor and citizens held London Bridge against their return, and after a savage fight Cade failed to force his way again into the city. At this juncture the King's ministers played the old trick of 1381. They promised pardon and reform if the rebels would disperse. The majority had already had enough of the adventure, and Cade was deserted. He fled into Sussex and was killed fighting near Heathfield. The Duke of York was still absent and had played no part in the revolt, but the rebels had used his name, and all England was looking to him as a deliverer. This was the first popular rising in English history to be caused by political indignation and not by the bread-and-butter grievances of the rebels. What the great lords had done under Simon de Montfort the peasants did under Cade. It shows how far they had progressed since the days of villeinage. The free Englishman was at length a force in politics.

Five years passed uneasily amid disorder at home and disaster abroad. A son was born to Henry VI and Margaret of Anjou, a blow to the hopes of the Yorkists. The King became definitely insane in 1453, and York was appointed regent. He ruled with sense and moderation, and when the King recovered he laid down his office in 1454. But Henry, although he had regained his faculties, was helpless in the hands of his vindictive wife. He dismissed all the Yorkists and chose as his favourite minister the Duke of Somerset, the general who had fought the last campaign in Normandy and lost it in record time. It was too much, and York took up arms. At St. Albans in 1455 he defeated the royal forces, killed Somerset, and captured the King. Another fit of insanity, another Yorkist regency, and another partial recovery followed in quick succession. But Henry was now more than ever a spineless puppet, and his wife really wore the crown. She had energy but no discretion. Instead of keeping on civil terms with Richard of York, who had not shown himself unduly ambitious, she drove him again into revolt.

The Wars of the Roses began in earnest in 1459. They were essentially a struggle for power between two factions of the nobility, and the issue of good or bad administration, which had been prominent in the earlier stage, was quickly lost to view. Small armies of retainers and professional soldiers disbanded after the French war fought with bitter cruelty. Treachery and changing of sides were common. In some battles no quarter was given to the vanquished. After others the prisoners were executed within a few hours of their surrender. The mass of the people, townsmen and countrymen alike, took little part and only prayed for some strong man to end it all. There were ups and downs in the contest, and each one thinned the ranks of the baronage. In 1460 Richard of York declared himself King. Two months afterwards his severed head grinned from the gate of his city, duly adorned with a paper crown. His son Edward had better luck. A terrific slaughter at Towton in 1461 made him King in fact as well as in name. All the midlands and the south were his, and the Lancastrian remnant dwindled away in scuffles and pursuits on the northern moors. From 1464 to 1470 Edward IV reigned in comparative peace. It was, however, a reign of terror, and the state of the country showed little improvement. Apart from Edward, the luckiest man on the Yorkist side had been Richard Neville, Earl of Warwick. His clear brain and cool courage had turned the scale on more than one doubtful field. Forfeited Lancastrian lands had made him rich, and hundreds of the midland gentry wore his livery; his 'maintenance' was well worth their service. He as much as any man had made the Yorkist throne, and as king-maker he meant to exercise a power greater than a subject could fairly claim. But Edward IV was an ill man to dominate. Up to a point he was manageable, because he was fond of ease and pleasure. But once aroused he could be active and courageous, faithless and merciless as a beast of prey. He married the widow of a Lancastrian leader and showered favours upon her kinsmen, to the disgust of the old Yorkist party.

In 1469 Warwick asserted his power and made the King his prisoner. Next year there was a shift of fortune, and Warwick fled to France. There he made an alliance with Margaret of Anjou and the exiled Lancastrians. With French help he landed on the south coast, caught Edward unprepared, and drove him from the country. Warwick was now a declared Lancastrian. He brought the miserable Henry VI out of the Tower and set him on the throne again. But the restoration did not last long. Edward IV had fled to Flanders. The Duke of Burgundy and the Hanseatic League combined to equip him with an expeditionary force of German mercenaries. He landed in Yorkshire in 1471 and marched south to London without a battle. Thence he turned to face Warwick at Barnet and gained a complete victory. The king-maker was killed, and his army destroyed. There still remained Margaret of Anjou and her son Edward, now aged seventeen. They landed at Weymouth and were brought to action at Tewkesbury on the Severn. Once more Edward IV prevailed. In this final slaughter of the Lancastrians their prince perished, with the Duke of Somerset (third of that title to die in these wars) and many more. The victors celebrated their return to London by murdering Henry VI in the Tower. Edward was at length unchallenged King, and the old baronage had wasted to a shadow. At the end of his reign there were fewer than fifty lay lords, and many of them were newly promoted. In the fourteenth century the number had been nearly a hundred. Most of the old families were extinct or disinherited at the close of the civil wars.

Edward IV had two brothers, George Duke of Clarence and Richard Duke of Gloucester. Clarence had been a double traitor, first to Edward and then to Warwick. In 1478 he was made the victim of yet another of those mysterious prison murders whose details were never allowed to come to light. The general supposition was that he had been drowned in a butt of malmsey, which sounds too fantastic to be probable. A glass of the liquor, suitably prepared, would have been a more practical death-draught. Gloucester had been throughout the faithful henchman of his royal brother. He had fought and murdered, but had never turned his coat. After Edward's death in 1483 he showed more clearly the stuff of which he was made. The rightful king was Edward V, the young son of the late sovereign. Gloucester first assumed the office of Protector and next declared himself king as Richard III. In so doing he swept opposition from his path by a murder such as had now become customary. Expecting trouble from Lord Hastings, he ordered his arrest at a council meeting and beheaded him immediately outside the door. The coronation was preceded by a further batch of executions, intended to strike terror into all who survived. So far, Richard was but following the custom of the time. His next proceeding was a shock even to the conscience of the fifteenth century. It was nothing less than the murder in the Tower of the two young sons of Edward IV. These two princes, Richard's nephews, were the deposed Edward V and his brother the Duke of York. It was many years before the manner of their end was revealed, but everyone knew that they had disappeared, and could guess the reason. Hardened politicians who regarded the slaying of men as an everyday affair drew the line at the murder of children, and the crime left Richard with scarcely one genuine adherent who would stand by him to the end. His time was destined to be short. Overseas there waited in exile a man who watched events and made ready to strike when the moment should come. It came in 1485, the year which marks the transition from medieval to modern England.

V

THE ZENITH AND DECLINE OF THE ENGLISH MONARCHY

(From Henry VII to Charles I)

I. THE TUDOR PLAN

FEW intrinsically worthless men have had so great an influence upon the history of their country as John of Gaunt. In his own life he did much to degrade the tone of public affairs and to render possible the miseries of the fifteenth century. From among his descendants there was nevertheless to arise a sovereign who would rescue England from anarchy and set her on the way to becoming a great nation. John of Gaunt left a bastard son (subsequently declared legitimate) named John Beaufort. He was the ancestor of the three successive Dukes of Somerset who perished on the Lancastrian side in the Wars of the Roses. He was the grandfather also of the Lady Margaret Beaufort, through whom the Tudors derived what claim they had to the throne of England. The Tudor family itself was of Welsh origin. Its first prominent member was Owen Tudor, a soldier of the French wars. He was one of the lesser gentry, but he had greatness thrust upon him by gaining the love of Katherine of France, the widowed queen of Henry V. Owen Tudor married his princess, was imprisoned for his presumption, had a son Edmund Tudor, and was executed with a batch of other prisoners after a Yorkist victory in 1461. His son Edmund had pre-deceased him in 1456, but had first married Margaret Beaufort. From that marriage there was born in January 1457, three months after the father's death, Henry Tudor, Earl of Richmond, who was destined against all calculation to become King of England.

At the time of his birth Henry Tudor was a complete outsider so far as any claim to the throne was concerned. Before him stood the senior line of the House of Lancaster, in the persons of Henry VI and his son Prince Edward, and the House of York who were soon to succeed them. But by 1485 battle, murder, and execution had thinned the ranks of the descendants of Edward III. Richard of York was in possession of the crown, but his only son had just died. He had himself murdered two of his nephews in the Tower. A third, Edward Earl of Warwick, the son of the murdered Duke of Clarence (of the butt of malmsey), was a boy kept in close confinement. For the rest there survived only a few male claimants, and their pretensions were as shadowy as those of Henry Tudor himself.

The Tudor family had been Lancastrians in the wars, and when yet a boy the young Henry had been sent overseas to escape the fate with which the victorious Yorkists would have visited him. He grew up at the court of the Duke of Brittany, and in 1485 was twenty-eight years old. His life had not been safe or easy. He lay continually under the peril that some diplomatic bargain would hand him over to his enemies. Keen wits were his only salvation, and he grew up watchful, subtle, and reserved. It is surprising that he did not become also a heartless ruffian like so many of his contemporaries. But he had in him a streak of kindliness which his circumstances repressed but did not quite eradicate. His temper was cool and humorous. He could fight with decision when occasion demanded it. But in general he hated fighting. Its waste and uncertainty were abhorrent to his orderly nature. He was by conviction a man of law and peace. His destiny called him to a perilous venture, but he determined that if he succeeded he would close the age of bloodshed and open that of healing and prosperity. Such was the man who watched for two years the murderous progress of Richard III.

In the late summer of 1485 a small squadron cleared from the mouth of the Seine. It carried 2000 men, and there were perhaps a score of ships of an average burden of a hundred tons. They were merchantmen of the period, broad and deep in the hold, lofty at bow and stern. Each mast spread a single bellying sail, and perhaps already they showed the green and white Tudor flag which Spaniards and 'Portugals' were to know on all the oceans of the world in time to come. The men were a scratch lot, a rabble picked up in the Norman villages. The leaders were English, the Earl of Oxford, a dozen or so of knights, clerics, and lawyers—and Henry Tudor. Such was the forlorn hope that set out to make one more English revolution and bring the century of revolutions to a close. It was the last but one of all the successful invasions of England, and the next was not to occur until 1688.

With the wind in the east Henry turned down Channel and
rounded the Land's End. After a week's sailing he came to
Milford Haven on the evening of 7 August. In Wales he was
on his own soil, and some Welshmen joined him. Those who
did not lifted no finger to stay his progress. He crossed the
Severn at Shrewsbury, and Englishmen came in also. But in
general the people waited on the event. A generation of blood
and terror had sickened them of claimants, and they trusted
none; but most of them wished the Tudor well. Richard III
expected the invasion but could not tell on which coast it would
land. He had therefore taken station at Nottingham in the
centre of his realm. He called up his levies and advanced to
meet his foe. His force was the greater, but not the more trust-
worthy. He was 'bought and sold' ere ever he fought, as an
anonymous warning told him on the night before the end. With
the shadow of death on his face he set forward to the clash of
Bosworth Field on the morning of the 22nd. His last word to
his troops was that they would get no mercy and were to give
none. True to that pirate watchword he fell on, striking hard
and swift like a cornered snake, and the life was beaten out of
him in the midst of the Tudor ranks. A knot of his accomplices,
too deep in his crimes to temporize, fell with him. The bulk of
his host fought feebly, and some did not fight at all. Sir William
Stanley, who had betrayed him, picked up the crown from the
debris of the field and set it upon Henry's head. It was the last
day of medieval and the first of modern England. It was
characteristic of both. The battle had been decided by despera-
tion and treachery. After it men were surprised that there was
no wholesale execution of the prisoners. The reign of the politic
king had begun.

Henry VII desired peace at home and abroad, and knew he
could get it only by studying the interests of those of his subjects
who desired it likewise. The reign of Richard and the casualties
of Bosworth had still further reduced the numbers of the
baronage. In Henry's first Parliament there were only a score
of lay peers and about twice as many bishops and abbots. He
determined not to increase the number, and to reduce the
power of the survivors. They had to take oath not to give their
livery to armed retainers or to make any bargain with other
men for armed support. They swore also not to practise maintenance, that is, interference with the course of justice. Livery

and maintenance had been the mainstay of the fighting factions and now they were to go. Henry meant what he said. Livery ceased almost at once. Maintenance, less easy to prove, died out more gradually, but the following generation knew it no more.

A powerful agent in restoring the rule of law was the Star Chamber. The King's Council had long had jurisdiction over cases in which great offenders might be involved. An Act of 1487 gave regularity and definition to this work. By it the councillors were empowered to try cases of riot and trespass, bribery of juries, unfaithfulness of the King's officers, and breaches of law by great men.[1] It is a mistake to suppose that the Star Chamber began as an engine of tyranny or that it dealt chiefly with political offences. The reverse is the truth. Its records exist—thousands of 'Bills of Complaint' and 'Answers' neatly written on parchment sheets. In the vast majority the complainants are humble persons, small landowners, tenants unjustly evicted, defrauded heirs, tradesmen robbed of their goods, victims of private malice or mob violence. All such could appeal to the Star Chamber and get cheap and speedy justice from the men who sat in council with the King. Henry could have devised no greater reform for the benefit of the numberless small men of the middle class, the backbone of the England that was growing up. Protection and encouragement of the middle class are a keynote of the whole Tudor period. It is the age of the merchant, the squire, and the yeoman. Many even of the great nobles of the time were newly promoted from the middle ranks. The sun of feudalism had set.

Property was made more secure by the reforms described above. Crimes against the person were a much more difficult problem. The whole land was full of tramps, poachers, thieves, and highwaymen. The habit of fighting was ingrained. Every man went armed and drew his weapon on the slightest occasion. Duels, murders, and assaults occurred everywhere and every day. There were no police. In their stead were the justices of the peace, chosen in every shire from the ranks of the gentry. Everything depended on their personal activity and zeal for order. In the bad times they had been paralysed by the power of the fighting retinues. The Tudors did all they could to strengthen them. In the sixteenth century the local justices

---

[1] The origins of the Star Chamber are obscure. See 'The So-Called Star Chamber Act', by C. H. Williams, in *History*, vol. xv, No. 58, pp. 129–35.

became the men-of-all-work of the administration. They seized and sentenced petty offenders in their own neighbourhood, met four times a year in quarter sessions for more serious cases, held rebels and murderers for trial by the judges at assizes, published new laws and proclamations, watched for spies in time of war, mustered their neighbours in arms in an emergency, collected horses and foodstuffs for the King's troops, and performed all the duties of a civil service. It was all voluntary and unpaid work, and in the spirit of the new England it was ever better done. To be a zealous justice was to be 'worshipful'.The Tudor sovereigns and their councillors knew by repute, if not personally, every gentleman of every shire, and the gentry took pride in their work because they knew that their efforts were known and noted. Their most continuous duty, the repression of crime, was an uphill task. Under Henry VII and Henry VIII the state of the country improved, although it would be considered frightful by modern standards. Under Elizabeth progress was more marked, and some semblance of security for life and limb was at length attained. The greatest obstacles to the punishment of crime were the twin rights of sanctuary and benefit of clergy. Any evil-doer could take sanctuary, from which it was difficult to hale him forth. Any 'clerk' or literate person could claim exemption from the criminal law and escape with a penance from the bishop's court. The first two Tudor kings limited but did not quite abolish these abuses. They died out in the century after the Reformation.

So much for peace at home. Peace abroad was no less a part *foreign* of the Tudor plan, and notably so under Henry VII. He knew *affs* that half-a-dozen revolutionary movements of the fifteenth century (including his own Bosworth venture) had been patronized by foreign powers. He worked hard to avert such aggressions for the future. Henry, therefore, is the first English sovereign who made foreign alliances in order to preserve peace; the alliances of the past had been for waging war. His greatest success was his pact with the rising power of Spain. Ferdinand, King of Aragon, and Isabella, Queen of Castile, had united the country by their marriage. In 1492 they completed the work of centuries by a last crusade which conquered the Moorish kingdom of Granada in southern Spain, the final remnant of the Mahometan rule of the peninsula. Henry sought their friendship, and cemented it by marrying his son Arthur to their daughter Katherine. The strongest monarchy in Europe had thus an interest in maintaining the Tudor throne. After years of bickering he scored a similar success with Scotland by marrying his daughter Margaret to James IV. This did not indeed yield a permanent peace, but it did result in the ultimate union of the Crowns when James VI of Scotland succeeded Elizabeth as James I of England. The Spanish alliance continued unbroken until the first decade of Elizabeth, a matter of eighty years. It certainly achieved what its author expected of it by giving England a strong supporter amid the perils of a turbulent age.

With other countries Henry VII had trouble at first but success at last. The great lords of Ireland were virtually independent and had sided with the Yorkist party in the English wars. They pushed the claims of two pretenders against Henry's throne—Lambert Simnel, a baker's boy who claimed to be the Earl of Warwick, and Perkin Warbeck, son of a Flemish boatman, who said he was that Duke of York whom Richard III had made away with in the Tower. Henry overcame the Irish and treated them with mercy and justice, together with a certain caustic humour. When the Irish lords came reconciled to London he had them served at table by Simnel, the poor creature to whom they had once done homage as their king. 'Ah, my masters,' said Henry, 'I think ye will crown apes in Ireland at the last.' The King's deputy, Sir Edward Poynings, was meanwhile regulating the powers of the Irish Parliament. By Poynings' Law, 1494, that body was rendered incapable of meeting or of discussing any measures without the previous approval of the King's Council. Henry VII did not make Ireland orderly, but he left it better than he found it. Henry VIII in his turn made spasmodic efforts at Irish reform. Then the Reformation succeeded in England but failed in Ireland, and the breach between the two countries was irreparable. The difference of religion, rather than the difference of race, is the underlying cause of all the bloodstained record of the past four centuries. The Welsh have as strong a Celtic element in them as the Irish, but how different have been their relations with their Anglo-Saxon neighbours.

With the Low Countries Henry VII had a difficult task to secure peace. They were controlled by the Archduke Maximilian (Emperor from 1493) who had married Mary, the daughter of Charles the Bold, the last Duke of Burgundy. There was a personal enmity between Henry and Maximilian, and in addition the House of Burgundy were the traditional allies of the Yorkist party. Edward IV's sister Margaret had been the wife of Charles the Bold, and as his widow she lived still in the Netherlands, where she gave support to Lambert Simnel and Perkin Warbeck in turn. She professed to recognize these two impostors as her nephews, although she knew without a doubt that they were not. Henry cleverly availed himself of commercial interests. The Flemish cities needed English wool and half-made cloth. Henry stopped the supply, and Maximilian's own subjects pressed him to make up the quarrel. The great treaty known as the *Magnus Intercursus* was the result. The merchants gained unfettered trade, and the two sovereigns promised not to countenance each other's enemies. On the east, as on the west, Henry's diplomacy made his throne secure. Further royal marriages merged the Burgundian alliance with the Spanish. Maximilian's son Philip wedded Juana, the daughter of Ferdinand and Isabella. Charles, the son of Philip and Juana, became King of Spain in 1516 and Holy Roman Emperor in 1519. The Tudor monarchy was thus the centre of a league of three maritime powers, Spain, England, and the Netherlands, and when, under Elizabeth of England and Philip II of Spain, the Anglo-Spanish alliance gradually turned to enmity, the English still held to the Netherlanders and aided them to throw off the yoke of their Spanish master. From that day to this England has always used her strength on behalf of the independence of the Low Countries.

In spite of the fact that in the Tudor period there were seven wars with France, that period is mainly one of Anglo-French peace. For the wars were half-hearted and of short duration, diminishing echoes of the savage contest of the earlier age. The ambition to conquer France was given up, save perhaps for a brief moment in the youth of Henry VIII. Of the hundred-and-eighteen years of the Tudor dynasty only twelve were years of war with France, divided into seven episodes, mere diplomatic demonstrations when compared with past efforts. The Tudor instinct in calling a halt to the ancient feud was sound. Soldiering in France had led to anarchy at home. The new orderly England could only be an unmilitary England. So in the sixteenth century the fighting spirit had to satisfy itself chiefly on the sea. Disorderly sailors robbed along the coast, but they did not permeate the whole country like the soldiers of the Hundred Years War. The battlements of England's towns and castles mouldered into ruin, the bowman forgot his skill, the knight hung his armour on the wall. But the ships multiplied, navigators learned the ocean tracks, gunners found the cunning that the archers had lost. He who would grow excitingly rich no longer led a company to France; he fitted out a squadron for the Indies.

mercantile

It was by their commercial policy above all else that the Tudors moulded the destiny of England. Before their time foreigners carried on the greater part of the trade between England and other countries, and this was a principal cause of the weakness of our fifteenth-century governments at home and abroad. A nation which exploits its own resources is strong and respected. A nation which allows them to be exploited by others is not only despised but its independence is endangered. Henry VII understood this thoroughly. Where he got his knowledge we can only guess. By origin he was a mere fighting baron, and by upbringing a mere hanger-on of courts. He had few books and no professors of political economy. Yet from the outset he displayed a grasp of commerce, finance, and the principles of economic power such as no European sovereign had evinced before. In the classic phrase of Francis Bacon, his first biographer, 'he could not endure to see trade sick'.

An obvious evil was the low state to which English sea-power had sunk. There were few ships and few seamen, and the shipbuilders turned out craft that were inferior to the hulks of the Hanseatic League or the galleys and carracks of Venice and Genoa. Henry lost no time in passing through his first Parliament a Navigation Act which reserved to English vessels an entire branch of trade, the import of wines and woad from Gascony. It was an important business, for the French wines were in great demand and the woad yielded a dye for English cloth. This Navigation Act, unlike that of Richard II, was enforced for the best part of a century, until changes in trade rendered it obsolete. Not only had the ships to be English owned, but their crews had to be 'for the more part' (the majority) of English, Irish, or Welsh sailors. Henry also encouraged the use of large ships by granting bounties to the merchants who acquired them. His peaceful foreign policy made no great demands upon the Royal Navy, but he did not neglect that force.

He built few ships, but they were of first-class design. His *Regent* and *Sovereign* were among the most powerful vessels afloat. Upon this nucleus Henry VIII accumulated a fleet which made England the chief sea-power of his time, equipped not only with fighting craft but with dockyards and a Navy Board of tried officials. Elizabeth continued the tradition. The English Navy of 1588 cost far less than the Spanish Armada, which it overwhelmed. Its efficiency was due to long experience and to the care of officers like Sir John Hawkins, who had grown up as heirs to a century of knowledge. The Tudor naval policy was all of one piece. The fighting admirals saved their country in 1588, but behind them stood the shades of Henry VII and Henry VIII who had taught England the principles of sea supremacy.

Ships of war were expensive. Only a rich nation could afford them. In time of peace they must be laid up and the men discharged. Yet without seamen the ships would be useless. It followed that a busy maritime trade was an essential of sea power, to produce both the wealth to support it and the men to use it. Hence the Navigation Acts for the encouragement of the mercantile marine. But this alone was a small part of the Tudor commercial policy. Henry VII began, and his successors continued, an effort to transfer the foreigners' share of our trade to English hands. In northern Europe the Hanseatic League was the greatest trading power. Its ships carried goods between all the ports from Riga down to Seville. Its merchants in England paid lower duties than the English themselves. It monopolized the sale of the furs, timber, hemp, pitch, and corn from the Baltic coasts and the dimly-known plains of Russia beyond. Henry VII was not strong enough to challenge the Hansa to open war. With its ships and its money it had more than once promoted invasions of England. He therefore confirmed its privileges by a general charter. But, having done so, he set himself to whittle them away in detail. The Navigation Act was one such detail, for the Bordeaux wine trade had been largely in the League's hands before the passing of that measure. Other aggressions followed, and by the middle of the sixteenth century English trade in the North Sea had to some extent revived. In 1557 we hear of no less than fifty English merchantmen penetrating to the Baltic, formerly a Hanse preserve. The later Tudors overthrew the League's hold upon England,

Edward VI and Mary cancelled its privileges. Elizabeth partly restored them, then withdrew them again, and finally in 1598 expelled the Easterlings altogether from England, and closed their great London factory of the Steelyard. Only then was England commercially an independent country.

The *Magnus Intercursus* with the Netherlands has already been mentioned, together with Henry VII's treaty with Spain. These pacts gave English merchants fair treatment in the ports of two of their chief customers. They endured until the Counter-Reformation set all Europe in a blaze of religious warfare and commercial interests vanished like chaff in a furnace. But by that time (in Elizabeth's middle years) the work was done. England had become strong enough to stand apart from Spain, and London took the place of Antwerp as the chief business centre of the north. The Merchants Adventurers who had traded in Flanders shifted their depots into Germany, and the skippers who had brought cargoes from Seville became priva-teers who picked up the same goods on the ocean. From that it was but a step to establishing plantations in America and fac-tories in India, and so the Empire was born. The germ of it all lay in the wisdom of the King who could not endure to see trade sick.

'India' was a word of magic in those Tudor days. It meant more than it does now. It stood, along with 'Cathay', for the whole vast mystery of Asia, the land of great cities, great emperors, and fabulous wealth, of silks, spices, perfumes, pearls, and gems, a lure to a lusty nation turning from feudal warfare to the call of the sea. Vasco da Gama, the Portuguese, sailed to India by the Cape of Good Hope when Henry VII was king, but it was many a year before Englishmen were fit to follow him—it was eighty years, in fact, before Francis Drake sailed a Plymouth keel across the Indian Ocean. Meanwhile the nearer Asia could be reached through the Mediterranean. There, in the Levant seas at its eastern end, one could trade with Arabs, Turks, and Egyptians, and buy the spices that came from the unknown. Venetians had been doing so for centuries and making vast profit by selling these luxuries in England. Under the Tudors the English began to trade in the Levant. It was their first really long trade-route, through the Straits of Marrok, sometimes called of 'Juberaltar', by Minorca and Malta to Cyprus and Alexandria, the road that the Suez Canal

was in after days to render the principal artery of empire—
twelve months out and home for a stout ship. Under Henry VII
the stout ships began to ply, and he backed them with his
ubiquitous diplomacy. The Venetians were naturally hostile
and levied crippling tolls. He applied the screw by threatening
to cut off their supplies of English wool. The threat sufficed, and
resistance ceased. The Levant trade established itself. Under
Elizabeth the traders were incorporated as the Levant Company, a powerful body which endured until the nineteenth
century.

It was a long way to India by the Cape of Good Hope, and
there were many geographers who believed in a shorter route by
the west. Columbus tried that way for Spain in 1492 and
announced that he had reached the Indies. Although in truth
there was half the world between the real Indies and his islands,
they are called the West Indies to this day. In 1497 John Cabot,
a Venetian, sailed on the same quest in the *Matthew* of Bristol
with a charter from Henry VII. He followed a more northerly
track and discovered the mainland of America in the neighbourhood of Cape Breton. But none realized that it was a new
continent. It was thought to be the coast of Asia. Cabot went
again in 1498, but failed to open a spice trade; for in his new
land there were no spices, and no wealthy Chinese cities or
great emperors. Gradually the truth appeared, and America
was looked upon with disfavour as a barrier in the path to
Asiatic wealth. Nevertheless Cabot's New Found Land provided something to exploit, a marvellous fishery where the cod
teemed so thick that enthusiasts declared that a ship could
hardly force her way through them. Before Henry VII was
dead an English company was already 'adventuring' to the
New Found Land, and afterwards the fishery became a regular
business for all the west-country seaports. At Madrid there is
preserved a map drawn on an ox-hide in 1500 by the Spanish
pilot Juan de la Cosa. It shows the North American coast dotted
with English flags and marked with names such as Cape England, Cape Lizard, Cape St. George, and The Sea Discovered
by the English. They are the memorials of John Cabot and his
Bristol sailors.

When America was recognized to be a separate country the
westward search for Asia took a new form. It became a problem
of penetrating through or round the new land, and the quest of

the North West Passage began. Sebastian Cabot, son of John, made a voyage with this object, probably in 1509.[1] He claimed that he had found the passage open before him, but that his men had mutinied and forced him back. He had most likely been in Hudson's Strait. For well over a century the North West Passage was sought. Under Henry VIII there were at least three expeditions. Under Elizabeth two captains made persistent efforts—Sir Martin Frobisher and John Davis—whilst Sir Humphrey Gilbert wrote a *Discourse* to prove by scripture, science, and history that the passage existed. In 1583 he was drowned whilst trying to make his word good. Repeated failure only called forth new adventurers. The greatest of all was Henry Hudson in the reign of James I. He passed through Hudson's Strait and entered Hudson's Bay. There he was turned adrift by his men in an open boat and never heard of more. But he died in the belief that he had solved the problem, for he thought his bay was an arm of the Pacific. Alas, it was not, and the next explorer was brought to a halt by yet another mass of Canadian mainland which he named expressively 'Hopes Checked'. The great quest never yielded a path to the wealth of Asia, but it did make men. They founded the Empire all the more surely after the hard schooling of early failure.

Such was the England which the Tudors rescued from anarchy and turned to worthy enterprise. It was still a land of open spaces, of great woods and moors and fens, of wide pastures, of cornlands tilled on the age-old plan of common field, with never a fence or a hedge. By every common was its village with church and manor-house, and in every dozen miles or so one came to a market town, a red-roofed gem set where the trackways met or the bridge passed over the stream. The people were few, not one person on an average where ten herd to-day. They lived hard and died young. Famine, plague, sweating-sickness, and the law swept them off year by year and taught them not to set a high value on mere life. They worked from dawn to dark on working days, and made their holidays occasions to remember—the Christmas feast and mumming, the carouse of harvest-home, the football match in which village

---

[1] The Cabot voyages are a much disputed but fascinating piece of history. The general reader should be warned that no two investigators have given the same account of them. He should study all versions and form his own opinion.

fought village and the field was the countryside, the welcome to
the sovereign when he rode on progress through the shire, the
judge's assize that never passed without some hangings to entertain the virtuous. The laws might be harsh, but the men were
free, so free and high-spirited that severity was needful. 'These
people have more liberty than is good for them,' wrote a Spanish
ambassador—such things were not done in his country. Because
they smote hard the Tudors have been called despots. They
were not. They had no army, no police, very few paid officials.
They ruled, as they had to rule, by public approval. They
called Parliament for every important matter, and there was not
one great change in their time that was not duly enacted by
Commons, Lords, and Crown. When the English monarchy
passed from their hands to those of the Stuarts its true position
was seen. The Stuarts lacked the Tudor talent for discerning
what might be done and what might not. They set themselves
against the spirit of England, and England rose against them.
The monarchy perished in the struggle, to be revived, but not
in its ancient form.

II. THE STATE AND THE CHURCH

Henry VII was a man of much formal piety, scrupulous to
observe the customs of religion and the duties it exacted from
his rank. In his time there was no question of a conflict between
Church and State. Churchmen, indeed, were prominent among
his councillors, notably the great Cardinal Morton, Lord
Chancellor and Archbishop of Canterbury, who is held by
some to have been his good genius. Henry, grasping as he
sometimes was of the property of his subjects, never made any
move to attack that of the Church. Like the Lancastrian
kings, he persecuted the Lollards, and several martyrdoms are
recorded in his reign. What mutterings there were against the
clergy were raised by zealous churchmen themselves, bishops
who sought power to reform religious houses which had grown
slack in pursuit of the pious way of life. In 1490 the Pope,
aware that much was wrong, issued an order for the visitation
and correction of the English monasteries.

Henry VIII also was in his early years no enemy of the
Church. His support of the Pope's international policy led him
into his first war with France in 1512–14, and during that war

he found in Thomas Wolsey a minister who was at once a statesman and an ecclesiastic. Wolsey maintained his ascendancy
by his capacity for hard work and his assertion of his clerical
dignity as against that of the lay nobles. As Cardinal, Archbishop of York, and holder of many other great offices, he
claimed a position equal to any which high birth could have
conferred. He relieved the King of all the work of administration and undoubtedly improved the condition of the country.
But he used this achievement only as a means to an end. His
chief interest was in foreign affairs, and his ambition was to be
Pope. He sought to make his country predominant in the
councils of Europe and by her power to secure his own advance-
ment. But he was opposed to statesmen as able as himself, and
events turned in a direction he could not foresee. For a dozen
years, however, his power increased, and the alliance between
the Crown and the Church appeared unthreatened.

Meanwhile the world moved. The revival of classical learning
had gained force on the continent in the fifteenth century, and
in the early sixteenth it spread to England. The importance of
the movement lay less in the knowledge gained than in the
mental attitude wherein it was approached. The new learning
substituted reliance upon evidence for appeal to authority. In
practical politics the way was prepared for the examination of
questions upon their merits rather than in accordance with
precedent. When such had become the spirit of the time there
was one question which could not fail to be reopened—that of
the wealth, the privileges, and the exemptions of the Church,
apart altogether from the validity of her doctrines. To understand what happened in England it is necessary to bear this
distinction in mind, that the position of the Church in the
national fabric was one matter, and religious belief quite
another; for there were many persons, and Henry VIII was
one of them, who grew dissatisfied on the first point whilst
unwilling to change on the second.

For nearly two hundred years Englishmen had been thinking
that the clergy were over-endowed and over-privileged, and
that their conduct did not square with their professions. The
abuses that Chaucer had derided and Wycliffe denounced had
continued. But whilst the clergy as men had not regained
public respect, the spiritual hold of the Church as an institution
seemed as great as ever. The Lollards, never quite stamped out,

were yet an obscure and despised sect. They had not shaken
the faith of their countrymen in the beliefs they had questioned
—in transubstantiation, in the worship of the saints, in pilgrim-
ages, and all the routine of medieval religion. Such was the
appearance, and few suspected that behind it a real decay was
setting in. That decay became manifest as the sixteenth century
advanced.

In England the attack opened on privilege rather than on
doctrine. In 1514–15 a case of clerical oppression evoked a
surprising outburst of passion. Richard Hunne, a London
citizen, had been arrested for offences against the Church and
was found dead in his prison. The clerical authorities said he
had committed suicide, but the popular belief was that they
had murdered him. The man was accused of Lollardism, but
it was not for that that the people sympathized. It was because
an Englishman had been harshly treated by an authority that
stood outside the law of the land. The anti-clerical party moved
in Parliament to abolish benefit of clergy and bring all criminals
under the King's law. The attempt failed, but it caused many to
reflect on the question of reform. It opened the eyes of Henry
himself to the fact that he was not fully master of his realm.

Meanwhile Martin Luther in Germany was opening the
doctrinal attack. There as here the ground was already prepared, and Lutheranism had a rapid success. Within four years
from 1517 it became the most important question of the time.
Lutheran ideas soon crossed to England and became grafted
upon the ancient stock of Lollardism. Perhaps for that reason
they did not at first make much headway. With the mass of
Englishmen Lollardism was already condemned. Moreover,
Germany was represented in England by the Easterling traders
of the Hanseatic League, an extremely unpopular body.
National feeling worked in two opposing directions. It condemned the clergy because their power weakened the state.
It cherished their doctrines because they were the national
creed. The workings of this intensely English sentiment are
the clue to the English Reformation. By 1521 the reformers
were yet a small minority, but their activities seemed worthy
of government notice, and a ceremonious burning of heretical
books was carried out in St. Paul's Churchyard. The King,
still entirely orthodox, wrote an essay against Luther and was
rewarded by Pope Leo X with the title of Defender of the Faith.

Wolsey, the great ecclesiastic, stood, unpopular but unchallenged, at the King's right hand.

Henry VIII marriages

In spite of this it was from the King's hand that the blow was to fall, a fact of which the King himself was yet unaware. Shortly after his accession Henry had married Katherine of Aragon, the widow of his brother Arthur. Such a marriage was contrary to the canon law, but a papal dispensation had been obtained. For fifteen years all went well, except that the children of the royal pair died one after another with dismaying regularity. Only one, the Princess Mary, a sickly girl destined to be queen of England, survived infancy. For the King and for the nation it was a cause of anxiety. If Henry were to die childless nothing could prevent the outbreak of a new series of civil wars, and all the good work of the Tudors would be ruined. If he left only a daughter the prospect would be nearly as bad. No queen had ever yet ruled England in her own right, and none could tell how the experiment would work. If she married a foreigner he would seek to dominate the country. If she married a subject jealous factions would be sure to make trouble. Such was the shadow that hovered over the English realm. For Henry personally it was equally black. He had a strong sense of duty to his people. He began to doubt whether his marriage was lawful. The deaths of his children seemed to be the punishment of God for transgression. He was entirely sincere. It is easy to scoff and to say that Mistress Anne Boleyn had caught his fancy. That also was true, but it did not render his doubts of his marriage hypocritical. To underrate that feeling is to misunderstand the religion of the time.

By 1527 Henry's doubts were pressing, and he resolved to take advice. So began the matter commonly known as the divorce, although strictly speaking it was no divorce since the King's contention was that there had been no marriage. At first sight it promised no trouble, for what the Pope could do the Pope could undo, and it would normally have been an easy business to obtain from Clement VII a decree pronouncing the King unmarried, whereupon he could have wedded Anne Boleyn. Henry had so far been a good servant of the Church, and Clement was personally anxious to do what was required. But the Pope was not a free agent. The interminable wars between Spaniards and Frenchmen for the control of Italy had produced a decisive event in 1527. An imperialist army had sacked Rome, and Clement was a prisoner of the Emperor Charles V. Charles was the nephew of Katherine of Aragon and unwilling to see her removed from the throne of England. Hence arose a deadlock over the King's matter, and that deadlock grew into a permanent breach between the realm of England and the Church of Rome.

Wolsey was eager to see the King remarried, although not to Anne Boleyn. His preference was for a French princess, as a move in his complicated foreign policy. Anne therefore hated Wolsey, and the King began to doubt his loyalty. Wolsey could not do the impossible by extracting a decree from a captive Pope. His failure was his ruin. He fell in 1529 and died in 1530 on his way to the Tower, where a trial for treason awaited him. Henry called Parliament in 1529, and by so doing made the nation the partner of his troubles. It was quite willing to back him, for the question was of jurisdiction, not of doctrine. Public opinion, or at least a weighty part of it, was ready to attack the power of the Church. The King and most of his people were agreed that matters of state must be decided within the realm, and that England must be no longer subject to the dictation of an outside authority. When we realize that it was not really the Pope, but the Emperor, who was preventing the King's new marriage the national standpoint is intelligible. England saw her future security menaced by the action of a foreign prince. At the outset there had been a good deal of sentiment in favour of Katherine, and a feeling that Henry was not acting fairly. That feeling was swamped as soon as it became apparent that Pope and Emperor were controlling an important piece of English business.

The King's policy was now to make the Church in England subject to the state. There was an interval of a year or two in which new men came to the front and their opinions took shape. Into the vacancy left by the fall of Thomas Wolsey there entered Sir Thomas More, a scholar of inflexible principles who became Lord Chancellor; Thomas Cromwell, a politician of no principles at all but of a wonderful audacity; and Thomas Cranmer, a man of sincere goodness, whose convictions were changing in the direction of Protestantism and whose principles therefore appeared wavering and inconstant—the Thomases have never had such an innings as they had in the reign of Henry VIII. In 1531 the King struck the first blow at the

Church. He charged the entire order of the clergy with having countenanced appeals to Rome and with having admitted the authority of a papal legate, Wolsey. This was to infringe the Statutes of Praemunire, and the penalty was imprisonment and forfeiture of goods. To attack a wealthy section of the population for breaking an ancient law, which had not been consistently enforced from the day of its enactment, was a bold stroke. Henry did it with success because he had the lay majority behind him, and particularly the middle classes, the squires and the merchants who filled the House of Commons. The clergy gave in without a fight. They confessed their guilt, paid a large fine, and acknowledged the King as Supreme Head of the English Church, 'as far as the law of Christ allows'. In 1532 they further promised to submit the canon law to the King's revision. 'We have well perceived,' said Henry, 'that they [the clergy] be but half our subjects, yea and scarce our subjects. For all the prelates at their consecration make an oath to the Pope clean contrary to the oath they make to us, so that they seem his subjects and not ours.'

Thomas More, the layman who believed in the independence of the Church, resigned office and withdrew to his books and his learned friends. Thomas Cranmer, the churchman who was beginning to think that the King was right, suggested that Henry should ignore the Pope and determine the marriage question in other ways. It was his first step to the archbishopric of Canterbury. Thomas Cromwell, the adventurer who aimed at power, revolved a gigantic scheme in which the King and all England were to be his instruments. The King must confiscate the wealth of the Church, to the last acre and the last shilling. Excommunication would follow. No matter; the gage must be taken up, and King and people, in spite of themselves, must turn Protestant and join the German Lutherans in a league of northern Europe strong enough to defy the Roman south. Seas of blood might flow, on scaffold and battlefield alike. But a new England would emerge, guided and preserved by the genius of Thomas Cromwell. He was a great man, a great scoundrel. Nothing could justify such a course but a burning love of country and faith in the new religion. Cromwell had no religion and no patriotism. Church, King, and England were but pieces in his game of power. For seven years he played it and then, genius as he was, he fell.

First the marriage question was settled. In 1533 the King wedded Anne Boleyn without further argument. Parliament passed the Act of Appeals, which denied any jurisdiction of the Pope in England. Cranmer, newly made archbishop, held a court which pronounced that Henry had never been married to Katherine. Behind the gentle Cranmer, honest in his decision, but doubting the high-handedness of pronouncing it, stood the burly figure of Cromwell. The next business bears Cromwell's stamp. Parliament passed in 1534 the Act of Succession, the Act of Supremacy, and the Statute of Treasons, the joint effect of which was to bring all questioners and doubters within the shadow of the axe. The Commons passed these measures with a free will. They did not see what use Cromwell was to make of them, and no one yet realized his calibre. Henry no doubt knew his man, but the man was useful. He might go on—to a certain point; after which the King had no doubt who would be master. More refused the oath of succession and was beheaded, a portent that not even a personal friend of the King might oppose the necessities of state. The Pope, in a last effort to assert himself, sacrificed John Fisher, the aged Bishop of Rochester. He created Fisher a cardinal, and Fisher lost his head for accepting the dignity.

After the marriage the next step was to deal with Church property. From 1535 to 1539 there proceeded the suppression of the monasteries. First Cromwell carried out a visitation. The visitors inspected every religious house and produced a mass of evidence of dishonesty, worldliness, and immoral living. Some of it was true, but it was not the whole truth. An entire order of men, thousands strong, are not without exception bad. There were many good monks whom the visitors passed over in silence. Cromwell made an unprincipled man's mistake in painting the case too black. He could quite honestly have suppressed the monasteries on the ground that they housed an idle order who did nothing to justify the wealth they drew from the community. However, so it was done. Parliament listened to a lurid catalogue of monkish sins, and with shouts of 'Down with them!' the worthy Commons sanctioned the confiscation. The lands fell to the Crown, and the monks were turned out to leaven the English mass with such godliness as they possessed. Many heads fell, for Cromwell was vigilant to smite down disaffection. The northern counties, where alone the monks were popular, rose in the revolt called the Pilgrimage of Grace. The government put them down with the power of London and the south. Much of the spoil was bestowed in endowing squires and nobles, for it was essential that the new England should have its leading class. Much also was spent in rebuilding the navy and fortifying the coast in case Rome should find armies to intervene.

The final step was to clinch the whole revolution by ranging England on the Protestant side. It was the logical consequence, but Englishmen have never been logical. The King was no Protestant, neither were the nobles, nor the bishops, except Latimer and Cranmer, nor the mass of the Commons. Cromwell was in face of a rooted obstacle which he could not upheave. He had no lever but the King's support, and the King had no mind to be his tool. He never had been that, and Cromwell had deceived himself in thinking so. In reality the King had used him, and now had no further use for him. In 1539–40 the great game of power ended in nightmare, the pieces all in revolt, no longer moving to the master's touch, at length plucking courage to strike him down. In the former year Parliament passed the Act of the Six Articles. It was the King's measure, not Cromwell's, for while it slew Catholics for denying the royal supremacy it slew Protestants for denying transubstantiation. The old religion was to continue, even though the King was Pope. Abroad danger threatened, and it looked as though a Catholic coalition would invade the realm. Half unwillingly the King was induced to marry the German Anne of Cleves as a move towards a counter-coalition of Protestants. The danger passed, and the King drew back. He disliked Lutherans, and he divorced the lady. Cromwell had failed, and since he had shed much blood his failure meant his death. The Duke of Norfolk, head of the anti-Protestant majority in the Council, suddenly charged him with treason; and at once the whole pack rose on him, and all England seemed baying for his blood. It was quickly done—no trial, a brief Act of Attainder in Parliament, and then the block. At the last he showed the base streak that tainted his greatness. He who had signed a hundred death-warrants whined for mercy and offered any abasement if only he might have his life. That Tudor England was beginning to forget the quality of mercy was his work more than any man's. He perished, as Norfolk told him, by the bloody laws he had made.

So things stood for the rest of Henry's life, the seven years that ended on a January morning in 1547. Never had the King been greater than in this last phase, never had he toiled harder for the state nor been more truly the leader of his people. He and they had sailed into rough waters, but they trusted him and he them. War came with France and Scotland in 1543, desertion by the imperial ally in 1544, and the peril of a great invasion in 1545. In every shire the militia mustered, the ancient fyrd of free subjects, 120,000 strong, bowmen and billmen, ready to march to the coast. Commissioners went round to raise a loan. Taxes were high and trade at a standstill, but the nation paid. 'If this be not sufficient,' said the commons of Surrey, 'His Grace shall have more.' The peril came and passed. The French landed in the Isle of Wight, looked across the Solent, and went home. Next year they signed a peace that left Boulogne in English hands, but they meant to have it back, and more. In England Lollardism was turning into Protestantism, and affairs of Church and state were 'jangled in every alehouse'. All was provisional, nothing settled. A stormy reign closed in a lowering sunset, with the signs of a stormy morrow.

Henry's Catholic England without a Pope could not stand. The balance was certain to go down on one side or the other, but time might be trusted to soften the descent. Every year gained was a gain to the prospect of a peaceful solution. From Cromwell's time the Protestants grew stronger, still a minority, but no longer a feeble minority. The orthodox Catholics were also a minority. Most Englishmen feared extremes and hoped for a reasonable settlement. Although the King was never Protestant he grew more tolerant. At his death he left a council in which Protestants were strong, and an heir nine years old, Edward VI, to be brought up amid Protestant relations. Already under Cromwell an English Bible had been placed in every church, and in 1545 the Litany was ordered to be read in English. No sooner was Henry dead than the Protestants advanced. Their lay leader, the Duke of Somerset, became Protector of the Realm. Their clerical leader, Cranmer, worked on an English Prayer Book. The Six Articles—'the whip with six strings'—were repealed. The chantries and religious guilds went the way of the monasteries. Enthusiasts entered the churches, tore down pictures, and defaced images—damage which is often unjustly laid to the account of Oliver Cromwell's

Puritans a century later. Somerset was for restraint and decency, but the times were too wild. He soon fell before the ambitions of the Duke of Northumberland, a much less reputable man. Under Northumberland the ultra-Protestants bore sway and a crowd of adventurers scrambled for loot. Cranmer's first Prayer Book came out in 1549, and his second, more Protestant, in 1552. Protestantism was well served by Cranmer, an honest man; but very ill by Northumberland, a rogue. On Edward's death in 1553 the Duke betrayed his religion and lost his own life by a wild attempt to exclude the Princess Mary from her right. England was weary of rogues and zealots. It thought of Henry, and with one voice called his daughter to the throne.

The daughter of Katherine of Aragon had led a life of tragedy. As a child she could just remember a golden age when all had gone well. As a girl she had seen her mother cast aside and herself declared illegitimate. She had endured the spite of Anne Boleyn and sometimes had thought her very life in peril. In truth no life had been safe with Cromwell at the helm. Her father had bullied and cajoled her, although at bottom he always wished her well. He never shook her religion. Tudor courage and Spanish faith were a grim blend. Even in the great days of the Protestants she defied them openly. Now at last she was Queen. Her people were in mortal sin, and on her it lay to bring them to salvation. All things new must be undone, all things old restored. The Catholic bishops came out of prison and the Protestants went in. The new laws and prayer books were swept into limbo, and that ancient scourge of the Lollards, the *De Heretico Comburendo*, was dug out of the records and copied fair. The Queen married her Spanish cousin Philip and welcomed, as Archbishop and Papal Legate, Cardinal Reginald Pole, who had spent a lifetime in exile writing slanders on Henry VIII. Cranmer was burnt at the stake to make room for him. Cranmer, Latimer, Hooper, Ridley, and many another, three hundred in all, paid the price of the faith and the follies of their kind. The Protestants had been bad winners, but they were good losers. In their prosperity they had excited disgust. In the flames they made the Reformation. 'Be of good comfort, Master Ridley,' said Latimer amid the Oxford faggots, 'We shall this day light such a candle in England as shall never be put out.'

The words have been often quoted and are worthy of quoting,

not for the glory of a creed but of liberty. More and Fisher had
been equally firm in the opposite cause. Either could have had
his life for denying his opinions. Each preferred death to bondage. Few men nowadays can endure to read the arguments
that then poured so hot from earnest pens, fewer still would
be ready to slay for the phrasing of a creed. But every
Englishman has something in his bones and blood that the
Reformation martyrs have bequeathed him. His judgement is
his own; he cannot yield it into the keeping of the state. It was
not so in the day of the martyrs themselves. They were the
exceptions who brought out into the nation's view the tradition
of freedom that had lingered underground since Wycliffe's time.
Most others of their time were not ashamed to speak as they
were commanded. Many a man took his share of abbey lands
from Henry, was Protestant under Edward, Catholic under
Mary, and Protestant again under Elizabeth. Only by slow
degrees did the new tradition take hold.

It seemed that there was no luck in Spanish marriages. That
of Philip and Mary produced no heir, not even a girl. It acted
as a check upon English enterprise beyond the ocean, and it
brought humiliation in a war waged solely in the interest of
Philip. Northumberland had restored Boulogne to the French.
In 1558 they took Calais. It was no material loss, for it was not
worth keeping. But it had been English for two hundred years,
and the blow to pride was sore. The country began to hate
Spain and was thoroughly sickened with the burnings. There
were more Protestants than ever, and at length the indifferent
majority were beginning to argue that there could never be
peace under a Catholic government. When Mary died, ten
months after Calais fell, the nation hailed with acclamation her
Protestant sister Elizabeth, the daughter of Anne Boleyn.

Elizabeth settled the matter, for the time was ripe. Under
the guidance of her Secretary of State, Sir William Cecil, who
had been Protestant with Northumberland and had gone to
mass in Mary's reign, she summoned a Parliament which represented the great middle section of the nation. It restored the
English Prayer Book, with some concessions to the older practices, and passed the twin Acts of Supremacy and Uniformity.
The latter made the Anglican service the only permitted form
of worship, although with very mild penalties upon dissent.
The former placed the Church of England under the control

of the state and denied any outside jurisdiction. It did so in impressive words which long formed part of the English tradition: 'No foreign prince, person, prelate, state or potentate, spiritual or temporal, shall use, enjoy, or exercise any manner of power, jurisdiction, superiority, authority, pre-eminence, or privilege, spiritual or ecclesiastical, within this realm.' With that the majority were content. After thirty years of strife the religious question was coming to stable bearings. The martyrs of both causes had not died in vain, neither had the tyranny that killed them been altogether evil. For it was because governments had struck without mercy at individuals that factions had not grown strong enough to fight. In condemning the cruelties of Henry and Mary we must never forget that England passed through the Reformation without a civil war.

III. THE FREEDOM OF THE OCEAN

In the fifteenth century, whilst Englishmen had been invading France or killing one another in the Wars of the Roses, the adventurers of Portugal had been doing something more promising. Under the inspiration of their Prince Henry 'the Navigator' they had explored the west coast of Africa. Year after year the expeditions went forth, and bit by bit they pushed the bounds of discovery farther to the southward. By 1460 they had passed Cape Verde. By 1480 they were on the Equator. In 1487-8 Bartholomew Diaz passed the southern end of the continent and made sure that he had the Indian Ocean under his keel before he returned with the news. His news meant that the sea way to India was found, and his King renamed his Cabo Tormentoso (Cape of Storms) and called it Cabo de Bona Speranza or Cape of Good Hope—the hope of opening trade with India. Ten years later, in 1497-9, Vasco da Gama led the first squadron to Calicut and brought home the first cargoes of eastern spices to travel round the Cape in European ships.

Christopher Columbus in Spain undertook to open a still easier path to eastern trade. In 1492 he discovered to the westward what he thought to be the islands of Asia. Within a dozen years it became apparent that he was mistaken and that his islands and the continent beyond them were something hitherto unguessed at. In the reign of the Emperor Charles V these western discoveries revealed surprising wealth. Hernando

Cortes conquered Mexico and found it full of gold and silver. Francisco Pizarro went down the west coast from Panama and conquered Peru, a region of still greater riches. The Portuguese discovered Brazil whilst sailing southwards to the Cape of Good Hope.

These events meant much to all Europe. They shifted the springs of enterprise and progress from its centre to its circumference, from Italy and the Mediterranean to the Atlantic coastlines of Portugal and Spain, and then to those of England, France, and the Netherlands. For two centuries the story of European expansion is that of a competition between five nations, the Portuguese and Spaniards as the pioneers, followed by the English, French, and Dutch as their supplanters.

England and France awoke early to the new conditions of growth. The Dutch were rather later; they had first to gain their independence by a long war against their Spanish masters. The pioneer nations, Portugal and Spain, staked out a vast claim before any others were ready to take part. From successive Popes the Portuguese obtained bulls entitling them to possess all heathen lands *usque ad Indos*, to the very limits of India itself. When Columbus returned in 1493 the Spanish sovereigns applied for a similar grant, and Pope Alexander VI (a Spaniard) issued bulls giving Spain everything to the west of a line to be drawn through the Atlantic from north to south. In 1494 the two powers signed the Treaty of Tordesillas which fixed the line at 370 leagues west of the Cape Verde Islands— rather more than half-way across the Atlantic. The rights of other nations were ignored, and for well over a century Spain and Portugal contended that they had none. The whole extra-European world, discovered or undiscovered, was 'prescribed', written down in advance as Spanish and Portuguese property.

Henry VII, friendly as he was to Spain, never agreed to this. He granted charters to Cabot and the Bristol men to discover and annex for England. In one of these grants he distinctly laid it down that he would respect the rights of others to lands *actually in their possession*, and to nothing more. In other words he stated the doctrine of effective occupation as against that of prescription as the test of colonial titles. England has ever since advocated that test, and it is now part of the law of nations. The French were equally emphatic. Francis I inquired whether

Adam had left a will nominating the Kings of Portugal and Spain as heirs to all his property, and French adventurers lost no time in giving point to the sarcasm. The early English voyagers found nothing of commercial value across the Atlantic except the Newfoundland fishery, and in accordance with Henry's doctrine they did not intrude in the Spanish West Indies. The French were more aggressive. Charles V and Francis I were frequently at war, and from 1521 Frenchmen were a scourge to Spaniards in the west, where they robbed and killed by land and sea. For half a century before Drake was heard of this went on, and the Spanish Indies had been sacked from end to end before ever an Englishman had been seen there. When the Reformation began in France the sea-faring population were especially drawn to the new doctrines. By 1570 many of the French sailors were Huguenots, and this added to the savagery of their warfare with the Catholic Spaniards.

Under Henry VIII the English did little, for the Anglo-Spanish alliance kept them from imitating the French. Nevertheless there was some trespass on Portuguese claims. William Hawkins of Plymouth carried on a trade with West Africa and Brazil for several years. Southampton men followed his example. They brought back Guinea pepper and 'elephants' teeth' and valuable dyewoods, to say nothing of curiosities like parrots and monkeys and a live Brazilian chief with a precious stone embedded in his chin. They claimed, both in Guinea and Brazil, that they were doing no wrong to Portugal, since they traded with native tribes whom the Portuguese had not subdued. Portugal thought otherwise, claimed the right to both coasts, and sent out ships of war to beat off the intruders. It may have been for this reason that the English desisted. After a dozen years' activity they adventured no more.

Under Edward VI the condition of English trade grew alarming. The transformation of ploughland into sheep pasture deprived many hands of employment and led to an over-production of wool and cloth. At the same time the European markets were unsettled by the wars arising from the Reformation. It was vitally important to find new markets for English goods, and these could only exist in distant continents. In 1553 a new merchant company dispatched Sir Hugh Willoughby to seek a north-east passage to Asia. He was frozen to death on the Murman coast, but his second-in-command, Richard Chan-

cellor, discovered the White Sea, and landed in Russia. He
went overland to Moscow and made a treaty of commerce with
the Czar Ivan the Terrible. This led to a valuable new trade,
and the merchants were thenceforward known as the Muscovy
Company. In the same year 1553 Thomas Wyndham reopened
the Guinea trade. He did so at a new place, the Gold Coast,
which had not been reached by William Hawkins. He died in
the course of the voyage, but his ship brought back a large
quantity of gold. Mary became Queen of England, and her
husband, Philip of Spain, took the part of Portugal in its protests against the venture. The government therefore ordered
the stoppage of the African trade. In spite of this it went on,
and there were numerous expeditions to the Gold Coast for
many years. With their sovereign siding with the foreigner it
was left to the traders to state the English case. 'We be merchants,' they said, 'who, by common usage of the world, do use
traffique in all places of the world. We have of late resorted to
sundry places both towards the south and north parts of the
world, and with them traffiqued, and from them returned
quietly, thinking that without any offence we might use there
the same liberty that we use and do find in all other places.'
It was a gently-worded challenge to the monopoly of prescription, but it was seriously meant, as Portugal and Spain were
to find.

John Hawkins, the son of William, trespassed upon the monopoly on both sides of the Atlantic. He went to Guinea for negro
slaves and took them to the West Indies, where he sold them to
the Spanish colonists. Both the aggrieved governments denounced him as a pirate, but they overstated their case. The
truth was that their own subjects found it profitable to infringe
the monopoly, and without their help Hawkins could not have
carried on his business. He was accused of capturing Portuguese
slave-ships on the Guinea coast, but in some cases at least there
is evidence that there was merely a show of violence and that
the Portuguese really sold him the goods. On the Spanish side
he committed no act of piracy. The planters were eager to buy
from him. The officials, to save their faces, made a pretence of
resistance, but easily gave way, and generally wrote him a
certificate of good conduct at his departure. He was on quite
good terms with most of these Spaniards and repeatedly expressed his desire to do King Philip a service. He probably had

in mind some service against the French corsairs who were then ruining the trade of the West Indies. King Philip, however, was obdurate. He would maintain the monopoly at all costs. He sent out strict orders to treat the Englishman as the pirate which he was not. In 1568 the Viceroy of Mexico, a high officer just arrived from Spain, fell upon Hawkins in the port of San Juan de Ulua. It was an act of treachery, for the Viceroy had entered the harbour with a promise to observe the peace. Hawkins lost four of his ships and many of his men. He escaped, along with his young kinsman Francis Drake, to plan new visits to the Indies for purposes quite other than those of peaceful trade. This event, with another in Europe at the same time, marks the rupture of the Anglo-Spanish friendship which had lasted since the days of Henry VII.

The fact that the monopoly rested on the Pope's grant, and the other fact that England under Elizabeth became a Protestant country, imported an element of religious bitterness into the commercial dispute. The bitterness has nevertheless been somewhat exaggerated. Englishmen treated Spanish prisoners with kindness, and Spanish commanders generally behaved well to Englishmen in their power. It was the Inquisition that tortured and slew the unfortunate captives, not as Englishmen but as heretics. When the long quarrel grew into open war it was more decently waged upon the sea than were the religious struggles on the continent of Europe, where atrocities were the rule rather than the exception. Between Frenchmen and Spaniards the case was different. There was a deadly hatred between them. The Huguenot rovers killed every priest who fell into their hands, and often their other prisoners as well. The Spaniards retaliated, and some shocking massacres resulted.

With trade in the Indies denied to them, the English adventurers took to plundering. John Hawkins entered the government service and remained at home to organize the navy for the war which loomed in the future. Francis Drake and many others sought fortune in the west. Many of their exploits are but dimly known, but Drake in 1572–3 came into the limelight with a landing on the Isthmus of Panama and the capture of a large consignment of gold from the Peruvian mines. Drake, unlike Hawkins, was a pirate at this stage of his career, for war had not been declared. His own view was that he was taking reparation for the treacherous attack at San Juan, and it is evident that the Queen sympathized. He certainly took a good deal more than he had lost. He did it with great good humour. The only Spaniard against whom he had a grudge was the Viceroy of Mexico. If he could meet him, he said, he would teach him how a gentleman should keep his word.

Drake's next exploit was the voyage of circumnavigation in 1577–80. He passed the Straits of Magellan and took great booty on the Peruvian coast. With his ship ballasted with treasure he then sought a way home by the North West Passage, trying it from the Pacific side. He soon gave up that attempt and crossed the ocean to the Spice Islands of eastern Asia. There he made a treaty of commerce with the Sultan of Ternate in the Moluccas, who was an enemy of the Portuguese. Still pressing westwards he crossed the Indian Ocean, rounded the Cape, and turned northwards up the Atlantic to England— 'the world encompassed'. Opinions vary about the motive of this great voyage. The old view was that the plunder of Peru was the primary object, and that all the rest was merely to find a way out when the work was done. Recent research suggests that the Queen, who certainly stood behind Drake, sent him to open an English route to the Spice Islands, and that the treasure snatching was his own unauthorized contribution to the plan. There is no doubt that great importance was attached to his treaty with the Sultan, and that it had much to do with the foundation of the East India Company twenty years afterwards. In 1584 there was a project for Drake to lead another expedition to the Spice Islands, but it came to nothing owing to the outbreak of war with Spain.

The Spice Islands and the best way thither occupied many minds in the middle years of Elizabeth. Gilbert, Frobisher, and Davis all worked for the discovery of the North West Passage, and the Muscovy Company sent out another expedition to try the North East in 1580. Sir Humphrey Gilbert was an ardent believer. His *Discourse* has been mentioned in a previous section. A map drawn for him not long before his death has recently been discovered. It depicts no less than three separate passages from Atlantic to Pacific through or round the North American continent. It was known after Frobisher's attempts that the way round the north of Labrador, if it existed, would be rendered difficult by ice. The belief in a more southerly channel through what is now the United States was therefore more attractive. It led to a scheme for planting a colony on the American coast-line, a project which Gilbert contemplated at the time of his death, and which his half-brother Sir Walter Ralegh took up afterwards. Ralegh, although not in the first rank as a man of action, was a deep and original thinker. His Virginia colony was to serve three purposes. It would provide a settlement for the unemployed of England, always numerous from the Reformation onwards. It would serve as a base of exploration for the Passage. It would also be 'a bridle' to Spanish power in the West Indies, for the winds and currents compelled shipping from the Caribbean to pass near the North American coast, and an English post there would threaten the treasure route.

Ralegh never went to Virginia himself, but he sent expeditions under others and planted a colony in 1585. The outbreak of war in that year prevented his plantation from being properly nourished in its infant stage, and the undertaking was abandoned. Twenty years later, in time of peace, Virginia was soundly established, although by that time Ralegh was in the Tower and his task had fallen to others. His restless mind had in the meantime been drawn to another project. He had heard stories of a wealthy native state in the unexplored parts of South America. To find this Empire of Guiana, to take it under English protection and to utilize its gold against the Spaniard, became the dream of his later life. He led an expedition to the Orinoco in 1595, but brought home nothing but encouraging reports picked up from the Indians.

With the beginning of the Spanish War in 1585 the early series of English attempts to trade, explore, and colonize beyond the ocean came for the most part to an end. Their importance lies more in their promise than in their performance. They fired the imagination of the people and convinced them that their future lay upon the water. Gone for ever were the dreams of empire in France. The men of the newer England thought of colonies in America, North and South, and in the West Indies as well; of trade in gold and slaves on the coast of Africa; of the still richer trade in the spices and gems of the east. Active minds set themselves to educate their country in the necessary studies of geography and navigation. There was much to be done, for England was backward in such learning. Robert Thorne, an English merchant at Seville, was a pioneer. In 1527 he addressed to Henry VIII a *Declaration of the Indies*, in which he laid it down that 'no land is unhabitable, nor sea unnavigable'. Richard Eden in the discouraging reign of Mary collected foreign books and translated their wisdom into English. John Dee the Elizabethan philosopher was a high authority in all branches of practical science, consulted by merchants and seamen, a maker of maps and a solver of problems in navigation. In his writings is found the earliest use of the phrase 'the British Empire'. Greatest of all these students was Richard Hakluyt the clergyman. He was no Dutchman, as his peculiar name might suggest, but of an ancient Anglo-Welsh family.[1] He spent all his time and most of his income in collecting, translating, and publishing every scrap of knowledge he could gain about the wonderful worlds beyond the seas. There was no money in it; such books did not pay the cost of printing. It was a labour of patriotism. The list of his works is long, but he is best known to-day by his *Principal Navigations of the English Nation*, from which we draw much of our knowledge of the deeds of the time. Drake and Gilbert and Ralegh consorted with these men and strove to turn their aspirations into fact.

But after all the nation counted for most. Leaders must have followers, and it was the valour of unknown heroes that made possible the renown of the great. Every voyage in those days involved all the risks of war. Even a harmless trade with Spain or Portugal might lead 'to the thumb-screw and the stake, for the glory of the Lord'. The cabin-boy of a ship lying at Seville was punished by his master. He went off in a temper to the Spaniards and told them there were forbidden books on board. The ship was searched and some Bible or prayer book found in the captain's chest. The Inquisition received him. Cecil complained to the Spanish ambassador in 1563 that a number of Englishmen had been burnt in Spain.

A venture through the Mediterranean might lead, and often did, to capture by Turkish pirates and life ended as a galley-slave. One such slave has left his record, John Foxe, who after fourteen years of bondage saw his chance and took it, raised a revolt among his fellow-slaves, seized a galley, and dashed out of harbour for the open sea. He was luckier than most. The tropical passage to Africa or the Caribbean was more perilous

[1] Hakluyt seems to be a corruption of Ap Cluyd, from the Forest of Cluyd in the Welsh marches.

still. Death was less a risk than a certainty for most of those who
sailed. John Hawkins in 1567 led four hundred men and boys
out of Plymouth Sound. Less than a hundred saw their native
land again. They were steady, well-conducted men. It was
not 'drink and the devil' that did for them, but poisoned arrows,
tropical fevers, hunger and thirst and Spanish guns. In Wyndham's pioneer Guinea voyage of 1553 there was no fighting,
nothing but peaceful trade from first to last. But of a hundred
and forty who sailed only the forty came home. Drake's
Panama raid of 1572 was a brilliant success, but only thirty of
his seventy-three men lived to boast of it. As for the failures,
we may quote John Davis in the Straits of Magellan in 1591.
The Straits beat him, not to his dishonour; for he made an
English port with fifteen survivors of his crew of seventy-six.
These figures read like the record of infantry battalions in the
Great War. They are the price of duty in the sixteenth century
as in the twentieth. There is no romance about them.

IV. THE COUNTER-REFORMATION

The Catholic Church, on surveying the breaches wrought in its
ancient fabric by Martin Luther and Henry VIII, was obliged
to admit that the fabric had not been of unimpeachable
material. The last four important Popes of the old order,
Alexander VI, Julius II, Leo X, and Clement VII, had displayed conduct varying from the frankly criminal to the weakly
time-serving, but they had all been of the world worldly and
in no sense a pattern of Christian conduct to the Christendom
of their time. From such men no honest reform of the Church
was to be expected, and the larger opinion of the time demanded
the calling of a general council. The council met at Trent in
1545, but the wars of the succeeding years interrupted its work.
It was resumed after the pacification of 1559 and concluded its
sittings in 1563. The Council of Trent decided definitely
against any concessions to the Protestants. It affirmed the
Catholic view on disputed points of doctrine, enacted a stricter
discipline for the clergy, and left the papal supremacy untouched. To use a modern political term, it provided a platform
for those who sought to revive the power of the Church. There
were many who were willing to devote themselves to that work,
particularly the members of the Society of Jesus, founded by the

Spaniard Ignatius Loyola in 1540. The zeal of the Jesuits had an effect beyond their own ranks. The energy of churchmen, from the Pope downwards, was devoted more singly to the interests of the Church, and it became impossible thenceforward for a man of the character of Alexander VI to mount the papal throne. Whilst aims were purified and energies concentrated, the methods of the revival were borrowed from the past. The Holy Inquisition, as elaborated in Spain, was extended to Portugal, Italy, the Netherlands, and the Spanish colonies in America.

Lutheranism was a visibly failing force by the time of Luther's death in 1546. The Protestant advance was thenceforward led *Calvinism* by a younger man, John Calvin, a Frenchman who took up his abode at Geneva. Calvin's own doctrines were too extreme and eccentric for widespread acceptance, but in moderated form they were the inspiration of the resistance to the Counter-Reformation begun at Trent. They penetrated certain sections of French society, the nobles of the south and west, the richer burghers of many towns, and the seamen of all the ocean provinces but Brittany. They found adherents in Bohemia and in the Rhineland, and thence spread to the Spanish Netherlands of Philip II. The Marian persecution in England had the effect of introducing them here, for many Protestant clergy fled overseas, found refuge at Geneva or Frankfort, and came back in 1559 imbued with Calvinistic tenets—the germ of English Puritanism which was one day to grow so great. In Scotland the same process produced a rapid success, the most easily won victory of the Reformation. John Knox, an early Protestant, was exiled for his belief, lived in England under Edward VI, fled from Mary to Geneva, and returned to Scotland in 1559. He put himself at the head of a revolt against the ancient Church, already attacked by nobles greedy for abbey lands. In 1560, with English aid, the reformers triumphed and expelled the French troops who sought to maintain the old order. The effect was lasting. Scottish Calvinism reinforced that of England, and alliance took the place of enmity between the two peoples.

These two European movements, of the Counter-Reformation on the one hand and of Calvinism on the other, were the cause that the evolution of England in the next half-century was largely shaped by outside forces. Elizabeth's own intention in her settlement of 1559 had been not very far removed from that

of Henry VIII. She designed a church which should be acceptable to English conservatism by embodying a strong tinge of
Catholic practice, and to English nationalism by repudiating
the papal authority. But the Counter-Reformation would
respect no such settlement. It aimed at the reconquest of England and all the revolted areas of Europe. The continental
Calvinists were weak though heroic. They looked to England
for aid, and England realized that if they fell she would fall too.
She had to support them and fight the Catholic powers; it was
a condition of her own freedom. Patriotism therefore meant
Protestantism, and in the course of the struggle England became
what she had not hitherto been, a Protestant country.

The evolution may be seen in the mass and in individuals.
The people of Devon were mainly Catholics in 1549, when they
revolted against Cranmer's new Prayer Book. Thirty years later,
having taken the lead in the maritime defence against the
Counter-Reformation, they were ardently Protestant, and
Hawkins and Drake, Puritans both, were their heroes. In
London the process was similar. The city had quietly watched
the burning of Protestants in the last years of Henry VIII, and
even the hanging of a man merely for eating flesh on a Friday.
The Smithfield fires of Mary aroused questionings. But it was
the war of the Dutch Calvinists against the Inquisition, the
dispatch of troops to help William of Orange, and the tales of
refugees from the most ferocious cruelties yet on record that
made London what it was for the ensuing century, the stronghold of English Puritanism. In the north and north-west,
remote from the struggle, Catholicism lingered in appreciable
strength. In the east and the south men realized that they must
fight it or lose their independence.

In the first ten years of Elizabeth's reign the new conditions
were only gradually understood. It was five years, in fact, before
the Council of Trent concluded its labours. When the Queen
mounted the throne the Anglo-Spanish alliance was still active,
although the burnings and the loss of Calais had rendered it
unpopular. Philip indeed was making a show of broad-minded-
ness; he had allowed his wife to bear the odium of the persecution, and he had not yet begun strong measures against his
Netherland subjects. The death of Mary was a blow to his
political schemes, and he tried to maintain the English alliance,
first by offering to marry Elizabeth and then by refusing aid to

the enemies who sought to depose her. So long as England and Spain could hope for one another's help the struggle between Protestantism and the Counter-Reformation was postponed. The date of the change is 1568–9. Before that date the leading men of England were neither extremely Protestant nor markedly anti-Spanish. After it they were both.

If the sentiments of the English were shaped by foreign events, their actions were moulded by their geographical position. England stood literally at the cross-roads of international power, at the point of intersection of two lines of political influence. To the south lay France, whose House of Valois was ambitious to dominate Europe. France had an outpost in Scotland, ruled by Mary Stuart, the widow of a Valois king and the daughter of a princess of Guise, the most powerful family in France. The connecting link was the North Sea, bordered by the long east coast of England. The Royal Navy of England, based on the Thames estuary, could command and cut the Franco-Scottish communications. Obviously, if the French could gain control of England they would be in an unassailable position, with a compact north-to-south empire giving law to all the rest of Europe. In the first ten years of Elizabeth they had a fair chance of achieving this control, for their Scottish deputy Mary Stuart, a descendant of Henry VII, had in Catholic eyes a better right to the English throne than had Elizabeth herself. To become Queen of England was the constant aim of the Queen of Scots. Hence her intrigues with the Catholic north of England, and hence also Elizabeth's support of the Calvinist followers of John Knox. It was high politics under a religious guise. Elizabeth checkmated the peril by ensuring the triumph of the Scottish Reformation.

The other line of political influence ran from west to east, and again England stood midway between its extremities. Philip II was left by his father Charles V as sovereign of a mighty empire which had the disadvantage of being ill-knit. Its head-quarters were Spain, whose armies were the best in Europe. It owned part of Italy and dominated the rest, and from the Italian sea-ports it drew a fleet of galleys which commanded the Mediterranean. Its possessions in America supplied gold and silver, but the broad Atlantic was an unsafe highway, long beset by the French corsairs, soon to be assailed by the English also. But the real strength of the Spanish empire was in none of these regions.

The importance of England to the France-Scotland and Spain-Netherlands combinations at Elizabeth's accession

SCOTLAND under Mary Stuart

Dumbarton Leith

ENGLAND

Bristol London
Dover
Plymouth Calais

Amsterdam
Antwerp
NETHERLANDS
(Philip II)

Rouen

St.Malo

FRANCE
(Valois)

Rochelle

Bordeaux

Miles

0   100   200   300

Coruna

Bilbao

SPAIN
(Philip II)

PORTUGAL

Lisbon

Seville

Cadiz

It lay in the commercial energy of the Netherlands, whose cities were wealthy and civilized beyond any in Europe. And the connecting link between Spain and the Netherlands ran through the narrow seas of the Channel, bordered by England on one side and France on the other, a perilous bottle-neck for the greatest stream of commerce then flowing in the world. Thus it was a matter of life and death for the Spanish Empire to have the service of England and its navy. For that Philip had married Mary of England, and offered to marry Elizabeth, heretic though she was. For that he maintained the alliance for the next ten years, much as he hated the English and all their works.

England occupied the central square in a game of noughts-and-crosses. If either side, France-Scotland or Spain-Netherlands, could write its mark on England, it could cry victory and dominate Europe. For ten years Elizabeth defended her square against both with the ingenious diplomacy of which she was a master. Then the board caught fire and flamed up in the wars of the Counter-Reformation—all except the English centre. Elizabeth's ingenuity continued more masterly than ever. She fed the flames overseas, gave her rivals plenty to do in putting them out, and prevented them from carrying the torch across the water and setting fire to England. At the end England stood free, Protestant, and unscathed. That is the Queen's title to fame. She did not start the fire. No single person did, not even Philip II. The world was in an inflammable state, and any short-sighted action was bound to cause a catastrophe. The policy of the Counter-Reformation was the direct agency, but we can hardly blame the Catholic Church for seeking to recover what it believed to be its own.

The great fire of the religious wars began slowly. Mary Queen of Scots, Catholic and French, bickered for years with her subjects, Protestant and allies of Elizabeth. She was guilty of follies if not of crimes, and at length her subjects had had enough of her. They rose in arms and deposed her, and in 1568 she fled to seek refuge in England. To seek refuge, and something more. For she never gave up her claim to the English crown. Whilst expecting to be treated as a guest and to be given aid against her Scots, she intrigued all the time with the English Catholics and plotted to oust her hostess from the throne. No wonder Elizabeth made her a prisoner. It is not the harshness but the moderation that is remarkable. In the France or Spain of that day such a problem would have been quickly settled by a dose of poison. The presence of Mary in England soon caused trouble. In 1569 the Catholic lords rebelled in the Rising of the North, to depose Elizabeth and make her rival queen. They were dispersed without much fighting, and Mary remained in custody. That was the only instalment of the religious wars that took place on English soil. For the rest the story is of ceaseless plots defeated by ceaseless vigilance.

On the Continent affairs were much more serious. In 1562 Francis Duke of Guise massacred a body of Huguenots who were holding a service at Vassy. The Huguenot leaders took arms, and the first religious war broke out. Elizabeth, glad to see her Valois opponents occupied at home, sent aid to the rebels. They, however, had the worst of it, and the war ended in a compromise that settled nothing. A second scuffle in 1567-8 had a similar termination, but it left angry feelings in its train. The Huguenots began to think of making a determined struggle and achieving a real toleration for their faith. A third war began before the close of 1568 and was fiercely contested for two years. Although the Huguenots were beaten in the field they had sapped the power of the Valois monarchy, and they finished stronger than ever. In the course of this third war they discovered the value of sea-power. From their port of Rochelle they sent forth swarms of privateers to prey upon Catholic commerce. To the Huguenot rover all papists were the enemies of God, and the papist subjects of Philip II were especially desirable enemies on account of the rich trade they carried between Spain and the Netherlands. From 1568, therefore, the Counter-Reformation, strong on land, found itself attacked at sea. Englishmen joined the Huguenots, and the Channel was swept by privateers of both nations who cut the communications of the Spanish empire. Elizabeth did not declare war, but she made no effort to check the rovers. For the explanation we have to look to the Netherlands.

From the year 1559, when Philip II finally took up his abode in Spain, his Netherlands were in a state of unrest. His officials offended the Flemish burghers and nobles by cutting down their rights of self-government. The Netherlands had always been proud of their liberties, and it was now evident that Philip meant to make the seventeen provinces into a single state governed by a Spanish despotism. In addition he was determined to root out Protestant heresy, and to that end he established a modified form of the Spanish Inquisition. In the Netherlands, as in England, the Protestants were a minority; but they were very obstinate and ready to suffer all things for their faith. Calvinism spread rapidly among them, and it was much more a fighting creed than Lutheranism, which enjoined obedience to the civil power. Calvinism was the creed for rebels, and it proved very acceptable to the Dutch of the northern provinces, which contained all the chief seaports except Antwerp. The whole people, some for political reasons and some for religious, were simmering with discontent against their Spanish masters. Philip determined on strong measures. He regarded himself as the commander-in-chief of the Counter-Reformation, and he thought it scandalous that there should be heretics in his own dominions. In 1567 he dispatched the Duke of Alva with a Spanish army to crush resistance. Alva was a fine soldier who believed in discipline. 'I have tamed men of iron in my day,' he said, 'I shall know how to deal with these men of butter.' At first he succeeded. The iron carved and pounded the butter, although in the end it found a substratum of concrete. Alva's Council of Blood lopped off the heads of nobles and burghers, the Inquisition racked and burnt heretics rich and poor, a rising led by William Prince of Orange failed miserably—and then, in 1569, the Dutchmen copied the Huguenots and took to the sea. It was, had they known it, the death-blow to Philip's empire. The Protestant seamen of three nations held the narrow seas, and Alva, victorious on land, was cut off from his master in Spain.

Why did not Elizabeth oblige her royal brother-in-law and clear the Channel, as with her navy she could easily have done? Because she knew that the Counter-Reformation meant to conquer England, and that Alva's Spanish soldiers were the force designed to do it. The motley crowd of privateers were defending her shores at not a penny of cost to herself. A real regular navy would have made short work of them, but Alva had none, and neither had Spain. Elizabeth kept hers in port, reserved for higher purposes. Meanwhile she made a privateering stroke herself. Alva's troops were threatening mutiny for lack of pay. Philip borrowed money in Italy and hopefully dispatched it up-Channel, ninety-five chests of it, in half-a-dozen unarmed trading vessels. It was his first lesson in practical sea-power. The Huguenots hunted the treasure-ships like rabbits and chased them into English ports, Falmouth, Plymouth and Southampton. The treasure was stuck; left to itself, it would never get through. Elizabeth would not turn out a single cruiser as escort, and so it had to be landed in England. There the Queen settled its disposal by borrowing it herself from its original Italian owners. She repaid it in due time, but Alva went without his money. He taxed the Netherlanders instead, and goaded them into a fresh revolt that kept him busy for many a day. It was what the Queen wanted. Alva was a great man, but he could not hold down mutinous soldiers, fight Dutch rebels, and invade England at the same time.

This treasure business took place in the winter of 1568-9, just as John Hawkins came home from Mexico with his tale of treachery and massacre at San Juan de Ulua. The Dutchmen, the Sea Beggars as they were called, began privateering soon after, and the wars of the Counter-Reformation never ceased for the remainder of the century.

Philip and Alva were very sore at the loss of the money, but they dared not declare war. That would have brought the English navy out to add to their misfortunes. Instead they proclaimed a stoppage of all trade with England and encouraged Catholic plots for the overthrow of Elizabeth and the enthronement of Mary Stuart. Mary, it was true, had been no great friend of theirs. She belonged to the rival Valois interest. But the Valois power was sinking into hopeless decay, and she could expect little help from it. The Huguenots were growing more powerful, and the Valois family was at the end of its tether. Its last members were three feeble brothers who reigned in succession, Francis II, Charles IX, and Henry III. None of them had any force of character, and their mother, Catherine de Medici, alone prevented France from falling into chaos. She had no strength for outside adventures, and Mary Stuart looked to Spain for deliverance.

From 1569, therefore, began the period of the plots. The first is known as the Ridolfi Plot. In 1570 Pius V excommunicated Elizabeth, and a copy of his bull was found on a summer morning nailed to the Bishop of London's door. Roberto Ridolfi, a Florentine banker, came over in 1571 ostensibly on financial business, but secretly as the Pope's agent to organize the conspiracy. He arranged that the Duke of Norfolk should lead a rebellion, depose Elizabeth, and place Mary Queen of Scots on the throne. Norfolk's reward was to be the hand of Mary, but he was timorous and stipulated for a Spanish invasion to support him. Ridolfi, therefore, went first to Alva at Brussels and then to Philip at Madrid to arrange for their help. Alva had no great faith in the project, but Philip II gave his consent and even discussed with his council the feasibility of having Elizabeth assassinated by way of an opening. He also bargained with John Hawkins to provide the necessary ships of war to cover the invasion. Here he was completely taken in, for Hawkins was no traitor and was simply getting even with Spain for his losses at San Juan. Hawkins kept Sir William Cecil informed of his proceedings and induced Philip to release some of his English prisoners. Cecil was aware of the plot and arrested Norfolk in time to foil it. Norfolk was executed, a weak man who had been the tool of others. Mary Stuart might as justly have been put to death, but Elizabeth would not hear of it. The Spanish ambassador, also implicated, was merely expelled from the country, after which the whole affair was allowed to blow over.[1]

Sir William Cecil, created Lord Burghley in 1571, was the pilot who had weathered this storm. It was the first of many such, and his difficulty was always the Queen's disregard of danger. She would not take proper precautions for her own safety, or allow him to arrest men whose guilt was obvious. In particular she would not give up hopes of a reconciliation with Mary Stuart, although Mary never ceased to plot revolution. The English Catholics were placed in a difficult position by the Pope's bull, which forbade them to support an excommunicated queen. They had to choose between their religion and their allegiance. Some gave up their religion. Others became active revolutionaries, encouraged by Jesuit priests who penetrated England in disguise and worked hard to stir up trouble. They were plucky men, for when caught they were executed.

[1] The Ridolfi Plot had many ramifications not described in this brief account. The full story may be read in the pages of Froude; it is a detective thriller in real life. Mr. Belloc contends that Hawkins was at the outset a genuine traitor. He does not prove it; and Hawkins, as his whole record shows, was not the man to sell his country. Of the letters that must have passed between the various parties, probably not one in five has been preserved. Hence the scope for unsupported assertion.

It is, however, unfair to charge Elizabeth and Burghley with religious persecution. They had shown their tolerance in the first ten years of the reign, when the only penalties had been a system of fines, hardly ever enforced, for non-attendance at church. It is true to say that they did not execute Catholics for their religion, but only for treason. If they had not done so the treason would have been successful and England would have plunged into civil wars such as those which ravaged France and the Netherlands. Even so, the executions were comparatively few.[1] The vast majority of the Catholics lived undisturbed, even when their views were perfectly known. The government understood their difficulties and had no wish to drive them into revolt. The Inquisitors took the opposite course in the Spanish Netherlands, and the independent Dutch Republic was the consequence.

On these lines history proceeded for the next fifteen years. In 1572 Catherine de Medici and Henry Duke of Guise tried to wipe out the Huguenots by the Massacre of St. Bartholomew. Thousands perished, but the cause survived. Rochelle continued to send out its corsairs, and in a few years Henry of Navarre began his victorious career as leader of the French Protestants. In 1572 also the Sea Beggars[2] were strong enough to take to the land. They captured Brille and Flushing, and a revolt spread through all the Dutch provinces. It was never put down, although Alva strove hard enough. He was recalled as a failure, but other Spanish commanders did no better. William of Orange slowly wore down the Spanish tyranny. Philip offered a reward for his death, and he was murdered in 1584; but his work could not be undone. Whenever Dutch energy flagged Elizabeth sent English help, unofficially and without declaring war. At home she was growing stronger. England was prospering in peace, and the ruin of the Netherlands transferred their trade to London. Philip realized too late that he had approached his problem from the wrong side. He could not conquer the Netherlands while England supported them. He should have built his Armada and closed with England a dozen years before he did. He would have had a better chance, for

[1] The average was seven per year from 1575, when the Jesuit revolutionary movement commenced.

[2] A contemptuous term applied to the Dutch rovers, and adopted by them.

the English navy was not in a good state when John Hawkins took charge of it in 1577. The ten years' work he put in before the Armada came rendered the fleet much fitter to face the trial.

As it was, Philip fought his Dutchmen, but relied on plots to overcome Elizabeth. In 1583 the conspiracy of Francis Throckmorton, for the same general objects as that of Ridolfi, ended in the execution of the ringleaders and the expulsion of another ambassador. At the same time John Somerville planned to shoot the Queen, was detected, and hanged himself. He was a minor ill-doer unconnected with Spain. In 1586 Anthony Babington hatched a more dangerous conspiracy with John Ballard, one of the Jesuit missionaries. Sir Francis Walsingham, who was now Burghley's second in state business, was early aware of it. He allowed it to go forward in order to gain proof of Mary's guilt. When the time was ripe he denounced her. Babington and Ballard were of course executed, but Elizabeth was still reluctant to proceed against Mary. She yielded at length to the national demand. Mary was tried and beheaded at Fotheringay early in 1587. Her trial has been represented as unfair, but of her general encouragement of these plots there is not the slightest doubt. By present standards no trial was fair in those days, for modern rules of evidence had not been thought of. Mary's continental friends did not question her guilt; their only doubt was whether Elizabeth would be fool enough to let her off again. To Philip II her death was not unwelcome. He had resolved to invade England, and he preferred to do it in his own interest rather than in that of Mary Stuart. When he heard of the execution he went forward with the plans for the Armada. England and Spain were already virtually at war. Its outbreak is generally dated from 1585, but there was no declaration, merely a drift from lesser to greater hostilities. Until the very sailing of the Armada the war could have been called off, and many thought it would be.

V. THE WAR WITH SPAIN

It is not the object of this account to give the full details of the Spanish War, but to indicate briefly the objects of the combatants and the means and methods they used to accomplish them. The story has a living interest, for even at this late date there are points in it which, to take a liberty with Mr. Kipling,

The Armada War 1585-1604

'could tell us a lot that would save us a lot on the things that we ought to know'.

In number of ships the English navy stood in 1585 at about half the strength at which Henry VIII had left it. Elizabeth and Burghley had no monastic spoils to expend, and they were obliged to economize. They contented themselves with less than thirty vessels, large and small. Until the middle of the reign the quality of these ships had not been good. Jobbery and corruption prevailed in the dockyards, stores were charged for but not bought, and some of the large ships were mere wrecks unable to put to sea. Even the famous *Revenge* was alleged to have been built of unseasoned plank 'of no continuance'. In 1577 the Queen (or rather Burghley) appointed John Hawkins Treasurer of the Navy. He was a man of business as well as a seaman, and he put down dishonesty with a strong hand. He made enemies, but he cared little for popularity when the national defence was at stake. He was accused of pocketing the gains which he forced others to disgorge. His own claim was that he had reduced expenditure and increased efficiency. The financial records prove the first contention, and as for the second, the test was to come in the Armada campaign of 1588. After that there were no more charges against Hawkins. England, therefore, entered the war with a small royal navy of high quality. She had also a great number of armed merchantmen and sea rovers owned by private individuals. They did much damage to Spanish commerce but very little regular fighting. It is a false claim, although often repeated, that the privateers beat the Armada. The men of the time gave the credit to the navy and complained of the 'simple' (i.e. negligible) service rendered by the others.

Spain had a strong force of galleys, oar-driven craft, chiefly supplied and manned from her Italian possessions. With this fleet she disputed the command of the Mediterranean with the Turks and gained in 1571 the crushing victory of Lepanto. But for various reasons the galleys were useless outside the Mediterranean, and there was hardly any attempt to employ them against England. For ocean work there was a small squadron of sailing warships provided to escort the treasure fleets, and when Philip II became King of Portugal in 1580 he took over twelve good Portuguese vessels and made them his own. He built a few more before 1588, but his effective fighting ships of that year were not more numerous than those of England. The Armada, like the fleet of its opponents, was made imposing to the eye by crowds of merchantmen that could do little service. Philip never found a Hawkins to do his naval business efficiently. His ships were costly and rotten, and the victualling was scandalous even in that incompetent age. In armament there was a great contrast between the English and Spanish services. The English believed in pounding the enemy with heavy guns and in avoiding hand-to-hand fighting. The Spaniards had a lingering medieval contempt for gunnery. Their aim was to board, sword in hand. They filled their ships with soldiers and neglected their artillery.

In 1585 it was obvious that the plots, plundering raids, and unofficial help to the Dutch were developing into serious war. Philip seized the English merchantmen in Spanish ports, and Elizabeth determined on reprisal. She had two seamen of the first rank in Hawkins and Drake. Drake was the more prominent as a leader of fleets, and Hawkins as their organizer. Hawkins had also done some original thinking on the problem of overthrowing Spanish power. He looked for the enemy's weakest spot and decided that it lay in the treasure-route from the West Indies to Europe. The treasure from the West was the life-blood of Philip's empire. With it he financed his armies in the Netherlands, helped the Catholic cause in the French civil wars, and might perhaps build a navy strong enough to conquer England. Once cut the treasure-route and Philip was beaten. The great financiers of the time considered this reasoning sound. There was then no system of credit and paper money and the raising of vast national loans. Without hard coin one could not have a fleet or an army.

Hawkins proposed as early as 1579 to send an English force to the Caribbean, to capture the treasure fleet if possible, and in any case to destroy the Spanish ports and the local shipping that fed the trade to Europe. But this was not all. The Azores were an island group half-way across the Atlantic, at which the Spaniards from the west and the Portuguese carracks from the east were alike obliged to touch. He therefore advocated a continuous blockade of the Azores by successive squadrons of the Queen's navy. Each squadron should stay out four months and then be relieved by another, with never an interval between them. If this were done, he claimed that not a ducat would get

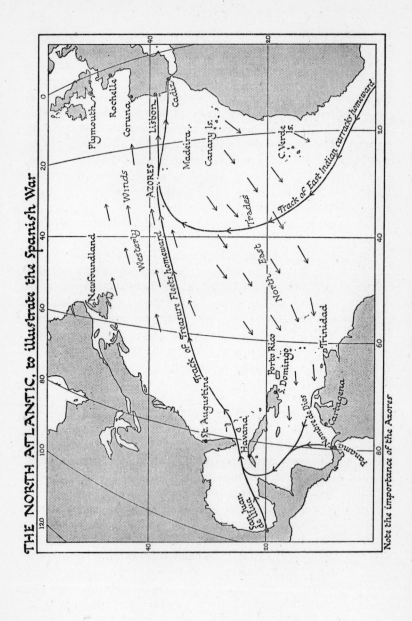

THE NORTH ATLANTIC, to illustrate the Spanish War

Note the importance of the Azores

through to Spain and that Philip would be compelled to sue
for peace. Finally, Hawkins was opposed to fighting on the
continent of Europe. 'Let us', he said, 'have as little to do in
foreign countries as may be (but of mere necessity), for that
breedeth great charge and no profit at all.' The advice was
good, for Tudor England was not a military nation, and its
armies were generally unsuccessful. The Queen and Burghley
neglected the hint. For them the war at sea was always a side-
show from which victory was not to be expected. They spent
four times as much on armies on the continent as they did upon
the navy, and at the end they had little to show for it. At the
same time they starved the navy, tried to get the work done on
the cheap by privateers, and never made the continuous effort
that Hawkins laid down as essential to speedy success. Their
war lasted nineteen years.

At the outset, however, they promised vigour. Drake was
allowed to make the opening stroke in the Caribbean. His fleet
was chiefly of privateers and comprised only two ships of the
navy. But Spain had no fleet in the West Indies, and so there
was no sea fighting to be done. Drake's fighting in 1585-6 was
all on land, and he handled his little expeditionary force
brilliantly. He first visited the Spanish coast and proved that
Philip could be insulted in his own harbours with impunity.
Then he plundered the Cape Verde Islands and sailed across
the Atlantic with the trade wind. He took Santo Domingo in
Hispaniola, Cartagena on the Spanish Main, both capital cities,
and St. Augustine in Florida, and whatever in these places was
not redeemed by ransom he burnt. He destroyed a quantity
of shipping and carried off no less than 240 guns from the forti-
fications. His booty almost paid for the expedition, and the
damage he had done cost a whole year's treasure-output to
make it good. As Hawkins had predicted, Philip had been
caught with his Indies imperfectly defended; and if the pressure
had been kept up he never could have defended them, for
without money coming in he could have equipped no fleets.

Hawkins wished to close the gap, before another western
expedition could be organized, by holding the Azores station
or at least blockading the coast of Spain. But the statesmen
were afraid lest the Guise party in France, now Philip's allies,
should try a raid across the Channel. They mobilized only
one-fifth of the navy and with it ordered Hawkins to 'ply up

and down' in the Channel. Not until the end of August, 1586, was he allowed to go to the Spanish coast, and by that time the rich Portuguese carracks from the East Indies had slipped in untouched. Their cargoes supplied Philip with some of the money he had lost in the west. Meantime the Earl of Leicester was leading an expensive army in the Netherlands. It was argued that it was necessary to avert a Dutch collapse, but in fact it did little service, and the Dutch would have been better helped by half the money it cost. The other half might well have given Spain the death-blow at sea.

In 1587 Philip determined on the invasion of England. He squeezed his subjects in a huge financial effort and began to gather the great Armada at Lisbon and Cadiz. Drake urged to be allowed to smite it before it was ready, and the Queen yielded, half against her will. She still hoped to make peace by bargaining, but Drake could persuade her when other men could not. The campaign of 1587 was Drake's masterpiece. He entered Cadiz and destroyed thirty large ships, mostly merchantmen. He found Lisbon too strongly fortified to be treated in like manner. There were many Spanish ships there, but they lacked the guns and stores that would have enabled them to put to sea. Drake, therefore, cruised off Cape St. Vincent and paralysed all efforts to transport these things from the Mediterranean until it was too late for the Armada to sail that year. Then he sailed for the Azores and captured an East Indian carrack with a lading of fabulous wealth. But nothing was done this year or the next to stop the homecoming of the western treasure. The Queen, in fact, was displeased with Drake's success because she feared it would spoil her peace negotiations.

The glory of Elizabeth and Burghley lies in the thirty years of diplomacy by which they had kept England out of trouble in a turbulent world. When war did come it was due to their merits that the country was strong enough to meet it. But they themselves did not shine in managing the war. That was inevitable. All history proves that the diplomatic mind is too subtle, sensitive, and pliable for the hard decisions of war. To postpone resolution, a habit fatal in a commander, is often a merit in a diplomatist. Burghley continued in office until his death in 1598. It might have been better if he had retired ten years earlier, but on the other hand England produced no man but

Walsingham with the makings of a great war minister; and
Walsingham died in 1590. Walsingham, although he knew less
about the navy than did Burghley, was always more ready to
listen to the sailors' plans. He was also convinced that the
Counter-Reformation could be beaten only by hard blows and
not by negotiation.

The Armada was positively to sail in 1588, and Philip secured
the respite essential to its preparation by amusing Elizabeth
with hollow peace discussions. It was his only diplomatic
success, and since his fleet was rotten and its commander
incompetent it led him only to a greater disaster. But for the
moment all went well. Spain had gained the initiative, England
was on the defensive. The whole strength of the royal navy was
turned out, but Elizabeth held it in port in spite of the protests
of Howard, Drake, Hawkins, and all the captains. Lord Howard
of Effingham, the Lord High Admiral, was the commander-in-
chief this year. He was not a seaman of lifelong training, but
he had studied his job and was wise enough to know his limitations. He framed his plans by the advice of his senior officers,
among whom Drake as vice-admiral ranked highest. The
Armada appeared in July and sailed up Channel to pick up
the Spanish army from the Netherlands and land it in Kent.
The English followed, 'plucking its feathers,' but avoiding close
action. Then, in the Straits of Dover, they found their opportunity when the Spanish formation had been broken by fire-
ships. At the Battle of Gravelines they won a decisive victory.
They did not sink many ships, but their gunnery inflicted heavy
losses and they themselves suffered hardly at all. The Spaniards,
inferior in manoeuvre, never had a chance to board. They
realized that they were fighting unarmed, for their guns were
too small and too few to inflict damage. They had suffered
heroically, but it was useless to continue. The Netherland
waters were shallow and dangerous, and the great Spaniards,
once entangled among the sandbanks, would have been destroyed in detail by the smaller English craft and the Dutchmen
who knew to an inch the depth of every channel and the set of
every current. The Armada fled up the North Sea, round
Scotland, and south by the Irish coast to Spain. It was then
that the shortcomings of their government slew thousands of
these brave men whom the English guns had spared. The ships
leaked, sank, or drove ashore, there were no pilots for the

northern coasts, the putrid victuals poisoned those who were not drowned. Less than half the fleet returned to Spain.

Next year Drake had his way and was given the command of the counterstroke. He remembered how brilliantly he had handled a landing force in 1585, when he had shown how a small army conveyed hither and thither in ships could multiply its efforts five-fold. He proposed to play the same game in Portugal, which was restive under Spanish domination. To rouse a revolt, to make Portugal a second Netherlands, promised the ruin of Philip II. The reasoning was persuasive but superficial. Patriotic Portuguese disliked Spanish rule, but there was lacking that Calvinistic fire which filled the Dutch with fury. Catholic Portugal was not, in fact, ready to die for Protestantism against Catholic Spain. To raid distant colonies was quite a different thing from invading the peninsula itself. That was to attack Philip at his strongest point, and England had no army with which to do it. A rabble of untrained men, without discipline or victuals, landed at Peniche and marched to Lisbon. It found the place ready and retired in disorder. Thousands died before reaching England, and the disaster was almost as great as that of the Spaniards the year before. Drake had ventured off his proper ground. It was left to a later age to show how a Peninsular War should be conducted. What Hawkins thought of it he had already stated. He was a large-minded man. 'I told you so' was not in his vocabulary. He uttered not a word of criticism on Drake's return.

The government might now have given the plans of Hawkins a trial. He promised success by a continuous blockade of the Azores, to cut off the western treasure and the wealth of the East Indies. Elizabeth and Burghley made only a pretence of doing it. They sent out small fleets, mostly of privateers, for summer cruises only, and left the way clear for the treasure to pass through in the intervals. Lack of faith, not of money, was to blame, for they were spending much on armies in these years, not only in the Netherlands but in France, where they fought for Henry of Navarre. The Spaniards adapted themselves to the conditions. They sent fast dispatch-boats to the West Indies with warning of the English movements, and regularly got their money through in the winter months. With this money Philip began to build a fighting navy much more formidable than the pretentious Armada of 1588.

By 1595 men were saying that Spain had been 'wakened, not weakened', and it was time for energetic measures. Drake and Hawkins were commissioned to repeat the West Indian raid of ten years before and stop the treasure at its source. This time the story was sadly different. Everywhere the Spanish ports were well garrisoned and fortified, and warned by small craft that outstripped the English fleet. Moreover, Philip was able to send out an ocean fleet himself and so impose a time-limit on the English operations. These failed successively at Grand Canary, Porto Rico, Cartagena and Panama, whilst the usual epidemics carried off hundreds of men. Hawkins died early in the voyage, and Drake before its close. The failure was the penalty of ten years' delay. In 1586, or even in 1589, the expedition could hardly have failed of success. Drake and Hawkins were both past their prime and so different in temperament that they could not pull together, but the real blame lies on the government that had not used them earlier.

Before the result was known another stroke had been launched with better success. The news of Philip's shipbuilding was alarming and gave promise of a second Armada. The policy of 1587 was repeated in 1596. Howard turned out once more, and with Ralegh and the Earl of Essex swooped on Cadiz in the best manner of Drake. The city was taken and gutted, and the Spaniards burnt much of their valuable shipping to prevent its falling into English hands.

It was the last vigorous stroke of the war at sea. Thenceforward the tale is of short cruises to the Azores, privateering raids which did little damage in the Indies, Spanish help to Irish rebels, and a great deal of commerce destruction. But neither side could deal a vital blow at the other. Meanwhile on land the Counter-Reformation was at last brought to a standstill. In France Henry of Navarre defeated the Spaniards and the Guises, declared himself a Catholic, and secured toleration for the Protestants by the Edict of Nantes. In the Netherlands Spain could not be beaten out of the Belgian provinces, which were Catholic, but she could not subdue the Dutch, and the Republic of the United Provinces was in effective being when Philip II died in 1598. It was many years before Spain admitted defeat, but her admission was not the thing that mattered.

Dutch independence and French toleration both rested on one basis, that England remained free and Protestant. The cardinal

fact was proved, that the Counter-Reformation could not strike
across the sea. So, in spite of all muddling and loss of opportunities, there is no doubt about the issue of the Spanish war.
It was a victory for the Reformation. But it might have been
won much earlier by an intelligent use of sea-power.

VI. THE TUDOR ACHIEVEMENT.

Some months before her death Elizabeth made her last speech
to Parliament. 'Though God hath raised me high,' she said,
'yet this I count the glory of my crown, that I have reigned
with your loves. . . . To be a king and wear a crown is a thing
more glorious to them that see it than it is pleasing to them
that bear it. For myself, I was never so much enticed with the
glorious name of a king or royal authority of a queen, as
delighted that God had made me his instrument to maintain
his truth and glory, and to defend this kingdom from peril,
dishonour, tyranny and oppression.' The members listened
with mixed feelings. They knew that she spoke truth. She
was nearly seventy, haggard, painted, worn out in the task she
still pursued. They could answer from their hearts, 'God save
Your Majesty,' but every generous man among them felt a
twinge of compunction at his heartstrings. For they had been
in open revolt against certain trade monopolies she had seen
fit to grant, and this was her manner of yielding. It was the
Tudor manner. The people had resisted their sovereign, and
yet she was their sovereign still, and they her loyal subjects.
Such was the spirit of the English monarchy, a thing to be felt
but not defined, once broken never to be restored.

The Queen was busy every day with affairs of state. Hers
was the final voice in every decision, sometimes the only voice
to carry some course that all her advisers condemned. Her
ministers were what the word means, servants, not dictators of
her policy. All ministers of the Tudors were expected to speak
their minds freely, to bring forth what wisdom was in them,
and to leave judgement to the sovereign. Even Henry VIII
had no use for a man who always agreed with him. He listened
to all counsels, weighed all suggested courses, and followed his
own. The Crown was the nation as an individual. The Crown
must seek the best advice and then be perfectly independent
in its action. 'Upon the king!' mused Shakespeare's greatest

king, 'Let us our lives, our souls, our debts, our careful wives, our children and our sins, lay on the king! We must bear all. O hard condition, twin-born with greatness, subject to the breath of every fool, whose sense no more can feel but his own wringing!'

Such an authority had need of roots deep in the national life. It found them in the local justices, whose duties have already been described. All routine business flowed upwards like the rising sap of state through the county leaders, the sheriff and the lord-lieutenant, to the Privy Council, in which sat with some dozen others the two or three intimate ministers who always had the ear of the Crown. The justice supervised his parish, the mayor his town, the lord-lieutenant his county, the Council the whole realm. The realm was then almost as wide, for all matters of news and action, as the Empire is now; from Plymouth or York to London and back was a week's riding. As the Tudor period advanced and government tackled ever new problems of administration and order, the central Council had to save itself from being overwhelmed with business by throwing off outlying branches to sift, settle, or transmit the regional problems. The Council sitting as a court in London was the Star Chamber. Its representative in Wales was the Council of Wales and the Marches, remodelled by Henry VIII in 1535 as part of a reform which divided Wales into its twelve shires and gave them representatives in Parliament. A similar offshoot was the Council of the North, reorganized after the Pilgrimage of Grace in 1536. The disposal of confiscated church property was placed under another branch called the Court of Augmentations. Finally, when Elizabeth settled the religious question by the Acts of Supremacy and Uniformity, she established the Court of High Commission to watch over their working. All these bodies were attended by Privy Councillors who maintained touch with the central institution.

The above were channels for official views and official action. But a people rapidly growing into a nation, intelligent and self-conscious as it had never been before, needed an outlet for its own opinions to be freely expressed. Parliament performed this function, its upward thrust of non-official representation dovetailing with the downward reach of the administrative roots. Under Henry VII Parliament was not very prominent. His problem was chiefly administrative, the restoration of order.

He called few Parliaments, but dealt with them judiciously and obtained without trouble the few new statutes necessary to his plans. Only under Wolsey's influence did Tudor government show a definite distrust of Parliament and a tendency to suppress it. Wolsey's ideals were rather foreign than English, and the public instinct was sound which viewed him as leading the state into doubtful courses. After his fall the great age of Parliament began with the assembly of 1529, which sat for seven years and passed the Acts that separated England from Rome. Thenceforward Parliaments were frequent although not regular, and the House of Commons became predominant because its members were more numerous and of more diversified talents than the Lords. On the whole the Tudor Parliaments preserved the right of free criticism and free decision. Their alleged subservience is a myth invented to square with the other myth of Tudor tyranny. They rejected many a measure promoted by Henry VIII. He humoured them sometimes with the royal air of condescension that sat so naturally upon him, but he never sought to coerce them. His royal state and dignity, he said, were never so high as when Parliament was sitting, when King and people were visibly working together. Elizabeth, more nervous and less patient, had many a sharp passage with her Commons. She would not have this said or that discussed, and she committed to the Tower honourable members who discussed them nevertheless. But the union of hearts was firm beneath the tantrums, as that last sacramental scene of withdrawing the monopolies testified.

The English people were more like a family, or like a great school, than they afterwards became. Distinctions of rank were strongly observed, distinctions of class very slightly. Edmund Dudley, an obscure lawyer, became the familiar spirit of Henry VII. Henry VIII beheaded him and made his son an earl. Elizabeth's chosen intimate the Earl of Leicester was his grandson. Thomas Cromwell, a blacksmith's son, reached the highest position a subject could attain. Hugh Latimer, a yeoman's son, died a bishop. Francis Drake, born in a peasant's cottage, shook the world. These are the few whose talents carried them highest. There were thousands of others who rose from rank to rank to the level for which they were fitted. The feudal baron of ancient lineage had gone, and class distinction based on distinctive manners and ethics had not set in. A

rising man could learn the etiquette proper to the rank he had
attained; his manners required no revision. Members of Parliament spat on the floor of the House as their constituents spat in
tap-rooms. The Queen could talk to foreign ambassadors in
their own tongues, and she could also swear at her councillors
in the idiom of her pikemen in Flanders. Table usages at Court
differed little from those in a tradesman's house. The squire's
younger son was often a merchant's apprentice. Whether he
rose to be a capitalist or remained a journeyman depended
solely on his merits. At sea this divorce of class from rank was
very evident. It was a common thing for a man to be commander of a ship in which his brother served in the forecastle.
Drake would not have his gentlemen carrying their land rank
to sea. All who were not ship's officers must 'haul and draw'
together. Corporal punishment in all ranks was the usual
method of discipline. The farmer thrashed his labourer, the
craftsman his apprentice, and the squire his children, daughters
as well as sons. Henry made Cromwell a peer, but frequently
punched his head. No lady-in-waiting was safe from Elizabeth's
bejewelled hand. It was not all to the bad. If people were
privileged to lose their tempers as superiors, they had learned
to keep them as subordinates.

The growth of London is a feature of the period, and it had
much to do with the success of the Tudor government. In the
fifteenth century London had been by no means predominant.
Political power had been spread among the great nobles, who
drew their strength from their country estates and the subordinate gentry who wore their liveries. Foreign trade had been
distributed over a large number of seaports. The wool had been
sent to the Calais Staple from half a dozen important havens on
the east coast. The Italians had brought their Mediterranean
wares to Southampton, whose customs receipts fell not far short
of those of London. Bristol had done a great deal of the business
with Bordeaux, Spain, and Portugal.

The breaking of the feudal baronage transferred government
business to the Crown, whose courts and offices were in Westminster and the City. Tudor Parliaments met invariably at
Westminster, and there collected all the wealthy and influential
men of the country. The powerful abbots disappeared and left
the rule of the Church solely to the bishops, who were often in
London to confer with the government; many of them kept

permanent town houses. Young men of wealth were welcome at the royal palaces, and it became the custom for them to complete their education by reading law for a year or two at the Inns of Court. All this created employment and stimulated London enterprise.

Above all, foreign commerce centred more and more in the capital. The old trades declined, and the new ones, needing government support, fell to the London merchants who had the ear of the King's ministers. The export of raw wool was transformed into the export of manufactured cloth. Blackwell Hall became the central mart for cloth from the whole country, and the London branch of the Merchants Adventurers, originally one among many, overshadowed the rest and monopolized control of the business with Flanders and Germany. The Muscovy Company of 1553 was founded as a London concern; so also were the Levant Company of 1581 and the East India Company of 1600. Southampton declined rapidly with the decline of Genoese and Venetian trade, and the Englishmen who supplanted the Italians were chiefly Londoners; one reason was that they often hired the armed vessels of the navy, and naval business was transacted in London. The new trade to West Africa was nearly all done from London, and Hawkins, although a Plymouth man, settled in the capital and financed his slaving voyages by the aid of government officials and London merchants. Again, London was the nearest rival, as an international exchange, to the cities of the Netherlands, and when Spanish folly ruined Antwerp its business migrated across the narrow sea to the security of the Thames. By the end of the century London was doing three-quarters of the country's foreign trade. Its people were firmly Protestant and increasingly Puritan. Their interest was in domestic peace and the maintenance of law. Their wealth and their loyalty were the chief support of the Tudor throne, against which no Pilgrimage of Grace or Rising of the North had any real chance of success. The twin cities of London and Westminster, with their dependent villages, attained for those times an enormous population, about one-third of a million people. Late in Elizabeth's reign it seemed to have gone too far, and laws were passed to forbid the building of any more houses in the capital. But such rules were never seriously enforced, and the 'great wen' continued to swell.

The instinct that doubted the wisdom of heaping all the national wealth on a few square miles of ground had much to be said for it. The glittering fabric of trade was in those stormy times precarious, and none knew it better than Elizabeth and Burghley as they watched the fair cities of the Netherlands sinking in flames and blood. The armies which did these things might yet visit England, and in that day of wrath all would depend on the numbers and the spirit of squires and yeomen and peasants. Though the domestic strength of the government might rest on the capital, the national strength of England sprang from the soil. For two centuries longer the statesmen never forgot it, and whilst the 'moneyed interest' created power, the 'landed interest' was always fostered to maintain it. Until a hundred years ago it was a maxim that England must be self-supporting, able to live of her own whatever tempests might rage without. Now we have lost that advantage, whilst gaining much in its place. The thing may have been inevitable, but it is none the less deplorable.

The countrymen passed through a bad time in the mid-sixteenth century, and not the least of the Elizabethan achievements was to reform and re-settle the exploitation of the soil. The volume of commercial enterprise and the standard of comfort throughout Europe were rising, with a consequent increased demand for cloth or the wool with which to make it. The transmission of the precious metals in bulk from across the ocean began with the capture of Mexican gold by Cortes in 1519, continued with the looting of Peru by Pizarro in 1532, and settled down into a regular stream with the working of the silver mines in both regions a few years later. This influx of gold and silver spread over all Europe and caused money to grow less valuable, or in other words, prices to rise. Both these world-causes aided local factors peculiar to England in producing a limited economic revolution in that country. When the villeins had ceased to render personal service they had become rent-paying tenants. But the rents they paid to the lord of the manor were fixed and not rightfully to be raised, neither could the holder be lawfully turned out. The fall in value of money thus turned to the disadvantage of the landlord and lured him by hook or by crook to break the bargain. At the same time the rising price of wool and the growth of the cloth manufacture formed a strong incentive to give up the tilling of the soil and turn it into sheep pasture—which again could only be done by evicting the smallholders.

There were complaints of this 'enclosing' in the early years of Henry VIII, but the abuse was then of small extent. The dissolution of the monasteries and the transference of vast estates to new owners produced a period of confusion. Many of the new landlords took advantage of it. They were merchants who had bought land as an investment, or yeomen rising to the status of esquires and not yet imbued with the tradition that their rank had its duties as well as its rights. They quite illegally evicted tenants, re-let the farms at higher rents, or combined them into great sheep-runs which employed few hands. The result was two-fold: unemployment among the evicted, many of whom became tramps and vagabonds; and neglect of corn-growing, leading to higher food-prices. The French war of Henry's last years increased the distress by checking the cloth-trade that might have compensated for the agricultural disturbance. The government also met expenses by debasing the coinage, which made prices rise higher than ever. It was the custom of nineteenth-century historians to vilify Henry for this course. We can realize now that he probably could not help it. His mixing of copper with his silver shillings was exactly the same as the printing of too many paper sovereigns by our own government in the Great War—it raised prices, but it had to be done. Henry VIII left the land problem unsolved. Under Edward VI it grew worse. With Henry's hand removed the unscrupulous rich increased their enclosures and drove the peasantry to revolt. Protector Somerset sympathized with the oppressed, but the oppressors were too strong for him and struck him down. Under the Duke of Northumberland there was an orgy of profiteering in land—four years in which a pack of greedy scoundrels had things all their own way. In Mary's reign the progress of the evil was checked, but little was done to remedy the damage already committed.

The next forty years saw prosperity slowly return. The swing of the pendulum had much to do with it. As soon as corn was dear it paid to restore tillage, and gradually the proportion of green and brown on the face of England settled down to that which was best for the common weal. The actual amount of the change in either direction should not be exaggerated. A very little enclosure was sufficient to fill the land with outcries, and the records of economic change are always deceptive in that they give us the complaints of those who lose, but not the satisfaction of those who gain. There were many gainers in this Tudor revolution, but they pocketed their winnings in silence. The enclosures were in fact limited, and most of England remained as 'open field' until the eighteenth century.

But Elizabeth's statesmanship did not fold its hands over the problem. It assisted recovery by a series of wise measures. First, the coinage was restored. All the base pieces were called in and new pure silver issued from the Mint, at considerable sacrifice to the Treasury. The Statute of Artificers (or of Apprentices) of 1563 was a really constructive effort to deal with the problem of vagrancy. It enacted that every craftsman engaged in the skilled trades must serve a seven years' apprenticeship. Boys were apprenticed at the age of ten or under and invariably lodged in the houses of their masters. The rule, therefore, tended to improve the quality of workmanship by ensuring proper training, and to give boys steady habits before they grew old enough to roam. The Act further provided that all persons who could not prove their apprenticeship to a trade might be compelled to serve as agricultural labourers. They were to be hired for a year at a time and must produce a 'character' when changing their employment. Finally, the justices at quarter sessions were to fix fair rates of payment and to compel masters and men alike to accept them. Later Acts contained clauses for breaking up large farms into smaller ones and for attaching to every labourer's cottage four acres of land for his own use. It may be thought that these measures remained mere words, to be ignored by the influential landowners who filled the bench of justices. But in fact, such was the new public spirit which grew with the new patriotism that these regulations were very generally observed until the eighteenth century. Parliament plainly stated its motives: 'that by the maintenance of husbandry the greater part of the subjects of the realm might be preserved from extreme poverty, and the wealth of the realm be dispersed and distributed in many hands.' The landed interest was not to be solely the landowner's interest.

Throughout the reign there was also built up the system of Poor Laws for dealing with those persons who still could not find employment. The parish was the unit. At first the church-wardens were allowed to raise voluntary contributions for the poor. Next the justices were empowered to assess householders and compel them to pay poor-rate. They were also to find employment for the able-bodied and compel them to accept it, under pain of corporal punishment. The whole series of rules was overhauled and made permanent by the Poor Law of 1601. By these means crime was reduced and industry re-settled after the economic revolution. Food became more plentiful, although a bad harvest might still cause famine, and English manufactures improved in quality and bulk. The expansion of overseas trade took off the surplus, brought in luxuries in exchange, and raised the standard of comfort of the whole people.

The political achievements of the Tudors have little apparent connexion with the extraordinary progress of their people in literature, art, architecture, and music; and yet one can hardly imagine these pursuits attaining the excellence they did if the country had remained in the condition typified by the Wars of the Roses. The fifteenth century, save only in architecture, had been a desert with a few oases. The sixteenth witnessed an increasing fertility that ripened as the seventeenth set in. Historical writing improved from the wretched threadbare chronicles of Lancaster and York (far poorer than those of earlier times) to the descriptive accounts of Hall and Holinshed and the critical scholarship of Richard Hakluyt. Poetry advanced from merely amusing rhymes and ballads through the verse of Wyatt and Surrey under Henry VIII to that of Spenser under Elizabeth. Drama, as we know it, began with the Tudors and culminated in Shakespeare. English music achieved a reputation higher at the time than that of English literature; it was not merely that there were great musicians, but that there were many more musicians than in any succeeding age. The whole nation displayed a taste that enchanted foreigners. Architecture changed rather than enlarged its genius. The building of fine churches decayed; that of fine houses flourished as never before.

Schools underwent a revolution connected with that of religion. Among its pious works the fifteenth century had been given to founding schools. They were generally connected with chantries or other religious institutions. In the suppressions of 1536–53 these school endowments were confiscated, but there was a certain amount of re-foundation on secular lines. Hence appeared the so-called grammar schools of Edward VI. Most of them are of older date, with their endowments re-settled

under that King, often less generously than before. Under
Elizabeth more grammar schools were founded and education
generally improved. Latin ceased to be the mystery of the
Church and the debased jargon of lawyers, and became the
heritage of every layman who could learn. As English vowel
sounds became differentiated from those of continental tongues,
the English pronunciation of Latin followed suit, and thus became a second familiar language to many who would never have
twisted their tongues round a foreign pronunciation. And Latin
is a speech of civilization which no nation can afford to neglect.

The religious settlement of Elizabeth was on the whole a
success. By the end of her reign the strict Catholics had become
a rather small minority, and the Anglican Church had established its hold upon the country. The western rebels of 1549 had
denounced the English service as 'a Christmas game', but the
hostile sentiment quickly gave place to reverence. The Protestant tendency was towards Puritanism. That does not mean
that there were many nonconformists. Very few of the early
Puritans separated from the Church of England. The majority
regarded themselves as its members and placed their own inter-
pretation on its ceremonies. Burghley and Walsingham, the
Queen's chief ministers, must certainly be classed as Puritans, but
they held it their duty to support the Church. Another miscon-
ception may be mentioned. It is that the Puritans affected a
severe manner and plain costume, cut their hair close, and
disapproved of worldly entertainments. That was true only of
a limited section at a later period and, even so, has been
exaggerated. The Elizabethan Puritans, of whom we may cite
Drake and Sir Philip Sidney as examples, were as fond of
jollity as most men. Their views sprang largely from their fear
of the Counter-Reformation. They regarded Rome as the
enemy and disliked anything in the English Church that
savoured of the ancient connexion.

In concluding this survey of the English of the Tudors we may
compare them with their ancestors of the fifteenth century,
whose warfare had been for booty and devoid of patriotism, and
whose politics had been a compound of murder and treachery;
with those of the fourteenth century, with its class hatred between
bond and free; and of the thirteenth, when only a few men had
been awake and enlightened and the mass had been mere servile
animals. The spirit of a nation had at length emerged.

VII. THE DECLINE OF THE MONARCHY

The essence of an active monarchy is that all depends upon the monarch. For that reason monarchy at its best may be the most enlightened form of government, and yet it is the most precarious, for sooner or later the throne is bound to fall to one who is unequal to his task. That misfortune befell England in 1603, when Elizabeth gave place to her cousin James of Scotland.[1] James I's radical disqualification as an English king was that of being a foreigner. If he had been a great man he might have overcome it, as did William III in after days. But, though a man of intellect and learning, he lacked the swift judgement, the business instinct, the sympathy with men demanded of an active king, and at the same time he believed he had those qualities in perfection. He argued when he should have decided. He decided hastily and ignorantly in matters wherein he should first have sought information. By either fault he brought himself and his office into contempt. The English had a high standard of kingship. James soon revealed himself as far below that standard, whilst ever prating of his 'kingcraft'. Henry of Navarre is said to have dubbed him 'the wisest fool in Christendom'. It is one of the epigrams that stand the test of time.

In the turbulent fifteenth century James would have endured no longer than a snowflake in a furnace. A hundred years later the monarchy was so well rooted that there was no swift collapse, but only a prolonged decline. So slow was it that he died fatuously content with himself and all his works, although he left his son to face a different reckoning. The year 1603, the change from Tudor to Stuart, therefore marks no abrupt break in English life. The impression was of continuity. The mon-

[1] The claim of James I:

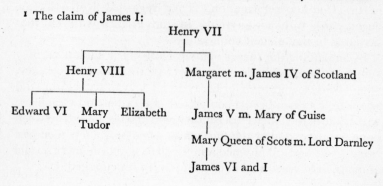

archy had deteriorated, but might soon improve. Elizabeth herself had passed her best days before she died. She retained her subjects' sentimental loyalty until the end, but the young men had begun to lose some of their respect and to long for a livelier court. James, it was hoped, would settle down and turn out well. The country was prosperous, and with peace would grow more so. All the mechanism of the law and the national business was working steadily. All the projects of discovery, new trades, and colonies were as promising as ever. Culture, comfort, luxury, were on the rise. England still had a statesman in the younger Cecil (Sir Robert), captains in Howard and Ralegh, intellect in Francis Bacon, art in Shakespeare and many more. The machine would run whilst its new director learned his job.

The tragedy was that he thought he had nothing to learn. He had grown from infancy as King of Scotland and had acquired a sound knowledge of the politics of that country. But Scotland was utterly different from England. Its nobles were still in the untamed feudal stage, its Parliament was a powerless body without any of the rights or traditions of that of England, its Kirk was ruled by assemblies in which laymen and preachers sat together whilst bishops had no place. James had passed through humiliating experiences, handled as a puppet by baronial factions, baited by free-spoken divines, censured at their pleasure, as he put it, by Jack, Tom, Will, and Dick under cloak of godly liberty. At the same time he had watched Elizabeth from afar enjoying power and respect such as he had never attained; and he had totally misinterpreted the conditions of her success. Thwarted in practice, he had formed a grand theory of the rightful status of a king, and he came prepared to apply it in a country of whose political habits he knew nothing—not even that it had any. His theory was that a monarch was free, unbound by any human restraints. He was accountable to God alone, and the dictates of his own thought and conscience were his sole guides. Before ever he reached London there occurred an act symbolic of Stuart kingship. A pickpocket was caught in the crowd that thronged to greet the King, and was instantly hanged without trial on the royal command—five centuries of English law wiped out by a wave of the hand. James probably thought he had made a good impression as a lion of justice.

Men had been accustomed to speak freely, if respectfully, to the Tudor sovereigns. Tom and Will and Dick had kept their distance, but their representatives had always stated their views. The working of the constitution had been a matter of give and take. A framework of general principles had been observed, tacitly accepted rather than debated. Within it there had been latitude for common-sense decisions based on counsel. There had been as little definition as possible. Tudor England had not consciously shaped its institutions, save in the matter of the Church; they had grown to fit the circumstances. When Shakespeare wrote *King John* he included not a reference to Magna Carta. Minds did not run on such things in 1594. Thirty years afterwards the Charter would inevitably have been the centre of the plot, with stirring talk at Runnymede.

The Tudors had abstained from definition. James was for ever defining his own rights and other people's duties. He is an instance of the peril of logic in human affairs. Logical thought commonly leads to mistaken action, for the simple reason that human instincts are incapable of exact definition. The logician combines the ideal citizen's needs and wishes in a beautifully reasoned state paper, only to find that the real citizens perversely refuse to conform to the ideal; upon which the logician loses his temper, as in the French Revolution. Rousseau's logic went so far as 'to compel men to be free'.

James I and Charles I ruined the English monarchy by defining it. 'Although a good king,' wrote James whilst still in Scotland, 'will frame his actions according to law, yet he is not bound thereto but of his own will and for giving example to his subjects'. It followed, therefore, that no one might criticize him for breaking inconvenient laws: 'As for the absolute prerogative of the Crown,' he told an English court, 'that is no subject for the tongue of a lawyer, nor is it lawful to be disputed. . . . It is presumption and high contempt in a subject to dispute what a king can do'. To a remonstrant Parliament he declared, 'I will govern according to the common weal, but not according to the common will.' Charles I lost no time in taking up the parable: 'Remember that parliaments are altogether in my power, for their calling, sitting and dissolution: therefore, as I find the fruits of them good or evil, they are to continue or not to be.' Churchmen and political philosophers found backing in scripture and history for the claims of divine right. A writer, officially approved by the Archbishop of Canterbury in 1607, said of the King: 'He is above the law by his absolute power . . . and though at his coronation he take an oath not to alter the laws of the land, yet, this oath notwithstanding, he may alter or suspend any particular law that seemeth hurtful to the public estate.' Sir Robert Filmer wrote under Charles I: 'Kings are above all laws. They have a divine right to absolute power, and are not answerable to human authority.' James had said much the same of Parliamentary privilege: 'he could not allow of the style calling their privilege an ancient and undoubted right of inheritance . . . their privileges were derived from the grace and permission of his ancestors.'

Much of this was not new, and some of it was theoretically true. It was the manner of saying it that roused opposition, and above all, the disposition of the men who said it. Elizabeth in a rage had made high claims on her prerogative, but there had been no answering mutiny, for all knew that she could be trusted to act wisely. When, however, kings who were palpably unwise and untrustworthy took to defining their high authority, they were simply provoking their opponents to some unpleasant definitions in reply. The disparagement of the law aroused the ire of lawyers. They delved in the long-forgotten past and produced some ancient skeletons which they contrived to dress in surprisingly new clothing. It was then that Magna Carta became what it had never been before, a statement of the liberties of the whole English people and of the privileges of a Parliament that had not been thought of in 1215.

The constitutional lawyers found voice not on the judges' bench but in the House of Commons. The judges dared not speak too loud, for they were dismissable at the royal pleasure. One of them was so dismissed, Sir Edward Coke, to become a leading exponent of anti-royal views in Parliament. The Commons defined themselves with progressive emphasis. 'Your Majesty,' they said politely in 1604, 'would be misinformed if any man should deliver that the kings of England have any absolute power in themselves'. In the following years the King exercised the power of imposing customs dues (hence called impositions), and the Commons requested in 1611 'that all impositions set without the assent of Parliament be quite abolished and taken away'. By 1621 the tone was stiffer, and the resolution ran: 'That the liberties of Parliament are the ancient birthright of the subjects of England; that the affairs of the realm and of the Church are proper subjects of debate in Parliament; and that every member of the House hath freedom of speech to treat the same.' Under Charles I the crisis rapidly developed. 'England', said a member in 1625, 'is the last monarchy that yet retains her liberties. Let them not perish now!' Three years later Sir Thomas Wentworth declared: 'We must vindicate our ancient liberties. We must reinforce the laws made by our ancestors. We must set such a stamp on them as no licentious spirit shall dare hereafter to invade them.' So far had matters gone in the first generation of Stuart rule. 'The laws of our ancestors' had become the touchstone. Under the Tudors men had reflected rather on the follies of their ancestors in the Wars of the Roses, and had sat content.

There is no fire without fuel, and there is no political discussion without material subjects of disagreement. What were the subjects on which King and people were at odds? First and least important may be mentioned the control of trade. The merchants of London were growing rich and powerful. Foreign trade had always been reckoned part of foreign policy in general, and clearly within the scope of the King's prerogative. James I claimed that to levy customs on trade was solely in his own discretion. It was a stretch of the prerogative, but there was something to be said for it. His impositions were bitterly contested, but he had his way; the judges decided in his favour. The richest trades were the monopolies of privileged companies, with whom no outsider might compete. In earlier days this had been necessary, for a private individual would have been unable to secure fair play in foreign ports. But times were changing and commerce everywhere becoming more secure. The monopolies now appeared unjust and the 'interlopers' carried on a ceaseless agitation against them. James and Charles frowned on the interlopers, but at the same time failed to secure the love of the regular companies, whose interests they often sacrificed in treaties with foreign powers. The mercantile community thus became anti-royalist.

Next came the question of direct taxation, which touched the property of every man. Here, as with trade, the trouble was partly due to the fact that times were changing. The old theory had been that the King should live of his own, that he should carry on the government on the income from crown lands, feudal dues, and the recognized duties on commerce. Only in time of war was it thought right that direct taxes should be levied. Henry VII, a financier of genius, had managed in this fashion and even accumulated a surplus. Henry VIII had needed additional money for war expenditure and had raised much of it from the spoils of the Church. Elizabeth, by the strictest economy, had carried on a long war with very moderate demands for direct taxation. Moderate as they had been, the Commons had resented them, and when James I made peace with Spain it was expected that he should then live of his own. But he could not do it. Money was worth only half as much as it had been a century before, and the activities of government were much greater. The time had come for the nation to submit to be taxed, and it was quite prosperous enough to afford it. Sooner or later the Tudors, if they had continued, would have had to take their people into their confidence and explain the position. There would have been some grumbling, but probably the thing would have been honestly faced and a change agreed to.

The Stuarts would not explain because their notion of divine right forbade it: they were accountable only to God, and to man they had but to issue commands. The Stuarts also could not explain, because their hands were not clean. James was a reckless spendthrift. His court expenses were enormous. He lavished vast sums on useless favourites who did not a stroke of public service. His officials made fortunes by plundering the state. His peace expenditure was far higher than Elizabeth's war expenditure. If he had explained, the Commons would have demanded an inquiry, and the rottenness they suspected would have been revealed. Coke and the lawyers had been making historical researches. They would have been ready with 'laws of their ancestors' which had given the fourteenth-century Commons the right to supervise the royal expenditure, and divine right would have cut a sorry figure with its account-books open to public inspection.

James and Charles, therefore, took a high tone, demanded money as of right, and raised it unlawfully when it was not granted. In 1608 the Book of Rates placed new impositions on merchandise without a parliamentary grant. In 1610–11 an attempt at a bargain failed. By the Great Contract the King was to surrender the feudal dues in return for a fixed income from direct taxes. He would have been the gainer, but both sides were suspicious and the bargain broke down. He dissolved his first Parliament in anger. In 1614 he called a second. The Commons refused to vote a penny before their grievances should be redressed. James exploded in wrath and dismissed them. It was called the Addled Parliament, since it had hatched nothing. The third Parliament in 1621 did a little, but not much. It made a niggardly grant of about one-fourth as much as the King demanded, pronounced opinions on foreign policy which he highly resented, and impeached the Lord Chancellor, Francis Bacon, for corruption. These things were enough to warrant a speedy dissolution. The impeachment of the King's ministers was another ancestral revival, for the proceeding had not been used since 1449. James childishly asserted divine right by tearing out an offensive page from the Commons' Journal with his own hand. But the visible effect of divine right was to recall forgotten parliamentary rights. His fourth Parliament in 1624 again criticized foreign policy, impeached another minister, declared monopolies illegal, and voted some money. Poor old James was growing worn out in the struggle. He behaved meekly, parted with his Commons on comparatively good terms, and died a few months afterwards, a worthy man betrayed by false reasoning.

Charles I had the advantage of long residence in the country he came to rule. But he looked through Stuart glasses and knew the real England as little as his father had done. James had at least known Scotland, but Charles was completely out of his reckoning even there, and his Scots were destined to be the beginners of his downfall. His manners were good, his tastes artistic, his morals without reproach. He was less ready of speech than his father, and proportionately more violent in action. His views and policy were those of James. Had they been utterly different he could hardly have made a success of the English monarchy, for its spell was broken. He succeeded to the command in a battle already lost.

His first Parliament in 1625 took the offensive with an insult. It granted tonnage and poundage for one year instead of for life as with all previous monarchs since Henry VII—a vote of no confidence before the reign had well begun. Charles spurned the grant, dissolved Parliament, and collected forced loans in a manner unknown for seventy years. The collection produced

little, and he called another Parliament in 1626. Here Sir John
Eliot took the lead and proposed a grant of money, coupled with
the impeachment of the Duke of Buckingham, the King's friend *Buckingham*
and minister. Charles, to save Buckingham, dissolved without the
grant, and made all kinds of illegal exactions in lieu of it. Again
the system broke down, and a third momentous Parliament met
in 1628. Before considering its record we must hark back to the
greatest cause of English dissensions in all these years—religion.
Religion produced the heat and fury which made men ready
to resist the Stuarts to the death, just as in happier times it had
made them ready to die for England against Spain. Elizabeth's
Anglican Church of 1559 had been purposely ill-defined. There
were large blanks in the formal instructions that bound the
clergy, blanks that could be filled to suit the taste and fancy of
the individual clergyman. So the Queen had conciliated some
Catholics and most Protestants, and had gathered all but the
extremists into the national fold. Seven thousand out of eight
thousand of Mary's Catholic clergy had accepted Elizabeth's
settlement and become Anglican clergy. Mary's Catholic
bishops had been of sterner stuff, and all but one had been
replaced by Protestants. The struggle against the Counter-
Reformation increased Protestant feeling, and by 1603 most
laymen and many of the clergy were of the thorough-going
Protestant type known as Puritans. But the bishops had moved
in the opposite direction. The Queen was no Puritan, and she
promoted men who fell in with her views. They were not
Roman Catholics, but they had a liking for vestments and ceremonies which recalled the ancient past of the Church. And,
like the Queen, they believed in discipline and were severe with
the Puritan clergymen who disliked ceremonies and thought
more of preaching principles which they derived straight from
the Bible.

James I continued the policy of promoting High Churchmen.
He was himself a Protestant, but the democratic tendencies of
the Scottish Kirk had scared him into the belief that Puritanism
must mean disloyalty. The Puritan clergy petitioned for
changes in ceremonial. He summoned a conference at Hampton Court, but used it only to air his learning, having already
decided against the petitioners. His famous dictum, 'No bishop,
no king', meant that he regarded bishops (of the right stamp)
as the apostles of absolute monarchy. They were. They could

quote the Bible like any Puritan, and they drew from it the doctrine of passive obedience; to question the lightest word of a king was a sin, however little of a crime the laws of disorderly ancestors might account it. Charles I was much more of a High Churchman than his father. His artistic nature revelled in ceremonial, and he believed with all his heart that Puritan plainness was simply irreverence. James had occasionally persecuted the Roman Catholics, especially after his narrow escape from the Gunpowder Plot. Charles let the penal laws lie idle, and was unjustly suspected of being a Catholic himself. If only he had been as easy with the Puritans he might claim to be a pioneer of religious toleration. As in other matters, he acted where his father had talked. James threatened the Puritans at Hampton Court that he would 'harry them out of the land'. Charles did it fairly effectively. The first fifteen years of his reign are those of the great exodus to New England.

This, then, was how the religious question came home to the ordinary man. He had to attend his parish church on Sunday. There he was obliged to behave decorously in face of ceremonies which he believed idolatrous, conducted by a priest in the vestments of Rome. If there was a sermon it was not of a style to comfort his Protestant soul, but an exposition of divine right and passive obedience, enforced by arguments which he held to be fallacious but dared not interrupt. He went home with lowering brow and read his Bible. He turned, not to the passages of tolerance and meekness, but to the fierce old Israelitish tales of war against the foes of Jehovah, and to the prophecies of judgement to come. The sabbath was for him no day of love and charity but a festival of impotent wrath. And this went on, week after week, year upon year, for two long reigns, until the hour of judgement struck. We moderns, in like circumstances, should not display a tithe of the discipline and self-restraint required in those days from fully half the thinking population of England. It made them men, but not pleasant men, not fit denizens of merry England. It made them the men who would one day boast in gloomy pride that the other half of their blood-brethren had been 'as stubble to their swords'.

The handling of foreign policy added to Puritan discontent. James I made peace with Spain in 1604, wisely, because the object of the war had been attained in the establishment of English Protestantism against the Counter-Reformation. But as the years went by it became clear that the Counter-Reformation was not finally disposed of. It had recoiled but to gather new force, and a fresh instalment of the religious contest broke out when the Thirty Years War began in Germany in 1618. The struggle opened in Bohemia and thence spread to the Rhineland and the Netherlands. The Protestants had the worst of it in the early stages, and since it was upon the Calvinists rather than the Lutherans that the chief attack was launched, the sympathy of English Puritans was all the keener. On the Catholic side the Spaniards were prominent. Their troops served in western Germany, and from the Spanish Netherlands they recommenced the war with the Dutch Republic. France took little part until the ministry of Cardinal Richelieu began in 1624.

English feeling would have welcomed the Elizabethan policy of support to the Calvinists and a naval attack upon the Spanish colonies. James I rejected it. He had a creditable hatred of war, and sought to check the whole outbreak by acting as a neutral mediator. His daughter Elizabeth was married to the Calvinist Elector Palatine, who had been expelled from his territories by Spanish armies. He tried to marry his son Charles to the Spanish Infanta and so make himself the head of an all-round family connexion which should stifle animosity in both camps. James's heart was better than his head. His motives were praiseworthy, but he miscalculated the forces with which he had to deal. His policy of mediation could only have succeeded if backed by overwhelming strength and a determination to use it. James had neither the resolution nor the wherewithal to fight. His treasury was empty, and the fine navy which had beaten the Armada had well-nigh disappeared, engulfed in a wave of jobbery and corruption that has no parallel in English history. Thus the Spaniards amused the English King with negotiations that were meant to fail, whilst his own subjects grew ever more suspicious that he was betraying the Protestant cause—as, unintentionally, he was.

Charles I in 1625 meant business. He was enraged at the rejection of his suit for the Infanta, and he declared war on Spain. It might have been the means of healing the breach with the Commons, but it was not. Charles entrusted everything to the Duke of Buckingham, whom the Commons entirely distrusted. A great expedition to Cadiz failed shamefully, beaten rather by its own incompetence than by the enemy. Not content with this, Buckingham picked a quarrel with Cardinal Richelieu, and the country had thus two first-class powers to fight. There was much talk of the Elizabethan exploits, and a London bookseller published *Sir Francis Drake Reviv'd*. But it was easier to revive Drake in print than on the quarter-deck, and Buckingham's captains failed uniformly in everything they attempted. He himself had just returned unsuccessful from an expedition to Rochelle when the Parliament of 1628 assembled. The Commons met in a determined mood. Much as they had at heart the Protestant cause abroad, they had made up their minds that reform at home must come first. Without that they could expect nothing good anywhere. Their leaders, Eliot and Wentworth, were bent upon pulling down Buckingham, or in other words, upon making the King's ministers accountable to Parliament. In the Petition of Right they restated the English constitution as against absolute authority—no taxation without parliamentary grant, no imprisonment without due process of law. Charles accepted the Petition of Right, and then during the parliamentary recess infringed its terms as if it had never been drafted. In the course of the recess two things happened: Wentworth changed sides and joined the King; and soon afterwards Buckingham was assassinated by one of his own officers, a Puritan unbalanced by brooding on his country's dishonour. Wentworth's motive is not clear, but thenceforward he devoted his abilities to dragging the government out of the slough into which it had fallen. It was Wentworth who had made that daring allusion to licentious spirits tampering with ancient law. He spent the rest of his life in aiding Charles to do that very thing, and died for the thoroughness with which he upheld the claims of divine right.

If Wentworth had forsworn the cause, Eliot had not. The Houses re-assembled in 1629 with the violation of the Petition of Right as the culmination of their grievances. The King saw at once that he could not work with them and gave orders for a dissolution. Then occurred a memorable defiance. The royal messengers were demanding admittance, and the Speaker made ready to rise and thereby close the proceedings. But the Commons had first a word to say. One member locked the door and stood guard upon it, whilst others forced the Speaker to his seat and held him there. Eliot then proposed resolutions that whoever should advise the King to infringe the laws or make innovations in religion should be accounted a traitor to the realm. The resolutions were passed, the doors opened, and the third Parliament of Charles I dissolved. It was eleven years before Lords and Commons were to meet again, but those parting resolutions were not forgotten. Oliver Cromwell was one of those who passed them, and he did not forget. Sir John Eliot did not live to see their fruition. The King ordered him to the Tower and kept him there until his death three years later. He could have had his liberty by making submission, but he was not the submitting type of man.

To Charles I the logic of the situation seemed simple. He could not work with Parliament, therefore he would work without it. There was no reason save that of finance to compel him to summon the Houses, and he thought he could see his way clear to financial independence. That being granted, he flattered himself that he had done with Parliament for good and all. He disbanded his forces and made peace with France and Spain. For revenue he relied upon the customs and the income from the crown lands, recognized sources, and also upon a number of expedients that caused bitter discontent. Chief of these was the sale of monopolies. They had more than once been declared illegal, and even the popular Elizabeth had had to give them up. Charles, under pretext that all regulation of trade pertained to the royal prerogative, created monopolies in almost every article of commerce, in necessaries as well as luxuries. These monopolies were sold to capitalists or given to courtiers with the result that everything became dear and bad. Another financial extortion was practised in fining land-owners for encroachments upon the royal forests, even when the trespass was centuries old and difficult of proof. Ancient feudal law contributed to the harvest. The rights of wardship of minors and the control of their marriage belonged to the Crown and were used in a manner that amounted to blackmail. Men of quite moderate property were compelled to accept knighthood, which involved paying heavy fees, or to compound for being excused. The Star Chamber, once a court operated for the public good, became an engine of tyranny for the enforcement of these exactions, until all England grew passionately desirous of its abolition.

Ship-money is the most strongly denounced of Charles's

irregular taxes, but in fact it was the most justifiable. The King had a genuine regard for the navy and was ashamed of the poor showing it had made at the opening of his reign. Spaniards and Dutchmen in the course of their wars were treating neutral England with contempt, plundering her merchantmen and even fighting in her harbours. The Barbary corsairs, who had once lurked only within the Straits of Gibraltar, were now ranging the ocean, taking prizes in the Channel, and even carrying off prisoners from English soil. In a single year they captured seventy English vessels. Charles therefore equipped the navy, set it to patrol the home waters, and attacked the pirates in their own port of Sallee. But incompetence was rife in his squadrons, the officers were mostly amateurs, and the seamen were vilely treated. In the Cadiz and Rochelle expeditions they had sickened in thousands from the badness of the victuals and had been turned out to die in the streets on their return. The management of the ship-money fleets did not revive their loyalty, and so the force that could have saved Charles his throne turned against him when the day of crisis came. Meanwhile ship-money provided a constitutional quarrel. John Hampden refused to pay it, and there was a famous trial in which the tame judges decided against him. Hampden belonged to the inner ring of the Puritan leaders. He was a friend of John Pym, Oliver Cromwell, and the Earl of Warwick. His reverse gave them an added grievance and bound them more closely together.

Two men stand out in the King's counsels, Thomas Wentworth, created Earl of Strafford, and William Laud, promoted Archbishop of Canterbury. Strafford was sent to govern Ireland. He did it efficiently, improved that country's trade, and smothered its chronic discontent. He made himself terrible to all who resisted, and was never weary of urging his policy of 'Thorough' upon the King. The Irish army which Strafford said he could raise became a nightmare to the Puritans, who realized that an army was the one thing needed to make absolutism permanent. The former ally of Eliot became one of the two most hated men in the country. The other was Laud. Laud was a pious, sincere, and upright man without a grain of imagination or humour. All who disagreed with him were wrong, and not merely wrong but criminal. He made no distinction between wide principle and petty detail. On the one and the other Englishmen must conform or suffer. There were like minds among the Puritans, minds devoid of all human charity and sense of proportion. The result was a truly devilish hatred. Puritans gave vent to coarse abuse, unworthy of men of intellect. Laud resorted to unreasoning violence, out of all proportion to the offence. The Star Chamber and the Court of High Commission dealt with his victims, inflicting impossible fines, personal mutilation, exposure in the pillory, and lifelong imprisonment. The case of William Prynne is the outstanding example. His envenomed pen cost him all the above penalties. Cheering crowds heartened him on his path to prison, a demonstration that might have struck Laud as ominous. But Laud, like his victim, cared nothing for consequences. They were both men of perfect courage.

Laud's unreasoning obstinacy caused the downfall of his master. Not content with dragooning England, he sought to harry Scotland as well. The King agreed. It was monstrous that Presbyterians should wallow in heresy whilst Puritan error was repressed. A new Laudian prayer-book was therefore devised for Scotland, and its use ordered in 1637. Resistance was prompt and general. The Kirk assembly provided a focus of revolt such as England lacked when its Parliament was not sitting. In 1638 all Scotland swore to the Covenant and took arms to maintain it. Charles thought that the militia of northern England could deal with the matter. But the ancient fyrd, which had often fought Scots for the honour of England, had no mind to die for the Prayer Book of Laud. When the Covenanters crossed the Tweed with sword in right hand and Bible in left there was no pretence of resistance, and the true power of divine right was revealed. Charles sent for Strafford, whose Irish sojourn, it appeared, had made him forget the temper of Englishmen. For Strafford advised the calling of a Parliament. It met in the summer of 1640, and at once John Pym took the lead. Reform as thorough as Strafford's tyranny was his demand, to precede the voting of a single shilling for the Scottish war. The King would not submit, and the Short Parliament was dissolved.

Once more Charles and Strafford tried to raise an army, this time from the south. A few ragged bands were impressed, but sufficient Protestant gentlemen could not be found to lead them, and Catholics were defied and even murdered by the mutinous troops. Once again there was no headway against the Scots. The truth had to be faced. Absolutism without an army had broken down. Before the end of 1640 there was another general election, but it was no short Parliament that it returned. It was the famous Long Parliament, with whose gathering at Westminster the great days of the English monarchy were done.

VI

REVOLUTION AND EMPIRE

(*From 1640 to 1714*)

I. THE CIVIL WARS AND THE RULE OF THE PURITANS

Puritan Revolution (Pym's revolt)

THE Long Parliament, for its first three years, was Pym's Parliament. This man, cool, vigilant, valiant, and knowing whither he was bound, had become the mainspring of the Puritan party during its long sojourn in the shadows. With its emergence upon the stage of action he took it and England into the hollow of his hand. Yet he was no dictator before whom his followers trembled and obeyed. He and they were set to destroy dictatorship. His ascendancy was that of a leader of free men who saw always one move ahead of the others and could cast their sentiments into clear demands. If he made mistakes he sometimes made them consciously, for he had often to choose between a lesser and a greater evil. His death in 1643 was a loss to England. How he would have played the game to the end no one can guess, but he would surely have ordered it more wisely than did those who survived him.

Lords and Commons in 1640 were unanimous for reform. Their first task was to strike down Strafford and Laud, the two heads of tyranny. Laud was easily dealt with. To send him to the Tower was in effect to abolish him, for he was a small man though he had occupied a great place, and out of that place he counted for little. Strafford was a more urgent problem, for he was a giant whom no cell could be trusted to contain. Pym began with his impeachment for treason. It was manifestly untrue that Strafford had been a traitor to the King as a person, and ardently as the Houses desired his death they could not consent to pervert the facts to that end. But Pym's doctrine was that the King should be viewed not as a person, but as the embodiment of the nation, in which case the charge was good. It is a conception with which we are now familiar, but the men of that day were not ready for it. The impeachment was doomed to failure, and Pym had regretfully to fall back upon the only alternative, that of execution by law but not by trial and proof. In the spring of 1641 both Houses passed a Bill of Attainder declaring the earl worthy of death.

To become an Act it needed the King's assent. Would he yield? London encircled Whitehall, roaring for blood. Charles was no coward, but his wife was in danger as well as himself. He consented and signed his faithful servant's death-warrant. The citizens turned out to gloat over the scene on Tower Hill, and horsemen spurred through every shire with the news, 'His head is off!' Strafford was physically dead. Morally the King had died too. He moved through the ensuing years as a man without will, faith, or honour. It may have been only the effect of his natural inertness. It may have been also that he felt himself indelibly stained by Strafford's death. He certainly expressed remorse for it as his own end approached.

Swift dispatch was the word in 1641. After the minister of tyranny the tools of tyranny fell in quick succession. The Star Chamber, the High Commission, the Councils of Wales and the North were all swept away. Ship-money, distraint of knighthood, all unparliamentary taxes, were again declared illegal, this time by a Parliament which took means to substantiate its word. For it passed also a Triennial Act to provide that three years must never elapse without a meeting, and another Act whereby the existing Houses could not be dissolved without their own consent. Charles signed everything without resistance. After Strafford's death no other surrender cost him a pang. To him all were empty forms which he forgot as soon as he had complied with them. In other compartments of his mind he was thinking of Irish armies, of winning over the Scots Covenanters to fight for him, and at the same time of bringing in Catholic aid from the continent. No dreamland can ever have yielded a stranger notion than that of combining the inheritors of John Knox with those of the Bartholomew Massacre.

The above-named abolitions represented the effective material work of the Puritan revolution. They were all permanent, and when the monarchy was restored in 1660 it was accompanied by no restoration of the institutions destroyed in 1641. 'The Restoration' is, in fact, a misleading term, for the old English monarchy was never restored. Pym had killed it.

Up to this point the men of the Long Parliament had been very nearly unanimous. Those who were afterwards to fight for the King and those who were to fight against him had been agreed on the death of Strafford, the pulling down of Laud and his bishops, and the vindication of regular law against the prerogative courts. There had been no Royalist party. If matters could have rested at this point there would have been no Civil War. Unhappily, they could not so rest; for religion was at the back of all politics, there were two views of religion, and the idea of toleration had not yet emerged. The thorough-going Puritans proposed to complete the work of 1641 by abolishing all bishops 'root and branch' and placing the Church under the control of laymen; and with the bishops they wished to sweep away the English Prayer Book. The policy at once divided Parliament, for there were many who loved the Prayer Book and held that Protestant bishops were essential to church government. These men had hated Laud and his set, not as bishops, but as suspected papists and enemies of liberty. They were satisfied with the removal of Laud, but would not hear of any supersession of the Prayer Book. It was out of this division of opinion that the Cavalier and Roundhead parties were formed in the autumn of 1641. Cromwell and Hampden headed the Root-and-Branch enthusiasts, Lord Falkland and Sir Edward Hyde the defenders of the Prayer Book. All alike had been foes of absolutism a year before. Pym, whose eyes were on something greater, the destiny of English freedom, had to make his decision. He foresaw that with the powers of bishops unimpaired there would be nothing to prevent the King from promoting a new set of Laudians and dominating everything through their grip upon freedom of speech. Pym, therefore, sided with Root-and-Branch. The test of party strength came with the Grand Remonstrance, which the Puritans carried by a majority of eleven in November, 1641. Its most hotly debated clauses were those that outlined an 'intended reformation' of the Church, but Pym probably drew most satisfaction from one which laid it down that the King's ministers must be 'such as the Parliament may have cause to confide in'.

Whilst men were thus defining their theories an occasion was arising to demand instant practice. In October and November the Celts of Ireland rose and slaughtered thousands of the Protestant colonists. The truth was horrible enough, but rumour magnified it tenfold. It was patent to all that an army must be sent to rescue survivors and recover property. It was no less obvious that the army could then be put to other uses. Who should control it, King or Parliament? If the King, then the triumph of the bishops was assured; if the Commons, then Root-

and-Branch might become an accomplished fact. It was a clear issue of aye or no, not admitting, like 'intended reformation', of any disguise in clouds of verbiage. All English law and custom were with the King, who alone had the right to raise armies and commission officers. Many who doubted the King respected the law, and with heavy hearts prepared to give their voices for his claim. At that juncture Charles restored the balance by outlawing himself.

On 3 January 1642 he impeached five members of the House of Commons of high treason. It was an unconstitutional act, for the right of impeachment belonged to the Commons alone, and the Lords therefore refused to order the arrest. But the King would not accept the rebuff. The spectre of Strafford haunted him, and he meant to lay it in the blood of Pym and Hampden and their three companions. Next day he issued from Whitehall at the head of four hundred swordsmen—courtiers and expectant officers of the new army—and marched to the Commons to seize his victims with his own hand. But that he was a few minutes too late, and that he displayed one gleam of sense at the last instant, his life might well have ended then and there. The saving circumstances were that the Commons had been warned of his approach and had sent off their five by boat to the City, and that Charles entered the House alone after bidding his bravoes halt at the open door. Had they crossed the threshold nothing could have averted a battle with the high-spirited members within, and the King would have been in the midst of the *mêlée*. But Charles was ever dignified in his utterest folly. He strode to the chair and looked round. The faces he sought were not there. Without temper he acknowledged himself foiled, and walked coolly out, perhaps knowing that he had done more towards his own destruction than the men he would have beheaded; for he had been guilty of a revolutionary act in offering violence to members within their House. After that, Westminster, Whitehall, London were no places for him. Within a week he left the capital. He moved to the midlands and on to the north, there to gather all who would fight for him.

So men took sides, gravely and sadly, without any of the joyous jingoism that has ushered in so many wars. All had reason to doubt the issue, even though they might win the war. Roundheads knew well what they sought to destroy, popery, prelacy, and the divine right of kings. But, having destroyed, what were they to build? There was no answer, and to fight for a negative yields but hollow satisfaction. Still more were the best of the Cavaliers a prey to doubt. Falkland and Hyde and many another were no swashbucklers. Peace was their desire, and a decent, sober England wherein law should prevail and old sacred things be respected. For that they had parted company with the Roundheads, in whose innovations they saw nothing but destruction. They had stood by the King from the Grand Remonstrance onward, for the King was by his office the embodiment of order. But they knew very well that if he won the England of their dreams would be in peril as dire as under Strafford and Laud. Two things had decided them, love of the English Prayer Book and loyalty to the throne, although over Charles as a man they shook their heads. It was a tragic choice, and more than Falkland for one could endure. There was only one path to the peace he craved, and he gained it by a Puritan bullet at Newbury. Others less fortunate went down with their cause into the mire, faithful to their ideal and to the fool to whom their ideal bound them.

Such a war could yield no permanent material victory, but only lessons, monitions, and new principles for future guidance. These alone can be noted here, for all else was futile and transient and bore no part in the evolution of England.

First, and dominating all else, was the importance of sea power. If the navy had stood by the King he would have triumphed in six months. London, with its men and its wealth, was the strength of Puritanism. London lived by foreign trade and by that alone. A blockade of the Thames without a shot fired on land would have entailed unconditional surrender. The possibility has been little regarded, simply because it did not take place and never has taken place at any time since, except when for a brief six weeks in 1797 the mutineers at the Nore held the estuary. They were but a faction, held together for a moment by a handful of desperate ringleaders. In 1642 the entire fleet declared for Parliament and remained steady in its choice until Parliament was supreme. Maltreatment of the seamen by Stuart callousness is the most obvious reason. But one may surely believe that sailors' loyalty went deeper than that, and that it was the shame inflicted on the service by Stuart incompetence that moved the decision.

THE CIVIL WAR

Lowland
Scotland
anti-Royalist

°Edinburgh

Carlisle °Newcastle

Ireland
Royalist
or
Neutral

York
Hull

°Dublin

R
O
Y
A
L
I
S
T

A
R
E
A

Lincoln
Chester °Nottingham

oLeicester

P
A
R
L
I
A
M
E
N
T
A
R
Y

A
R
E
A

Cambridge

Oxford

Hague

Amsterdam

Dutch sympathies
divided owing to
division between
Orange and
Republican parties

oBristol London

Towns Parliamentary
country Royalist

Dover
Portsmouth

Dunkirk
Calais

Scilly Is.
A few Royalist
cruisers intercepting
London commerce

Exeter
Plymouth

Sea communications secured to Parliament by the Navy

Channel Is.
(Royalist)

Havre

FRANCE Royalist in sympathy

Miles

0   50   100   150   200

On land things moved slowly at first, partly because either side had to create its army, and partly because there were few who clearly saw what they were fighting for. In 1642 there was only one serious clash of arms, a battle at Edgehill which decided nothing. There fell Sir Edmund Verney, a Cavalier of the Falkland type, who had said to Hyde: 'I have eaten the King's bread and will not do so base a thing as to forsake him . . . but I will deal freely with you—I have no reverence for bishops, for whom this quarrel subsists.' In 1643 there was more energy, and a great plan of campaign whereby the Cavaliers were to sweep through the southern counties to the Kentish shore of the Thames estuary, and through the east midlands to the Essex shore, and thus cut off London's trade by commanding the river. It came to nothing, but it shows how Charles would have used the fleet if it had served him. The foiling of this plan entailed half-a-dozen fierce fights, and Cromwell founded his reputation by stopping the southward advance through Lincolnshire. Civilian England was now turning military, and the land was full of the horrors of a war which was no child's play, amateurs though the soldiers were. At Marston Moor, where the Cavaliers lost the whole north in 1644, more than four thousand men were killed on the field, besides many who died afterwards, and the conflict was so concentrated that all was done between sunset and dark on a summer's evening.

These sufferings gave the Parliament men a positive purpose to fight for—to end the war at any cost and as speedily as possible. To that they bent their energies, leaving the peace to be settled afterwards. Pym worked to that end in the last days of his life in 1643. His contribution was an alliance with the Scots, who undertook to serve Parliament on condition that the Presbyterian system should be set up in England. It was a necessary pact, for it was the Scots who shared with Cromwell's Ironsides the saving of the day at Marston Moor.

The politicians who succeeded Pym did their best to honour his covenant. But among the bulk of the English Puritans there was no love for Presbyterianism, whose temper was as narrow as Laud's. Particularly in the fighting regiments there was arising a multiplicity of independent sects, none big enough to dominate, and all, therefore, desiring toleration. It was here that the age-old doctrine was first challenged, that all England must be of one faith. The Independents were the first tolerants—and Oliver Cromwell was one of them.

Cromwell had achieved greatness at Marston Moor, not by mere hacking and hewing, although he did much of that, but by the cool brain that discerned every critical point and smote in at the right moment. His rise entailed a quarrel with the bigoted Scots, who thenceforward drew apart from the struggle. He supplied their place by forcing through a reorganization of the whole army as the New Model of 1645. The war, he said, would never end as long as the men were unpaid and undisciplined, and their generals mere politicians who were half afraid of beating the King. Charles must be regarded as an enemy and not as a sovereign: 'If I met the King in battle I would fire my pistol at him as at any other'—a speech shocking to the luke-warm. He had his way, and the New Model, of soldiers led by soldiers, fought its first battle at Naseby (1645). After that there remained but to round up fragments, and the war was over.

It had produced the first regular army in an England that had not fought seriously by land since the days of archery and plate-armour. But it was an army different from any that has existed since. Cromwell extended his Ironside system through the whole of the cavalry, wherein every man had to be of sober character and godly life and to pay twelve pence for swearing a profane oath. The cavalry were the winners of battles, for all was in their favour, the open fields of the midlands with no hedges to break a charge, the neglect of the artillery arm, and the defencelessness of the musketeer, who had as yet no bayonet to render his ranks impenetrable. The infantry were at first of a lower class, pressed men and vagabonds, but the Ironside spirit permeated them also in the end. One-third were pikemen and two-thirds musketeers, and it commonly happened that the pikes were too few to save a square from the horsemen. Hence the losses of the infantry were the heaviest in a close battle. They were called 'the poor foot', then as now. But it was the discipline of the New Model that made it unique. In drill and conduct it was strict to the point of Prussianism, and yet any man might argue religion with his officer or preach to the regiment, and any who had the wits might publish political tracts and propound theories of government for the common-wealth. The men were deliberately encouraged not to forget that they were free citizens whilst bound soldiers, and it became a custom for elected privates to sit in council with colonels and generals to formulate the policy of the army towards King and Parliament. Officers who could hold their men under such conditions must have been officers indeed, and the men could have been no common soldiers.

The consequence was that when the war ended the whole army, and not only two or three generals, exercised a voice in the settlement. The politicians were greatly disgusted. Their plan was to make some bargain with the captive King and to establish a Presbyterianism as intolerant as the Laudian church. The Independents would have none of it. Whilst more democratic than the civilians, they were disposed to be more charitable. They had treated their Cavalier prisoners generously in the surrenders of 1645–6, so that among the fighting men there was a chance of general reconciliation. The members of Parliament, on the other hand, had taken a needless revenge upon Laud, whom they beheaded in 1645. He had long ceased to be a danger to any one, and his death was a blunder if not a crime. For Laud, like Latimer, lighted a candle, which has burned with a steady flame ever since. But for his martyrdom his views might not have been perpetuated as they have been by a well-defined section of the Church of England.

Dissensions between Parliament and army spoilt any chance of a settlement in 1646–8. But it must be admitted that there never was much chance, for Charles I was impossible to bargain with. He gave fair words to Parliament and then to the army, but he did not mean to submit to any control. His plan was to divide his enemies and regain absolute power. He was neither clever enough to conceal his purpose nor steady enough to follow one policy at a time, but he did succeed in stirring up a second civil war in 1648. Welsh and English Cavaliers took arms, and a Scottish faction crossed the border to aid them. But the Puritans were too strong. The English rebels were not allowed to concentrate, and surrendered piecemeal. Cromwell fell upon the Scots at Preston and killed or captured them all. Then, at the close of the year, the army turned to deal with 'the man Charles Stuart' who had deluded every one. The victorious army had hitherto been a good-natured giant, earnest and simple-minded and rather easily taken in. That phase ended with the Second Civil War. Thenceforward a grimmer mood prevailed. The sword had decided between 'the honest party' and 'the malignants'; the axe should ratify the decision.

In the House of Commons the Presbyterian majority were still for some system of rigid intolerance. They recognized that the army rather than the King was their enemy. They hoped to make the King their instrument. But these remarkable soldiers had an unsoldierly insight into the workings of the politician's mind. They knew their own minds and acted without hesitation. Colonel Pride beset the doors of the House with his musketeers, and turned away all but a minority of the members. Pride's Purge left only the Rump of the Parliament. The Rump, some sixty strong, appointed a High Court of Justice for the trial of the King. The result was sentence of death for levying war upon the people of England. Execution followed swiftly upon sentence, and the head of Charles Stuart fell on 30 January 1649. A few days later the House of Lords was abolished as 'useless and dangerous', and the government of England was declared to be a Commonwealth, with a single chamber, the Commons, and a Council of State chosen by it. Thus did England embark upon the experiment of throwing over the political habits evolved through the centuries, and of putting in their place the fruits of logical thought based upon abstract principles. The history of the next eleven years was to prove that the attempt was futile and that, for our people at least, the path of progress must be followed, not by destroying old things, but by grafting new things upon them.

The execution of Charles I was plainly illegal, for the crimes for which he was condemned were unknown to the law. But it is unjust to stop at that, and to brand his slayers as murderers. For the execution was but the culmination of a whole series of illegalities, which grew inevitably out of one another and for which no one can be held finally responsible. The Civil War was illegal, the attempt to arrest the five members was illegal, divine right itself was an utterly illegal claim. Charles was the victim of a chain of error which had begun when he was a child. His dignity and courage, his piety, his melancholy artistic nature, have appealed to sentimentalists, who have glorified him as the Royal Martyr. They forget that he was not the only martyr of his time, and that thousands of others paid for his failings in the duty of his high office. It was not so hard a fate to die decently at Whitehall as to lie broken in the slush of

Marston Moor. The men who killed him were mistaken perhaps, but they acted from a sense of duty, not from motives of revenge. Their humanity was broader than that of any ruling men before them. They recognized that the poorest peasant was a man equally with the King, that he had his life to live, and that it was the duty of his rulers to safeguard it. These amateur soldiers, Cromwell and Ireton, Harrison and the rest, were always citizens first. They had passed through the temple of Mars and seen the sacrifices done therein, and they were passionately set on calling to account the King who had placed a theory above his subjects' welfare, and who was certain to do it again if he were spared. It was expedient that one man should die for the people.

The new Commonwealth was encircled by a sea of troubles. Ireland, which Englishmen regarded as a subject-state, had been torn with disorders since the massacre of 1641, and none had had leisure to take it in hand. The Covenanters of Scotland were no subjects of the English. They were not bound by anything done at Westminster, and on the news of 30 January they accepted 'the young man Charles Stuart' as their King—Charles II, whom they were hopeful of moulding in their likeness. That meant war, for Charles II, King of Scots, would never rest until he was King of England too. On the ocean the prospect was also stormy. Prince Rupert with a squadron of Royalist ships [1] was preying upon English commerce. France abetted him and was virtually making war, although without a declaration. The colonists of the West Indies and Virginia revolted against the new government, and civil war extended to the farthest confines covered by the English flag.

The Commonwealth statesmen followed the only course for revolutionaries. They faced every challenge and truckled to none. Cromwell went to Ireland in 1649 and smote right and left with heavy hand. He stormed Drogheda and put its garrison to the sword with the rigour of the dreadful law of war. He claimed that initial severity would save bloodshed in the end by scaring others into submission. It is true that Ireland was quiet for a generation thereafter. It is also true that it was only in Ireland that the Puritans mingled no mercy with their

[1] The western seaports had sent out privateers under royal commissions to take prizes in the Channel. In 1648, when Parliament and army were at odds, a few ships of the navy also went over to the Royalist side.

justice. Elsewhere they were ready to spare the vanquished, but in Ireland they were relentless. The feuds of Ireland, Catholic against Protestant, Celt against Saxon, have ever brought out the worst in all men's natures. The massacres of 1641 and 1649 do but exemplify that sorry rule. Cromwell turned next to Scotland. He routed the Covenanters at Dunbar in 1650, but he regarded them rather as erring brethren than as enemies. 'I beseech you, in the bowels of Christ,' he wrote to the Kirk Assembly, 'think it possible you may be mistaken.' Charles II threw himself upon the pure Royalists after Dunbar. With them he made a dash into England, to end in ruin at Worcester in 1651. There was hot search for him after the fight, but faithful Royalists got him away to France. It was as well for his opponents, for the course on which they were now embarked might well have compelled them to behead him also. On the sea in these months Prince Rupert was being hunted by Blake from port to port. In 1652 he hauled down his flag and retired to exile. Ayscue with another Commonwealth squadron subdued the colonies. After three perilous years the new state had weathered its storms.

But at the heart of things there was no peace. All men desired 'a settlement', but they could not agree on its terms. Most Englishmen, Cavaliers and Puritans alike, were conservatives. The past, the golden past of loyalty and contentment, was their common ideal, but they looked to different chapters of the past. The Puritans, in seeking to restore the England of the Tudors, had overthrown the un-English Stuarts, and they had nothing that was satisfying to put in their place. An illegal revolution could not bring back the legality they craved for; that was their dilemma. Active minds had produced paper schemes in profusion, 'Heads of the Proposals', 'Agreements of the People' galore. But no such agreement could command more than a minority, and meanwhile government had to go on. Any revolutionary government was illegal and therefore a tyranny. The victors were tyrants who had fought for liberty.

The Rump and the army had combined to kill Charles I. Before long they were at odds. The soldiers would not disband without a settlement, to leave the country in the hands of a knot of politicians whom most men distrusted. The civilians writhed under military control as the worst form of despotism. Neither party cared to face the free choice of their fellow-countrymen. The Royalists, beaten but numerous, would never give up their ideal of a Stuart restoration. In 1653 the Rump tried to pass an act making their own powers permanent. Cromwell in anger expelled them by military force, and no pretence of a lawful authority remained. What then? He alone had power, and he must govern. It was not what he had fought for, and he recoiled at the prospect. 'I have sought the Lord that he would rather slay me', he declared, 'than put upon me the doing of this work.' But he had to do it. The officers produced yet another paper constitution, the Instrument of Government, and Cromwell took office as Lord Protector, with provision for the regular summoning of parliaments.

In the task of restoring England's position in the world, and of regaining the respect of foreign nations, Cromwell's Protectorate was a great success. In enforcing law and preserving order at home he was also successful. Yet in the object dearest to his heart he failed. He could not reconcile the English people to a new-fangled form of government, highly efficient though it was. In theory the Protector's Parliaments should have been freely elected. But if they had been they would have contained Royalist majorities, which would have cut short the Protectorate in summary fashion. It was not only the Cavaliers who were against Cromwell. The Presbyterians were enraged at his religious toleration, which enabled a variety of Independent sects to thrive and multiply; and this grievance drove the Presbyterians into the Royalist camp. Cromwell was therefore obliged to disqualify known Royalists from election, and even after that his Commons comprised numerous members whom he prevented from taking their seats. These twice-sifted Parliaments commanded no respect, for every one knew they did not represent the nation. Thus Cromwell was never able to shake off the taint of illegality that clung to the whole revolution. The English mind was set upon monarchy. Cromwell realized that when he exclaimed, 'What if a man should take it upon him to be King?', meaning himself. It is possible that if King Oliver could have reigned for twenty years and left a son as able as himself, the dynasty would have taken root. But Protector Oliver reigned only five years. When he died in 1658 he was succeeded by his son Richard, who had neither the ability nor the will to rule. He soon resigned, and through 1659 the country was a prey to rival factions, politicians and soldiers, with hopes of 'a settlement' more remote than ever.

Restoration

Inevitably men's minds turned to the one solution of the difficulty, the restoration of Charles II. It was a thing dreaded by some, but hoped for by more. At length General Monk, head of the troops in Scotland, took the decision. He marched on London, declaring for a free Parliament. Every one knew what that would mean, and so it turned out. Cavaliers and Presbyterians had between them a majority, and they combined to recall the King. In May, 1660, Charles II landed at Dover, and the Puritan Revolution was over.

There were joy-bells and bonfires and delirious rejoicings, and it seemed as if the whole country was anxious to prove its loyalty by denouncing everything done in the past twenty years. Much indeed was overthrown in the tide of reaction, but out of all the blood and sacrifice two permanent things remained.

One was respect for the law. Every revolution is at some point illegal, but this one had been more so than it need have been. The result had been years of uncertainty and a final loss of the Puritan cause. Henceforward the nation was extremely loath to suffer any breach of law. The Puritan army itself had learnt that lesson. It could have dissolved the free Parliament of 1660 and prevented Charles from landing. But a belated reverence for the law tied its hands. It looked on in silence at the Restoration, and then quietly disbanded into private life. Not the least victory of those splendid soldiers was that last victory over self for the people's good, that noble surrender to the Cavaliers whom horse and foot had chased from so many fields. The maxim that law must prevail saved the English mind from many temptations in the years to come, and when in 1688 revolution again became inevitable the breach of the law was so momentary and its reassertion so prompt that legality was strengthened by the achievement and has never since been overthrown.

The other permanent consequence of the Puritan revolution was religious toleration. It did not come at once, but the way was prepared for it. The Independents of the New Model Army had proclaimed it as a novel principle, in the teeth of Presbyterians and High Churchmen, persecutors both. Cromwell had been the maker of the New Model, and as Protector he was as tolerant as the circumstances allowed. He gave fair play to all the Puritan sects. Under his rule George Fox founded

the Society of Friends, the so-called Quakers whose mild principles aroused an insane hatred among those who misunderstood
them. In theory he prohibited the Prayer Book, for unrestricted
worship would have given cover to Royalist plots; but in practice he allowed many an Anglican congregation to carry on
unmolested. He recognized the Jews as entitled to their own
way of thought, and revoked the ancient rule that debarred //
them from living openly in England. As a Puritan he could have
small love for the Catholics, but even they had an easier time
under the Protectorate than in many former periods. So long
as they did not seek to overthrow the state they suffered little
interference in the private practice of their faith. All this was
changed for the worse at the Restoration, and an era of persecution set in. But it proved to be the last blaze of the old evil
fire. The seed of toleration lived on beneath the surface, and
after another generation it bore fruit and made England at
length a truly free country. That alone is sufficient to justify
the Puritan Revolution.

II. THE ENGLISH EMPIRE AND THE MERCANTILE POLICY

The end of the Spanish War and the beginning of the Stuart
period in 1603–4 made some alteration in the course of English
activities upon the sea. But what took place was a resumption
rather than the beginning of something new. Before 1585 there
had been a colony in Virginia and plans for trade with the east.
Then came the war as an interruption. After the war the old
plans were taken up again.

The East India Company was indeed already in being. It
had received its charter from Elizabeth in 1600, and when she
died its first expedition was on its way home from the Asiatic
islands. These islands, Sumatra, Java, and the Moluccas, were
the goal of the early English voyages, which sought to follow
up Drake's treaty with the Sultan of Ternate and establish a
spice trade. Ultimately the plan had to be changed, for the
Dutch founded a stronger East India Company than the English, and after twenty years of rivalry succeeded in ousting them
from the islands. Meanwhile the English factors had begun a
trade in India itself, but only as a second string to their bow.
After 1623 it became the first. The original factory at Surat
was followed by others at Madras and in Bengal. In spite of

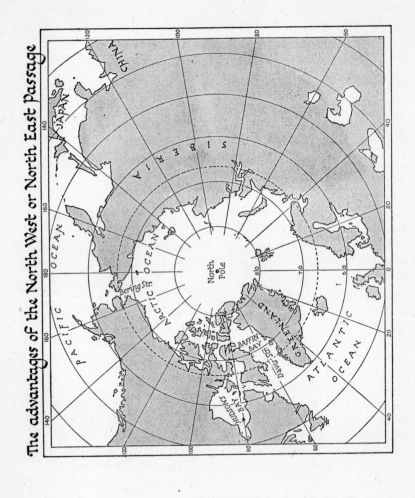

The advantages of the North West or North East Passage

some early disasters the East India Company grew very prosperous, but only as a trading body. It was not until the eighteenth century that it was destined to become a territorial power.

The East India Company sent out its ships by way of the Cape of Good Hope—the South East Passage to Asia. But many geographers were confident that a shorter way would be found by the North West, round the Arctic coast of North America. We of this generation rely too much upon flat maps for our impressions of the world's surface. The men of older times studied with the aid of globes. They might be cumbersome, but they gave truer ideas of world-geography. One of the things revealed by the globe was that the distance from England to the Spice Islands by the North West route was much shorter than by the Cape, and the quest of the North West Passage was actively pushed in the reign of James I. Many explorers tried it, and the greatest of them was Henry Hudson. He passed through Hudson's Strait and entered Hudson's Bay beyond. He thought it was an arm of the Pacific and that the way to the east lay open. Before he could make sure his men mutinied and turned him adrift in an open boat, never to be seen again. Those who followed in his track found that he was mistaken, and at length had to admit that the Arctic ice was too great an obstacle to a trade with Asia by that route.

Meanwhile America, North and South, began to press its claims to attention. The greatness of Sir Walter Ralegh has often been misunderstood. As a man of action he was not successful, and his exploits at sea will not compare with those of Drake and Hawkins. But as a thinker he stood in the first rank. He was a strategist of empire. He had three objects: to attack the power of Spain, then so formidable to England, to found colonies for the relief of distressed people at home, and to examine North America for the passage that might still be found to lead through it to the Pacific. His Virginia colony was intended to serve all three purposes, but it withered away in the Elizabethan war. During that war, in 1595, he led an expedition to South America and explored the delta of the Orinoco, then reckoned as a part of Guiana. He was very urgent that England should colonize that region. A good map shows his motive. The Spanish treasure fleets entered the Caribbean Sea through the chain of the Lesser Antilles, and left it by the

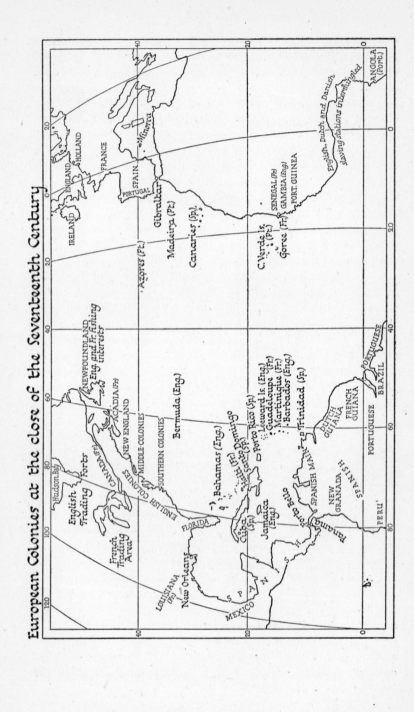

European Colonies at the close of the Seventeenth Century

Florida Channel, near the Virginia coast, a course which the prevailing winds and currents compelled them to take. An English post in Guiana would be a base of attack on the Spanish trade route as it approached the West Indies, and a similar post in Virginia would permit attack on the homeward bound treasure ships. Between them they might strangle the trade that produced the wealth of Spain. Ralegh pointed out that colonies located some way up navigable rivers might be so strongly fortified that the Spaniards would be unable to capture them.

The execution of these plans fell to others, for Ralegh displeased James I and was sent to the Tower. Guiana attracted most attention at first. In 1604 Charles Leigh attempted a colony there, and in subsequent years Robert Harcourt and others did the like. All these efforts were ultimate failures. The best known was Ralegh's Guiana voyage in 1617–18 which ended in his defeat and execution. Perhaps the most promising was Roger North's Amazon Company of 1619, which sent home some rich cargoes and was then dissolved by James I at the bidding of Spain. The Guiana Company of 1626 struggled on for several years, until lack of capital and Portuguese attacks on its settlements compelled it to desist. With a little government support these ventures would have turned out well. It is interesting to speculate on the form the British Empire would have taken if its principal colonies had extended up the Amazon from the Brazil and Guiana coasts. That was quite a possibility, for between 1620 and 1630 there were half a dozen thriving plantations in the great delta of the Amazon. Few people nowadays have ever heard of them.

Whilst the South American effort was dying out, more permanent things were being achieved in North America. In 1607 a new Virginia Company planted its colony at Jamestown on Chesapeake Bay. The Virginia settlers had a terrible time in their early years, and nothing but the stout heart of Captain John Smith prevented the abandonment of the venture. The early hopes were those of finding gold and of discovering an easy passage through America to the Pacific. Both were illusory, and only after a dozen years did Virginia find its true vocation in tobacco-planting. As a tobacco colony it was a moderate success, and it became a refuge for Cavalier exiles during the Commonwealth period. In 1632 another tobacco colony was

N. Amer

founded in Maryland, to the north of Virginia. Its promoter was Lord Baltimore, a Catholic peer, who desired to make a place of refuge for his co-religionists.

The colony as a refuge for the oppressed was an idea that had already appealed to the Puritans. In 1620 a small band known as the Pilgrim Fathers settled at Plymouth, near Cape Cod on the New England coast. The first winter killed half of them, but the remainder persevered and were joined by others. The home government took small notice of these people, who governed themselves as a little independent state whilst acknowledging their allegiance to the King. It is the earliest example of dominion status, if one may apply such a term to a community two or three thousand strong. More important was the adjacent Puritan colony of Massachusetts, founded in 1628. Its promoters were men of substance who obtained a charter from Charles I. They acted vigorously and attracted many emigrants, so that after a dozen years there were 16,000 people in their colony. Boston, its chief town, became a busy seaport, dealing in the salt fish of the coast and the furs and timber of the interior. The Massachusetts Puritans were quite as intolerant as their enemy Archbishop Laud. Any who disagreed with the church elders were cast out. Dissentients of this sort fled southwards and founded Rhode Island, whilst other Massachusetts men trekked westwards to the fertile valley of the Connecticut and created yet another colony there. New Haven, planted by later refugees from Laud's tyranny, completed the tale of the New England colonies, a compact block of states well able to take care of themselves. 'The New English Canaan', as scoffers called it, was a combination of religious zeal and business aptitude. Puritanism was the motive of its establishment and hard common sense the method of its management.

Promising as were the American colonies, they were outshone during the first generation by the English settlements in the West Indies. In 1624 Thomas Warner, one of the Amazon venturers who had left that river, took possession of the island of St. Christopher (St. Kitts). He had much trouble with the Carib savages and was glad to welcome a crew of Frenchmen, who divided the island with him. In 1627 another band of English pioneers occupied Barbados, a fertile island which had the advantage of being uninhabited. Other establishments followed—in Nevis, Montserrat, and Antigua. At first they did a thriving trade in tobacco. But about 1640, the tobacco market being overstocked, they turned their attention to sugar, and a period of brilliant prosperity set in. Barbados, the premier sugar island, although no larger than the Isle of Wight, attained a population and trade far exceeding those of Virginia. It became likewise a refuge for exiled Royalists when the civil wars turned against their cause.

Such was the condition of the colonies when Charles I was executed and the Commonwealth proclaimed. The only friends of the Commonwealth were the Puritan New Englanders. All the other colonists declared for Charles II and defied the Rump and its Council of State. They were confident that the new government, with several wars already on its hands, would have no force to spare for the west. Charles I, even in his best days, had never sent a ship-of-war across the Atlantic, and his authority in the colonies had been more nominal than real. But the colonists had mistaken the men with whom they had now to do. It was quite true that the West Indies had seen no English fleet since the days of Drake. It was also true that the Commonwealth statesmen regarded themselves as the inheritors of the Elizabethans, and looked upon the Stuart interlude as a nightmare that had passed away.

They took two measures to establish their authority over the rebellious colonies. They passed Navigation Acts to regulate trade; and they strengthened the navy to enforce the Acts. The Navigation Act of 1650 prohibited all foreign trade with the English colonies, a considerable blow to the planters, who had been selling sugar and tobacco to the Dutch and buying negro slaves from them. The further Navigation Act of 1651 prohibited the import into England of any produce from the non-European continents save in English ships. These laws were a novelty, for they meant that the colonies were to be strictly subordinate to the mother-country. The plantation colonies prepared for a fight, but here the navy stepped in. Sir Harry Vane and other Puritan statesmen reorganized the fleet and infused new life into the dockyards. Within three years they doubled the number of ships on the navy list and made them incomparably more efficient than in the corrupt days of the Stuart kings. Whilst Puritan officials were building ships, Puritan soldiers were taking over their command. That colonels and captains of the New Model Army should be able to transform themselves into good sea-officers is almost incredible, but it is a fact. Blake, Deane, and Ayscue, and in later years General Monk, proved themselves admirals fit to be mentioned with Drake and Hawkins and to hold their own with the Dutch, who were infinitely better sailors than the Spaniards had ever been. In 1651-2 a squadron of the new navy blockaded Barbados and forced the colonists to submit. The other rebellious islands surrendered on hearing the news. The fleet then went on to Chesapeake Bay, where it had an easy success over Virginia and Maryland. Almost without bloodshed the colonial revolt had been put down. The Commonwealth had demonstrated how the use of sea-power could make the empire a reality and direct its trade into channels that would convey tropical wealth to England instead of to her rivals.

For a generation the Dutch had been the greatest sea-power in the world, and the revival of English sea-power was a challenge to their position. Cromwell and the army had no wish to fight the Dutch, whom they respected as fellow-Protestants. Cromwell's plan was rather to seek an alliance and to divide the spoils of the oceans on equal terms. But the Dutch would not admit English equality, and the London merchants would not accept an inferior position. Hence a petty quarrel about a salute to the flag brought on the first Dutch War in 1652. It was stubbornly fought, rather in the desperate spirit of Grenville and the *Revenge* than in the easy confidence with which Howard had beaten the Armada. In the end the new Commonwealth navy under Blake proved the stronger, and the Dutch in 1654 acknowledged the right of England to control her own trade and colonies.

Cromwell, who had become Protector during the war, made the terms of peace easier than they might have been. His view of these matters was Elizabethan. For him Spain was still the enemy and the Protestant religion was in danger. To fight against Protestants was therefore scandalous, and he sought to extend the empire by attacking Spain in the manner of Drake. In 1654-5 he launched his 'Western Design' for the conquest of the Spanish colonies. Spain was weak and England strong, and the 'Western Design' looks like the plan of a bully. But to judge it so is unjust to Cromwell. He was by inclination a man of peace who would much have preferred 'to keep sheep rather than to govern men'. His sense of a mission drove him on. He had no conceit of his own abilities, and yet he had routed all opponents and come to the head of the English nation. He could only explain it as the work of God, who would hold him to account for the use of the power entrusted to his hands. To a seventeenth-century Puritan that use was obvious. It must be to strike down Spain, the citadel of Catholicism. In actual fact Spain was no longer a danger, and the headship of the Catholic world was passing to France. Cromwell had a suspicion of the truth, but the traditional view prevailed, and he made the upholders of the Inquisition his quarry.

He gave orders to Admiral Penn and General Venables, the commanders of the expedition, to 'gain an interest' in the Spanish colonies. They began by attacking Santo Domingo, the chief city of the Spanish West Indies. But everything went wrong, and they were beaten off with some disgrace. Then they found an easier prey in the island of Jamaica, which they captured without difficulty. Cromwell meant this to be merely a beginning of much greater conquests. Jamaica, however, absorbed all the energies of the force, for the climate killed so many men that the survivors could barely hold what they had gained. The 'Western Design' had proved a disappointment. It brought on a war with Spain in Europe. Although Blake destroyed a treasure fleet, English trade suffered heavily from privateers, and war expenditure had made the government nearly bankrupt when Cromwell died. Another part of his foreign policy needs mention. In 1654 he concluded a treaty with Portugal by which England gained great advantages. Englishmen were allowed to trade in Brazil and West Africa and in the Portuguese stations in India. In return we gave Portugal some help in asserting her independence against Spain. This treaty closed the long period of Anglo-Portuguese hostility which had lasted from the days of Henry VIII. England and Portugal have ever since been friends, and often allies in time of war.

The restoration of Charles II entailed no break in the policy of colonial expansion and of trade protection by means of Navigation Acts. It produced rather a fresh outburst of energy. The new government made peace with Spain on the condition that we kept Jamaica. It confirmed the alliance with Portugal, and Charles married a Portuguese princess with whom he gained Bombay and Tangier as a dowry. Bombay became a stronghold of the East India Company, whilst Tangier served as a base for the fleet in the Mediterranean, a position afterwards filled by Gibraltar. In 1660 the Restoration Parliament passed a Navigation Act to supersede the measures of 1650 and 1651. It restricted the colonial trade to English ships and compelled the colonists to send most of their goods to England only, whence they might be re-exported to foreign customers. Other Acts followed, and a whole code was built up, to be known as the Laws of Trade and Navigation. They ensured to the mother-country the monopoly of business with the growing empire. In this imperial policy of Charles II the most active figure was James, Duke of York, the King's brother and heir to the throne. James and Charles proved themselves good friends to the East India Company, which enjoyed its most prosperous period after the Restoration. They also formed the Royal African Company to monopolize the supply of negro slaves to the western plantations. In 1670 a charter was granted to the Hudson's Bay Company for the fur trade of the North West, and Prince Rupert, the veteran of the Civil War, became its governor.

The expansion of English enterprise provoked a second war with the Dutch. It began in 1664–5 and ended with the Treaty of Breda in 1667. In the fighting the honours were divided, and so also were the spoils at the close. England gained the colony of New Amsterdam, renamed New York, but lost that of Surinam in Guiana, a thriving plantation which had been founded by Royalist exiles during the Commonwealth. The third and last Dutch War (1672–4) was due to European politics and had little effect upon the colonial empire. On the whole the navy maintained its prestige during these struggles. It was not always victorious, but it did not slip back into the feebleness of the early Stuart period. The Duke of York rendered good service as Lord High Admiral, both in action and at the Navy Office. In the latter sphere his right-hand man was Samuel Pepys, who would be remembered as one of England's greatest civil servants had he not left a diary which has made him even more famous as a writer.

The most enduring work of the Restoration overseas has yet to be described. It consisted in a new outburst of colonization which made the North American coast a continuous line of English settlements. In 1663 eight prominent men were created Proprietors of Carolina, and their efforts produced the distinct colonies of North and South Carolina. These filled the gap between Virginia and the Spanish holding of Florida. When New Amsterdam was taken in 1664 its adjacent territories became the two English colonies of New York and New Jersey, which almost filled the space between New England and Maryland. In 1681 the line was completed by the foundation of Pennsylvania which, although mainly an inland colony, had an outlet to the sea by the estuary of the Delaware River. North of Massachusetts the area of New England was extended by the settlement of New Hampshire and Maine, which had been claimed but scarcely occupied earlier in the century.

The peopling of these colonies took place in a new manner. Although some emigrants went out from England, the majority of the settlers were not English-born. Many were from the older colonies, particularly from New England, Virginia, and Barbados. They were colonists of the second generation who were beginning to be over-crowded in the original settlements. American population, in other words, was now vigorous enough to expand on its own account, a portent significant to the future of the Empire. Of the remainder of the new hands probably a minority were English. New York contained some thousands of Dutchmen, French Huguenots went to all the American colonies, many Germans and Swiss settled in Pennsylvania, Irishmen were everywhere to be found, there was a distinct Scottish element in Carolina, and all the sugar and tobacco colonies received a large influx of negro slaves. Turning to the emigrants from the mother-country, we may notice that they were nearly all of special categories, and that hardly any were ordinary subjects of the King who swarmed off to new homes of their own free will. The victorious Puritans of the Civil War transported thousands of Royalist prisoners to work virtually as slaves in the colonies. After the Restoration this continued to be a usual means of getting rid of criminals, who escaped a death-sentence by accepting slavery. In 1685 the collapse of Monmouth's rebellion produced another large body of exiled prisoners of war. Meantime the Quakers were suffering severe persecution. Many of them sought a refuge in New Jersey, and still more in Pennsylvania when their leader William Penn secured the grant of that province in 1681. The Irish and Scots who emigrated in this period were also for the most part victims of religious persecution.

From all this we may draw a general statement to the following effect. The growing Empire was peopled either by foreigners or by British undesirables. This does not mean that the Quakers and their like were not thoroughly worthy and often heroic men, but it does mean that in the eyes of the government they were undesirable citizens, and that they were thrust out in company with rebels and criminals. It was a foolish policy to fill the colonies with bad characters, or with good characters who left their homes with a grievance, for from such a colonial population no ardent loyalty could be expected. The explanation lies in the economic theory fashionable at the time. It was no longer believed, as in Elizabeth's reign, that England was overpopulated and must get rid of its surplus. Restoration thinkers held, on the contrary, that every good citizen was a source of wealth to his country and that the numbers ought to be increased rather than diminished. But at the same time the mother-country needed colonists to send home raw materials and buy her manufactures. Therefore the colonial population must be expanded. And, on this reasoning, it could only be done by exiling undesirables who gave trouble at home, or by admitting foreigners from the continent of Europe. This policy underlies the whole history of the old colonial empire which was broken up by the War of American Independence; and the policy was largely to blame for the state of feeling which produced that disaster.

Apart from this radical defect, the Restoration statesmen made a great success of the Empire. Its colonies were all self-supporting and most of them prosperous. Its shipping and commerce expanded until they eclipsed those of the Dutch. Wealth accumulated overseas and poured into England, where capital became available to fertilize ever new enterprises and ultimately to finance the Industrial Revolution of the eighteenth century, the greatest event of modern history. The new money supported a powerful navy, and the merchant sailors were available to man it and capture fresh colonies in time of war. The North Atlantic became almost an English lake, surrounded by the national possessions and traversed by connecting trade-routes. From the Restoration the pace of English development became more and more rapid, until it plunged into the furious rush of recent times.

III. THE FALL OF THE STUARTS

When General Monk's free Parliament of 1660 recalled *Restoration 1660* Charles II it did not restore the monarchy which had perished with Charles I. There was no repeal of the Triennial Act of 1641, whereby not more than three years might elapse without a meeting of the Houses. There was no revival of the Star Chamber, the High Commission, or the lesser prerogative courts which had served as instruments of tyranny. The very fact that Parliament had made Charles II King implied that in the last resort it could unmake him. Divine right was practically dead, although some Royalists could still be found to render it lip-service. Above all, it was clearly understood that taxation might be levied only by grant of the House of Commons. The ancient feudal dues were abolished, and forced loans and ship-money were equally things of the past. Charles II, the only Stuart who possessed tact and really genial manners, understood the position. His was a limited authority. He did not like it, but he refrained from openly saying so. At heart he was as much an absolutist as his father. But he worked to restore absolutism by means so subtle and secret that when he died on the morrow of accomplishing his aim the majority of his subjects regarded him only as an easy-going gentleman, too light-hearted and pleasure-loving to be a danger to liberty.

Charles II was actually a Roman Catholic when he ascended the throne; but again he refrained from saying so. He desired to have Catholicism tolerated, and perhaps in the future day of power to make it the state religion. In 1660 he realized that it could be tolerated only in company with the various nonconformist sects which had developed out of Puritanism. His minister and faithful companion in exile, the Earl of Clarendon, the same Edward Hyde who had helped to pull down Strafford in 1641, was neither Catholic nor Puritan, but neither was he an ardent persecutor. His view was that King and Parliament should work together in harmonious balance, and should rule the country on the Tudor principle of give and take. It was this which made him accept the views of Parliament in matters of religion, and so he lives in history as the author of the Clarendon Code of persecuting statutes. He promoted them against his better judgement. As for the King, he assented to persecution whilst heartily detesting it.

The persecution was bitter enough, but it sprang from the Commons. In 1661 a new Parliament was elected in the flush of Cavalier triumph. Its members were by no means enthusiastic for divine right, and they took care to keep a tight hold upon the King's revenue. But they were full of zeal against their old Puritan enemies, who had fined them mercilessly after the Second Civil War. The Cavalier Parliament, therefore, enacted law after law to make life intolerable for all who did not belong to the Church of England. Exclusion from public office and the learned professions, imprisonment for holding dissenting services, continual harrying by Anglican magistrates, became the lot of the nonconformists. Men of property for the most part joined the Church, and it was left to the humbler members of society, John Bunyan the tinker and his like, to suffer for their beliefs. The social cleavage lasted into the nineteenth century. To be a nonconformist meant to be ineligible for a university education and a professional career, to be restricted to a despised trade as the best means of livelihood. The sects thus excluded inevitably became narrow and intolerant in reaction to the intolerance with which they were treated. 'The nonconformist conscience' is a phrase often used as a gibe to the present day; but the Cavalier High Churchman was largely to blame for the unpleasant outlook of the ranters he derided. At least the nonconformists proved sturdy, obstinate Englishmen and took their gruel unflinchingly. They really suffered more than did the Puritan gentry under Charles I. But they neither rebelled nor, with the exception of the Quakers, did they emigrate. They hung grimly on in the hope that times would alter. For there was this to give them hope, that it was Parliament and not an arbitrary power that was tormenting them. Sooner or later Parliament would cease to show a Cavalier majority, and then toleration would return. The time of waiting was to be longer than most of them expected.

Charles II, by far the most interesting of the Stuarts, was two men if not three. To his courtiers and to the public he appeared a merry trifler given up to pleasure and wholly incapable of work. This Charles was most often seen and has formed the stock figure of many histories. But a man who loved to stride through the English countryside for hour upon hour at a pace that his companions found killing was something more than a lounger; and in matters of administration he was as competent as any ruler of his century. He gave much more attention to business than most people thought. He had the gift of economy of effort. In five minutes' talk aside from a revel he would settle things to which a more pompous man would have devoted two hours at the council board; and things he did not choose to handle himself he would delegate to the right men unerringly chosen. Much of the prosperity of Restoration England, of her rapid recovery from civil and foreign war, of her great expansion of trade and empire, must be attributed to Charles II. His father or his grandfather would certainly have made a mess of these things. This was the Charles known to ministers and officials, the gifted men whom he employed in the background whilst the masquers and boon companions performed before the public. An administration which used such servants as Samuel Pepys, Sir George Downing, and Sir Joseph Williamson was in no idle hands.

There was yet a third Charles unknown to any but himself, the man of ambition, patience, and callous cruelty. He carried his secret to his grave, but it came near to switching the evolution of England into surprisingly new courses. The merry monarch who was so popular with crowds and so genial to self-important magnates despised the part he was called upon to play. In his heart he longed to be a despot of the continental type, ruling by terror and surrounded by a nation of slaves. The French tradition of his day was his model, the tradition founded by Richelieu and carried on by Louis XIV with the motto 'L'État c'est moi'. The Cavaliers were his enemies as much as the Puritans; more, for they were the stronger. To the outward Charles they were the loyalest of subjects, for they regarded him as the head of their order. To the secret Charles they were detestable, for they represented a spirit which he would have to break before he could say with his French cousin 'I am the State'. For the poor nonconformist underdogs he had little aversion. They were powerless, and he might make them useful. For twenty-five years Charles worked in the dark, and then he died suddenly, a middle-aged man, with his work half done. His brother James took up the ambition, proclaimed it in blatant arrogance, found himself deserted by all his prospective slaves before he had chained them, and fled ignominiously after a three years' course of folly. That is the thread of English politics from the Restoration of 1660 to the Revolution of 1688.

Although France might be the model, France was by no means the cordial ally, even in secret. The ambition of Louis XIV was too great to allow of that. Not satisfied with a subservient France, he designed to rule a trembling Europe, and Charles II had no mind to be a deputy-despot. The two worked as confederates, but always with a view to over-reaching one another, and Charles played with a double-edged tool in using French resources to accomplish his aim. But French help he was obliged to have. France had taken the place of Spain as the leading anti-Protestant power. She was directed by the specialized policy of the Jesuits rather than by that of the Catholic Church as a whole, and the Jesuits of this period were both extreme and unscrupulous. Their methods appealed to Charles as a politician much more than as a believer, and he became a political Catholic, devoid of sincerity but convinced that the Jesuit procedure was best adapted to the sort of monarchy he wished to create. As for the English people, they recognized Louis and France as the foes of liberty, but could hardly believe that their pleasant king was ranged on the same side. The anti-French feeling grew throughout the reign, amid much puzzlement that the government should be so blind to the peril.

The King's need was an army, and his difficulty was lack of money. The Cavalier Parliament kept him short of cash, and its worthy squires had a fixed disgust for soldiers, who reminded them too much of Cromwell's ascendancy. A regiment or two were kept on as lifeguards, but the rest were disbanded. The Earl of Clarendon would not have countenanced any absolutist designs, for he was as much attached to Parliament as to the King. During his ministry Charles therefore played a waiting game, although he did make some overtures to the Pope in 1662. Clarendon fell in 1667, hated by the Puritans as their persecutor, hated by the Cavaliers as too moderate, disliked by the King as too honest. It was then that Charles really began his secret moves to power. At the demand of Parliament and public opinion he entered into alliance with the Dutch against French encroachment in 1668. Two years later he concluded the secret Treaty of Dover with Louis XIV. By this pact the two monarchs agreed to fall suddenly upon the Dutch, Louis to seize the Netherland coastline and Charles the islands adjoining it. Furthermore Charles was to restore the Catholic

religion in England, whilst Louis was to provide him with
French money to make him independent of Parliament, and if
necessary with French troops to crush resistance. The betrayal
of English religion may perhaps be excused in the name of
toleration, although toleration would have been short-lived had
the plot succeeded. The furtherance of French conquest admits
of no excuse. In the seventeenth century, as in the eighteenth,
the Netherlands in French hands would have been 'a pistol
pointed at the heart of England', and every one knew it. If ever
a king committed treason against his people it was Charles II.

The plan bore fruit in 1672. Louis invaded the Netherlands
by land. Charles declared war without consulting Parliament,
and at the same time issued a Declaration of Indulgence to
excuse Catholics and Puritans alike from the operation of the
penal laws. The calculation was that the old English jealousy
of Dutch trade would make the nation the unconscious tool of
despotism. There was a momentary enthusiasm for the war,
but soon men began to doubt. Why help France to greater
dominance? And why this favour to Catholics? Before long
the French ally grew far more unpopular than the Dutch enemy.
The Dutch, indeed, fought with the heroism they had displayed
against Alva a century before. They cut the dykes, drowned
their fields, and brought the French hosts to a stand. Their
young stadtholder William of Orange (the third of that great
name) led them in battle and schemed for them in council.
He awoke Europe to a sense of the French peril and formed a
coalition of Protestant and Catholic powers which curbed the
aggression after six years of struggle.

England soon dropped out of the plot. In 1673 Parliament
met, full of suspicion, to cancel the Declaration of Indulgence
and to pass the Test Act depriving all Catholics of public
office. The Houses had no knowledge of the secret pact of
Dover, but their instinct warned them that all was not right.
In 1674 public opinion forced Charles to make peace. He
submitted with an easy grace and abandoned the Catholic path
to absolutism. Thenceforward he sought other means to his end.

In these years the two great English parties began to take
shape. The Tories stood for a single opinion, that the Church
of England must be supreme and intolerant; and they sprang
from a single ancestry, the Cavaliers of the Civil War. Their
strength was in the squires and gentry of the countryside, and

they believed that the King was their natural leader. Squires and parsons joined in harrying dissenters and preaching the doctrine of passive obedience: '... and damned were they who dared resist, or touch the Lord's Anointed.' Unhappily for the Tories neither Charles nor his brother James was prepared honestly to play the part of Defender of the Faith. The Whigs were a more varied crew. Their most brilliant leaders were great nobles who took little stock in religious belief and were therefore disposed to be cynically tolerant. They found support in the plebeian nonconformists, who were especially strong in the towns. Between these two extremes stood the country Whigs, landowners of new families who had bought Cavalier estates cheaply in the Civil War, had turned Churchmen in 1660, but still had the honesty to disapprove of persecuting the Puritans from whose ranks they had sprung. These Low Churchmen were the hope of the dissenters, who were themselves disqualified for seats in the Commons. The cement of the Whig party was thus toleration for all Protestants, whilst that of the Tories was intolerance. The antithesis extended into secular politics, where the Tories stood for authority and the Whigs for liberty; and into foreign affairs, where the Tories admired yet feared the absolutist French, whom the Whigs feared more keenly and hated wholeheartedly. Anthony Ashley Cooper, successively Lord Ashley and Earl of Shaftesbury, became the leader of the Whigs in opposition to the half-suspected designs of Charles and the ascendancy of his Tory dupes.

The year 1678 found England in a whirl of suspicion, with Tories proclaiming that a new revolution was brewing, and Whigs declaring liberty to be in peril. The King had given up the idea of toleration for Catholics, and was leaning on the Tories, whose price was the full enforcement of the anti-Puritan laws. Over all lowered the inscrutable figure of Louis XIV, his enmity to England realized, his plans and methods in doubt. Charles II passed for a Protestant, but his brother was an avowed Catholic; and he was heir to the throne. The Catholics of England were an unknown factor. They formed no organized party and voiced no political opinions. Yet none could suppose them content with their position, and their very silence made them suspect. Their numbers were exaggerated in popular belief, for the age of censuses and statistics had not dawned. All tempers were raw with persecution. The judgement even of prudent men was unbalanced, and panic was in the air. Into this cauldron of mischief stepped the devil in the person of Titus Oates.

In the course of a roving career Oates had joined the Jesuits, who had cast him out as soon as they discovered his character. He returned to England, studied politics, and embarked on the boldest design ever carried through by an English criminal. He declared that there was a Popish Plot whereby the Catholics of England and Ireland were to massacre the Protestants, burn London for the second time, murder Charles II, and enthrone his brother James, all with the aid of French troops. He produced lists of the conspirators, scores of innocent persons who for the most part had no finger in politics. In normal times he would have been challenged for his evidence, but he had correctly gauged the situation. The panic of the moment and the sense of peril threatening from an unknown source played into his hands. To the English of that day Louis XIV was a very real menace. Their city had been destroyed, none knew by whom, a dozen years before. Their fathers had told them of the Irish massacre of 1641. Their grandfathers had known the Gunpowder Treason of 1605. In the seventeenth century Protestantism was always in danger. Oates had luck as well as judgement. The magistrate to whom he opened his story was murdered by unknown miscreants; and it was believed, of course, that the papists had done it to stop his mouth. Edward Coleman, the Duke of York's secretary, was one of those denounced, and when his papers were seized they were found to contain treasonable matter, vague enough and common enough among the intriguers of the period, but absolutely damning when fitted to the accusation Oates had launched. It is possible, indeed, that some of the Catholics were hatching a plan of some sort, but not that it bore the implications Oates alleged.

The Whigs took up the tale with enthusiasm. The Tories believed it also and were paralysed; for the heir to the throne was implicated, and he stood next to the King as leader of their party. London crowds thronged to gaze upon the corpse of their murdered magistrate and to invoke the vengeance of heaven for his death. Honest citizens lay awake through the night listening for popish slaughterers to begin the general massacre. Through the courts defiled the procession of Catholic victims, condemned with scarcely a hearing on the testimony of Oates, executed without respite ere the madness could subside. Two men only kept their self-possession. One was Titus Oates, pensioned, flattered, fawned upon. The other was the King, who knew from the outset that the plot was a lie. Yet it would have been awkward to say so, for in the existing panic Shaftesbury might have turned Whigs and populace upon their royal master, and a savage revolution might have ensued. Charles, therefore, affected belief and daily signed the death-warrants of his own co-religionists whom he knew to be innocent. He and Oates were a well-matched pair.

Shaftesbury and the Whigs rode into power over the bodies of the victims. They determined to make the most of their good fortune, and they overdid it, to their own ultimate destruction. They struck at the Tories through their leader, the Earl of Danby, who had been induced to further the secret intrigues of the King for French money. To save Danby from an impeachment, in which many ugly facts would have come to light, Charles dissolved the Cavalier Parliament in 1679. It had sat for eighteen years and had become increasingly Whiggish in tone as the old members died off and were replaced at bye-elections. There followed three short Parliaments in which the Whigs had the majority. Had Shaftesbury played a cool game he might have secured permanent toleration and guarantees against tyranny. But he struck too high and outran his popularity. His Exclusion Bill proposed to deprive the Duke of York of the succession on the ground that he was a Catholic. The Duke had two Protestant daughters, of whom Mary, the elder, was married to William of Orange. The natural course would have been to transfer the rights of James to his daughter. But Shaftesbury made it plain that his candidate would be the Duke of Monmouth, an illegitimate son of Charles II. This was more than sober men cared for, since it would certainly have caused a civil war on the death of the King. The Exclusion Bill was therefore three times blocked by the dissolution of Parliament, and it was then the turn of the Whigs to be paralysed by their leader's blunder. For the respite had given the Popish panic time to blow over, and the country was growing ashamed of the excesses into which it had been led. The Monmouth candidature was a revolutionary policy. The more it was looked at the less it was liked, and moderate men thought it better to risk tyranny by supporting the King than to ensure revolution by backing Shaftesbury.

So Charles dissolved his fourth Parliament in 1681. At last he was on the road to absolute power. His lifeguards were unobtrusively growing into a small army. He had money from Louis XIV, who had been scared by the possibility of a Whig triumph and an anti-French policy. Non-party opinion was passive, and the Tories were exultant. High Churchmen though they were, they vowed confidence in the Catholic heir, preached non-resistance in the highest degree, and filled the gaols with Quakers and nonconformists. The Rye House Plot of 1683, a genuine conspiracy of desperate Whigs to murder the royal brothers, evoked transports of loyalty. Charles made use of it to ensure that the next Parliament should be submissive. He deprived scores of the boroughs, the stronghold of the Whigs, of their ancient charters, and substituted new ones which provided in effect that the members returned should be nominees of the Crown. When Parliament should at length meet it would be a docile body such as no Stuart had ever faced before. Meanwhile there was no hurry, and a preliminary extermination of Whigs could best proceed without parliamentary eloquence. Shaftesbury fled overseas and died in exile. His less nimble friends died on the scaffold in expiation of the Rye House Plot.

The King had come into his own, and the land basked in the calm sun of royalty. It was fated to be but an Indian summer. In 1685 Charles died after a violent illness at the age of fifty-five. He was the greatest and worst of the Stuarts. He had the courage of his line, but in subtlety he stood alone. What would he have done with fifteen years of his triumph? We may surely say that he would have made England a successful state. But it would not have been the land we know. The England of William III and Marlborough beat French despotism by hard blows, and showed the world that a free nation was more efficient than a nation in chains. The England of Charles II would have outwitted France—and grown like it. Charles was a compound of intellect and appetite untroubled by conscience. He received the sacraments of the Catholic Church he had never truly served, and died jesting at his own agonies.

James II succeeded to a stable throne, and in three years his throne and his family and their theory of government had fallen for ever. James was the reverse of his brother, a Catholic first and a politician afterwards. But his honesty alone does not explain his downfall. That resulted from a sequence of follies which look as if they were due to physical failure. He was not much over fifty, but his brain was worn out before its time. As a king he showed himself devoid of common sense and common courage. Yet as Duke of York he had served with credit in murderous fighting, had managed colonies and trading companies with wisdom, and had saved his beloved force, the Royal Navy, from the worst effects of disloyalty and corruption. Had the Rye House plotters shot him down we should deplore him as a good king lost.

The defect of James's policy is simply explained. He was master of the three kingdoms under the existing conditions, but he was not content with that. He determined also to make England a Catholic country. And he was not prepared to work patiently to that end; he would achieve it violently and without delay. Charles II, as we have seen, had followed the same object in 1670, but had given it up as not practicable and had achieved mastery by the aid of the Church of England and the Tories. James presumed to undertake a project which his much abler brother had condemned as unsound.

In 1685 Parliament was called and proved itself thoroughly Tory and loyal. It voted the King ample supplies which enabled him still further to increase the strength of his army. But when James demanded the repeal of the Test Act, it refused. The Tory High Churchmen were prepared to wink at a certain limited favour to Catholics, but they would not see the great offices of state thrown open to them. During this year Monmouth and the Whig exiles gambled for the throne with a rebellion in the west country. At Sedgemoor the King's regulars defeated them. Before the battle was over Monmouth fled, leaving the Somerset peasants to die for him. He was taken and executed after grovelling for mercy. There are doubts whether he was really Charles II's son, and his conduct supports them. He deserved his fate, and yet to kill him was a blunder. For his death relieved the Whigs of the error Shaftesbury had imposed upon them. They could now support a much stronger candidate for the throne in the person of the Princess Mary, whose husband was one of the most influential men in Europe. James would have done better to keep Monmouth in the Tower or even to let him escape overseas, where he would only have weakened the opposition.

A still greater blunder was the Bloody Assize in which Judge Jeffreys took vengeance on the rank and file of the rebels. The tale of executions sickened even the English of the Popish Plot, by no means a squeamish generation. Even the rabid Tories grew alarmed, for in those years Louis XIV, having revoked the Edict of Nantes, was persecuting the French Protestants in a manner reminiscent of Alva in the Netherlands. Two neighbouring sovereigns, cousins, both Catholics, both advised by Jesuits, both despots, both stony-hearted—even the most optimistic were obliged to bracket them together and ask whether their conduct was not the fruit of a jointly concerted policy.

With his triumph over Monmouth the King cast discretion away. He thought himself unassailable and forgot that the price of despotism is ceaseless vigilance. He created a prerogative court, that of the Ecclesiastical Commission, in defiance of the Act of 1641. He 'dispensed' with the Test Act in scores of appointments of Catholics to army commissions and civil posts. He promoted Catholics to university fellowships and even to benefices in the Church of England. The result was that he overstrained the loyalty of the Tories and dared not summon the very Parliament which his brother had refashioned as an instrument of tyranny. He revived the discredited policy of a general toleration. The Declaration of Indulgence of 1687 suspended wholesale the penal laws which had hitherto been dispensed with in individual cases. The gaols gave up their nonconformist prisoners, and Puritans and Catholics worshipped openly before the world. The Tories were exasperated, and the Whigs were not content, for they saw that the King was using toleration only as a temporary device to pave the way to a Catholic dominance. What that would mean they had only to look to France to understand. England was full of Huguenot refugees whose stories were illuminating.

In the summer of 1688 the plot quickened. The second Declaration of Indulgence led to the protest and trial of the Seven Bishops. Their acquittal was hailed with delirious joy, even in the army, the pillar of despotism. The King's second wife bore him a son, who would take precedence of the Princess Mary and continue the Catholic succession. The story at once went round that the infant was a pretender smuggled into the queen's room in a warming-pan, and at the same time the leading Whigs and Tories combined to invite William of Orange to invade the country and safeguard the Protestant succession.

Thus began the Revolution of 1688, which to many seemed as hopeless a project as man could well conceive. Louis XIV could have prevented it by attacking Holland and pinning down William to its defence. He neglected to do so until too late. The English navy, loyal to James, might have stopped the expedition on the seas. A contrary wind kept the fleet at its anchors at the Nore for a few vital hours during which the Dutch armament slipped through the Straits of Dover. The English pursued with every chance of catching William in the act of disembarkation. The east wind carried him to Torbay, and at once changed into the west in time to hold up the English at the Isle of Wight.[1] James had an army which on paper was stronger than William's. On Salisbury Plain it deserted *en masse* without firing a shot. James became a prisoner to his son-in-law. He had only to remain so with the certainty that the Tories would in time rally to his deliverance. Instead he escaped and crossed to France, leaving his adversary unhampered to control the situation. In two months the bloodless Revolution was over, which at the outset few betting men would have backed at odds of ten to one against.

Then followed the settlement. The Whigs, eager to assert the power of Parliament, talked John Locke's philosophy of government based on contract to respect the fundamental laws. By violating them, they argued, James had forfeited the throne, and the people in Parliament should appoint his successor. The Tories, half repenting what they had done, which was clean against their own doctrine of non-resistance, would not allow that a king could be deposed. But James's flight enabled them to save their faces. It was equivalent, they said, to an abdication, and therefore the throne was vacant. Both views found expression in the preamble to the Bill of Rights of 1689, but in all other respects that document was a Whig triumph. It laid down that the King might not be a Roman Catholic, that he

---

[1] Napoleon waited two years in 1803–5 for a similar combination of weather chances. He might well have waited ten. William did not await the chance, which arose after he had started. He believed he was under divine protection, and the 'Protestant wind' became a proverb.

might not suspend or dispense with the laws, that subjects might present petitions, that elections and debates in Parliament should be free from royal interference, that prerogative courts were illegal, that a standing army (without Parliament's permission) was illegal, that taxes might be levied only by parliamentary grant, and that Parliament should be held frequently. The Princess Mary was declared Queen as the rightful heir, the Pretender being ruled out; but her husband, who had no claim of his own, was made King with equal powers, and his title was entirely parliamentary. Moreover, the offer of the Crown to each of them was conditional upon their accepting the above rules of government. Finally, the Toleration Act granted liberty of worship to all but Catholics, but they were in practice allowed the privilege as well as the nonconformists. Henceforward religious penalties in England consisted in disqualification for the universities and public office, a serious breach of liberty, but light in comparison with what had gone before.

The settlement proved permanent. William III was a man of his word. The Whigs forbore to demand vengeance for past sufferings. The Tories still hankered after persecution, but never obtained it. The Stuarts in the male line never reigned again on English soil. For a century afterwards politicians were used to perorate on 'the principles of the glorious Revolution', until those principles became so much the fabric of the English mind that men ceased to be conscious of them. Some of the credit for the success belongs to Louis XIV, for it was his menace that hammered the brawling factions into community of action as Englishmen.

IV. THE STRUGGLE WITH LOUIS XIV

Louis XIV, in asserting 'L'État c'est moi', was speaking the truth, for he was the embodiment of the France of his age. But his was not an original mind, and though he executed he did not conceive. The two men who laid the plans of that brilliant merciless régime were Richelieu and Colbert. Cardinal Richelieu had prepared the ground. As the minister of the feeble Louis XIII he tamed the nobles who had been so disorderly in the Wars of Religion, the French counterpart (a hundred years later in date) of our own Wars of the Roses. He broke also the independence of the Huguenots and made all ready for the persecution which was to expel them from France at a later time. He founded the system of administration which centralized all authority in Paris. He was alive to the importance of sea-power and colonization, but his achievements in this sphere were not great. He initiated the foreign policy by which France was to push forward to her objective of possessing all lands west of the Rhine and controlling the destinies of a disunited Germany to the east of it. All these things were of permanent importance. Perhaps more important was the moral tone which Richelieu imparted to the French government. He made the state logical, impersonal, and therefore pitiless. No human interest must stand in the path of France, and his France was less a nation of human beings than a system of ideas and ambitions.

After Richelieu's death there was a reaction when Cardinal Mazarin ruled during the minority of Louis XIV. Mazarin had the will but not the power to be a Richelieu. He lacked the ferocious personality which had made bold men tremble before his predecessor. He was too supple and cunning, he forgave too readily. The nobles knew that they could revolt without risk to their heads. There was a last civil war, the Fronde, which Mazarin extinguished by guile rather than by force. When he died in 1660 he had not forwarded the internal discipline of France, but he had rendered great services to her foreign ambitions. His Peace of the Pyrenees with Spain marked the end of Spanish greatness, just as the Peace of Westphalia a dozen years earlier had left Germany weak and divided. Mazarin handed on to Louis XIV a rich legacy of provinces won, a rich prospect of provinces ripening for seizure, and a kingdom fortified like a citadel from which to give law to dependent neighbours on every side.

With Mazarin's death Louis began his personal rule. He had been educated in the tradition of Richelieu, and he was an apt pupil. He knew that a ruler must work, and he worked hard. He had a talent for authority such as Mazarin had never shown. He overspread the land with a cold, silent discipline strangely at variance with the garrulous vivacity which Frenchmen normally display. The monarch's approval meant success to any subject; his frown meant ruin, however high the offender's rank. Priestcraft appealed to him as an engine of rule. But his France was rather a Jesuit state than a Catholic state. The French Jesuits were playing for their own hands and paid scant respect to the commands of Rome. Louis yielded as little allegiance to the Pope as did our own Henry VIII. His Gallican Church was a department of his government, and the priests were his police. One man in every fifty was a priest or monk. The 'religious' were more numerous than the soldiers of his mighty army.

So far Louis was the reincarnation of Richelieu, but there was something lacking, and that was supplied by Colbert. Jean Baptiste Colbert was efficiency personified, a clear thinker, a tireless worker, an unsparing crusher of obstacles. He applied himself to the departments that had been weakest in the governments of Richelieu and Mazarin—those of trade, finance, and the marine; and Louis, who could originate nothing, appreciated Colbert's originality, and allowed him to carry his ideas into effect. Colbert held that a great army was insufficient to give France world-supremacy. She must have also a navy and wealth. He undertook to supply them. The profits of trade, in the view of that age, were a fixed amount not capable of expansion, a cake at which competing nations cut for the largest slice. To diminish a rival's share was therefore to increase one's own, and the best way to do that was to establish monopolies. The colonial trade was an obvious subject for national monopoly. Therefore France must have colonies, and navigation laws to exclude foreigners from them. The Indian trade was lucrative; France must have an East India Company, and must obtain Asiatic goods by no other channel. Private enterprise was injurious because individuals wasted their substance in competing with one another; all French traders must therefore be organized in corporations, the drilled battalions of commerce. The state must see that outsiders did not undersell Frenchmen; therefore high protective duties were necessary. The profits of transport were great; therefore they must be reserved to French shipping. A fighting navy was essential to protect these interests and strike down those of competitors. Trade-begotten wealth would pay for this navy, and merchant seamen would man it in time of war. These ideas, as we have seen, were current in England, but it was Colbert who first enunciated them as strictly as mathematical propositions, and enforced them to the last detail with the authority that absolute power alone could confer. The parliamentary, undisciplined English passed navigation laws with much unseemly wrangling and debate, and broke them quite as often as they obeyed them.

THE NETHERLANDS & RHINELAND. The prize
of many European Wars from the 16th to the 20th century

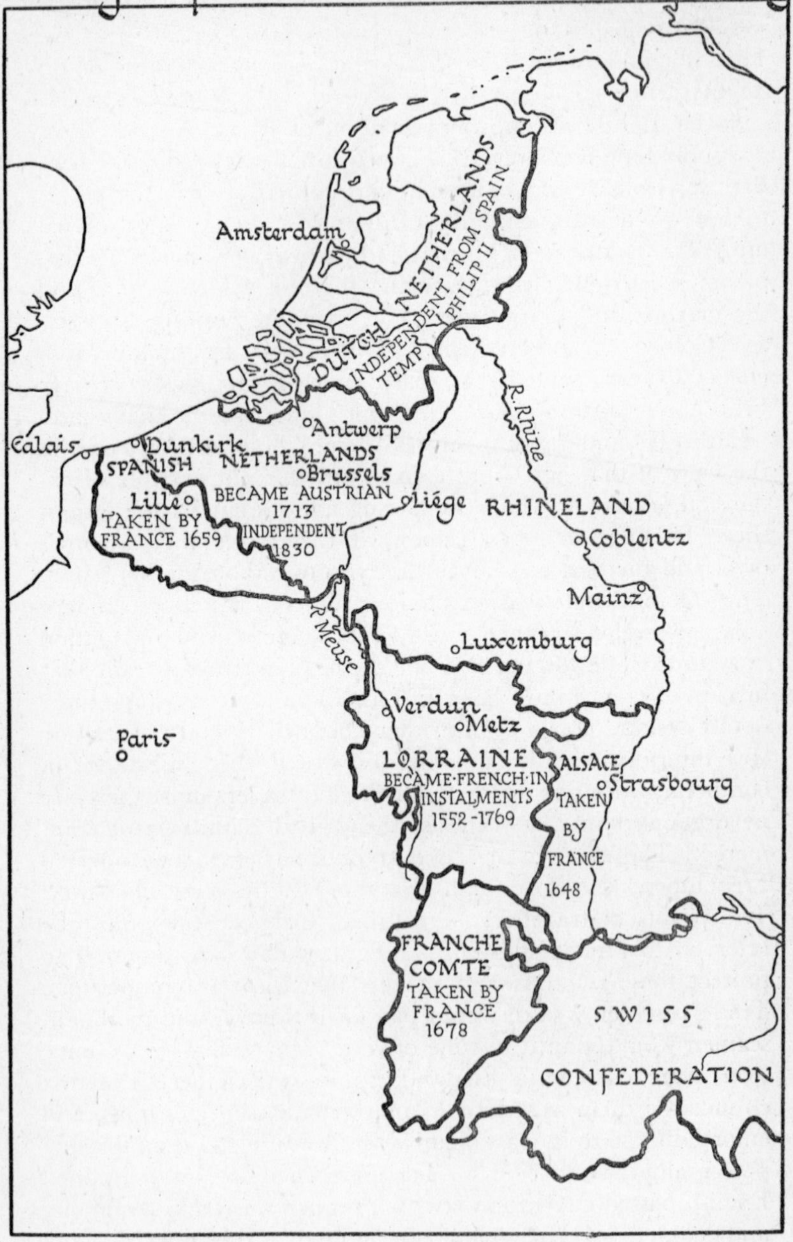

Amsterdam

DUTCH NETHERLANDS
INDEPENDENT FROM SPAIN
TEMP. PHILIP II

R. Rhine

Calais

Dunkirk

SPANISH

Antwerp

NETHERLANDS

Brussels

BECAME AUSTRIAN
1713
INDEPENDENT
1830

Lille

TAKEN BY
FRANCE 1659

Liége

RHINELAND

Coblentz

Mainz

R. Meuse

Luxemburg

Paris

Verdun

Metz

LORRAINE

BECAME·FRENCH·IN
INSTALMENTS
1552-1769

ALSACE

Strasbourg

TAKEN
BY
FRANCE
1648

FRANCHE
COMTE

TAKEN BY
FRANCE
1678

SWISS

CONFEDERATION

Under Colbert there was no argument and no exception. Men did what the state thought right. For a season French trade prospered, and the French navy was a fine force.

This was the neighbouring nation which Englishmen viewed across the Channel from the time of Cromwell onwards; no easy neighbour either to fight with or to live in friendship with, a malevolent neighbour to any people who should dare to claim freedom and equality. Englishmen being what they were, hatred was inevitable.

England grew especially uneasy at any advance of French power in the Netherlands. In 1668, when Louis was encroaching upon the Spanish provinces of what is now Belgium, the nation heartily approved of Charles II's Triple Alliance with Holland and Sweden, designed to check the French. Two years afterwards Charles bartered the true interest of his country for the promise of Louis' help to establish Catholicism. The secret Treaty of Dover produced the joint Anglo-French attack on the Dutch in 1672, coupled with Charles's Declaration of Indulgence of the same year. In the battles with the Dutch the French fleets left all the fighting to their allies, and men began to say that the true enemy was France. Charles was compelled by his people to make peace in 1674, and four years later there was even a clamour for the government to join the Dutch against France. At the same time the affair of the Popish Plot testified to the general uneasiness at French designs. In his later years Charles II took large sums from Louis XIV, who was also in the habit of bribing English ministers and members of Parliament. By these means the national hostility was smothered, whilst public indignation at the aggressions of Louis and his treatment of the Huguenots grew ever louder.

James II took a more independent line than his brother had done. He had no desire to fight France, but he declined to be subservient to her. In order to teach James a lesson Louis refrained from stopping the expedition of William of Orange, as it was in his power to do. Louis did not believe the attempt would be successful, but he miscalculated, and the English Revolution was the turning-point in his victorious career. With William III on the throne England took her place in the Grand Alliance against France. She contributed the sea-power necessary to success. The French fleet was stronger than the Dutch, but not so strong as the Dutch and English combined.

The war was waged on land as well as sea, for Louis, having allowed James to be driven from the English throne, did his best to put him back. The Highland clans rose for James in 1689. They defeated the Lowland Whigs at Killiecrankie. But Viscount Dundee, the Jacobite leader, was killed at the moment of victory, and there was no one left to keep the Highlanders together. The clansmen wished to go home with their plunder —a musket, a greatcoat, or a pair of shoes formed a rich prize in their eyes—and the chiefs were too jealous of one another to go on. The Highlands remained quiet thenceforward. In Ireland there was more serious business. The Catholic provinces declared for James in 1689. They desired rather to make him King of an independent Ireland than to restore him to the throne of England. 'England's necessity is Ireland's opportunity' was the watchword of a later crisis, but it was acted on at this time to the motto of 'Now or never; now and for ever'. Only the Protestants of Ulster stood for William of Orange, and they have been known as the Orangemen ever since. James crossed from France and held a Parliament, which ordered severe confiscation of Protestant lands. Londonderry, the Ulster stronghold, was hotly beset and was relieved from the sea when at its last gasp. Louis sent French troops and money.

William was detained by English business until the summer of 1690. Then he crossed over to Ireland and routed James at the Battle of the Boyne, a polyglot affair in which English, Scots, Dutchmen, Frenchmen (Huguenots and Catholics on opposite sides), Ulstermen, and Celts decided the fate of Ireland. James fled at once to France. His supporters held out for another year and surrendered at Limerick in 1691. Thenceforward William was King of Ireland, and the Protestant ascendancy began. Following, as it did, upon the Catholic ascendancy under James, and upon memories of confiscation and massacre, it was naturally no pleasant thing. For close on a century the Irish Catholics had a terrible time. It is false history to blame the woes of Ireland upon one party when both were guilty; but what has caused more woe than anything else is the Irish habit of treasuring up bitterness over grievances after they have been removed.

On the sea, as in Ireland, the war went against Louis XIV. At the outset he had an excellent fleet. Colbert indeed was dead, but his spirit lived in the service he had organized. The French navy seemed well able to contend with the English and

Dutch combined. In 1690, whilst William was in Ireland, the French won the Battle of Beachy Head. Had it not been followed a few hours afterwards by the Battle of the Boyne, the result might have been serious. But Louis had lost Ireland, and he made no effort to invade the English coast before his great rival could hasten back. Two years later there was a plan of invasion. James was to land in England with French soldiers and French gold, and trust to the Tories to rally round him. Few would have done so, for they were Englishmen, much as they hated the Whigs. The English navy saved them the trial. At Barfleur it scattered the French squadrons, and at Cherbourg and La Hogue it destroyed many of their fugitive vessels. James II looked on with mixed feelings. His hopes of restoration were being hammered to fragments—but it was by the men and the ships that in happier days he and his faithful Pepys had organized for victory. After that Louis discarded the teaching of Colbert and spent all his money upon his armies. The French battleships were laid up in port, and their crews went to sea as privateers. They did much damage to English trade, but they did not affect the issue of the war.

The settlement of Ireland and of the contest by sea left William free for the task that lay nearest his heart, that of stemming in his own Netherlands the rush of French aggression. In that cockpit of Europe he fought round after round with the best generals Louis could send against him. The details belong to military history. The result may be summed up by saying that whilst Louis won the victories William won the war. By 1697 his dogged defence had its reward in the Treaty of Ryswick. Both sides laid down their arms without gain or loss of territory. But Louis was obliged to recognize William as King of England, and thereby to recognize the English Revolution, the overthrow of the Stuarts, and the blighting of French hopes of European domination. Moreover this treaty of 1697 was the first in which Louis had closed a war without adding new provinces to his kingdom. The power of France was not broken, but it had passed its zenith.

Ryswick gave but a breathing-space before the next contest. On three occasions in modern history the decay of a once mighty power has plunged all Europe into war. In our own day it was the Austrian Empire, whose decline paved the way for the events of 1914. At the close of the eighteenth century the tragic fall of the French monarchy produced twenty-two years of conflict. At the close of the seventeenth the weakness was with the Spanish monarchy. In the person of Charles II of Spain the Hapsburg line, descended from Philip II and the Emperor Charles V, was at its last gasp. Charles was a dying man, and he had no son to succeed him. His vast empire was impoverished, weak, and destitute of nerve and enterprise, a prey to any strong neighbour who should make a push to seize it. Such a neighbour was in readiness across the Pyrenees.

Louis XIV had a plausible claim to the succession; so also had the Austrian Hapsburgs at Vienna; whilst a minor prince, the infant son of the Bavarian Elector, had the best claim of all. Two interested onlookers, England and Holland, had no claims whatever, but they were unwilling to see Louis upset the balance of power by gaining the prize. There was much at stake. The Spanish Netherlands marched with Holland by land and faced across the narrow seas into the mouth of the Thames. In feeble Spanish hands they were harmless; in strong French hands they would be a menace to both the sea powers. In the Mediterranean most of Italy was Spanish, and the two naval bases of Minorca and Gibraltar gave shelter only to innocuous Spanish ships of war. Across the Atlantic the wide colonies of Central and South America slumbered under Spanish rule. They yielded little wealth to their possessors, but again, if competent Frenchmen should exploit them the position would be very different. Englishmen and Dutchmen had need to bestir themselves or they might be overwhelmed without a blow struck, solely by the chance of cousinship between the French and Spanish dynasties. William III determined to act in time. His English were in a difficult mood, sick of war, blind to the great peril, more intent on domestic quarrels than on world politics. He promoted Partition Treaties to solve the problem in advance by dividing the spoil. Then, in 1701, the Spanish king at last died and left a will which ignored the treaties and bequeathed everything to the grandson of Louis XIV. Louis had to make his decision, to observe the treaties or to claim all under the will. After long debate the decision was announced in a memorable scene. Louis led forth his grandson from his inner cabinet and presented him to the expectant courtiers with the words, 'Messieurs, voici le roi d'Espagne'. It was the death-sentence of a generation of brave men.

William was yet in doubt whether England would follow him. Louis kindly decided that she should. Old James II died at Saint-Germain, and the French monarch publicly recognized his son the Pretender as King of England. He meant it only as a polite form, for at the same time he recognized him also by the complimentary title of King of France which English kings had claimed since the days of Edward III. But the effect in England was decisive, since it added the touch of sentiment necessary to consolidate material interests. The Tories were at the moment in power. They had at first shown no opposition to the French candidature for the Spanish throne. They even acknowledged the new King of Spain as Philip V. But Louis quickly showed that he really meant to unify the French and Spanish Empires, and to crush the commerce of both English and Dutch. The compliment to the Pretender seemed a studied insult to the English people, whose own Tory Parliament had just passed the Act of Settlement to exclude the Stuarts for ever from the throne. The country immediately became resentful. William dissolved Parliament at the close of 1701, and the general election returned a majority for war. Before the campaign could open William was dead. His horse stumbled over a mole-hill and threw him. The Jacobites made a toast of 'the little gentleman in black velvet' who had caused the tragedy; but in fact they had no reason for congratulation, for its effect was to place the English cause in the hands of a greater than William III. The feeble Anne succeeded to the throne, but the commander-in-chief of the armies and the diplomatic head of the anti-French alliance became John Churchill, Duke of Marlborough.

The War of the Spanish Succession began in earnest in 1702. Marlborough's tasks were those of William III—to humour the European princes and keep them steady to the purpose of beating Louis, to command the armies in person, and to manipulate English politics so as to prevent party dissension from weakening the national effort. He had to do all this, not with the advantage of being a king himself, but from the position of a subject to a queen who was notoriously feeble in will-power and ignorant of public affairs. For nine years Marlborough coped with this tremendous problem, and when his enemies achieved his fall success had already crowned his efforts. As a soldier he was the equal of Cromwell and Wellington. As a statesman he surpassed them both.

The English objects were, first, to keep the French out of the Netherlands, the region most vital to our safety; secondly, to prevent Spain from becoming a province of France; and thirdly, to acquire naval bases and colonies for the strengthening of English sea-power. Marlborough took command always in the Netherlands. All his battles were fought there save that of Blenheim; and that, although far away on the Danube, was in essence a part of the Netherland defence. For Blenheim foiled a French advance on Vienna which, if successful, would have knocked the whole coalition to pieces and so have gained the Netherlands in the general ruin of the allied cause. Year after year, in battles and sieges, Marlborough made good the defence of the Low Countries, and at the end he was over the frontier and ready to advance on Paris itself. In Spain the English effort failed. Most Spaniards preferred the Bourbon candidate for their throne; and the Hapsburg claimant, the Archduke Charles of Austria, found support only in Catalonia. With English troops Charles obtained Barcelona and reached Madrid, but he did not long remain there. The French party gained the decisive victory of Almanza in 1707, and thenceforward no efforts availed to shake their position. The command of the Mediterranean was essential to this Spanish undertaking and also to the eviction of the French from Italy. The French fleets had a great base at Toulon, centrally placed for cutting the allied communications. The English navy seized Gibraltar in 1704 and Minorca in 1708, and by so doing secured the means of maintaining its command of the Mediterranean. There were no great naval battles in this war, simply because the French saw no hope of success in fighting them. Ever since 1692 Louis had allowed Colbert's fleet to go to ruin, and his neglect permitted free communication to all his scattered enemies and lost him the war. Had the French been able to dispute the control of the seas Marlborough could not have led armies to the Netherlands.

The most favourable moment for ending the war came in 1708. Louis saw France on the point of being invaded, and sued for peace. But Almanza had given Spain to his candidate, and the English Whigs were determined to reverse that decision. Their formula was 'No peace without Spain', and they insisted that Louis himself should assist in turning his own grandson out of Madrid. It was too much to ask. Louis called on his suffering

people for a last effort, and they responded nobly. At Malpla-
quet in 1709 Marlborough indeed drove the French from the
field, but at terrible cost. His casualties were twenty thousand
men, a staggering total in proportion to the armies and populations of those days. A cry went up against the war and against
those who had needlessly prolonged it. The Tories, like John
Hawkins in days of old, had always held that it was not England's business to pour out blood and money on the continent.
They could point to the security attainable by sea-power alone,
and they denounced the Whigs for making England the catspaw
of continental ambitions. Could England have survived if she
had left Louis to conquer Europe? It is an undecided question.
The problem arose again, in the time of Napoleon, in the war
of 1914, and in that of 1939. On every occasion the answer of
British statesmen was in principle the same, that we must fight
on the continent to preserve our liberty at home. The application has indeed varied in intensity. The numerical strength
of the British armies so employed was small in the struggles
with Louis XIV and Napoleon, immense in that of 1914-18,
and (averaging the whole war) moderate in that of 1939.

In the War of the Spanish Succession the Tories had their way
when the work was already done and France powerless for
further offence. At the general election of 1710 they overthrew
the Whigs. Then they stopped all serious fighting, recalled
Marlborough, and opened peace negotiations. The Treaty of
Utrecht was signed in 1713. It effected a partition such as
would have averted the whole war if only Louis XIV had been
reasonable in 1701. The Spanish Netherlands were given to the
Hapsburg Emperor and became the Austrian Netherlands, with
the proviso that the great port of Antwerp should be closed. So
were England and Holland rendered secure, for Austria was not
a sea-power. The Italian provinces also became for the most
part Austrian. The throne of Spain, together with the Spanish
colonies, remained with the Bourbon Philip V, but he had to
renounce all claims to succeed to the throne of France; the two
kingdoms were never to be united. Great Britain retained
Gibraltar and Minorca and thus remained the dominant sea-
power in the Mediterranean. She received from France the
Hudson's Bay trading factories (originally English, but lost in
the war), the French colony of Nova Scotia, and the whole of
Newfoundland (hitherto divided). She received also from

Spain the Asiento or monopoly of supplying slaves to the Spanish colonies. It was a much-prized concession, although it proved valueless. It was set off by a counter-concession of French rights to fish on the Newfoundland coast.

Such were the material fruits of the great contest with Louis XIV. They were solid enough, for they left England the chief sea-power of the world, with freedom to develop her trade and wealth in the period of peace which followed. The intangible results were greater still. They moulded the whole course of subsequent history. Until Louis was humbled, absolute monarchy was regarded as the path to national greatness, and parliamentary liberties as the inevitable cause of weakness. The English in 1688 had decided for liberty, but no onlookers had expected them to thrive by it. After Utrecht there was a revolution in European thought. This English system was worth studying; despotism was discredited. Hence began a movement which gathered strength throughout the eighteenth century. The French themselves were its leaders. Although they did not love England they admired her government and became ever more critical of their own. The challenge to despotism, begun in England by Pym's Puritans and carried on by Shaftesbury's Whigs, was extended to the European stage by William III and made good by Marlborough's victories. Thence it was taken up by French thinkers, Montesquieu, Voltaire, and Rousseau, and many more, until it exploded in the French Revolution which gave the death blow to the old order throughout the world. It is a definite sequence of cause and effect, to be seen on the high peaks of history as they stand up clear in the light above the murk and mist that encircle their lower slopes.

V. GREAT BRITAIN

The days of the final struggle with Louis XIV were also the last days of England as a self-contained and separate political unit, the England-and-Wales united by Edward I and consolidated by Henry VIII; for in 1707 the Act of Union merged England with Scotland in the single kingdom of Great Britain. Nevertheless, when full weight has been allowed to the importance of Scotland (which has grown steadily during the past two centuries), it must be said that since the Union the predominant partner has been England, and that the Scottish nation has

grown into one of the world's great peoples by its association
in the lines of enterprise originated by its neighbour. To this
general statement there are two obvious exceptions, in the
Scottish religion and Scottish education, but otherwise it holds
good. After 1707 we speak of the British nation, British policy,
and the British Empire, but it is still in the main the evolution
of England that we must follow. It is noteworthy that our
foreign friends are to this day more used to thinking of us
as the English than as the British. To Frenchmen we are
'Les Anglais', and the German war-prayer was 'Gott strafe
England'.

The time of the Union is a fit occasion to take stock of the
England and the Scotland that entered into it, and to note how
they had developed in the century of troubled politics which we
have hitherto been tracing. The population of England and
Wales at the beginning of the eighteenth century was about
five and a half millions, of whom one-tenth were inhabitants of
London. Of the remainder few were townsmen, for London was
the only great city in the kingdom. The next largest, Bristol and
Norwich, had about 30,000 people each, and after them there
were not a dozen towns with more than 5,000 apiece. The vast
majority of Englishmen were countrymen and drew the greater
part of their living from the soil. Property was divided among
several classes. The peers were almost all great landowners, but
there were only 168 of them in 1707. Probably half the land
was owned by the gentry, the squires of whom Addison's Sir
Roger de Coverley stands as a type. The petty freeholders or
yeomen together owned much, but their individual shares were
small. The Church of England and various colleges and corporations held a good deal of landed property. The Crown
lands had greatly diminished in extent since the Tudor period
and were no longer of much importance.

Of the country people the most important classes were the
squires, the yeomen, and the landless folk, who ranged from
tenants of farms to mere cottagers and labourers. The squires
were distinguished from the yeomen by their superior birth,
and their capacity to sit in Parliament, to act as justices of the
peace, and to hold commissions in the fighting forces. These
qualifications were not easily defined, but were clearly understood in a society which had no difficulty in distinguishing the
'gentry' from others. When the law attempted a distinction, as it

did in the Game Acts, it had to take the value of land owned as its
criterion, and it drew the line between gentlemen and yeomen
at the possession of land worth £100 a year. Wealth in other
forms did not constitute a gentleman of the sort who might kill
game or sit in the House of Commons. The squires were predominantly Tory in their politics and High Church in religion.
Their wealth and power steadily increased from the Restoration
onwards. This was partly due to the growing predominance of
their House of Commons, and partly to their function as justices
of the peace. In the earlier period the justices had been closely
supervised by the Privy Council, but after the Civil Wars the
Council did not recover its old position, and local affairs were
left much more to the unfettered control of the local gentry.
The yeomen were therefore a declining class, hemmed in by
restrictions upon their ambitions and activities. They had been
the backbone of the Puritan armies, and the nonconformist or
at least Low Church tradition continued strong among them,
which caused them to be Whiggish in their politics. Many men
of this rank had risen to eminence in the Tudor period. Fewer
did so in the eighteenth century, when the career open to
talents was not nearly so marked a feature of English life.

The Church presented a curious contrast after the Revolution
of 1688. The rank and file of the clergy were nominated by the
squires, who were commonly the patrons of livings. As a class
they were therefore High Church and Tory, haters and would-
be persecutors of nonconformists. The bishops, on the other
hand, were chosen by the Crown or its ministers, who, save for
a few years of Anne's reign, were predominantly Whig. The
bishops were thus more tolerant and Low Church than their
clergy, and this circumstance mitigated a good deal of the petty
persecution that was still possible even after the Toleration Act
of 1689.

Tradesmen and manufacturers were not limited to the towns.
Every village had its craftsmen, its smith, saddler, joiner, and
tailor, who catered for the local demand in most articles that
are now mass-produced in great factories. The word manufacturer has entirely changed its meaning in the last two hundred years. At the time under discussion it did not signify a
capitalist at the head of a big business. It meant a person who
made things with his own hands. The chief national manufacture was that of cloth, and some of its processes were still,

as in the Middle Ages, carried on in the homes of peasants and farmers. The poorest cottage had its spinning-wheel for the preparation of yarn. The yeomen kept hand-looms for weaving. Only the finishing was done by special workmen who gave their whole time to their craft; and many of these were countrymen rather than townsmen. This domestic system of manufacture continued through the eighteenth century to yield bye-industries to the humbler folk and to prevent them from being wholly dependent on the wages they could earn as farm-labourers.

The function of the towns was rather to be centres of commerce than of production. The market-town was the focus for exchange of the corn and cattle and manufactures of its district. The larger towns added to this business the wealth they attracted as seats of county and legal administration, or from the presence of a cathedral with its staff of dignitaries creating employment. The smaller seaports, which had seen much of their trade diverted to London since the beginning of the Tudor period, began to recover it in the eighteenth century. Bristol was an early example of this revival. It was favourably placed for ocean commerce. Its merchants carried slaves between Africa and the West Indies, and imported raw sugar to be refined in the sugar-works for which the town grew famous. Liverpool rose later, and it also laid the foundation of its greatness in the slave-trade. A scarcity of wood for fuel grew serious as population rose, and coal therefore became more important. This revived the prosperity of Newcastle and its neighbours, where the mines lay close to the harbours. The revival of the navy from the Commonwealth onwards was favourable to the dockyards and fleet-bases such as Chatham, Portsmouth, and Plymouth.

London, however, did not decline. It grew greater than ever, in population, trade, and shipping. The City proper, within the walls (which remained standing until the latter part of the century), was still the place of residence as well as of business for the wealthy citizens. The poorest people and the worst slums were to be found just beyond the City limits. Outside the poor belt, at least to the westward, there was beginning to arise the residential area of the world of fashion and court society, the West End of later days. In many respects London was already an overgrown city. Lack of sanitation rendered it terribly unhealthy, even after the Great Fire had led to the rebuilding of most of the houses. The death-rate far exceeded the birth-rate, and the population increased only by virtue of a steady immigration from the country. Lack of police, schools, and what may be called social missionary work accounted for the existence of a huge criminal element, which was always ready to give a dangerous turn to any popular excitement. The honest citizens might turn out to demonstrate on some political grievance, and under cover of this respectable motive the roughs would begin a course of sack and pillage. Shaftesbury had been given to organizing Whig mobs to impress the government, and the fashion continued until the Gordon Riots of 1780, an orgy of robbery and arson that came near to the destruction of the whole city; for it was only the stillness of the weather that averted a general blaze like that of 1666. Even in normal times theft and violence were common. Londoners were excitable and quarrelsome, and street fights were of everyday occurrence. After dark all sorts of criminals roamed at will, and young men of fashion set forth in gangs to seek adventure. All this is related by many witnesses, and yet there is more favourable evidence to modify the picture. A Swiss traveller who came to London in 1727, after visiting many continental cities, was struck by the cleanliness of the houses and the preservation of order, the goodness of the water-supply, and the general well-being of the people. All such things are comparative, and the fairest comparison is not of one century with another, but of one country with another at the same period.

To appreciate development, however, we must place one age against its predecessor. The London of Queen Anne exhibited some features entirely lacking in the London of Shakespeare. One was financial. Joint-stock companies had now become a usual method of business enterprise. By taking shares in a foreign trading company, an insurance or mining company, or a bank, a man might draw profit from an undertaking of which he had no personal knowledge and to which he contributed no skill of his own. The age of the stock-market had set in, and speculation in shares attracted moneyed persons of all classes who in former times would have invested only in landed property. The 'moneyed interest' now meant much more than the interest of actual merchants, and it became an ever more important factor in English life. The formation of the Bank of England and the placing of the National Debt on a firm basis of regular payments of interest, both achieved under William III, greatly assisted this change. The moneyed interest was mainly Whiggish. The Stuart kings had had a bad record for honesty, and it was generally feared that another Stuart restoration would mean the repudiation of state debts.

Another new feature was the importance of the press. Pamphleteering of all sorts, political, religious, and financial, had grown common in the Stuart period. Regular newspapers appeared during the Civil Wars of Charles I and never quite died out thereafter. After the Revolution of 1688 these activities redoubled, for men could be much bolder to write as they pleased. Charles II had founded the Royal Society, and scientific studies occupied a hundred minds for every one they had attracted under the Tudors. Literature likewise extended its scope, and Steele and Addison trained a generation of readers to appreciate writings inspired by the interests of everyday life rather than by the squabbles of parties and sects; whilst Defoe was preparing to clothe in fiction the romance of distant lands and peoples. The opera was an almost new type of stage entertainment. Meeting-houses opened their doors to a variety of religious sects which had hidden in holes and corners a century before. Altogether the London of the new age was a city of richer life and more active intelligence than it had ever been before.

Scotland was still a land of two nations. The Lowlands in most respects resembled rural England on a poorer and rougher scale. There were gentry, yeomen, and peasants under other names, but after 1688 there was less religious animosity, for there was no High Church to set against Puritanism. The democratic Kirk embraced nearly all Lowlanders. Edinburgh was a far more rustic capital than London, not yet the seat of the learning and taste that were afterwards to make her 'the Athens of the North'. Glasgow was a poorer seaport than Bristol, for she had no colonial empire open to the traffic of her shipping. The Scots Parliament, although of ancient origin, lacked the prestige of its English counterpart. It dealt only with domestic affairs, for all foreign policy was controlled from London. The Highlands supported an entirely different society. The clans were tribal, not national, in their way of life. They lived under the despotic authority of their several chiefs, as a patchwork of little states sundered by the rugged mountains. They obeyed no laws from Edinburgh, and regarded the Lowlands as an enemy country fit only to be raided for plunder. They lived chiefly by their sheep and cattle, with little agriculture and no manufactures or trade. United (as they seldom did unite), the clans could put a force in the field capable of beating a regular army in battle; but it was a force with little endurance for a long war, for it had no sources of supplies and munitions. The whole population of Scotland was barely a million.

Since 1603 England and Scotland had been ruled by the same kings. But the bond had been purely accidental; the Scottish Stuarts were lineal heirs to the English throne, and that was all. For many purposes the two nations remained foreigners to one another. When the Commonwealth deposed the Stuarts in England it recognized the exiled Charles II as King of Scots, and a temporary union was afterwards attained by the conquest of the northern kingdom by the armies of Cromwell and Monk. At the Restoration the former state of affairs returned—two kingdoms under the same King. After the Revolution of 1688 it grew apparent that this could not continue, and that union or complete separation must take place.

The merchants and adventurers of the Lowlands had long cast their eyes upon colonial trade as the means to national greatness. They were excluded by the Navigation Acts from any share in the business of the English Empire. Merchants had to content themselves with European commerce, which for them did not amount to much. The hard fighters and leaders of men whom Scotland has always produced had to take service under foreign flags, for their own country could offer no outlet for their energies. They were to be found over all Europe, fighting for Dutch merchants, German princes, and even Russian Czars, but not for their own Scotland. The national spirit demanded a change in these conditions. In 1695 Lowland Scotland undertook to become a colonial power. Under the guidance of William Paterson she founded the Company of Scotland for Trade with Africa and the Indies. The intention was worldwide in its scope. Scotland was to found trading posts in east and west, and her ships were to bring wealth from all the oceans. There was great enthusiasm, and a large capital was subscribed. In 1698 the first expedition set sail to found the first colony. Paterson chose the Isthmus of Panama or

Darien as the site. With the eye of a strategist he saw that
Darien might be made the focus for trade routes converging
from all parts of the Atlantic and the Pacific. He even talked of
cutting a Panama canal. The outcome was failure. The most
malarious climate in the tropics killed the majority of the
settlers, and the rest surrendered to the Spaniards, who owned
the isthmus and had not consented to its invasion. William III,
hard at work on his Partition Treaties, was annoyed at the
disturbance promised by the Scottish plans. The English East
India Company was alarmed at the threat of competition. The
English colonies in the West Indies had therefore given no help
to the Darien pioneers. The Scottish national effort had failed
utterly and had lost the people their money; and public opinion
blamed England as the jealous villain of the tragedy.

Whilst Scottish anger was at its height the English Parliament passed the Act of Settlement of 1701. It decreed that
William III should be succeeded by his sister-in-law the Princess
Anne, and that in the event of her death without children the
Crown should pass to the Electress Sophia of Hanover, an aged
sister of Prince Rupert and grand-daughter of James I. This
meant the exclusion of the Pretender, the son of James II, born
in 1688. But an English Act of Parliament was binding only
upon England, and Scotland was free to make different arrangements. By the Act of Security the Scottish Parliament declared
its right to do so, and opened up the prospect that on the death
of Anne the Hanoverian line would succeed in England whilst
the Stuarts might be restored in Scotland. That would ultimately mean war, for no Stuart would ever give up his English
claims and rest content with Scotland alone.

In 1707 the best men in both countries found the statesman-
like solution. By the Act of Union the two parliaments were
merged in one, that of Great Britain, and the Hanoverian succession became legal on both sides of the Tweed. Scotland had
only a minority of members in the united Parliament, and Scots
are sometimes tempted to describe the union as unfair. They
should remember that their ancestors gained solid advantages.
The Darien shareholders were repaid their lost money by the
English taxpayer. More important in the eyes of that time was
the admission of all Scots on a parity with the English to the
monopoly created by the Navigation Acts. Scotland became at
a stroke an equal partner in the Empire created solely by Eng-

lish money and enterprise. It was a big concession for mercantilists to make, but it has had its reward. Scottish leaders,
merchants, and seamen have since been prominent in the British
Empire, to which Scotland has become a mother-country with
lasting benefit to herself. To re-create a Parliament at Edinburgh would not be to undo the effects of the union. No power
on earth can undo them; they are part of the permanent fabric
of the modern world.

The Act of Settlement had been the work of a Tory majority.
The Act of Union was promoted by the Whigs. As the years
passed it was seen that Anne's death would produce a crisis to
test the statesmanship of both parties; for her children had all
died young, and the Hanoverian succession would be necessary
if the law was to be maintained. The crisis was due to the fact
that some of the Tories were repenting of their own work. They
came into power in 1710 as the result of national disgust at the
Whig war policy. They were united in the making of peace,
but divided on the succession matter. Most of them, with their
senior leader, Robert Harley, Earl of Oxford, were for letting
the Act of Settlement take its course and receiving as King the
Elector George of Hanover, the inheritor of his mother's claim.
But a minority, under Henry St. John, Viscount Bolingbroke,
were Jacobites who favoured the Pretender. Anne herself had
a natural reluctance to discuss a question that depended on her
own death, but when she did face it her preference was for the
Pretender. There was little doubt that he was really the son of
James II, and thus he was Anne's half-brother. The point was
mainly one of religion. The Pretender was a Catholic, the
Elector a Protestant. As Churchmen the Tories distrusted the
former, as Jacobites they disliked the latter. The old division of
motives which had paralysed them in 1688 was to be their ruin
in 1714.

For the last year of the poor queen's life the contest raged in
the Tory party, with the Whigs looking on, eager to seize the
advantage. At length Bolingbroke, the Jacobite, persuaded the
dying woman to dismiss Oxford, and the Protestant succession
was endangered. In six weeks, Bolingbroke calculated, he could
place the army, the navy, and the offices of state in Jacobite
hands and make all sure for a restoration. But the Queen died
in less than one week. Even then a man of the highest courage
might have made a desperate bid for victory. Happily for

England, Bolingbroke was more brilliant than sound. He lacked the iron nerve requisite for the moment. One of his followers had it, but only one, Atterbury, the Bishop of Rochester, who counselled riding down to Charing Cross and proclaiming the Stuart, the Act of Settlement notwithstanding. But Bolingbroke faltered, and the Whig lords pushed their way into the Privy Council and proclaimed the Elector. After that George I was King in law and fact, and the Protestant Succession was ensured.

The decision of 1714 marks the close of three-quarters of a century of revolution, from the meeting of the Long Parliament in 1640. In storm and passion, in doing and undoing, in treachery and persecution, England had at last hammered out a set of principles on which she would henceforth be governed. The head of the state was to be Protestant, and therefore not subject to those foreign influences so feared in the person of Louis XIV. The Crown was not to be absolute, but was to work in harmony with Parliament, through which the public will could find voice. Religious toleration, limited in some respects, was to prevail. The Church of England was to be the state religion, and nonconformists were to be disqualified from office; but there was to be no persecution of the old sort, involving peril to life, limb, liberty, and property. Finally, the state was to keep faith with individuals in money matters: there should be no taxation without public consent, and no defaulting on public debts. All these principles were directly or indirectly challenged by Bolingbroke's plans of 1714. His failure rendered them secure.

VII

THE EIGHTEENTH CENTURY

(*From 1714 to 1783*)

I. THE REIGN OF THE WHIGS

*T*HE *Vicar of Bray*, a political song written shortly after the accession of George I, should be known to every historical student, for it gives a witty summary of the turns of party fortune from 1660 to 1714. The good vicar is determined to retain his job, and so he changes his opinions with every revolution in the state. 'In good King Charles's golden days, when loyalty no harm meant, a zealous High Churchman was I, and so I got preferment.' But the golden latter days of Charles II did not last long, and in 1685 a new course became desirable: 'When royal James obtained the crown, and popery grew in fashion, the penal laws I hooted down, and read the Declaration.' The Declaration of Indulgence soon brought disaster to its author, but not to its adroit reader, for: 'When William was our king declared, to ease the nation's grievance, with this new wind about I steered, and swore to him allegiance.' Queen Anne, although she endured the Whigs for a season, at heart belonged to their opponents, as the vicar was quick to note: 'When gracious Anne became our queen, the Church of England's glory, another face of things was seen, and I became a Tory.' Anne died in 1714, and Bolingbroke failed to keep out the Elector, whereupon: 'When George in pudding-time came o'er, and moderate men looked big, sir, I turned a cat-in-pan once more, and so became a Whig, sir.' And the vicar ends a year or two later on a note of qualified constancy: 'And in this faith and loyalty, I never more will falter, and George my lawful king shall be, until the times do alter.' The times never did alter within that veteran's experience. The vicar and all his flock, which numbered many thousands throughout the length and breadth of England, were able to end their days in a tranquil reign of Whiggery to which there was no end in sight.

The Whig supremacy in fact lasted nearly sixty years, a thing surprising to us who are accustomed to see parties alternately victorious and defeated with every general election. The conditions were evidently different then, and it is well to attempt to

understand them. Then, as now, there was a House of Lords
and a House of Commons, and the King's ministers were obliged
to have a majority in the Commons, or else they could not carry
on. How was it then that in a nation comprising Whigs and
Tories the latter were never strong enough to instal a ministry
of their own leaders? The answer is that while the outlines of
the constitution were the same as now, the emphasis was
different.

At the present day the whole mass of citizens chooses its House
of Commons at a general election and, the majority in the
Commons having made choice of a leader, the King sends for
that leader and invites him to form a ministry. It is the inevitable course, for no other ministry would be able to get its bills
passed and its taxes voted. The flow of authority is from the
broad base of the popular will to the isolated man at the summit,
His Majesty's prime minister.

In the eighteenth century the process was reversed, and
authority flowed from the summit downwards. The King in
the first place chose his ministers. They looked for parliamentary support. Sometimes they could get it at once by a
judicious bargain with men influential in the Commons. Sometimes they might need to dissolve and hold a general election.
And if they were competent politicians they could so order that
general election that it would yield them their desired majority.
Therefore, so long as a party held together, kept in favour with
the Crown, and made no first-class mistakes, it could remain in
power indefinitely. George I and George II both had their
reasons for favouring the Whigs; George III, on the contrary,
hated them. The Whigs were thus continuously in power until
the accession of George III, and fell soon after that event. It
is a common mistake to suppose that the power of the Crown
was negligible after the Revolution of 1688. It was not, for in
normal times the government of the country depended upon it.
But there was this limitation, that if some powerful wave of
emotion really roused the nation, the popular will was strong
enough to burst through this delicate system of control and to
assert itself in defiance of King and ministers. Great Britain in
the eighteenth century was a limited monarchy, with the
emphasis usually on the monarchy, but with the limitation
always in the background. It was well understood, for instance,
that any tampering with the rules of government laid down in

the Bill of Rights would instantly arouse a storm. No such tampering was ever attempted; 'the principles of the Glorious Revolution' remained a standing limitation on the power of the Crown. In time of national peril also the sleeping lion would awake. We have seen how disgust with the war over-threw the Whigs and let in the Tories in 1710. We shall see again in 1757 how the country will beat the King on the choice of William Pitt as a minister in an even graver crisis.

Englishmen understood this constitution of theirs only in an instinctive fashion; they never succeeded in defining it in clear words. Foreigners failed to understand it at all. French admirers, looking for the secret of English success, were com-pletely led astray. They came to conclusions which proved disastrous when experimented with in their own Revolution of 1789.

The clue to the Whig supremacy is therefore the approval it won from the first Hanoverian sovereigns. The reason for that constant approval is that the exiled Stuarts existed as an alternative to the Hanoverians. The supporters of the Stuarts were known as the Jacobites, and all Jacobites were Tories. It is not equally true to say that all Tories were Jaco-bites. Some were, such as Bolingbroke, and some were not, such as Oxford. But in the crisis of 1714 Bolingbroke had seized control of the Tory party and schemed to bring back the Stuarts. He had failed, and his failure ruined the Tories. For when George I was safely installed he naturally looked upon the Tories as his enemies and gave all his favour to the Whigs. This state of affairs continued as long as there was the least danger to be feared from Jacobitism, as long as there was the slightest chance that a new revolution might replace the Stuarts on the throne.

In 1715, under the Old Pretender (Prince James), the Jacobites tried their fortune. The Highland clans turned out, and a body of English from the north-western counties joined them. But the revolt was unlucky and badly led, and it flickered out more from the Pretender's faintheartedness than by reason of the government's strength. Under strong com-mand, it seemed, the Jacobites would be a power to be reckoned with. In 1745 they tried again under the Young Pretender (Prince Charles Edward). The Highlanders turned out as before. The Prince was a good leader and inflicted a smart

defeat on the Hanoverian forces. But when he advanced into
England hardly a man joined him. In the thirty years since
1715 the Jacobite spirit had faded away, and all England had
grown used to the rule of the Georges. The little Highland
army had to retreat, and was routed at Culloden in the following
year. After that there was no hope of a Stuart restoration, more
especially as Prince Charles Edward lost heart and drowned his
high courage in drink. There was no more need for the Georges
to rely solely on the Whig party. George II was too old to
change his policy. But when he died in 1760 his successor did
change it, with disastrous results to the Whigs.

The lost cause of the Stuarts evoked splendid loyalty from its
adherents, and is worth remembering as a testimony to valour
and unselfishness. Those qualities have been celebrated in
many histories and romances. But from the standpoint of
political development the importance of the Jacobite rebels is
just this, that they gave the Whigs half a century of unbroken
power.

We have seen why the early Hanoverians chose Whig ministers. We have now to consider how it was that the ministers
could always count on a majority in Parliament. The House
of Lords offered no difficulty. The great nobles were mostly
Whig because it suited their interests. The principles of 1688
gave them an influence in the state which they might have lost
had there been any return to absolute monarchy of the Stuart
type; the power of the Crown was limited for their benefit as
much as for that of the country at large. As for the bishops, they
were nominated by the Whig ministers as vacancies arose. The
House of Commons presented a more delicate problem. There
were as many Tories in the country as Whigs, perhaps more.
But only a small minority, even of substantial men, possessed
votes. The system of election had never been overhauled since
the Middle Ages. In many boroughs the two members were
returned by the mayor and aldermen, in others by the freemen
(always a limited number), in others by a body of voters
qualified in various ways but seldom exceeding a hundred in
strength. It was all a matter of local custom, and it was quite
exceptional for every householder in a borough to have a vote.
These limited electorates were easily bribed or intimidated, and
constituted the rotten boroughs. Another large class of boroughs
were mere villages or decayed towns with very few inhabitants

left. Their handful of voters were generally tenants of some
great landowner, and voted as they were ordered. These places
were the pocket boroughs, so called because their members
were nominated by the local magnate and 'in his pocket'. The
county members were more freely elected by all freeholders of
land worth forty shillings a year. But in rustic society the great
families again possessed a weighty influence, and the poorer
freeholders often found it advisable to follow the nobleman's
lead.

The upshot of all this was that the elections as a whole were
controlled by a comparatively few men. The great landowners
(mostly Whig) owned many pocket boroughs. The moneyed
tradesmen who formed the corporations of the prosperous towns
were Whig by interest. In the towns with larger electorates the
King's ministers could bribe a sufficient number by appointing
them nominal revenue officers, with a small salary and nothing
to do for it but vote. Any boroughs not thus accounted for
could be influenced by the allotment of titles, pensions, or
offices of state to the men who controlled them. The mass
of the smaller gentry and their dependents (mostly Tory) had
little chance of returning their representatives save in those
counties not dominated by a Whig magnate; and the total of
county members was only one-fifth of the whole House of
Commons. It is little wonder that, once in the saddle, the Whig
ministries stayed there until a King arose to turn them out.
Then it was shown that the whole game of influence could be
played as effectively in the Tory interest as in the Whig.

It must always be remembered that this control of Parliament
held good only whilst affairs jogged along easily and the ministers ruled soundly. In a time of crisis, if it seemed that the
ministry was leading the country to ruin, the Houses asserted
themselves and voted according to their convictions. The
manipulation of elections was a thing so well established that
it was not thought dishonourable. These Lords and Commons
of the eighteenth century were men of honour, and when
England was in a tight place no minister could buy their votes.
It happened more than once that, right or wrong, the King and
the cabinet had to give way to the will of Parliament, which
prided itself on representing the people although it was not
elected by them. Such was the system, hard for us moderns to
understand, a complete puzzle to the French inquirers of that

day. It was illogical, but it worked. It probably worked better than any other would have done. For it was the spirit behind it that counted for more than the rickety mechanism exposed to view. Borough-owners took pride in nominating talented men to their seats. To win a great county election was a sporting honour that could only fall to a good sportsman; any other would have had his own class against him. The King's ministers were the servants of the nation also, for no King after James II set himself against the nation; and such ministers had no desire to fill the House of Commons with knaves if they could get good men to back them. The general tone of Parliament was high, in spite of the traffic in votes that produced it. Of all the prime ministers of the eighteenth century there was not one who made money by his services. Most of them left office poorer than they entered it.

There was one important process of government in which the Crown stepped behind its advisers in 1714 and has never since resumed its old position. All previous sovereigns had personally presided at the meetings of their ministers. Queen Anne had done so within a few days of her death, when she had dismissed the Earl of Oxford. The effect of this had been that each minister had been directly accountable to the sovereign for the business entrusted to him. There had been no need for a prime minister, since the sovereign filled that position. Under George I the situation was different. He did not understand English, and his ministers spoke no German. It would have been waste of time for him to attend their meetings. He therefore absented himself and received a report afterwards from the mouth of one who had been present. The man who thus acted as the mouth-piece of the ministry inevitably became the most important member of it, since the affairs of all departments passed through him to the King. So arose the office of prime minister. For a few years the meaning of the new departure was not recognized, and in theory the ministers remained equals. But Sir Robert Walpole, who came to the head of affairs in 1721, speedily consolidated his position as superior to the others. He was the first of the modern prime ministers, although he was always careful to disclaim that title. He welded his colleagues into the first of the modern cabinets. They had to look to him and not to the King as their master. His recommendation ensured their appointment or dismissal. He tried to insist that they should present a united front to the outside world by speaking in harmony on contentious subjects, whatever their private convictions might be. All this existed in practice long before it was admitted in theory. It was not until the reign of George III that the title of prime minister was assumed or the doctrine of cabinet solidarity generally recognized. But both these things were the products of the Whig ascendancy.

Walpole was the great man of the early eighteenth century, the steadying influence that kept England on the path of peace and freedom. Until he took office nothing was certain. An age of tumult and revolution lay behind him, and it was expected to continue. The Protestant King was an unpopular foreigner, the Jacobites were a power in the land, the High Churchmen were still thirsting to persecute dissenters. Walpole's level sanity was like oil on breaking seas. His merit was his sense of proportion. He saw things as they were, not as imagination would have them be. He had no fads, no pet theories to push to extremes. England was for all Englishmen. He would have no persecution, religious or political. The Church must not harry the nonconformists, neither must his own Whigs be severe with the Jacobites. Bolingbroke, who had backed the rebellion of 1715, was allowed to return from exile and live in peace. The land tax upon the Tory squires was not made unjustly high. Writers and pamphleteers might say what they liked without fear of prosecution. There were a few exceptions, of politicians hounded out of office because they would not knuckle down to the prime minister. But that was party discipline, not a breach of public liberty; and party discipline is much more strict to-day than it was in Walpole's time. Under his rule Jacobitism died out, religious freedom became an unquestioned principle, opinion was unmuzzled as never before. Until 1739 he kept the peace amid constant temptations to war. 'Fifty thousand men slain this year in Europe,' he said in 1733, 'and not one Englishman.' It was the War of the Polish Succession, a first-class row among the old-fashioned despots, and not one Englishman in a thousand has ever heard of it. It was not lack of enterprise that kept us out; mere flabbiness would certainly have drawn us in. It was Walpole's unsleeping vigilance and his conviction that peace was our true interest. Population grew and trade grew faster. By 1750 England and Wales had six and a half million people, and their foreign commerce had increased by fifty per cent. since the opening of the century. Average wealth per head was mounting, and with it the standard of comfort.

The result of all the religious quarrelling had been that among large sections of the nation religion had almost ceased to exist. That was Voltaire's opinion when he came over to England in the time of George I. The society and literary folk whom he met were for the most part atheists. The same was true, as we know by other evidence, of many of the poorer people. Towards the end of the Walpole period there began the Methodist revival, led by John Wesley and George Whitefield. Wesley was a Tory parson with no intention of becoming a nonconformist. He worked at first within the Church. His method was to travel unceasingly and preach to the largest open-air audiences he could collect. His appeal was emotional, and his hearers often groaned and shrieked as his eloquence convinced them of their sins. But the result was to add a new element to English life, or rather, to revive an old one, the personal piety of Puritan times. By the end of the century no observer could accuse the English of being an atheist nation, and the effect scarcely wore off for another hundred years. Wesley's methods were distasteful to the easy-going clergy who had left him so wide a field to cultivate. They made his task so difficult that his own adherents ultimately left the Church and formed a separate nonconformist body. But the stimulus was felt far beyond their own ranks, and within the established Church it gave rise to the evangelical movement which attracted recruits from the world of wealth and fashion. The fact that this new leaven worked peacefully and produced no explosion like the Puritan civil war is a testimony to the freedom and tolerance of eighteenth-century England.

There was much in that England for reformers to do besides preaching. Education was grossly neglected, and no one considered that the state had any duty in the matter. Private persons kept schools for those who could pay, and there was a steady trickle of new foundations of free schools, a work that had begun before the Reformation. But the supply was not on a national scale, and there was no national demand for it. The masses remained illiterate, and when herded in town slums they might become criminal and dangerous. The poor-law of Elizabeth continued in force, modified by later measures which were more economical than wise. Their effect was to restrict migration in search of work, for parish authorities were alert to prevent any poor newcomer from 'gaining a settlement' within their boundaries, lest he should become chargeable to their funds. Organized charity was beginning on a small scale the work in which it was afterwards to grow so great. Captain Thomas Coram established the Foundling Hospital for deserted children, and after the peace of 1748 he exerted himself to provide for discharged soldiers, to save them from crime and the gallows. In 1732 General James Oglethorpe founded the colony of Georgia as a refuge where debtors and bankrupts might begin a new life. Some of the great hospitals for the sick were likewise founded in this period, but in general it must be said that only the well-to-do could command medical services. When the hospital and dispensary movement grew more extensive at the end of the century there was a fall in the death-rate and a more rapid growth of population.

The English of the Middle Ages had been comparatively a sober people. The rich had drunk wine and the poor had drunk ale without ill effects to themselves. In the late Stuart period spirit drinking became noticeable. The liquor was imported and therefore not too cheap. But in the time of George I the distilling of alcohol in its crudest forms became a national industry. From 1720 to 1750 is the period of the gin mania, of the famous 'drunk for a penny, dead drunk for twopence' placards to be seen at the street corners. The stuff was sheer poison to body and soul. What it meant may be realized from Hogarth's cartoon entitled *Gin Lane*, with its tottering houses, inhuman women, neglected children, and the suicide hanging from a beam. The gin mania inflicted untold misery and was a serious set-off to the prosperity accruing from Walpole's peace. When the consumption had risen to two gallons a year for every man, woman, and child in the country, the government took action and checked the plague. But it was long before national sobriety returned.

The eighteenth century is a period of contradictions amongst which it is not easy to arrive at the truth. On the one hand we can discern Parliament and the public services full of dishonesty, bribery, neglect of duty, and favouritism. On the other hand we find that there were never lacking men of pure zeal and public spirit, strict in performing their own duties, and a constant inspiration to others to do the same. Shirkers and heroes are prominent on every great occasion; it is the proportion between them that is difficult to judge. It is perhaps true that much of the apparent knavery was sheer stupidity. There were few trained administrators and little consciousness that administration (the science and art of getting things done) was a matter with a technique of its own that required study. Hence such transactions as that of Anson's soldiers. Commodore Anson, sailing in 1740 to round Cape Horn and attack the Spaniards in Peru, was given as his military force a body of Chelsea pensioners, mostly over sixty years of age and many over seventy. Anson protested, but was told that those who were good judges of soldiers considered that the poor old men were suitable for the service. Hardly one survived the outward voyage. It was probably mere incompetence. Some official who knew nothing of the sea must have argued that the pensioners were experienced soldiers; their lack of marching power would be compensated by the fact that the ships would carry them to the scene of action; and there would be an economy in pensions.

The above is a choice example of eighteenth-century methods. England survived because her rivals of France and Spain were even worse. Only one country had an honest civil service and a competent administration, and that was Prussia under Frederick the Great. Prussia was fortunately not our enemy.

II. THE STRUGGLE FOR OCEANIC EMPIRE

It has been well said that the Treaty of Utrecht left Great Britain not merely one of the sea-powers but, at least for the moment, *the* sea-power. The marine of France had been almost wiped out. That of Spain remained feeble; it had hardly ever been anything else. The Dutch, our chief competitors in the Stuart century, were exhausted by the strain of land defence. After 1713 they made no effort to be a first-class power at sea. The day was far distant when Germans would believe that their future lay upon the water; the great Frederick would have scoffed at the idea. The Scots had joined forces with England.

The generation after Utrecht saw the exploitation of the British advantage and a revival of Bourbon enterprise at sea. Spain and France, although separated by the treaty, were both ruled by princes of the House of Bourbon, and English statesmen were perhaps inclined to be more perturbed by that fact than they need have been. France rebuilt her navy, revived her East India Company, and entered on new colonial schemes.

Spain made an effort to put her colonial empire in better order, and also to create a naval force in European waters. Great Britain steadily extended her trade in all directions, and felt jealous that her neighbours were doing the like. To a certain extent it was an unworthy jealousy; to a certain extent it was justified. It is quite true that the Bourbons did design to challenge our position by sea; it is also true that we sometimes used our advantage in an overbearing manner and so provoked their opposition.

British opinion hoped much from the South Sea Company, formed in 1711 to trade with Spanish America and ultimately with the rich lands thought to await discovery in the Pacific Ocean. The Asiento concession was obtained at Utrecht, and under it the South Sea Company had the monopoly of supplying slaves to the Spanish colonies. The Company was also permitted to send one ship a year to the mart held at Porto Bello when the cargoes of Asiatic produce arrived in Central America from the Philippine Islands. Acapulco was the receiving port on the Pacific side, and Porto Bello on the Atlantic side acted as the distributing point for European destinations. This was the trade that William Paterson had hoped to seize with his Darien scheme. The South Sea Company never did a profitable business, although it was always promising to bring in dazzling wealth. The fraudulent booming of its shares in the 'Bubble' of 1720 caused a great scandal and wrecked a ministry, but did not bring the Company's operations to an end. They continued for another thirty years and produced constant disputes with the Spanish government. All through modern history the wealth of tropical America has provided a perpetual delusion to British investors. The Elizabethans made some profit of it, but never so much as they hoped. The English Guiana colonies of the Stuart period all failed. Cromwell's Western Design failed. The Scots failed at Darien. The South Sea Company lost money on every voyage. A century later British optimists again crowded to try their luck in the new South American republics emancipated from Spanish rule; and they lost every penny they put in. So also did adventurers from the United States in the mid-nineteenth century. Only to-day is American 'big business' beginning to make a success of exploiting the tropical republics.

In the eighteenth century the lure was as potent as ever, in spite of the South Sea Company's failure. Unlicensed British traders ran cargoes into the Caribbean ports and were roughly handled when caught by the authorities. The case of Captain Jenkins, who was barbarously treated although innocent of smuggling, caused a great stir. Walpole tried to settle the matter by negotiation. But in his pursuit of peace he was not a true Whig. His opponents in his own party were bent on war, not because they cared much for the sufferings of Jenkins, but because they thought the feeble Spanish Empire would prove an easy conquest. In 1739 they forced Walpole into the War of Jenkins' Ear. The plan was to capture the seaports on both sides of Spanish America. It failed completely. Porto Bello was taken but could not be held. At Cartagena a strong expedition was ruined by tropical fevers and the inexperience of the commanders. Anson sailed round Cape Horn to attack the coast of Chile and Peru. Storms and hardships destroyed most of his force before it fired a shot. With only one ship remaining fit for service he could merely raid where he had been expected to conquer. His voyage was an epic of heroism, but he arrived home after four years with one-fifth of his men alive and nothing permanent accomplished. The Spanish Empire had made scarcely any defence, but fevers, distance, and scurvy rendered it unassailable by any force the England of that day could equip.

Meanwhile, with the decline of the peaceful ministers, Walpole and Cardinal Fleury, Great Britain and France were drifting into war. The younger Whigs, led by William Pitt, were denouncing the Bourbons as the enemies of England. The new generation of French soldiers were eager to reverse the defeats inflicted by Marlborough on Louis XIV. The Austrian Succession War provided the occasion. In 1740 Maria Theresa, heiress to the Hapsburg dominions, found her rights questioned by a variety of claimants. The Bourbon powers sought their profit in the confusion—Spain in northern Italy, and France in the Austrian Netherlands. Leagued together in the Family Compact, the Bourbon kings made a new bid for the domination which Louis XIV had lost. The threat to the Low Countries brought England into the field. George II went to Germany and won a victory at Dettingen in 1743, but until 1744 the British and French were not officially at war; they fought only as auxiliaries of the German disputants.

With the formal declaration of war a new arena of Anglo-French strife grew prominent. The struggle for India began, and went on with little interruption to a decisive result. Both the English and French East India Companies had been compelled by native troubles to fortify themselves, and in the Carnatic province their respective headquarters, Madras and Pondicherry, were close together on the same coastline. In former wars the two Companies had agreed not to fight one another in India, but on this occasion Dupleix, the French governor-general, forced on a contest.

The Anglo-French struggle for India may be divided into three stages. The first, which coincided with the Austrian Succession War in Europe, lasted until 1748. It was indecisive. The French took Madras in 1746, but were checked by the defence of Fort St. David, where the young Robert Clive first distinguished himself. The British were likewise foiled in a siege of Pondicherry, and then the Peace of Aix-la-Chapelle ended the war and provided for the restitution of Madras.

Dupleix was greatly disappointed at having to hand back his conquest. Within a year, although peace reigned in Europe, he began a new struggle. This is the second stage. Dupleix used French troops to place a native claimant on the throne of the Carnatic, calculating that his nominee would be only a puppet through whom the French would rule the country. The British at Madras answered by backing a similar claimant in their own interest. This unofficial war lasted five years and ended in the defeat of Dupleix, mainly by the military genius of Clive. Clive's defence of Arcot in 1751 was the turning-point. His heroism brought over the Indian warriors to his support, and the French steadily lost ground. In 1754 Dupleix was recalled by his own government as a disturber of the peace, and the second stage came to an end with the British stronger and the French weaker than at the outset. But the future of India was still undecided.

The third and decisive stage coincided with the Seven Years War in Europe. It began in 1756, when the French prepared an expedition for India. Before their men arrived the British received a heavy blow from a native prince, the Nawab of Bengal. This great province had hitherto been a neutral area, and the defences of the British factory at Calcutta were in a poor state. In 1756 the Nawab took Calcutta, and many of his prisoners perished in the atrocity of the Black Hole, a stupid blunder rather than a deliberate crime. Clive sailed from Madras with a punitive expedition, and in 1757 he overthrew the Nawab at the Battle of Plassey. The result was unexpected, nothing less than the conquest of Bengal and the beginning of our Indian Empire. The Company had not wished for this. It was a trading body with no desire to rule a native population twice as numerous as that of England. The aim had been to set up a new Nawab who would be friendly to the British. But it proved easier to break than to make, and the East India Company found themselves the real rulers of Bengal from Plassey onwards. Whilst Clive was busy in Bengal the great French expedition reached the Carnatic. Its commander, the Comte de Lally, besieged Madras and was driven off. He was then beaten in the field by Sir Eyre Coote at Wandewash (1760). After that he was hemmed in at Pondicherry, and obliged to surrender that town in 1761. The minor factories of the French had all fallen, and they had not a foothold left in India. The Treaty of Paris (1763) restored their factories but none of the adjacent territory. The British on the other hand were left the virtual rulers of two great provinces, Bengal and the Carnatic. They gathered up most of the trade of India and remained the only European power with any prospect of expansion there. As the future was to show, the Anglo-French struggle was decided.

During these years a parallel struggle had been going on for the possession of North America. It was also divided into the same three stages: the Austrian Succession War, an unofficial contest, and the Seven Years War. At Utrecht the French had given up the colony which we call Nova Scotia, but the surrender had not included the island of Cape Breton. Here France built the fortress of Louisbourg, 'the Dunkirk of North America,' to guard the entrance of the St. Lawrence. The British took Louisbourg in 1745, but restored it at the Peace of Aix-la-Chapelle. As in India the first stage had been indecisive.

No sooner had peace been signed than the real struggle for North America began. The British colonies filled the Atlantic coast and were expanding westwards into the interior. The French held the two main waterways of the continent, the Mississippi and the St. Lawrence. The map shows that to connect the two it was necessary to occupy the Ohio. Hence began

X

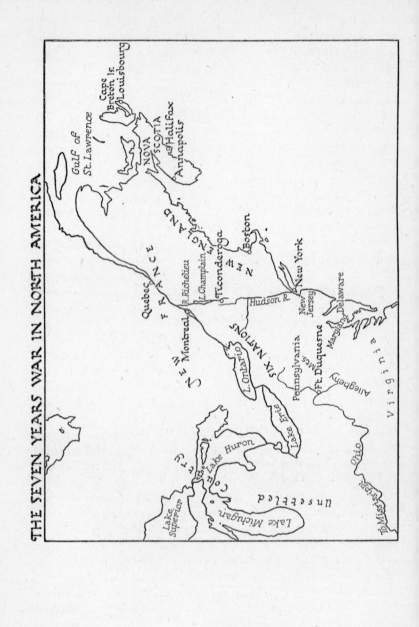

THE SEVEN YEARS WAR IN NORTH AMERICA

one of the inevitable wars of history, inevitable because no compromise was possible. If the French gained the Ohio they would stop all further British expansion. If the British were to expand they must have the Ohio and would therefore cut the French possessions in two. There was only one Ohio, and whichever side failed to get it would be ruined by the other. The river was the key of the continent. In 1749 French officers passed down its course from Canada to the Mississippi, warned off British pioneers, and claimed possession. A little later a party of Virginian colonists under George Washington intruded in their turn and expelled the French. There were years of petty fighting between the colonists whilst the governments in London and Paris were interested in other things. The result was that the French remained firmly entrenched at Fort Duquesne on the upper waters of the Ohio. In 1755 the British government, still without declaring war, dispatched General Braddock to turn them out. Braddock was defeated and killed. The second stage ended with the French victorious, and North America was potentially theirs.

The Seven Years War officially began in 1756. As between Great Britain and France, it was a struggle for sea-power and colonial empire—in America, the West Indies, West Africa, and India. But there was also at the same time a European contest in which France, Austria, and Russia combined to attack Frederick of Prussia and partition his dominions. France was thus common to both wars, and there was a further connecting link in George II's electorate of Hanover. Sea-power could save England from invasion, but not Hanover, and George expected his British ministers to provide for the defence of his German principality. The Duke of Newcastle, prime minister in 1756, made an alliance with Frederick the Great and offered subsidies to other German princes for the use of their troops. William Pitt threw himself into opposition, declared that North America was all that mattered to us, and denounced the wasting of men and money on Hanover. Naturally this did not endear him to George II.

The struggle being world-wide, its story is complicated. There were as many different 'shows' as in the Great War of 1914–18. A bare outline is therefore all that can be attempted here. The Newcastle government opened with two disasters. Its General Braddock had failed to take Fort Duquesne in 1755.

Its Admiral Byng failed to save Minorca in 1756, and there were minor failures in addition. Newcastle put the blame for Minorca upon Byng, who was shot for not having done his duty; but the ministry was really the culprit, for it had neglected the defences of both Minorca and Gibraltar, and Byng sacrificed the one to save the other after being sent out too late to save both. His disgraceful execution—murder is the true word—did the ministry no good, and Newcastle had to give way to Pitt. This illustrates the limitation of the British monarchy, for George II disliked Pitt and yet had to employ him at the nation's demand. It was already winter when Pitt took charge, and before the next year's campaigning began he was out. In the spring of 1757 the King suddenly dismissed him for unsoundness on the Hanover question. But the Crown could not now stand against the country, which was resolute to have its trusted Pitt in power. Neither Newcastle nor any one else could form a ministry without him; in a time of disaster neither voters nor members could be bought. George II had to submit, and the Pitt-Newcastle ministry began the four years' career which won the war. The season of 1757 was indeed lost, and Hanover was momentarily lost with it, but that of 1758 was the beginning of better things.

Newcastle was a party manager, expert in keeping a majority in the Commons; but as an administrator of armies and fleets he was hopeless. Pitt neither bribed nor flattered, and was unpopular with politicians, but in creating forces and finding leaders he was a magician. In 1758-9 he so disposed our armies and fleets that France was pinned and paralysed. His plan turned primarily on a strict blockade of the French coast, which prevented any aid from sailing to the French colonies. Thus freed from interference he sent his main army to North America. In 1758 Amherst and Wolfe took Louisbourg, and Forbes took Fort Duquesne. The outworks of Canada had fallen. In 1759 Wolfe sailed up the St. Lawrence and took Quebec, for which he paid with his own life. The remnants of the French surrendered next year at Montreal, and the object of the war was gained. But Pitt's ambition grew with success. His expeditions appeared everywhere, little armies carried by little fleets, able like frogs to swim over the water and hop out swiftly to the land, all under cover of the great blockade. One such force took the French African stations of Senegal and Goree. Another took

Guadeloupe, the best sugar island in the Lesser Antilles. A third took Belleisle, a sort of Isle of Wight off the coast of France, useful as a pawn to compel the restitution of Minorca at the peace. And with all this, Pitt was able after all to send British troops for the recovery of Hanover. They achieved it at Minden in 1759, a battle won by British infantry under a Prussian general. It is interesting to note how Pitt was thus drawn into the continental scheme of strategy which he had once denounced. He said in a moment of enthusiasm: 'We shall conquer America on the plains of Germany'; but that is hardly a true description of his policy, and America was in fact conquered by sea-power and the armies it conveyed to the west.

At the close of 1759 the French in despair broke the blockade, but to their own destruction. Choiseul, the new French minister, sought to end Pitt's successes by a blow at the heart in the shape of an invasion of England. Our possession of Gibraltar spoiled the plan in its opening move. The French fleet from Toulon, seeking to join the northern fleet at Brest, was seen passing Gibraltar, was chased by Admiral Boscawen, and destroyed in Lagos Bay on the coast of Portugal. The Brest fleet was thus left to try the invasion alone. It came out in November and was at once brought to action by Lord Hawke. His attack in Quiberon Bay was bold beyond all precedent. A rising storm, a lee shore, a cruel coast strewn with reefs, and a winter night closing down—all these would have made an ordinary admiral hold off and play for safety. They called Hawke on. He went in after the French and destroyed half their fleet with comparatively small loss to himself.

After that the colonial conquests were secure and could be added to year by year as long as the war went on. They were added to: 1760 saw the surrender of Montreal, 1761 the capture of Martinique and other West Indian islands. In 1762 Spain under a new anti-British king joined a lost cause by renewing the Family Compact. The result was the taking of Florida, Havana in Cuba, and Manila in the Philippine Islands, the latter by a British force from India. The trade of the enemy had ceased, that of neutrals was restricted, British trade was actually increasing under the shield of naval supremacy. It seemed that the mercantile doctrine of the Whigs, that wealth could be won by war, was vindicated beyond their wildest hopes.

But in the midst of the triumph doubts arose. Was it sound

policy to grasp a world-dictatorship at the cost of arousing world-hatred and an unsleeping lust for vengeance? Can one civilized nation permanently lord it over all its neighbours? The English tradition said no. It was to assert that negative that England had fought Philip II and Louis XIV. Pitt argued that we were so deeply in that the Bourbons were certain to plot revenge, and that the only safety lay in making them for ever impotent. He was the idol of the traders, 'the Great Commoner,' but to the Whig nobles he was an upstart. He was not descended from the spoilers of the monasteries, but only from an Indian profiteer under Queen Anne. He was proud and despotic, a king of men who made no pretence that other men were his equals. The feeling against him was deep though suppressed before George II died in the autumn of 1760. The new King, George III, called that feeling into the open. He cared neither for Hanover nor for the colonies, but only for English domestic politics. He meant to be the master of his ministers, not their shadow, and Pitt the dictator equally with Newcastle the borough-monger stood in his way. Within a year Pitt was thrust out, and within two years Newcastle, and George III proceeded to end what he coldly described as 'a bloody and expensive war'.

At the Treaty of Paris, signed in 1763, Great Britain renounced the aim of world-supremacy. France got back her Indian factories, the best of her sugar islands, her African slave-trade, and her Newfoundland fishery, the training ground of thousands of seamen. To Spain were restored Havana and Manila, with the hold over the rich islands in which they stood. But North America from the Atlantic coast to the Mississippi was made a British monopoly. Canada was kept, together with Florida, so that from the Gulf of Mexico to the Arctic shore there was no flag but the British to be seen. The forlorn hope of 1756 was more than realized; it was the ambition of 1759 that was given up. Pitt, powerless in opposition, prophesied ruin. To him the Newfoundland fishery was the worst of the surrenders. 'You leave to France the possibility of reviving her navy,' he said. He was quite right. The concessions were made of grace, not of necessity, and thus the Bourbons' pride was none the less humbled whilst the means of revenge were in their grasp. In twenty years the revenge duly took place. But the other course would have been equally calamitous. To dominate the world

was an impossible task even had the British genius been adapted
to it; and that it certainly was not. Even in the bragging, drum-
thumping eighteenth century, 'this country the terror of the
world' was not a sentiment of universal appeal. There was a
steady, sober undercurrent that recoiled from such things and
was destined to become ever more powerful in the British character. William Pitt differed from Cromwell and Marlborough
and Wellington in that he was not a typical Englishman. In his
virtues and his failings he represented a minority, even if he did
not stand alone.

III. THE TORY REVIVAL AND THE FALL OF THE
MERCANTILE EMPIRE

The accession of George III, a young man in his early twenties,
marked the beginning of the end of Whig ascendancy. The
Stuart claim was now but a phantom which no man took
seriously. There was thus no barrier between the King and a
Tory ministry if he should choose to employ one, for there could
be no suspicion that the Tories were disloyal to the Hanoverian
throne. There was on the other hand every reason for the King
to favour such a ministry, for he was of Tory principles himself.
That is to say, he believed that the King should be the working
head of the administration, that he should employ ministers
accountable to himself, and that the Houses of Parliament
should support these ministers simply because they were the
King's choice, and irrespective of the party influence of powerful subjects. In George's view the prime minister should not be
the source of authority, but simply the foreman of a body of
subordinates; he should be the King's mouthpiece rather than
the dictator of national policy as Walpole and Pitt had been.
These were principles congenial to the Tories and objectionable
to the Whigs. To that extent it is just to regard George III as
a Tory.

By 1760, however, it had become somewhat misleading to use
these party labels with any strictness of meaning. The Whigs in
Parliament were hardly a party at all in our modern sense of
the word. They were rather a series of groups attached to the
various great men whose families were traditionally regarded
as the heads of the Whig connexion. It seemed natural to these
great families that the rulers of the country should be drawn

from their ranks, but that was about the only principle common to them all; on many points of practical politics they were mutually hostile. Similarly there were other men whose grand-fathers had formed the Tory party of Bolingbroke's day. These people in 1760 inherited the Tory label, but the principle it had once stood for, the dominance of the High Churchmen, had almost faded away. What they really had in common under George III was dislike of the Whig families who monopolized power, and they were therefore prepared to support a King who would lead them against the Whig stronghold. The halo of divine appointment which had made Charles I stand out as a man utterly different from any subject had worn very thin. The Hanoverians owed nothing to divine right and everything to the Act of Settlement. George, therefore, in seeking to assert himself, could call forth little of the mystic loyalty of the old Cavaliers. He had to enter the arena as one among many competing politicians. He had to build up a following by the sordid methods of Walpole and Newcastle ; and the political struggle that ensued was one of persons rather than principles. The history of the first half of his reign is therefore very annoying to those who like clear-cut definitions and general statements; for such cannot be made. Not until the French Revolution came into the world, with its sharp contrast between democracy and aristocracy, was there a genuine division of principle between British parties.

George III scored an early but delusive success. He easily got rid of Pitt, who was disliked by his colleagues, and of Newcastle, who was growing old and losing his talent for management. The Earl of Bute, labelled as a Tory, was installed as head of the ministry before the close of 1762. But the King, although he wanted only a foreman, forgot that a foreman needs experience of his job. Bute was inexperienced. He lacked Pitt's genius for war and Newcastle's forty-years' knowledge of rotten boroughs, and the old hands in Parliament saw that he would not last long. Bute also had no faith in him-self, and the London mob soon reduced him to a nerveless wreck. The Londoners worshipped Pitt and hated his sup-planter. Bute made the Treaty of Paris, and Pitt denounced it. Bute was therefore saluted on public occasions with the display of lines of old boots hanging by cords, and with shouts of 'No Jack Boots and no wooden shoes!'—the latter a symbol of

French beggarliness. He had to enlist a bodyguard of prize-fighters to escort him through the streets. In less than a year he had had enough of it and insisted on resigning. The King was almost as unpopular, although a good deal more plucky, and his first experiment in discarding the Whigs had failed.

The Bute incident showed the Whig magnates what the King's game was. They had no mind to be supplanted in control by some outsider, but yet they were too jealous of one another to achieve real unity against the peril. Their strong point was that they were collectively in possession of the political machine, and that no one who was not a Whig had the requisite experience to run it. The King had therefore to employ Whig ministries for the next seven years. But he took care that no single ministry should last very long, and this lack of continuity broke the hold of the magnates upon the rank-and-file of politicans. Private members grew lukewarm in support of leaders who might not have time enough in office to reward them with places and pensions. The King at least was permanent, and the calculating sort of politicians turned to him as their patron. So the King gradually learned the art of management and built up the King's Friends from the wrecks of the disgruntled Whig groups. The King's party was by no means wholly Tory in label, although it was Tory in action. By 1770 it was strong enough to provide a working majority in the Commons, and the personal rule of George III began with the appointment of Lord North as the King's prime minister. North, unlike Bute, had received administrative training as a member of the last of the Whig ministries. With the King in possession of the political machine, able to control elections by the distribution of favours, and served by a fairly competent premier, the new supremacy bade fair to last as long as the old. The Whig leaders, thrust out of power and with little hope of return, harboured a deep resentment against their sovereign. They began also to preach political purity and to declaim against the corruption that was now the instrument of their opponents. In adversity they were finding a virtue that had never appealed to them in their days of prosperity.

The King's triumph was not destined to endure so long as many expected. During these years when attention had been fixed on the domestic struggle a great crisis had loomed up unnoticed overseas; and a first-class crisis, badly handled, was the one thing capable of overthrowing an eighteenth-century minister who enjoyed the favour of the Crown. The trouble was in the American colonies, where the results of the Seven Years War had produced problems beyond the wisdom of the five short-lived cabinets that filled in the interval between 1763 and 1770.

A government engaged in winning a great war spends money with a lavish hand and is generally popular on that account alone. A government in the early days of peace, which has to economize and to settle a host of contentious questions without aid from the fervent patriotism of the conflict, can hardly avoid being hated. That was the fate of the Grenville ministry which succeeded Bute in 1763. George Grenville, its head, was an able man, honest, methodical, and just, as good a premier as the country could expect to find. It was his misfortune that the post-war period introduced him to problems which had never been thought out and to awkward circumstances whose existence had not hitherto been even suspected. He did the wrong thing. That may be admitted. But it is also true that neither he nor any one else could have done the right thing, for public opinion would not have allowed it. Neither King nor statesmen, neither traders nor journalists, the people of England, or the colonists of America, were ripe for the application of the only policy that could have held the Empire together.

The Treaty of Paris had made America British as far west as the Mississippi. We were thus responsible for the welfare and good conduct of the wild Indian tribes in a vast stretch of unsettled country. The Grenville government took the humane view that these Indians must be protected from oppression by white pioneers, and it therefore issued a proclamation that a great part of the new territory was to be an Indian reserve, open to traders but not to settlers from the British colonies. The hard-bitten American frontiersman, who regarded Indians as vermin without human rights, was aggrieved. He had thought to invade the new territory with a few bottles of rum and to obtain from drunken chiefs the cession of thousands of acres. He found that game stopped by a government thousands of miles away, and he naturally resented the interference.

The Indian problem had more in it than that. The red man welcomed white traders who brought him drink and gunpowder, but he hated settlers who cleared the forest and drove off the game by which he lived. The French in North America had never been numerous enough to threaten settlement of the back country, and so the western Indians had generally regarded them with favour. When the war made everything British the Indians were alarmed. Before the good intentions of their new rulers could be made known the tribes flung themselves into a general rising. In 1763-4 the whole frontier was ablaze from the Great Lakes southward to Florida. 'The Conspiracy of Pontiac,' as it was called from the name of a prominent chief, inflicted enormous damage and cost the lives of many white men. The government expected the American colonists to turn out in arms for their own salvation. But they were tired of war and did little. The rising was put down by two or three heroic British officers and a handful of regular troops who had escaped the disbandment of 1763. The moral of it all was that the new American empire must have a permanent garrison to keep order, and that someone must pay for it.

Grenville had to find the money, and at the same time he was expected to reduce expenditure at home. The colonial theory of the time, which no one had ever questioned, held that if the mother-country defended the colonists with her armies and fleets she was entitled to a return in the shape of a monopoly of the colonial trade. The Navigation Acts were supposed to confer that monopoly, but for forty years their enforcement had been so neglected that their effect in controlling trade had been very small. Their real use had lain in their promotion of British and American shipping, but that shipping had traded with foreigners pretty much as its owners had pleased. In 1764 Grenville determined to make the Acts a reality. He brought them up to date by amending details, and sent out officials with orders for strict enforcement. American traders were incensed, but they could say little. To protest would be to admit that they had been breaking the law.

The check to smuggling meant an increase of customs revenue, but that was not enough to pay for American defence. Grenville decided that the colonists must also pay a direct tax, and he gave them a year in which to choose what form it should take. In 1765, having received no suggestions from America, he passed the Stamp Act through Parliament. It imposed on the colonies duties which had been levied in England since the time of Queen Anne. Even so, the estimated return was not sufficient to pay the cost of the garrison.

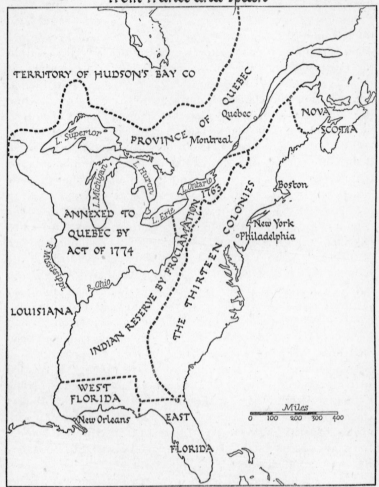

NORTH AMERICA AFTER THE SEVEN YEARS WAR.
Showing the disposal of the territories conquered
from France and Spain

TERRITORY OF HUDSON'S BAY CO

PROVINCE OF QUEBEC

Quebec

Montreal

NOVA SCOTIA

L. Superior

L. Michigan

L. Huron

L. Ontario

1763

L. Erie

Boston

ANNEXED TO

QUEBEC BY

ACT OF 1774

New York

Philadelphia

THE THIRTEEN COLONIES

R. Mississippi

R. Ohio

INDIAN RESERVE BY PROCLAMATION

LOUISIANA

WEST
FLORIDA

New Orleans

EAST

FLORIDA

Miles

0   100   200   300   400

In Canada and the West Indies the Stamp Act duly came into force, but in the old American provinces the effect was surprising. It was nothing less than a general refusal to pay. The collectors were everywhere insulted, their houses destroyed, the stamped documents burnt. From Massachusetts to Georgia there was no prospect of raising a penny from the new duties. Mob-rule was supreme, and there was no army to compel obedience.

The violence of the outbreak was out of all proportion to the sum involved, which was trifling. The real grievance, in fact, lay in the strengthened imperial control implied in the government's Indian and Navigation policy. But the direct tax was a novelty, and all the indignation was focussed upon it. For here it was possible to argue a principle. The privilege of every British subject was laid down in the Bill of Rights—no taxation save by the grant of representatives in Parliament. The Americans had no representatives in Parliament, and 'No taxation without representation' became the maxim for which they were ultimately prepared to lay down their lives. They took their stand upon constitutional right. But there was something equally convincing to be advanced on the other side, and that was legal right. The Parliament of King, Lords, and Commons was the supreme authority over every subject of the King. Whatever Parliament decreed was law, and there was no gainsaying it. To resist the law was treason and rebellion. This contradiction between constitutional right and legal right was the tragedy of the American quarrel. Either side was justified from its own point of view, and no man had ever given thought to a means of reconciling the contradiction. To think out a solution has occupied the best minds of the British race for over a century down to the present day, and even now the solution is not perfect. What wonder if the problem, arising like a sudden tornado in 1765, overwhelmed the men of that day and hurried them into war? We may blame their faults of temper, but we cannot blame them for standing up for their principles.

In Stuart times the Stamp Act would have caused discontent but not a revolt, just as in 1765 it caused discontent but not a revolt among the West Indian planters. It needs a nation to fight for constitutional rights; a mere collection of settlers can protest but cannot fight. The British in the West Indies were not, and never have been, a separate nation. The Americans became one in the eighteenth century. In 1700 there were about 200,000 of them; in 1765 they were nearly 2,000,000 strong. The numbers count for much, but not for everything. In the long century after the Restoration of Charles II the American colonies had developed along different lines from the English nation at home. Hardly any Americans returned to England, and the English who went to America were chiefly criminals and political exiles cast out against their will; there was no constant coming and going of normal citizens as in the Empire of to-day. The Americans of 1765 were mostly descendants of the pioneers from Shakespeare's and Milton's England, or of the Germans and Swiss, Dutchmen and Huguenots, Scotsmen and Irishmen, who had emigrated after the pioneer days. Some of them spoke no English, and none of them thought as the Englishmen of George III. Climate, trade, and agriculture gave them different interests in everyday life. The native problem had no counterpart at home. War with France meant fighting on their own soil, not rejoicing in safety over distant victories overseas. On the borders there was no law save that of the rifle; a man fired first or he lost his scalp. There were no squires and no High Church parsons to dominate the countryside. Inevitably a different national life had evolved. Nobody realized it, least of all the Americans themselves, until the lightning-flashes of the Stamp Act revolt revealed the truth: on one side of the ocean a new American nation set upon working out its own destiny; on the other the ancient British government, giving futile orders to 'our subjects in the colonies', and utterly failing to comprehend that it had a foreign nation to deal with.

These things have been enlarged upon because they are the key to what followed, and that may be briefly summarized. For five years the American business was only a side-show to George III's struggle with the Whigs. Grenville was turned out in 1765 for reasons unconnected with his Stamp Act, and Rockingham came in. The Rockingham party was only a group, disliked by the King and unsupported by the other Whig groups. It had no power to begin a war with the Americans, and so it had to surrender to them. It repealed the Stamp Act in 1766. The Americans, having carried their point, protested their loyalty to George III. Their objection was not to him but to his British ministers and Parliament. They would have been content with what we now call dominion status, that is, self-government and equality with England under a general allegiance to the Crown; but that conception belonged to the future and would not have been agreed to in the eighteenth century. The quarrel therefore slept only until a new offence called it again into life. The occasion was Townshend's American duties of 1767, a new attempt at a colonial tax. The same rioting and resistance followed, and the duties yielded virtually no revenue. All except that on tea were repealed in 1770. At that date, with North as premier, the King took unhampered control. America was now quite out of hand, full of treasonable talk, and defiant of authority; but so long as the government was content to be flouted there was no armed rebellion. The limit was overstepped with the Boston Tea Party of 1773, when four shiploads of the East India Company's tea were thrown into the harbour by rioters whom the whole colony shielded. George III and Lord North passed the Intolerable Acts in retaliation, and sent troops to Boston to enforce them. The New Englanders gathered an army, and in 1775 the War of Independence began with a struggle for the possession of Boston.

Was it an inevitable war? Given the ideas of that period, it was. The colonists had become a nation, and no nation can consent to be governed from without. Yet there was hardly a man in England, from the King downwards, who understood that this new sense of nationality was the crux of the matter. They all looked at details, specific riots and outrages, particular laws and their infringement; they could not see the wood for the trees. The American leaders were in like case. Until the first shots were fired they also did not realize that nationhood was urging them on. Far from distinguishing themselves as Americans, they were hot for 'the rights of Englishmen'. They conceived themselves as playing the parts of Pym and Hampden against a tyrannous ministry which was introducing innovations. They talked of the days before Grenville as a golden age of contentment to which they were quite willing to return. Dominion status is the modern recipe for harmonizing nationhood with empire. The dominions are independent and self-governing, and yet they stand together in the British Commonwealth because all alike share the British way of life. Put on paper the idea does not seem very hopeful, and sceptics are always telling us that it will not stand a real strain; yet it always does. The eighteenth century, which liked its politics cut and dried, could not rise to such a mystic notion. Edmund Burke alone perceived the light. His speeches were full of the paradox that perfect freedom was the strongest chain to bind the mother-country to her offspring.

Yet nothing is more certain than that if the King had made Burke prime minister in 1775 he would have been at war with the Americans or turned out by the English within a year. William Pitt, who had become Earl of Chatham, passed also for an advocate of the colonial cause; but he had no glimmering of perception that a nation had been born. He denounced every measure to tax the Americans and at the same time asserted that Parliament had complete authority over them. Had he been in control he would sooner or later have had to fight. Three events in thirteen months clarified the issue and showed both sides where they stood. In June 1775, blood flowed in the desperate battle of Bunker's Hill. In the following winter Washington's regiments devised the new flag of the Stars and Stripes, which meant to every man who marched under it that the old allegiance was dead. On July 4, 1776, the Congress at Philadelphia enacted the Declaration of Independence, and the rights of Englishmen gave place to the rights of Americans.

The American nation had emerged clear-cut from the turmoil. So much was an accomplished fact, but independence was not yet accomplished. For nations can be conquered in our modern world and lie in chains for a century—the Poles are an example. George III set out to conquer the Americans, and he had a good prospect of doing so. The really keen patriots among them were a minority, they had no fleet and few munitions, and they resented discipline. George Washington alone saved them from collapse. Even he could not have done it had there been a Pitt against him. But in the three seasons of 1775, 1776, and 1777 the King's ministers and generals fumbled their game, missed their chances, and ended with the disaster of Saratoga, where a British army surrendered to the last man in the backwoods of the Hudson valley.

Saratoga could have been retrieved but for the labours of America's second saviour, Benjamin Franklin. He had gone to France as ambassador of the United States. He found the

Bourbon government eager to revenge its losses in the Seven Years' War, yet desperately afraid of another drubbing—for the demon Pitt was still alive. Franklin conquered official fears and stimulated public enthusiasm. The jaded, over-civilized society of the *ancien régime* was charmed by the wise simplicity of this plain-spoken smiling old man, who brought a breath of the forest into salons and cabinets. His white hair and drab clothes befitted a sage of antiquity returned to earth. He became the idol of stuffy Paris, where Rousseau was preaching the return to Nature as the need of the age. Franklin's personality and matchless skill were already triumphing when the news of Saratoga came to clinch the business. Early in 1778 France signed a treaty of alliance with America, and threw her navy into the struggle. Spain followed suit in 1779, and for the third time we were at war with the Bourbon Family Compact. Holland joined our enemies in 1780. Almost every other power in Europe adhered to the Armed Neutrality, our foe in all but the name, and nowhere in the wide world could we discern a friend. The wheel had turned indeed since the days of Quebec and Minden twenty years before.

In the English state also the wheel had turned. Pitt was down and other men were up. North was premier, an amiable man, but with no head for war and no heart for it either, beaten before he fought. The navy was in the charge of Lord Sandwich, an arch-priest of corruption and a betrayer of his own associates. His record of dirty tricks had earned him the nickname of Jemmy Twitcher, and his conduct to officers afloat was such that many of the best resigned their commands and were lost to their country. The army was under Lord George Germaine, an incompetent bully who had been cashiered by George II for misconduct at Minden. George III had taken him back, to his country's sorrow. With such a hopeful quarter-deck did the ship of state go into action against the world. Yet the crew nearly atoned for the officers. Outnumbered everywhere, placed in impossible positions by the government's strategy and then blamed for the result, the British forces made a wonderful defence in this last war of the old colonial empire. The result to the nation was defeat but not dishonour, and it was by no means fatal to the national spirit. The death-blow fell upon the government of royal nominees relying on the bribed King's Friends in the Commons. George III's experiment in reassert-

Y

ing the royal power, which might have lasted indefinitely, was shattered after seven years of the American war.

The effect of the Bourbon intervention was to divide the British effort and make it possible for Washington to hold his ground. Until the autumn of 1781 it was uncertain whether this would be enough to ensure American independence. Then there occurred the decisive event. Lord Cornwallis, after hard fighting in the southern states, came out with a diminished army at Yorktown on the coastline of Virginia. He expected to receive help from his superior, Sir Henry Clinton, at New York. But the French fleet from the West Indies appeared off Yorktown, and Washington, with a French and American army, moved against it by land. The British fleet tried to raise the blockade, but failed. Cornwallis was trapped and forced to surrender. His army could not be replaced, and his southern conquests were lost. In a moment the British were reduced to holding New York and one or two other seaports, with no further prospect of gaining the interior, and the future of the United States was assured. Yet it had been a narrow squeak, for Washington's dispatches show that he had almost lost hope and could not have continued much longer. It was French sea-power that had decided the issue, as the American historian Mahan frankly states.

Elsewhere the Bourbon navies predominated, although they did not make the most of their chances. In 1779 French and Spaniards ranged the Channel without challenge, and only mismanagement prevented them from landing armies in England. For three years Gibraltar was hotly besieged, and its deliverance was due chiefly to the heroism of its garrison. That of Minorca fought no less manfully, but was starved and battered into surrender, the survivors so weak that they could barely crawl from their trenches to 'march out' with the honours of war. Flushed with the Yorktown triumph the French fleet returned to the West Indies, where it captured every British island but Jamaica and Barbados. But there the decision was reversed by Rodney's great victory of The Saints in 1782, and the lost islands were recovered. Florida, however, went the way of Minorca and reverted to Spanish possession. In the east the Comte de Suffren led an expedition to drive the British out of India. His fleet disputed the command of the Indian seas as no French fleet had done before, but the land operations were

too late for success; Warren Hastings had defeated his native
enemies before the French arrived. In 1783 exhaustion compelled all the combatants to make peace.

The Treaty of Versailles marks the fall of the old colonial
empire of Great Britain. The United States were acknowledged
independent, and they contained five-sixths of the white men
who had lived overseas under the British flag. That is how the
thing appears to the modern view. From the standpoint of that
time, however, it was not so bad. The West Indian trade was
much richer than the American, and in the West Indies we had
suffered trifling loss. Our hold upon India was secure, and
Canada (for what little it was then worth) remained within the
Empire. The African slaving stations, more lucrative than gold
mines, were also untouched. British pride had been humbled,
but the mercantilists of the period could congratulate themselves on getting out of a bad scrape very cheaply.

Sea-power had been all-important, and its balance was
against England. There was no repetition of Pitt's blockade of
the enemy coast. Frenchmen and Spaniards sailed the seas at
will, and if they had had a Pitt to direct them could have
conquered the whole British Empire. As Pitt had foretold in
1763, France had rebuilt her navy and had made it a very
fine force. Spain also had done something to revive her sea-
power. On paper the British fleet was equal to its adversaries,
but only on paper. Many of the battleships were heaps of
rotten timber unable to put to sea. Others were sent out, only
to drown their crews. The *Royal George* is the best known
example, but there were others. The *Royal George* should have
been a hanging matter; for the bottom simply dropped out
of her as she lay anchored in calm water. But the truth was
hushed up, and Cowper's mournful ballad—'A land breeze
shook the shrouds, and she was overset'—embodies the false-
hood served out to the public. Brave Kempenfeldt and thousands more were slain not by the King's enemies but by the
King's Friends.

The ministry and its placemen were guilty of more than
neglect. When anything went wrong they defended themselves
by attacking the officers afloat. They encouraged subordinates
to make charges against their commanders, and they instigated
journalists to poison the public mind against any admiral who
came of a Whig family. For the first and last time politics

entered the navy. In the same manner Germaine handled the army. Sir Guy Carleton, one of Wolfe's Quebec officers, was a brilliant administrator and a sound commander. Germaine expelled him from office in favour of Burgoyne, who walked into the trap of Saratoga. Carleton was made commander-in-chief only after Yorktown, when all was lost.

In one sense, however, Yorktown was a victory. It drove out this gang which had led the country to disaster. The news came early in 1782. The opposition Whigs so far forgot decency as to cheer the announcement; they knew that it meant more than the loss of America. Lord North accepted it as the death-sentence of his ministry. The King would have kept him, but he insisted on resigning, and with him went the rest. The Whigs came in, and it was they who made the Treaty of Versailles. Their own record was nothing to be proud of. They had openly supported the enemy and placed faction above country. To such a nightmare had the king-in-politics reduced Englishmen who had once been so proud of 'the principles of the Glorious Revolution'.

IV. THE LAST DAYS OF OLD ENGLAND

The stirring events described in the foregoing pages represent the surface history of a nation which in its depths remained quite placid and unstirred. The England, and indeed the Europe, of the eighteenth century had little conception that change in the conditions of life is an inevitable accompaniment of life itself. Change was indeed proceeding, but it was too slow to be perceptible to those whose outlook inclined them to be unobservant. Before the period of the French Revolution the average thinking man regarded society as it stood as a very good thing, capable of improvement in detail, but not needing any radical alteration. He would have been surprised and shocked to learn that the next hundred years were to witness the tearing up by the roots of every human relationship, political, industrial, social, and international, and its replacement by something previously unknown. He would have protested, 'In the name of common sense, what is the use of it? We are doing very well as we are.'

This static habit of mind blinded men to the significance of what they were themselves doing. They thought they were touching up and perfecting the existing system; they had no suspicion that they were destroying it to make way for another. Even the French philosophers who did so much to usher in the Revolution were themselves very theoretical revolutionaries. For them the criticism of the existing order was an intellectual game, but they did not seriously mean to overthrow the world in which they lived. They were pretty comfortable in it, and with some improvements might be more comfortable still. That is what 'the perfectibility of the species' meant to them—that elegant pursuit that was to lead them to the prisons of the Terror and the reeking guillotine of Quatre-Vingt-Treize. In England there was less theorizing and more of practical experiment. The revolution was slower and more respectable, but none the less complete when all was done—and none the less surprising to those who did it.

In the countryside the squire and the parson ruled the village as firmly as ever, and with less friction than in days of old. The religious question had come to rest. The vicar was more easy-going and less inclined to view the dissenter as an outrage on heaven itself. The benighted fellow was left to his errors, tolerated as a member of an untouchable caste which providence had evidently ordained to exist. Through all the wide belt of the midlands the open-field manor continued, its cornland cultivated in the piece and marked off into the little strips of antiquity, its cattle herding indiscriminately on the common, its landless hangers-on squatting in hovels on the waste and picking up a living with their poultry and wood-cutting and poaching. Here and there some energetic squire would take up ideas on novelties in crops or scientific breeding. He would get his friend the local member to promote an Act for enclosing the manor and sharing it out into separate properties in order that he might be unhampered in his experiments. He had no notion that in so doing he was overthrowing old England; he thought he was simply improving his own patch of it. 'The improving landlord' was a current phrase.

In the towns the tradesmen kept their shops in ancient houses set in narrow, smelly streets. Behind them lay unspeakable courts and alleys, the hives of their journeymen and charwomen and errand-boys. On the outskirts, where the High Street ran into the fields, were dotted the fair brick Georgian dwellings of the doctor and the lawyer, the retired officer, and the gentleman who had a little money but no land. These old towns existed to serve the countryside, not to control it. They were ruled by close corporations, very exclusive inner rings of their inhabitants. They were averse from change and 'improvement', and lagged behind in the revolution that was to come. Yet even in them the outlines of the old order were growing blurred. Apprenticeship was no longer so strictly enforced as in the great days of Elizabeth's statute. The trade guilds had become clubs or charitable bodies, and did not supervise quality and price and output as in the past. The regulation of wages by authority was out of date. Forms indeed remained, but the life was going out of them. It was like a tide near the bottom of the ebb.

There were other towns, indeed, where strange new industries were growing up, but these were not commonly the ancient places fortified by Alfred or represented in the Model Parliament. They were upstarts that had been mere villages, unhampered by mayor and aldermen and freemen. Here some innovator was setting up a blast-furnace to smelt iron by the heat of coal. There a mill-wheel turned below a dam and gave motion to a set of mechanical spinning jennies for producing cotton yarn. There again were 'works' for turning out tools, utensils, firearms, and other goods in the mass, things such as had hitherto been made one at a time by solitary craftsmen in fulfilment of individual orders. Just as these trades were new, their practitioners were new also. They had taught themselves and had no tradition behind them. They owed nothing to the past and hoped everything from the future—on the understanding that it would be different from the past. The existence of such a class of men was a threat to old England, for they could not be content to let her alone. Yet in the 1780's no one took it as a threat. There were not many of them, and they worked in out-of-the-way parts, unseen by the great static English world. The blast-furnace might pollute the verdure of the surrounding fields, the owner of the cotton-mill might keep under lock and key the child slaves he obtained from the so-called guardians of the poor, villainous new slums might spring up like fungus round the manufacturing works; but it was all very remote from the consciousness of those who ruled England. The new steam engine was matter of passing interest to the readers of the *Gentleman's Magazine*, but it appeared 'ingenious' rather than important to cultured minds that had mostly an antiquarian bent. It was quite incredible that there could really be slaves in cotton-mills; the principles of 1688 forbade such a thing any nearer than the sugar plantations. As for the new slums in the new towns, had there not always been slums in the old ones? So long as their denizens did not come to church the parish parson was quite unperturbed about them. Meanwhile manufactured articles were getting cheaper and more varied, and the standard of living for respectable persons was improved.

Improvement, but by no means a radical alteration, was likewise the watchword of politics. The Whigs in opposition looked backwards not forwards, backwards to the palmy days of Walpole and Newcastle, when the King had known what was required of him. In 1780, when the King's Friends were weakening, the Whigs passed a resolution in the Commons that 'the power of the Crown has increased, is increasing, and ought to be diminished'. Rotten boroughs, places, and pensions had been fit instruments of government in the old days, but it was now obvious that George III and North were making altogether too crude a use of them. Burke therefore introduced his Bill of Economical Reform which proposed to abolish some of the means of bribery; but the Bill was all whittled away in the course of debate, and its outcome was nothing.

When North fell and the Whigs came into power in 1782 they had the opportunity for a general overhaul of the constitution, for public opinion, raw with the American disaster, was favourable to reform. A new young man, the second William Pitt, moved for an inquiry into the state of parliamentary representation; but the prime minister, Rockingham, behind whom stood Burke, showed how conservative the true Whigs really were. He cleaned up the institutions of England, but he left their design substantially unaltered. He cut down the civil list, which had provided the King with money for bribery, he forbade members of Parliament to accept government contracts, and he disfranchised the revenue officers, most of whom had represented dummy appointments made only as a means of paying for their votes. That was the sum of the Whig reforms, a mild pruning but nothing more. There was no abolition of the rotten boroughs or placing of the franchise on a rational basis. Parliament as it stood was the ark of the covenant to Whig statesmen, who told themselves that they represented the people, even though they had not to court the votes of an inconvenient number of them. Burke, the most ardent of the Whig reformers, had no wish to tamper with the unreformed Parliament. He was much more concerned with thrusting the King back to his proper place in the constitutional scheme.

Superficial though it was, the clean-up of 1782 does mark a turning-point in British politics. It was an admission that the old system had not been all good, and a protest against a too glaring parade of corruption. After it corruption was by no means dead, but it was much less prominent. It was decently concealed, a sign that it was something to be ashamed of; and soon it became a fashion with statesmen to rely more upon a sound policy than upon underhand bargains for securing political support. Rockingham also did good work by rearranging the departments of state in 1782. The Home and Foreign Offices date from that year, and they superseded a much less efficient allocation of duties between the Secretaries of State.

The younger William Pitt is a figure who defies classification. At a time when party labels were growing more meaningless than ever, it is impossible to attach one to him. He would have described himself as a Whig, but that was only because he was not a Tory of the King's Friends' type. He was much more of a reformer and much more of a patriot than the ordinary Whigs. He disliked the existing system, with which they were quite satisfied so long as they controlled it; and he disliked it not so much because it was dishonest as because it was inefficient. He had no use for feuds and vendettas. Many of the Whigs, led by Charles James Fox, had a personal hatred for George III simply because he had ousted them from power. Pitt, although he had no notion of being a puppet-minister like North, realized in his common-sense way that the King was king and that it was the duty of his statesmen to get on with him, for only so could the course of government run smooth. 'The King's government must be carried on' is a maxim familiar to our ears. Pitt always acted upon it, but to the Whigs of the Fox type the exact opposite was the ideal; their highest ambition was to prevent the King's government from being carried on. In charm of personality and brilliance of speech Fox excelled Pitt; in the qualities most weighty in a public servant Pitt was superior to Fox. Whatever services Fox rendered to his country were outweighed by the injuries he did her. But neither were vital, for, when all was said, he was a brilliant failure, and his period belonged to Pitt.

After two years of confusion Pitt attained power. The respectable Rockingham ministry of 1782 lasted only a few months and was dissolved by the death of its premier. Pitt had refused the offer of a minor post in it as beneath his pretensions —a boy of twenty-two, but with all the self-confidence of his father. Shelburne succeeded Rockingham and made Pitt his Chancellor of the Exchequer. In 1783 Fox split the Whigs for personal reasons. He carried his group out of the government camp and formed an alliance with the Tories under Lord North. Together they had a majority, Shelburne resigned, and the Unnatural Coalition forced itself upon the King. It was almost more than George could bear. To him Fox was a man devoid of honour and patriotism, the foe of all that a true Briton held dear, and yet the trusted North led this monster to his presence to receive the seals of office. He never forgave either of them, and from the first moment sought only for deliverance. For the public also it was a shock. The sight of the King's Friends embracing the King's bitterest enemies in order to obtain the sweets of office showed all men how deep the principles of these politicians were. The people shared the King's disgust, and for the first time George and his subjects were at one. Before the year was out the King dismissed the Coalition and sent for Pitt, a Whig indeed, but not a Whig who had cheered in rapture at the news of Saratoga and Yorktown. For five months the young premier suffered defeat after defeat from the Fox-North majority in the Commons. England was with him, but the rotten boroughs were with Fox and North. In those five months he took his measures as skilfully as Newcastle could have done. In 1784, with the borough-mongers won over, he dissolved. The boroughs gave him his majority, the voteless public ratified it with their shouts, the King was happy, and William Pitt the Second entered upon an unbroken reign of eighteen years.

Peace and reform; survey the old edifice, tear away the ivy, repoint the bricks, sweep the cellars and rout out the vermin, overhaul the accounts and build up the bank balance, inspect the estate and turn off the idlers, polish up old England and give her a new lease of life; that was the programme of 1783. It was a good work, and it was a good thing that it was done. But it was not, as the men of 1783 imagined, a prelude to an age of sunny contentment. Pitt's improvements were to a different end from that. For the summer of the eighteenth century was over. An equinox of roaring hurricanes was almost due, and a twilight winter of such bitter frost that most old things were to lie beneath the ground for ever when the spring of the nineteenth century should dawn.

VIII

THE GREAT RIFT

(*From 1783 to 1822*)

I. WORLD TRADE

IN 1844 Benjamin Disraeli declared that England was inhabited by two nations. They were a propertied minority, who owned everything and were very prosperous, and a propertyless mass sunk in abject misery. These two nations were mutually hostile, keenly conscious of injustice on the one side and of envy on the other, and engaged in an unhappy struggle, the one for the maintenance, the other for the acquisition, of what it deemed to be its rights. The rights of property and the rights of labour—between them there had arisen a rift in English life.

These statements were quite true in the early years of Queen Victoria, but they would have been untrue in the early years of George III. Until nearly the end of the eighteenth century there had been no such disunion. The older England had been one nation, divided indeed into well-marked classes, but not rent by that hatred between them that existed at a later time. Labour did not envy property, and property did not fear labour. Property also had been more widely, if not more equally, distributed. The rural England of the old order comprised four-fifths of the population, and it contained many grades of small proprietors—yeoman farmers, commonable owners in the open-field manors, cottagers with some definite title to pasturing or fuel-gathering rights—all imbued with that respect for themselves and others that springs from ownership. All these small owners, together with the village craftsmen and public functionaries, had their special places in society. They were necessary to one another and to their richer neighbours. Above all, their duties and their rewards were fixed by long tradition and not the subject of perpetual revision and wrangling. Society in the eighteenth century was a harmony. In the early nineteenth it had become a discord. Twice before in English history the same thing had taken place: in the fourteenth century, when villeins had striven against feudal lordship; and in the Stuart period, when religion had rent the national life in twain. Of the third and greatest rift the causes are numerous and complicated, but religion bears hardly any part in them.

At first sight it would seem that foreign trade also was unlikely to occasion any upheaval in the domestic affairs of England. In fact it lay near the very bottom of the question, and a brief survey of its development is essential.

The world trade of the Middle Ages had passed chiefly by the land routes uniting Europe and Asia. Columbus and Vasco da Gama and the explorers of the Renaissance had set going a new oceanic trade which soon became much more voluminous than the old. For a full century, however, it had dealt only in the luxuries of the rich, the gold and jewels, silks and spices, which excited the imagination of English seamen under the Tudors. The Stuart period saw the beginning of a change. The colonies in America and the West Indies sent home tobacco and sugar and dyestuffs, which were used by a larger proportion of the population; and the colonists demanded clothes, shoes, and hardware, which may be bracketed as manufactures commonly produced in England. The island colonies also devoted themselves so intensively to their sugar crops that they did not grow their own foodstuffs. They relied upon corn and butter, salt meat and fish, from outside, and they obtained much of their supply from agricultural England, which in those days could feed herself and still have a surplus for export. There was thus the rudiment of an oceanic trade in bulky goods, and of a demand for manufactures which should be steady in quality, price, and output. It now becomes evident that world trade might have an influence upon industry at home.

In the Stuart period, however, the thing was but a rudiment, a hint for the future rather than an effect in the present. It is a matter of arithmetic. In 1700 the population of England was $5\frac{1}{2}$ millions, and that of English America and the West Indies (including many negro slaves) about 350,000, or, in other words, the colonial markets contained only one-fourteenth as many people as the mother-country which supplied them. By 1775 America and the West Indies together contained over 3 million people, whilst Great Britain had 9 millions, a proportion of one to three. This meant that the importance of the colonial market had grown immensely. Nor did the independence of the United States make any change in this tendency. After the war the trade between Great Britain and the States grew as rapidly as before, and until well on in the nineteenth century the Americans remained an agricultural people who drew most of their manufactured goods from England and supplied her with raw materials in return. The chief raw material needs special mention. It was cotton. In 1751 America sent us 1,300 tons of raw cotton; in 1782, 5,400 tons; in 1800, 25,000 tons; and in 1810, 59,000 tons. When we realize that this stuff was paid for with British goods, and that the cotton itself was manufactured in British mills and sold to all parts of the world, we see the enormous effect that this new oceanic trade was bound to have upon home industries.

Elsewhere it was the same story. In the West Indies sugar was profitable and the planters grew rich. They were able to buy manufactured goods of many kinds, and they had to buy them in England. Even the slaves needed cotton clothing, and not every negro was a slave. Many of them had gained their liberty and worked for wages, wherewith they were able to gratify a taste for gaudy finery. The slave trade poured ever more negroes into the plantations. It was carried on chiefly by the shipowners of Bristol and Liverpool, who brought home their profits to invest in England and took out a variety of manufactured goods to exchange with African chiefs for their living cargoes. India, increasingly subject to British rule, sent home wealth in many forms, and stimulated British enterprise. Tea became a national beverage and was obtained by the East India Company from China. The whole far-eastern region of the world was rapidly opened as a market for British trade. Large as was the American expansion, that of tropical commerce greatly exceeded it as the century drew to its close. The Hudson's Bay Company and the fur traders of Canada pushed westward across the continent, and their Red Indian clients added their quota to the demand for British goods. Pioneers of commerce entered the Pacific in the wake of Captain Cook. British traders were firmly settled in California before 1790, and whalers reaped a harvest of useful raw material from the hitherto untouched waters.

As a result of all this enterprise the whole world developed new wants. Far-off Africans and Asiatics became purchasers of British-made tools, knives, and muskets. The white men of America not only multiplied but became more fastidious in their living. No longer content, for example, to eat off wooden platters, they developed a demand for the new pottery which the Staffordshire towns were beginning to turn out. The people of those European countries which had no colonial trade drew upon England for the articles made from colonial raw materials. The people of England itself began to consume in bulk products that only the rich had used in earlier times. The demand upon British industry was enormous. It could only be satisfied by introducing new methods of production.

The new methods meant that the word 'manufacturer' changed its significance. Instead of being a craftsman working with his own hands the manufacturer became an organizer of craftsmen, a proprietor of a factory where goods were turned out in mass to fulfil large orders. Such a manufacturer required something more than enterprise and knowledge of his business; he required capital. He had to erect his mill and machinery, pay his workmen, buy his raw material, and transport his produce to a distant market before he received a penny on his outlay. Without capital, which means the ability to wait for a profit, the new industry could not have come into being. At the time when this demand arose England was full of saved-up money awaiting use as industrial capital. Expanding commerce and the Indian conquests had produced it. Never had so great mercantile fortunes been made as in the eighteenth century; it was the period in which the millionaire first appeared as a phenomenon in modern life.[1] Smaller men also were saving money as they had not done before. Puritanism had frowned upon social display and encouraged habits of thrift; and the Quakers, strictest of the nonconformists, were noted as a thrifty and consequently wealthy community. Banks became common, and they afforded a means of massing the small men's savings under the control of the banker, who could lend large amounts of capital to the new business enterprises. The joint-stock company, first tried in England in the Tudor period, became very much more common in the eighteenth century. It was another means of combining small savings for large undertakings; the possessor of only fifty pounds could take a share in a great business. By these devices the saved-up capital of the nation became a fluid energy, capable of application in any

[1] Alderman William Beckford, the West India merchant who died in 1770, left a million pounds, and was probably the first Englishman to do so.

required direction and easily switched from one operation to another.

The quickened production and movement of goods depended upon yet another development, the improvement of means of transport. Since the great Roman roads had decayed in the Dark Age there had never been a decent system of highways in England. The upkeep of the roads had been the duty of the separate parishes through which they ran, and the local people were naturally unwilling to spend money for the benefit of through traffic which did not concern them. Such tracks as existed were therefore left at the limit of vileness. They were impassable mud-rivers in winter, and even in summer they required the use of excessive horse-power for the conveyance of heavy goods. The eighteenth century applied the joint-stock device as a remedy. Turnpike companies undertook to maintain hard roads, surfaced with rammed stones, and found their profit in the tolls they charged to vehicles. It was taxed transport, but better than no transport at all. Some twenty years after the beginning of the turnpike system the same plan was applied to cutting canals and improving rivers. The company maintained a clear waterway and charged tolls to the barges that used it; and heavy stuff was transportable with hitherto undreamed-of cheapness.[1] The same motive led to the improvement of harbours. Seaports which desired to attract shipping constructed docks and quays so that vessels might discharge straight upon dry land and avoid the tedious transhipment of goods into lighters. Liverpool, the port for much of the new trade, was the pioneer of the modern dock system. She extended her docks throughout the eighteenth century, whereas London did not begin hers until the nineteenth.

Some of these developments took place also in other countries, but in none were they combined as they were in England and Lowland Scotland. Canals had existed in the Netherlands for centuries and had given the Dutch people much of the commercial predominance they had enjoyed in the Stuart period. But Dutch enterprise had been crushed under the burden of land-defence in the wars of Louis XIV. The Dutch were on the winning side, but they gained nothing out of the Treaty of Utrecht, and their colonial empire failed to expand in competi-

---

[1] The canals gave the language a new word. The 'navvy' was the labourer employed on excavations for the new 'inland navigation'.

tion with those of their neighbours. Amsterdam had once been greater than London, but in the eighteenth century it fell far behind. The Dutch also had flourished by superior business methods as exchangers of merchandise. They had never been great producers, and when the British producers learned their methods of exchange the Dutch could no longer compete. France constructed good roads long before England, but the French roads were made for war and not for trade. They enabled the armies to march to the eastern frontier, but they were not planned to connect the inland cities with the great seaports. Surprising as it may seem after the disasters of the Seven Years War, France had thirty years later as great an oceanic trade as England. The explanation is that she retained the best sugar-islands in the West Indies, with African slaving posts to supply them with labour; and commercial wealth lay in the tropics. There are three reasons why this trade did not stimulate the new kind of industry in France. Her home population was three times as large as that of Great Britain, and consequently it could support an equal volume of trade more easily by the old methods of production. Next, there was a lack of fluid capital in France; there was no Puritanical thrift, the middle classes were unfairly taxed, and the banking system did not take root among a people who feared to put their savings at the mercy of an arbitrary government; Frenchmen had no Bill of Rights to safeguard their property against the state. Finally, when there were signs that industry was about to change in spite of these disadvantages, all was thrown into confusion by the political Revolution which began in 1789. In the rest of Europe there were no possible competitors with England. The German and Italian states had no colonies or oceanic trade. Spain had no sea-power or ability for commerce wherewith to develop her stagnant empire. Portugal, once so great in those respects, had fallen asleep. In the eighteenth century most of her trade was run by British merchants for the ultimate profit of their own country. These are the reasons why the greatest change in modern history began first in Great Britain.

Before going on to view the working of these influences upon the life of the people, it is necessary to glance at their effects upon the theories and actions of statesmen.

It must be said at the outset that no British thinker realized that he had a great revolution to deal with. There was no gift of prophecy, but only a closer examination of past methods and an attempt to modify them so as to make improvements in the present. If merely wise men had been supernaturally wise they might have taken time by the forelock and avoided many mistakes and much future misery. But that is to ask too much. No generation has ever been able to predict the events of the immediate future.

From the earliest times English governments had levied duties on commerce. They had had two motives—to raise revenue and to favour some merchants against others by means of discriminating rates. The Tudors had so arranged things that their own English merchants enjoyed the favour as against foreigners, but they had not gone so far as to encourage home producers by making exports free and taxing only imports; the duties were levied on both alike. At the Restoration there was the beginning of a more reasonable system, but the heavy war expenditure under William III and Anne resulted in the unscientific piling-up of duties on every branch of trade that would bear them. The Whig merchants were protectionist and were satisfied so long as foreigners paid more than they themselves did. The Tory landowners gained nothing by protection and lost by the dearness of all imported goods. It was therefore among the Tories of this period that there were heard the first suggestions that free trade might be a better policy. They tried, but failed, to establish free trade with France by the Treaty of Utrecht. In this matter the Whigs were too strong for them, and the free-trade clauses were struck out.

Sir Robert Walpole was by no means a free trader, but he was a sane protectionist. He made it his policy to encourage exports and to encourage also the import of raw materials. He therefore freed those categories from duty whilst keeping stiff rates on the import of manufactured goods. But his work was overlaid by the needs of war expenditure in the great struggles of the mid-eighteenth century. Harassed Chancellors of the Exchequer clapped on duties wherever they saw a chance, and by 1783 the British tariff had again become an unscientific welter of imposts which hindered trade far more than they protected it. So high were the duties on French goods that hardly any cargoes paid them. Most of the cross-Channel traffic was carried on by smugglers with the connivance of the coast population. The smugglers were commonly called 'free traders', which in fact they were.

Meanwhile the philosophers had been considering the question. In France the group called the Physiocrats came to the conclusion that protection was an unsound policy. They held that all state regulation of trade was bad, and they coined the watchword *laissez-faire!*—leave things alone; let private men manage their business without interference. It was the very opposite of Colbert's doctrine, and in the country of Colbert it obtained little support. It did not deserve very much, for the French philosophers did not study hard facts and collect statistics. They were prone to argue in a vacuum and base their conclusions upon abstract reasoning; and practical statesmen knew that almost anything can be proved by abstract reasoning. The person who comes to conclusions without troubling to ascertain the facts is a doctrinaire. Doctrinaire methods were a peculiar vice of the Frenchmen of the eighteenth century and were to become one with many British reformers of the nineteenth. But in the earlier period British thinkers were realists, and that is especially true of the greatest of them—the Glasgow professor, Adam Smith.

Smith was attracted by the *laissez-faire* theory and took sound means of deciding whether it was justified. He studied trade as it was actually carried on. He mastered the laws of various countries, collected statistics of duties and revenues, followed patiently the movements of all sorts of cargoes, found out who produced goods and who consumed them, who handled them, and why. He took nothing for granted, and was never idle enough to assume that because a law prescribed a certain transaction it took place in fact. In the course of his work he evolved many new conclusions, but they were not doctrinaire conclusions; they were hard, honest, scientific statements. The result is enshrined in his *Inquiry into the Nature and Causes of the Wealth of Nations*, published in 1776. It is a vindication of *laissez-faire* and free trade, but always with the cautious proviso that political necessity may sometimes override economic theory. For example, he held that the Navigation Acts made transport dearer, but he approved of them because they built up sea-power. For him the health of England came before its wealth. His book is still for the ordinary man the most convincing treatise on free trade. It attracts because its author was unconnected with party politics, and it is patent that he was incapable of using any unscrupulous argument.

The author of the *Wealth of Nations* was a philosopher who studied his subject for its intellectual interest. He had little hope that his doctrines would be tried in practice. But he had made a convert in the younger Pitt, who took office in 1783 with a determination to improve the trade and finances of England. All the combatants in the War of Independence were deep in debt. and it was financial exhaustion that had put an end to the struggle. France made little effort to recover. Her statesmen refused to economize and continued to borrow, with the result that in six more years they were bankrupt and had to summon the States-General which began their Revolution. Pitt's knowledge and firmness saved England from a like calamity. His policy carried his country rapidly through the bad post-war period and enabled her growing trade to wipe out the losses of the past. He established the Sinking Fund, whereby he raised every year a surplus of revenue over expenditure and set it aside for paying off debt. It is a device that, except in war time, has been maintained ever since, and although it has never extinguished the National Debt it has established the reputation of the British State as one that means to face its obligations. Indirectly, the taxpayer's annual sacrifice has enormously increased the wealth of the country. Turning to the customs, Pitt saw the absurdity of fixing rates so high that they were seldom paid owing to the persistence of smuggling. He reduced the duties and simplified their collection, with the result that smuggling decreased and the low duties yielded more than the high ones. He initiated a step-by-step method of achieving free trade. His first object was to remove all duties on commerce between Great Britain and Ireland. Here he failed, for the Irish Parliament was suspicious and refused to pass the proposals, and there was a good deal of opposition in England. He was more successful with France, with which country he arranged a free-trade treaty in 1786. But for the wars which overwhelmed Europe a few years later this might have been the first of a series of such agreements; as it stood, it was fated to be the only example. Pitt's free-trade policy was therefore little but a promise, but his general overhaul of finance was of immense value. He intended it to mean the recovery of old England.

In fact it eased the way of transition to a new economic system and made all secure for the stormy times that were to set in with the passing of the eighteenth century.

II. SCIENCE AND WORK

'The Industrial Revolution' is not a good description of the alteration in British manufacturing methods whose most intense period is covered by this chapter. The thing was too gradual to be called a revolution, a word which implies sudden change. It had no very definite beginning, although some of its features may be discerned at the opening of the eighteenth century. Still less had it a definite ending; in one sense it is going on to-day. Yet, if we compare the England of 1760 with that of 1820—the dates of the reign of George III—we can see that an enormous change had taken place in industry. The effect was that of a revolution, although the process was rather an evolution. In 1836 Charles Dickens wrote this passage in *The Pickwick Papers*:

It was quite dark when Mr. Pickwick roused himself sufficiently to look out of the window. The straggling cottages by the roadside, the dingy hue of every object visible, the murky atmosphere, the paths of cinders and brick-dust, the deep-red glow of furnace fires in the distance, the volumes of dense smoke issuing heavily forth from high toppling chimneys, blackening and obscuring everything around; the glare of distant lights, the ponderous wagons which toiled along the road, laden with clashing rods of iron, or piled with heavy goods—all betokened their rapid approach to the great working town of Birmingham.

As they rattled through the narrow thoroughfares leading to the heart of the turmoil, the sights and sounds of earnest occupation struck more forcibly on the senses. The streets were thronged with working people. The hum of labour resounded from every house; lights gleamed from the long casement windows in the attic storeys, and the whirl of wheels and noise of machinery shook the trembling walls. The fires, whose lurid, sullen light had been visible for miles, blazed fiercely up, in the great works and factories of the town. The din of hammers, the rushing of steam, and the heavy clanking of engines was the harsh music which arose from every quarter.

Half a century earlier there had been nothing comparable with this. But it is well to remember that even in Dickens' time the picture was true only of limited areas of England. The new towns still claimed no more than a quarter of the people. Rural England had also undergone a change, but of a different kind.

The Agricultural Revolution is more justly named than its industrial counterpart. When the squire and the parson of an open-field manor, containing scores of little properties worked in common, obtained an Act of Parliament for its enclosure, there was a local revolution indeed. Within a few weeks the assessors came down upon the village, heard the claims of the inhabitants, allowed some and disallowed others, marked off the area into permanent closed-in shares, and allotted them on condition that the fencing should be done within a given time. In that summary process the practice of centuries was abolished and the ground cleared for something new to take its place. In the period under review Parliament passed thousands of these Enclosure Acts affecting nearly half the surface of England, and the indirect consequence greatly affected the inhabitants of the other half. The people of the time were quite conscious of what they were doing. They argued vigorously for and against it. Enclosure fills a large place in the literature of a generation which seemed almost oblivious of the so-called Industrial Revolution, a term which was only invented at a much later date.

The industrial and agricultural changes worked together in their effects on the life of the people, and their outstanding features must be traced in unison. But first a governing factor needs mention. After increasing very moderately for centuries, the population began after 1750 to rush upwards at a rapid rate. The figures for England and Wales are approximately as follows: in 1750, $6\frac{1}{2}$ millions; 1770, $7\frac{1}{2}$; 1790, $8\frac{3}{4}$; 1811, 10; 1831, $13\frac{3}{4}$—a doubling of numbers in eighty years; two people to be fed in place of one from the same soil. What caused it is not clearly known, but it was a fact unparalleled in English history, and one which threw a great strain upon the social framework in which it took place.

In a country with the climate and the foodstuffs of England a supply of fuel is necessary to life. Until the eighteenth century there had been little difficulty in obtaining it. The great woodlands yielded enough to keep the population warm and to cook its food. In the Weald, between the North and South Downs, there was sufficient timber also to provide charcoal for an iron industry, which had supplied guns to the Tudor navy and railings to the new St. Paul's Cathedral built by Wren after the Great Fire. Coal was burnt in regions where it happened to

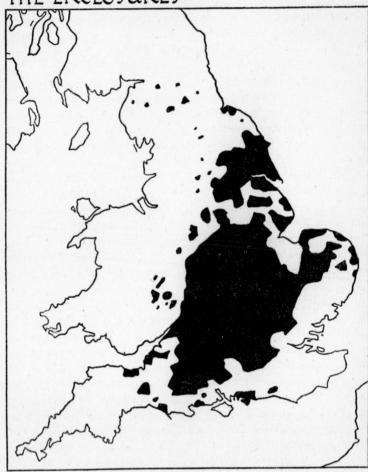

The shaded portions represent approximately the area converted from open-field to enclosures between 1740 and 1840. Of the remainder, much had been enclosed in earlier times.

exist near the surface, but the only large transport of coal was from the Northumberland coast to London, in the fleets of collier brigs in which Captain Cook served his apprenticeship to sea-life.

In the eighteenth century the growth of population upset this happy balance of the fuel question, with consequences that were important. The Sussex iron industry closed down, for the local woods were exhausted. The people of the Weald, thrown back solely upon agriculture, were impoverished by the loss of the money which their ancient manufacture had distributed among them. Elsewhere the surface coal was quickly used up, and deep mining became necessary. A new problem of pumping water out of the workings had to be faced, and the steam-engine was its only solution. For centuries the steam-engine had been an ingenious toy for men of science; it was now put to practical use, although in very primitive form. Deep mining proved a dangerous trade. Explosions and subsidences were of common occurrence. There were no safety appliances, no regulations, no inspectors to enforce them if there had been any. Men, women, and children worked underground amid conditions that would have shocked a West Indian slave-driver. Violent deaths were so frequent that even the farce of holding inquests on the victims was omitted. With increasing demand the mining industry spread rapidly. It was extremely profitable, but not for those who did the manual labour.

There were iron deposits, never touched hitherto, near the coalfields. Just as Sussex went out of business a method was found of using coal to smelt the iron ore. Blast furnaces arose like mushrooms in the Black Country round Birmingham, and in other black countries in northern England and southern Scotland. Nelson hammered the French, not with Drake's southern guns, but with northern ones, bigger and cheaper and more accurately cast. The carronade was the speciality of the Carron Iron Works, near Stirling. British iron became a portent of the new age. Its output was ten times as great in 1810 as it had been in 1740, and even that was only a beginning. It was no peasant industry, but one carried on in great works, financed by the growing capital accumulated in world trade. The ironworks turned out ploughshares and implements of every kind, things which had been made by the peasant crafts-men of the countryside. Their individual craftsmanship declined.

The farmer bought factory-made tools, and the villagers were the poorer for the change. The new iron was available for bigger things. James Watt improved the steam-engine and made it fit to give power to factories. By 1800 there were three hundred of his engines in use. When Dickens wrote the passage quoted above there were far more than that number in Birmingham alone. Iron and the steam-engine produced a whole new race of industrial wage-earners, recruited from the vanishing yeomanry and the impoverished peasants.

Iron stimulated the cotton trade. It gave material for inventors to use in new spinning machines, and it trained mechanics to erect and work them. Inventors had always existed, but they had had a poor time in the past. They had been only feckless cranks for whose ingenuity no man had a use. In the new age the inventor came into his own. Arkwright and Crompton and many more made cotton-spinning a factory trade. It was all gain and no loss, for it was a new trade and supplanted no one. But at the close of the century the machine began to get a grip on wool, and that was a different matter.

Wool-spinning and weaving had been the resource of the peasantry for centuries, the by-industry which had been carried on in the cottages and had saved even the landless man from existing solely on the wages of a farm labourer. The by-industry had supplied only a rough, unfinished cloth, and the numerous finishing processes had been in the hands of skilled whole-time workmen. Some of these processes were being worked in capitalist factories, but most of the labour was still of the domestic type when the great change set in. Wool-spinning became a factory trade as the eighteenth century gave place to the nineteenth. The fulling, shearing, dyeing, and other finishing processes followed suit. Last of all, the weaving deserted the hand-worker and was taken over by the 'works'. The old domestic cloth trade had been nation-wide, and especially important in two districts of the southern half of England—in East Anglia and in the counties bordering on the Bristol Channel. The new factory trade deserted the south and sought the north. Its centre became the West Riding of Yorkshire, where the streams gave water-power for the earlier type of factory, and where there was cheap coal for the steam-engines of the later type. The chief social effects of the cloth revolution were to create a new swarm of town workers and to deprive the countrymen of their best by-industry. But the constant improvements in machinery created a series of little revolutions within the new trade itself. Each new invention economized labour and led to a temporary turning off of hands. The unemployed blamed the machines, and there were frequent riots for the purpose of breaking them. The thing is well described in Charlotte Brontë's *Shirley*, another of the great novels of the period written from personal knowledge of its problems.

And so the list might be extended indefinitely. After iron, cotton, and wool, the machine and the capitalist factory absorbed every manufacture in turn. They created also a number of new trades, such, for instance, as the preparation of chemicals in bulk for use in industrial processes. The persons employed in the exchange of goods multiplied in proportion to those engaged in their manufacture. London had a good many minor industries, but its principal function was to be the centre of the country's commerce; and the population of London expanded at a rapid rate as the industrial changes made progress. Here as elsewhere the result was that classes drew farther apart. The rich merchant no longer lived in the City, with his staff under his own roof or lodging in the adjoining streets. He moved to the West End or to the suburban villages, whilst his clerks and warehousemen herded in the ever-growing slums of the East End. City sites went up in value until they became places of business but less commonly of residence. In London as in England one society was splitting into two.

The industrial classes were still a minority, and even when the nineteenth century was well advanced the land employed the majority of the people. How had they been faring in the meantime? Not well. The enclosure movement extended over a full century from its beginnings in the days of Walpole, but its most intensive period was in the generation after 1783. It was a necessary change if food supply was to keep pace with population, for the open field and the common pasture made for inefficient farming. Improvement in livestock called for scientific breeding and the segregation of herds. It called also for scientific feeding and the cultivation of root crops, for which the traditional agriculture made no provision. Improving landlords copied this innovation of root crops from the Dutch; Walpole's brother-in-law, known as Turnip Townshend, was one of the pioneers. Enclosure was therefore inevitable. But the manner of its accomplishment was bad, as Arthur Young, its chief advocate, himself admitted. Writing in 1801, he declared that nineteen out of twenty Enclosure Acts had wronged the poor. The assessors who weighed the claims rejected many which were morally good but lacking in legal proof; for it often happened that a poor family might have well-known traditional rights in a manor, but no written evidence to support them. Others whose rights to the common were admitted received shares of the enclosure too small to yield a living. They usually sold them for a small sum, spent the money, and became propertyless. Custom was giving place to law, and the law gave to those that had. It was an added misfortune that the factories were at the same time extinguishing the by-industries.

The result was that the land was divided into bigger properties in fewer hands, and that the numerous grades of the rural lower class were merged into one grade—that of the landless labourer whose only livelihood was the weekly wage the farmer paid him. By 1820 this depressed class of the landless agricultural labourers comprised the majority of the people of England. For reasons that will appear in subsequent pages their living was dear and their wages insufficient. They were in fact paupers perpetually cringing for 'relief' and hovering near the starvation line.

III. THE STRUGGLE WITH FRANCE—THE REVOLUTIONARY WAR

Just as economic changes were ushering in a time of stress the difficulties of England were greatly increased by the outbreak of the longest war in her modern history, the struggle with the French Revolution and Napoleon. Not only did this war take toll of life and wealth, but it introduced also political dissension to exasperate the bitter feeling caused by the industrial developments. The French destroyed their old government and their ruling class, and proclaimed a new gospel of liberty and equality for all. Their professions were belied in practice, but they were none the less attractive to the underpaid workman and the starving countryman of Great Britain. The wealthy on their side took alarm and dreaded a catastrophe like that which had overtaken their French brethren. Fear and anger led both parties to extremes; and so the 'two nations' of Disraeli's definition drew farther apart and engaged in a domestic contest that was not to be stilled for more than half a century. That is one aspect of our last French war. Another should not be forgotten, namely, that it was the new industrial wealth that enabled England to win victory over the greatest conqueror the world has seen.

The Revolution began in 1789 as an attempt to reform a monarchy which had confessed itself incompetent. But Frenchmen lacked the talent for grafting new things upon old. They were so impatient for results that they preferred to destroy the old to make way for the new. From compelling the King to accept new advisers it was an easy step to suspecting him of intriguing against them, and then to making him a prisoner and ruling over his head. That stage was reached by the summer of 1791. During the two years of its progress, authority had everywhere collapsed and the country had fallen into confusion. The National Assembly of 1789 had taken up those two years in eloquent debates on the new constitution, and when the constitution was finished something more than a debating society was needed to restore order and bring it into force. France was torn between childish optimism and unreasonable discontent: if only the aristocrats and plotters could be disposed of then the age of progress would set in. In this mood the country went to war in 1792 with Austria and Prussia, the backers of the exiled aristocrats. The enemy invaded France in the summer, and the extreme revolutionaries at once gained the upper hand. They massacred the royalists in the Paris prisons, deposed the King, and declared a republic. Then by a fluky victory they checked the invaders at Valmy and saw them retire over the frontier.

The new republican Convention was a democratic body in which the Jacobin extremists were strong. To the cry of 'La Patrie en danger!' they organized armies and struck down all Frenchmen who disagreed with them. Before the end of 1792 their troops were over the border into the Austrian Netherlands. In the following January they executed Louis XVI. Next fell the heads of the Girondists or moderate party; and then the Jacobins, led by Robespierre, instituted the Reign of Terror. The country, they said, was in danger from traitors at home and foreign monarchs abroad. Nothing could save it but the utmost severity and the concentration of all efforts upon defence. The newly born democracy therefore surrendered itself to the dictatorship of Robespierre and his group, a more effective tyranny than ever that of the Bourbons had been; and the men who plied the guillotine and invaded other people's territory chanted interminably the new Marseillaise hymn against tyrants. The contradiction between theory and practice made it easy for Englishmen to differ about the meaning and merits of the Revolution. All depended on whether one read the speeches or observed the acts of the regenerators of mankind.

In England the first effect of the Revolution was a split among the opposition Whigs. Fox took revolutionary theory at its face value and rejoiced at what was going on. The capture of the Bastille (and massacre of its garrison after surrender) seemed to him the best and greatest event in history until others still better and greater claimed his admiration. Even the death of Louis XVI and the countless executions of the Terror scarcely shook his revolutionary constancy. But only a minority of the Whigs held to Fox. Burke, essentially a conservative, declared as strongly in the contrary direction. In 1790, before the trend of events was clear to most men, he published his *Reflections on the French Revolution*, in which he predicted that tyranny and not liberty would be the outcome, a period of war and a military dictatorship. It was a remarkably accurate prophecy, or perhaps an inspired guess. Many of the Whigs thought with Burke and broke away from the leadership of Fox.

Pitt refused to theorize in either direction. He watched events and based his policy on verified facts. To him it seemed at first that the French Revolution was the business of none but the French, and he had no objection to the weakening of the anti-British Bourbon monarchy. Perhaps he over-valued that circumstance. The old French army was dissolving in the chaos, and the French treasury was emptier than before the outbreak. No one could predict that a democratic rabble would fight against regulars—that was to be one of the revelations of the future. Pitt therefore took a cool view and declared as late as 1792 that he looked for fifteen years of peace. Hardly had he spoken than the situation changed. At the close of 1792 the Convention passed a decree that all existing governments were their enemies and all peoples suffering under tyrants their friends. It was an incitement to the discontented in England as elsewhere, and it was not mere rhetoric, for at that moment the

French were invading the southern Netherlands and finding support among many of the people who disliked Austrian rule.

On more concrete grounds the invasion of the Netherlands was a challenge to Pitt. The Jacobin hosts pushed through to Antwerp and proclaimed in defiance of treaties that the navigation of the Scheldt was to be open and Antwerp a seaport in the full sense of the word. The breach of treaty was a breach of the public law of Europe. It was also an attack upon an age-old principle of English policy, that no great militant power must control the Netherlands. Pitt, man of peace though he was, prepared to fight. Burke supported him. Only the Foxite Whigs denounced the decision. The Jacobins were nothing loath, and war was actually first declared by them in February 1793, a few days after the execution of the King. Austria and Prussia were already engaged, and Pitt concerted with them and the minor powers the First Coalition.

If Pitt had foreseen the future he would have been a dejected man, for what he had conceived to be his lifework, of leading England to peace and prosperity, was at an end. But his knowledge of finance made him optimistic. Bankrupt France, he thought, could not sustain a lengthy fight; it would be all over in a year or so. It was quite true that the old-fashioned governments could not fight without money; it was a revolutionary truth, as yet unknown, that a people flaming with patriotism and a political religion can fight under any disadvantage if only they find good leaders. The First Coalition therefore went confidently into the ring, and was knocked out in a few rounds by an antagonist it had despised. Neither side put up a finished performance—a group of veterans, experienced but flabby, and a raw youngster who picked up his science as he went along. The gods looked down and laughed, and decided that both parties must have more training.

The story of the First Coalition must be briefly outlined. In 1793 British and Austrians invaded north-eastern France and besieged Dunkirk. They were soon driven back, out of France, out of the Austrian Netherlands, out of Holland—a continuous tale of retreat and disaster. In 1795 the remnants of the British force came home from a German port, whilst Belgium was annexed to France, and Holland affiliated to her as the Batavian Republic. Holland was the first of the Coalition powers to fall out. Prussia was the next, not by reason of defeat but of lukewarmness. Spain followed, and in 1796 actually joined France. Austria remained, but in 1796-7 she was forced to sue for peace by the unbroken series of Napoleon Bonaparte's victories in northern Italy. When the French path to Vienna lay open, Austria signed the Treaty of Campo Formio and the First Coalition was at an end. On the sea the British navy had gained the upper hand and blockaded the French coasts. Pitt used sea supremacy in a way that has been criticized. He sent the flower of the British army to make conquests in the West Indies. It achieved nothing of note, and in a few years it had lost nearly 100,000 men by disease. Those men, used in Europe, might have carried the First Coalition to Paris and overthrown the Revolution. They might—but most likely they would not; for the First Coalition was so feebly managed, and its members so jealous and selfish, that probably nothing could have saved it.

The French successes were fatal to the Terrorists. The excuse for the Terror was that the country was in danger. In the summer of 1794 the victory of Fleurus in Belgium removed the fear of invasion, and a month later Robespierre fell. He and his lieutenants followed their victims to the guillotine, and thenceforward milder methods prevailed. In 1795 the Convention gave place to the Directory—five Directors as heads of the government, supported by a parliament of two houses. The Directory governed less savagely but more corruptly than the Jacobins. The republican flame was burning lower, and the way was being prepared for a return to monarchy. The Directors, afraid of their own armies, continued the war. By 1797 France was surrounded by a ring of vassal states—the Batavian Republic in the north, Spain a subservient ally in the south, the Rhineland occupied, the Cisalpine and Parthenopean Republics carved out of Bonaparte's conquests in Italy. The Revolution had not modified French ambitions—they were still those of Louis XIV.

The year 1797 was described, until 1914, as 'the darkest hour in English history'. Our allies had gone, the whole Rhine delta was in French hands, Ireland was on the point of revolt, discontent was simmering at home, the great French armies were available for invasion, and the Dutch and Spanish fleets were at the disposal of France. The Spaniards indeed were routed at Cape St. Vincent in February by Sir John Jervis and Nelson, but as the year advanced the gloom deepened. The navy, the sole prop of our tottering power, mutinied. With the Channel fleet at Spithead it was rather a strike against bad treatment than an unpatriotic revolt, and the seamen gladly returned to duty when grievances were redressed. But in the North Sea squadron facing the Dutch there were some real revolutionaries who talked of carrying the ships over to France. For six weeks they blockaded London, and then the loyal men asserted themselves and the mutiny collapsed. In the autumn this squadron beat the Dutch fleet at Camperdown, and except for Ireland the prospect grew brighter, for invasion had become less likely.

Ireland was a terrible problem. Her grievances in the eighteenth century had been twofold—the oppression of the Catholics by the Penal Code and the suppression of Irish trade by regulations framed in the interest of English mercantilists. Until 1782 even the Irish Protestants had had little voice in their own government, and the Catholics had had none. But the weakening of England by the War of Independence had emboldened the Protestants to demand freedom for the Irish Parliament. Rockingham yielded in 1782, and Poynings' Law [1] was repealed. Thenceforward the Irish Parliament was nominally free to legislate for Ireland, but pocket boroughs and corrupt elections accounted for most of the seats, and real independence was still to seek. There was now, however, less bitterness between Catholics and Protestants, and the worst provisions of the Penal Code were repealed. Progressive Irishmen of both religions saw that a reform of their Parliament was essential to true liberty, and in 1791 the society of United Irishmen was formed to work for that end. The inspiration came from France, and it changed in unison with developments in that country. At first the United Irishmen worked by constitutional means. Then, as England declared against the Revolution, and the French themselves became bloody and terrorist, the United Irishmen became a revolutionary body, leagued with the enemy and pledged to set up an Irish republic.

Pitt was no enemy of Irish industry. He failed to secure complete freedom of trade, but the worst restrictions had been removed, and the Protestants of Ulster were partially satisfied. To the Catholics he granted the parliamentary vote in 1793, but he would not yield full Catholic emancipation, which meant the right to sit in Parliament. The Catholics would be content

[1] For Poynings' Law (1494) see above, p. 162.

with nothing less. So it came about that the most faithful
Catholic population in Europe looked for deliverance to the
revolutionaries who had overthrown the Catholic Church in
France, murdered its priests, and enthroned Reason in Notre
Dame. The intermediaries were the leaders of the United
Irishmen. But the passage of the sea was the difficulty. A
French army gathered at Brest and dodged the blockade in the
last weeks of 1796. The winter storms scattered the transports,
and not a man landed in Ireland. It was, however, a near thing,
and throughout the following year the Irish peasantry were on
the brink of rebellion, looking every day for the French. The
government employed regular troops and Protestant yeomanry
to disarm the malcontents, and in the search of houses many
atrocities were committed. The rebellion at last broke out in
1798, but the government measures had been fairly effective,
and the rising was limited to the counties south of Dublin.
There the Catholic peasantry, after committing atrocities in
their turn, were beaten at Vinegar Hill, and the movement
collapsed. When all was over a few hundred French troops
landed, but were made prisoners.

Pitt's intended solution of the Irish problem was to unite the
Irish and British Parliaments and then to grant Catholic
Emancipation. He accomplished the first but not the second.
In 1800 the Irish Parliament proved itself unworthy to live by
taking bribes to vote for its own extinction. It did not represent
the people of Ireland, but only a clique of borough-mongers,
and its end was no loss to anyone. Thenceforward for a hundred
and twenty years Irish members sat at Westminster. During
the first generation they were Protestants only, for Pitt did not
succeed in carrying Catholic Emancipation. George III vetoed
it, and his prime minister resigned in consequence in 1801.

The above are some of the external aspects of the struggle
against the French Revolution. Its effects upon the domestic
affairs of Great Britain were no less important, for they emphasized class divisions and moulded politics in a way which
endured after the wars were finished. It was during the long
war, and partly by reason of it, that the 'haves' and the 'have-
nots' ranged themselves in deep hostility to one another.

When the States-General met at Versailles in 1789, and when
their more liberal elements transformed themselves into the
National Assembly, the programme then adopted was to make

France a limited monarchy with complete equality, legal and religious, for all its subjects. It was this which attracted the support of Fox and his Whig followers, and their approval emboldened English dissenters to hope for similar rights under a reformed British constitution. In 1789 ominous disorders were already occurring in France, but optimists had some reason to hope that they would subside and that an age of peace and kindliness would ensue. Unhappily the course of events justified Burke rather than Fox, and the British reformers found themselves linked with a movement that sober men could see to be disastrous. The result was that reformers on this side of the Channel, however mild their intentions might be, were classed with the dangerous spirits who also existed here, and all alike were denounced as revolutionaries and Jacobins, enemies of Church and throne, and coveters of other men's property. By 1791 French *seigneurs* escaping from their burning chateaux were arriving in England as refugees, the property of the Church was confiscated, and Louis XVI, nominally King, was really a prisoner seeking vainly to escape. These things were not to the taste of the average Englishman, who was loyal to his King and the existing order.

In 1791 therefore events began to show that the Revolution was to be a dividing force in English life. Doctor Joseph Priestley, the great scientist and prominent dissenter, was one of those who had approved of the French transactions, chiefly because they held out the hope of religious equality. Soon after the flight and recapture of the prisoner-king in France the loyalist feeling in Birmingham made Priestley its victim, and a mob destroyed his house and scientific instruments, together with some meeting-places of the nonconformists. Mob-violence in this first outbreak was on the side of the ruling classes, who were so lax in dealing with the outrage as to suggest that it had their approval. Their attitude was short-sighted, for a precedent had been set that was to be used against them.

Meanwhile a revolutionary of a different type was coming into prominence. Thomas Paine, who had long before shown his quality as an Englishman by urging the American colonists to rebel, published *The Rights of Man* in 1791–2. In it he advocated the abolition of the throne and the House of Lords and the formation of a democratic republic. After some delay Pitt ordered the suppression of *The Rights of Man* and the prosecution

of its author, who fled to France, and narrowly escaped execution for giving offence to Robespierre. Paine was a full-fledged
revolutionary, but he was courageous enough to denounce the
Terror, and it was only a gaoler's oversight that saved him from
the guillotine a day or two before Robespierre himself was
overthrown.

The Rights of Man was even more of a best-seller than Burke's
Reflections on the French Revolution. Thousands of copies were
printed and passed from hand to hand. They were read by
a class to whom they came as a new gospel, the working men
of the mills and factories. *Laissez-faire* denied them even a
minimum wage or any limit to their working hours. Tom
Paine's republic promised them glittering benefits, such as old-
age pensions and free education, all at the expense of Property.
For the first time a large section of the poorer class became
interested in politics. In the older England they had been
content for the rich to represent them. They now suspected that
the rich were misrepresenting them. Radicalism was born.

Political clubs, an idea copied from the French, were the next
symptom of unrest. The year 1792 saw the foundation of the
Friends of the People, the Corresponding Society, and the
Society for Constitutional Information. The first-named, its
title boldly borrowed from *L'Ami du Peuple*, an ultra-Jacobin
journal of Paris, was the work of the aristocratic Whigs of the
Fox connexion. Their social rank made these democrats immune from prosecution, but the hand of authority fell heavily
upon humbler reformers. In 1793-4 numbers were brought to
trial for treason and sedition, both in England and Scotland,
and severe sentences of transportation were inflicted; but no
one was put to death. Viewed from the standpoint of to-day
transportation for a political speech was a barbarous punishment. In the light of 1793, when the Jacobins were lopping off
heads by the thousand, and England was genuinely in fear of
a similar tragedy, it was conspicuously merciful. After the fear
subsided juries would no longer convict, and the government
was reduced to suspending the Habeas Corpus Act in order to
keep suspects in prison without trial.

The execution of Louis XVI, the outbreak of war, and the
failure of the First Coalition made Englishmen rabid. In former
French wars there had been no such bitterness. The decencies
had been observed, and personal friendships between the in-

fluential men of England and France had been unbroken. This war was something new, a war for ideals, not for colonies, and defeat would mean the end of all that made life worth living. Common sense and tolerance were strained to breaking-point, and the ugliest passions assumed the cloak of patriotism.

In these circumstances political labels lost their former vagueness, and parties crystallized into sharp outline. The term 'Whig' came to signify a follower of Fox and a friend of the French. The former Whigs who could not take this side went over to the government. They and the Pittites and the old Tories combined into a new anti-reforming, anti-Jacobin party which assumed the Tory title. The fusion took a few years to complete. In 1794, for example, we find a political candidate expressing his horror of 'democracy and republicanism' and promising to support Pitt, but at the same time disclaiming any party label. But by the opening of the new century all such men were definitely Tories. The new Tory party was therefore what is called reactionary. It believed that Louis XVI's amiable weakness had let loose the revolutionary flood, and it determined that there should be no weakness on this side. It set its face against all reform, political and religious, and denounced as a Jacobin every advocate of new liberties. It was an extreme attitude, and whilst the country was in danger public opinion backed the extremists. They had a long run of approval, for the country remained in danger until 1815.

Were the Tories justified? Modern opinion generally condemns them, and especially Pitt, who broke with his reforming past and became the head of the reactionaries. The fact that Pitt could take such a course is a warning against too-hasty condemnation. Where he believed that a reform could be safely made he advocated it, as in the instance of Catholic Emancipation in 1801. Where he did not believe it safe his opinion is entitled to respect. It has been urged that the fear of revolution was groundless, since the structure of English society was quite different from that of the French. Pitt thought otherwise, and he had had an experience which his critics are apt to overlook. As a young man in 1780 he had seen London in the hands of the Gordon rioters, a revolutionary mob as dangerous as that which took the Bastille. A political demonstration by mainly respectable citizens had called out all the vast criminal class that lurked in the slums. They had held the streets for a week, destroyed an immense amount of property, and paralysed the arm of authority. Only the pluck of George III had saved the situation. He had shamed his ministers into action by declaring that he would clear the streets in person at the head of his Guards. It was an object-lesson in revolution, and if Louis XVI had been such a man he would not have died on the scaffold. The kingliness of George III had converted London into a loyal city, and now when he was old and failing his ministers applied his example in the uneasy north and midlands. If blame is due, it should not fall on Pitt in the 1790's, but upon his successors who continued to be reactionary after the danger was past.

The Tory rulers met the new situation in industry by two measures which were far less wise than their purely political statesmanship.

The massing of workers in the factory areas had led to the formation of trade unions for the purpose of raising wages by combined action. The principle of *laissez-faire*, which generally slept when it would have hampered government activities, was invoked against this interference with individual bargaining. Trade unions were described as a restraint upon trade, and by the Combination Acts of 1799–1800 all such bodies were made illegal and their members punishable with imprisonment. The motive was not purely economic, for the unions tended to fall under the control of Radicals who preached the doctrine of Thomas Paine, and it was partly for this reason that they were suppressed. But the economic restriction was a new infringement of liberty, and since it was also class-legislation it greatly embittered the downtrodden factory hands. Again, one must beware of ascribing the policy to merely sordid motives. William Wilberforce, the champion of the negroes and as unselfish a man as ever walked the earth, was the introducer of the Combination Acts. They are the chief blot on his statesmanship, but they leave his honour untouched.

The agricultural labourers were hardly yet a political body. They were too scattered, wretched, and ignorant for that. Enclosures and the loss of by-industries had pushed them down, and the high war-price of bread had brought them to starvation. Their masters, the Tory squires, were conscious of responsibility for their lot. They did not, like the millowners, invoke *laissez-faire*, but admitted that something must be done. The squires, however, were no economists, and in well-intentioned ignorance they committed a disastrous blunder. In 1795 the Berkshire magistrates met at Speenhamland, near Newbury. By ancient custom they should have fixed a fair rate of wages in accordance with the cost of living. Ancient custom was growing dim, and instead they adopted another remedy. They left the inadequate wage unaltered and drew up a scale of doles to be paid from the poor-rate. The dole was to be so much a head for the labourer and each member of his family, the amount to rise or fall with the price of bread. The Speenhamland system quickly spread through the country. Every farm labourer (the most numerous class in England) became of necessity a pauper, perpetually in receipt of parish relief. The degradation was an immense moral loss. There was also a material loss, for the relief in lieu of wages came out of public funds contributed by all ratepayers alike. The small farmer who worked with his hands and employed his sons instead of paid labourers was therefore penalized to support the servants of his richer competitors. The result was to hasten the process of concentrating property in fewer hands; the small owner went down whilst the big one went up. The Speenhamland system was adopted as a temporary device to tide over the year or two which were expected to elapse before peace and cheapness should return. But the wars lasted twenty years after 1795, and Speenhamland persisted for twenty more years after the wars.

There was little real hope of ending the war because a new aggressive force was arising in France just as the force of Jacobinism was growing weaker. Bonaparte had founded his fame by his Italian victories of 1796–7. In 1798, when Great Britain alone was holding out, he struck at her eastern interests. He sailed from Toulon to Egypt and there landed an army intended ultimately to drive the British from India. The plans seem to have contemplated the conquest of the whole Near East and a land advance on India, or the collection in the Indian Ocean of a French fleet based on the Red Sea. They never got very far because sea-power intervened. Nelson destroyed the French fleet at the Battle of the Nile, cut the army's communications with France, and cut also Bonaparte's line of advance from Egypt into Syria, which passed through the coast towns of Palestine. Bonaparte's army was bottled helplessly in Egypt, where it ultimately surrendered to a British force.

The Nile was the first great defeat the French had suffered.

With Bonaparte isolated and far away, the powers ventured to form the Second Coalition in 1799. Russia, whose Czar (Paul) hated all republicans, took part, and Russian and Austrian armies quickly cleared the French out of Italy.

The Directory, unpopular even in victory, grew hateful in defeat. Bonaparte left his army to its fate in Egypt and returned to France by running the gauntlet of the British cruisers. Instead of being arrested for deserting his command he was welcomed as a saviour. But he meant to save France on his own terms, which were that he should be her master. There was an unexpressed bargain between him and the French people: he might take control provided he gave first victory and then peace and an honest government. In November 1799 he overthrew the Directory. His supporters produced a new constitution, which pretended to be republican but actually created a monarchy. There were to be three consuls and a variety of elected bodies, between whom power was so subdivided that none had any. All decisions rested with the First Consul, who was Napoleon Bonaparte.

The fate of the Second Coalition was soon sealed. In 1800 Napoleon crossed the Alps and regained all his former Italian conquests by the single victory of Marengo. It was not in his best manner—in fact he was well beaten when a subordinate retrieved the day—but it sufficed; for at the same time Austria was routed on her German front at Hohenlinden. Once more the road to Vienna lay open, and Austria sued for peace. The Czar Paul was reputed to be mad, but he was sane enough to penetrate the sham of the Consulate. His enmity was for republics, not monarchs, and he recognized that Napoleon was monarch of France. He also made peace and called home his troops. For the second time England stood alone.

The First Consul meant to complete his peace by conquering England. He made plans for invasion, but he lacked sea-power. He saw hope in the north, where Paul became his ally and formed a league with Sweden and Denmark to revive the Armed Neutrality of 1780. Between them these northern powers had some show of a battle fleet. But Napoleon's hopes were dashed when in 1801 Nelson beat the Danes at Copenhagen, and Paul was murdered by his own courtiers. After that the plan changed. There should be a temporary peace with England, a thorough overhaul of France, and then the final trial of strength. The British government was ready enough for peace, and signed it at Amiens in 1802. We restored the best of our colonial conquests and consented to the French hold upon the Netherlands. Of the two objects for which Pitt had begun the war in 1793, the freeing of Antwerp and the checking of Jacobin ideals, the first was not attained, and the second was no longer necessary. Jacobinism was exhausted, but Napoleon, once a Jacobin himself, was its heir. In his hands was gathered the mighty force of the Revolution, to be devoted henceforth to the building of an Empire. A greater than Louis XIV overshadowed Europe, and the peace was not likely to be of long duration.

IV. THE STRUGGLE WITH FRANCE—NAPOLEON

The Peace of Amiens was broken after fifteen months, for neither party was satisfied with it. Great Britain had to complain of Napoleon's actions towards neighbouring states, whereby he showed that he did not mean to content himself with the conquests the treaty had allowed him. Napoleon had a grievance in the British refusal to evacuate Malta, which had been seized by our fleet in the course of the Nile campaign. Negotiation could have settled these questions had any good will existed, but the 'will to war' was reviving on both sides of the Channel, and in 1803, when Napoleon made bellicose threats, the British government took him at his word and declared war. His answer was to arrest numbers of British subjects who were travelling in France. These unfortunates remained prisoners for eleven years. To intern civilians on the outbreak of war has now become the rule, but it was a new measure in 1803; it had never been done in the more civilized warfare of the eighteenth century.

Napoleon had intended war and the invasion of England, but the British government had taken up the challenge before he was ready. His fleets were short of men and stores, and scattered in various ports, and to concentrate them in face of a British blockade proved an impossible task. His admirers are prone to assume that he never made mistakes, but in this matter his hasty temper had betrayed him. He publicly pledged himself to conquer England, and only then gave serious thought to the means of doing so. His plans would have been more effective if matured under the cloak of peace.

The French 'Army of England' was quartered along the shore

of the Straits of Dover, in sight of the land it was to win. To cross those narrow waters, patrolled by British cruisers, was the problem. Napoleon considered various solutions. At first it seemed a simple matter. Sooner or later there would come a calm or a fog. The sailing frigates would be blinded or deprived of motion, and the army could be rowed across in the thousands of light boats provided for its use. A technical detail proved objectionable: it was shown by practice that it would need at least a week for this swarming flotilla to work out of the narrow harbours of Boulogne and the adjacent ports. Fogs do sometimes last a week, but one cannot guarantee them at the outset; and thus the chance-of-weather plan would not answer. The next idea was to arm certain boats of the flotilla and use them as a mosquito fleet to drive off the cruisers. Napoleon spent a great deal of money on this, but his seamen pointed out that small boats, however numerous, could not seriously attack a heavy ship-of-war; and when such encounters did take place the result proved the soundness of the contention. Why could not Napoleon have set his own heavy ships to dodge the blockade as chances arose, and gradually accumulate at Boulogne? Geography forbade. The harbours of north-eastern France were all tidal, and the ships in them grounded at low water. Battleships with great guns on board would quickly have become wrecks if exposed to such a strain. The nearest French port fit to shelter a large battle-fleet was at Brest on the Bay of Biscay. Napoleon's position was unpleasant. The French people expected him to get on with the invasion. He distracted their attention with the gorgeous ceremony of his coronation as Emperor in 1804, but thereafter the problem returned. His last solution was the plan of 1805. Before dealing with it we must notice the British measures of defence.

The British government adopted the sound principle that England's frontier was the enemy's coast. The blockade began as soon as peace was broken. Nelson went to the Mediterranean to watch the French fleet in Toulon. Cornwallis with the largest British fleet lay off Brest, which contained the largest French force. Other squadrons detached from Cornwallis blockaded Rochefort and the Spanish port of Ferrol, where there were a few French vessels. A comparatively weak British force in the Downs was sufficient to account for the vaunted flotilla of Boulogne.

The admirals were quite confident that they could prevent

Napoleon from crossing the Channel, but the ministry took further precautions. On all low-lying parts of the south-east coast they built the Martello towers, some of which may be seen to-day. Each tower mounted a heavy gun, designed to play upon the flotilla as it approached and upon the troops as they disembarked on the beach. Across Romney Marsh, the most favourable spot for a landing, the engineers dug the Royal Military Canal from Hythe to Winchelsea. Its purpose was to serve as a moat to delay the invading infantry whilst the local defenders were reinforced by the main British army from the interior. The people of England were impressed with the reality of the danger, and men of all classes enrolled in volunteer corps to defend their soil. Pitt set the example by joining a Kentish regiment. His musket and equipment were long preserved at Walmer Castle, although history does not record that he actually drilled with them.

Pitt indeed had other employment. He had resigned on the Catholic question in 1801. The Tories remained in power under his friend Addington, a man of little weight. 'Pitt is to Addington as London to Paddington' was the current estimate, and the new war led to Pitt's reinstatement in 1804. Now that Napoleon was Emperor and a despot undisguised, Fox and his Whigs ceased to be pro-French. They would have joined Pitt in a ministry of national defence but that George III could not conquer his aversion for them. Pitt without Fox revived his former policy of a European alliance, which Fox disliked. In the summer of 1805 the Third Coalition (Great Britain, Austria, and Russia) was formed. Its immediate effect was to set a time limit to the invasion plans, for Napoleon would be obliged to march against the Austrians and Russians before the end of the year. Unless therefore he could reach England by September he would have to postpone the whole venture. The Third Coalition was an excellent stroke of policy on the assumption that there was a real danger of invasion. Pitt, like most of the landsmen, thought there was. If he had had complete faith in the navy he need not have formed the Coalition which, as the event turned out, played Napoleon's game. It delivered the Emperor from the unhappy predicament of being laughed at by his own subjects, for when he realized that British sea-power made invasion impossible he was able to save his face by alleging the Austrian attack as the reason for abandonment.

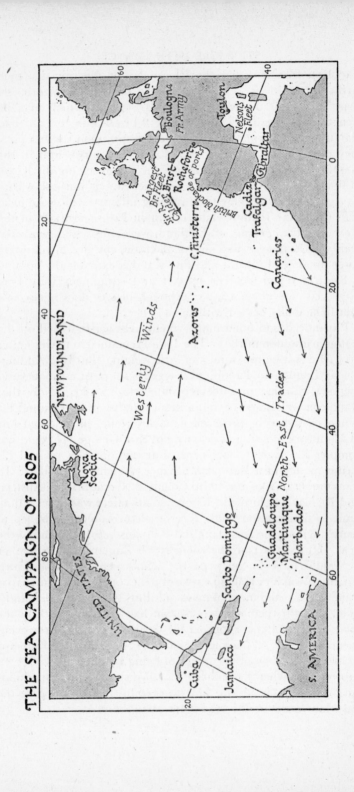

THE SEA CAMPAIGN OF 1805

All this was not apparent until the close of 1805. Meanwhile the invasion plan of that year was going forward. It was an example of the grand strategy that Napoleon used so well in the land warfare which he understood, but it overlooked certain technical factors pertaining to the sea, and it assumed that the British admirals would be as incompetent as the land commanders whom Napoleon had always beaten hitherto. The French squadrons received orders to leave their ports (as there were frequent opportunities for them to do), to elude the British pursuit, and to concentrate in the West Indies. Whilst gathering full strength there they were to attack the British plantations. Then they were to return as one mighty fleet to the Channel, sweep away the blockaders of Boulogne, and convoy the army across to England. Once across, Napoleon could be indifferent to the fate of his fleet. He despised the British army and reckoned on dictating peace in London within a fortnight.

The Rochefort squadron, a minor unit, duly escaped and reached the West Indies. There it waited the prescribed time, met no other Frenchmen, and returned to Rochefort, having contributed nothing to the plan. Admiral Villeneuve escaped later from Toulon with a larger fleet, picked up some Spanish battleships from their ports, and sailed for the west. Nelson, whose task it was to look after Villeneuve, did not allow himself to be eluded. He first made sure that the French had not gone again to Egypt, and then pursued across the Atlantic. Villeneuve had a good start, but Nelson gained rapidly upon him. It was only some misleading information supplied to Nelson at Barbados that prevented a battle in that neighbourhood. Villeneuve took the alarm and hurried back to Europe, but he was outstripped by a fast vessel which Nelson sent forward with the news of his approach. Meanwhile the largest French fleet at Brest had not come out at all. It remained in port under the watch of Sir William Cornwallis.

So far, Napoleon could still hope that the plan would work. Villeneuve might return to Brest and join forces with the French there, to make up a fleet of more than fifty sail. That should have been sufficient to clear the Channel. But to Villeneuve the plan seemed hopeless. The British Admiralty, warned of his approach, sent Sir Robert Calder to intercept him. They met off Cape Finisterre. Villeneuve lost two ships, and the action was broken off by bad weather. He then put into the north

Spanish ports to refit and obtain news. He found that all the
British fleets except Nelson's were between him and Brest, and
he knew that Nelson was certainly behind him in hot pursuit.
He gave up the whole plan and sailed southward to Cadiz.
There he was soon blockaded, and Napoleon was no nearer to
crossing the Channel than at the beginning of the year. Nelson's
determination to follow his quarry to the ends of the earth,
coupled with the concentration of the rest on the mouth of the
Channel, had foiled the Emperor's strategy. It had been designed to scatter the British fleets in bewildered search for an
enemy who had disappeared; it resulted in bringing them all
to the right place at the right time.

At the end of August Napoleon learned that Villeneuve had
declined to go on with a hopeless project. Meanwhile the
Austrian armies were moving westwards and the Russians were
getting into motion behind them. The Third Coalition proved
the Emperor's salvation. Furiously denouncing the unhappy
Villeneuve, he broke up his camp at Boulogne—he must have
been heartily glad to do so—and marched 'the Army of England' against an easier prey. Before the year was out the victories of Ulm and Austerlitz gave the French their fill of glory
and retrieved their Emperor's reputation for invincibility. The
English fiasco, it was agreed, had been the fault of the seamen;
Austerlitz showed what Napoleon would have done had he been
well served.

Fleets, unlike armies, do most of their important work without fighting great battles, as the invasion plan of 1805 had
demonstrated. But the year was not to close without one of the
greatest sea battles in history. The land war of the Third
Coalition rendered the Mediterranean an important highway,
a means by which the allied troops might be brought to attack
the French in Italy. A fleet at Cadiz was useless to Napoleon,
and in October he therefore ordered Villeneuve to leave that
port and move to the Mediterranean. Nelson was watching
Cadiz with inferior numbers; on the day of action his strength
was as two to three in proportion to Villeneuve's French and
Spaniards. But at Trafalgar, between Cadiz and Gibraltar,
Nelson's skill redressed the balance. He crushed two-thirds of
his opponents' fleet before the remaining third could come into
action. As he lay dying in the *Victory's* cockpit some twenty
ships-of-the-line were wiped off the roll of the Emperor's navies,

with the result that the remainder were so outclassed and outnumbered that no further sea plans were possible. Trafalgar
was not the end of the invasion scheme, which had ended two
months before, it was rather the beginning of a new chapter
in the Franco-British struggle. The complete command of the
sea which it yielded compelled Napoleon to seek new and unfortunate means of attacking his enemy; and it enabled his
enemy to adopt new and effective means of attacking him—but
only after long delay.

This explains why Austerlitz killed Pitt, as has been truly
said, and why Trafalgar failed to keep him alive. Pitt had hoped
from his Third Coalition an immediate end of the war. The
great land battle killed that hope; the great sea battle substituted only the hope of an end in the far-distant future. Pitt had
no doubt of that end. 'England,' he said, 'has saved herself by
her exertions, and will save Europe by her example.' But he
was worn out, and the end was not for him to see. 'Roll up that
map,' he groaned, as the news of Austerlitz came in; 'it will not
be wanted these ten years.' It was the map of Europe—and it
was ten years to Waterloo. He died in the first days of 1806.

It was time to bury feuds and pull together. The Whigs at
length came into the ministry, and Fox took command. But he
died six months after Pitt, and ere long Whigs and Tories fell
out again, and the Tories assumed sole power. Fox died a
patriot, and perhaps had always lived as one. But he had shown
his love for his country after a fashion that the plain man found
strange. His Whigs were indelibly dyed with the tint he had
given them, and until the wars were over they had nothing to
contribute to the common weal.

After the rout of Austerlitz the Austrian effort collapsed and
the Russians withdrew over their own border. In 1806 Napoleon dealt with Prussia, which had remained neutral while her
help would have been effective, and then challenged him when
left alone. The twin victories of Jena and Auerstadt accounted
for the Prussian army in a single day, and the victor entered
Berlin. Next year he beat the Russians at Friedland, a battle
that need not have been decisive had the Czar Alexander shown
as stout a heart as he was to display in later years. As it was,
the Emperor and the Czar made peace at Tilsit in the summer
of 1807. They agreed to divide the continent, and prospectively
the world, between them. Napoleon was to dominate central

and western Europe, and Alexander the east, where he was urged to revive those plans against British India which Nelson had cut short at the Nile. Meanwhile, with Alexander's support, Napoleon undertook to deal with the British in their island by means which he had already devised.

Napoleon realized how formidable was the wealth drawn by Great Britain from her foreign trade, and how sensitive the trading interest was to any attack upon its profits. That factor had played its part in the plan of 1805, for Napoleon had calculated that the news of French squadrons working havoc in the West Indies would cause such a panic that Pitt would be obliged to send his home fleets to the rescue; and it had been only the speed of Nelson's pursuit that had averted such a result by denying Villeneuve the time to commit any damage. After Trafalgar the Emperor was thrown back upon economic warfare as the only means of striking at his foe. He thought that means would be effective. The doctrines of Colbert appealed to his military mind. He believed that commerce could be 'manœuvred like a regiment', and that with all the ports in Europe under his control the nation of shopkeepers could be brought to its knees. In the autumn of 1806 he issued the Berlin Decree by which he forbade any country under his power to admit any British ships or goods. At Tilsit the Czar undertook to enforce the prohibition in his sphere of influence. Further decrees dated from Milan and elsewhere filled in the details, and the whole became known as the Continental System. In theory the European trade of Great Britain was cut off.

The British answer was no less sweeping. By the Orders in Council the British government declared a blockade of all ports that enforced the Continental System; if they would not trade with Great Britain they should not trade at all, and the navy would make the Orders a reality. Once again land-power was pitted against sea-power. It was a novel contest, in which the soldiers and sailors, unable to shoot at one another, sought their ends by starving non-combatants. The craftsmen, peasants, and merchants of the continent, the millowners and operatives of England, the traders of neutral countries, particularly of the United States, were all between the hammer and the anvil until this gigantic gamble with unknown forces should declare its result. And when after long years 'such a war had such a close' the scars it left were deeper than those of any previous contest.

We may consider the effects on England first. The stoppage of European trade was never complete, but it was sufficiently serious to produce some of the results Napoleon sought. The owners of cotton and cloth mills found their output exceeding their sales. Some went bankrupt, and many turned off their hands. The survivors, in desperate competition for such markets as remained, improved their machinery to cut down costs and turned out their goods with fewer hands than they had previously needed. With the labour market full of unemployed, and trade unions illegal, wages went down to starvation point. Industrial riots became common. The workman saw the new machinery turning him out of his job, and he gathered in hungry bands and broke the machines. Radicalism, stifled by Pitt, arose again. But it was not the gaseous political Radicalism of 1790 and Thomas Paine; it was a harsh economic Radicalism nourished by starvation. Crime, not eloquence, was its product, and its exponents went to Botany Bay for shedding blood in place of ink. The millowners were glad of soldiers to defend their machines, but they cursed the war and the ministry and its Orders in Council. The Tories were waging the war. They were in truth its offspring, but it was easy to call them its authors; and the manufacturers who had hitherto minded their private business in *laissez-faire* fashion became politicians and supported the Whigs. Harvests were bad, there was little corn to be had from the Baltic coasts, and population was growing. The price of the loaf went up, the large farmer and his landlord grew rich, but the farm labourer starved with the mill hand. Speenhamland alone kept him alive, and in so doing crushed the poorer middle-class with extortionate taxation. Napoleon had indeed struck a shrewd blow beneath the belt. The Tory statesmen—Spencer Perceval, Lord Castlereagh, Lord Liverpool—hardened their hearts and carried on. A broken trader murdered Perceval in the precincts of the Commons, but his colleagues did not flinch. *Delenda est Carthago*, the Corsican must be overthrown.

The Americans had done very well as neutral traders until the economic war set in. Both the Continental System and the Orders in Council hit them hard, and in their exasperation it was an open question whether they would declare against Napoleon or Great Britain. Certain additional factors decided them. The British navy claimed the right of searching neutral ships for its deserters. In the case of American vessels it was often difficult to prove the nationality of the suspected man, and some high-handed things were done. The expanding frontiers of the middle and southern States were in contact with fighting Indians, and the frontiersmen alleged that Canada instigated the red men and supplied them with arms. It was in fact the southerners who hurried the United States into declaring war in 1812, lured by the hope of conquering Canada; but the Orders in Council furnished the pretext. In three campaigns the Americans attempted the invasion of Canada, only to be repulsed. On the sea their cruisers won single-ship actions and their privateers destroyed much British trade. The interruption of trade was the most serious effect of the war, which had been preceded by a boycott of British imports. The loss of the American market deepened the misery of the manufacturing classes. One circumstance alone yielded some compensation for the injuries wrought by the Continental System. British sea-power cut off the ocean trade of France and her vassals. Business with South America, Africa, and the Far East became almost a British monopoly, shared in a minor degree by the merchants of the United States. It was a saving factor that was badly needed.

The Continental System was a two-edged weapon which wounded its author more deeply than his opponents. The Empire of Napoleon gave its subjects many benefits, the chief of which was honest and competent government. Had there been no irritant it is possible that central Europe would have settled down under his sway, for he had not deprived these peoples of liberty—they had never had any. But the attempt to enforce the System led to tyranny. There was a constant trickle of forbidden trade, which it needed all the vigilance of French officials to prevent from growing into a flood. Along all the North Sea coasts there was perpetual spying, denunciation, and arrest of persons who sought only to be left to gain their living in peace. In the Baltic the Russians quickly grew tired of it, and the Czar made little pretence of enforcing the decrees. In the Mediterranean it was the same story of growing restiveness and evasion. Commerce, it appeared, could only be manœuvred like a regiment if it was also disciplined like one. And the prolonged application of military rule in civilian affairs was the one thing needful to rouse against Napoleon those populations which had accepted his destruction of their old governments with indifference.

The first open defiance came from the feeblest state in Europe. Immediately after the Treaty of Tilsit Napoleon demanded of the Portuguese that they should close their harbours to British trade. They refused, and a French army at once invaded their country. Before the end of 1807 it seemed as though Portugal had become a province of the resistless Empire. Napoleon went further. To reach Portugal he had demanded passage for his armies through Spain, and the feeble Charles IV had consented. In the spring of 1808 Spain was full of French troops. Napoleon bullied Charles IV into renouncing the Bourbon claim to the throne, and proclaimed his brother Joseph Bonaparte as King of Spain.

Hitherto the Empire had expanded on this simple plan, the overthrow of governments unloved by their subjects, and the adhesion of those subjects to the vastly superior government provided by Napoleon. In Spain the formula did not work. The Spanish people, relieved of the worst of governments, showed no gratitude; they rose in arms against their benefactor. The Spanish army, as an institution, was as rotten as everything else in the state, but Spanish officers and soldiers proved themselves patriots, and the priesthood and peasantry joined them. The whole countryside rose in revolt, until the French controlled nothing more than the ground within range of their muskets. They were not sure even of that, as was shown at Baylen in the summer of 1808, when the Spaniards captured an entire French army twenty thousand strong. It was the first time such a dishonour had befallen the imperial eagles. The Spanish nation had risen against Napoleon, and the Portuguese nation was ready to follow suit. The era of brief campaigns closed by stunning victories was over. That of attrition and decline had begun.

In England the Tories heard the call from the Peninsula and answered it, much as the Whigs denounced their decision. In the autumn of 1808 Sir Arthur Wellesley cleared the French from Portugal, and in the winter Sir John Moore followed with such a thrust into Spain that Napoleon hastened in person to his brother's assistance. Moore had to retreat, and after his death at Corunna was unjustly blamed as if for a disaster; but it is now recognized that his move was so well timed and executed that it threw all the French plans into confusion and gave the southern Spaniards the breathing space they needed to consolidate their defence. Wellesley returned to the command in 1809. The French greatly outnumbered him, and he could make no rapid conquests; but on the other hand the Spanish resistance prevented the French from putting all their forces into the front line. The story of the years 1809–12 is therefore that of alternate advance and retreat. Wellington invaded Spain and beat the French opposed to him, the French forces coping with the Spanish insurrection then left that task and concentrated against him, whereupon he was obliged to fall back to Portugal and the sea. But each of his advances undid all the work the French marshals had accomplished in beating down Spanish resistance. The most perilous year was 1810, when Napoleon, untroubled elsewhere, sent Masséna, his most trusted marshal, to drive the British into the sea. Masséna seemed to have an ample force, but the famous entrenchments of Torres Vedras brought him to a halt. Without venturing an assault, the French withdrew, and Portugal at least was saved. 'Masséna is growing old' was the Emperor's comment. He would not admit that the Empire also was past its prime.

The Peninsula was 'the running sore' that infected the whole imperial system. In 1811 the Czar threw over the commercial decrees and braved the consequences. Central Europe was still submissive, and its conscripts were added to the French to form an army of invasion half-a-million strong. In the summer of 1812 the half-million entered Russia. By the end of the year one-tenth of them were straggling out; the rest were dead or prisoners. It was not the Russian government alone that had ruined Napoleon. The spirit of the whole people had resisted him, and the Czar, his Russians, and their terrible climate had formed a harmony of defence. Russia was not satisfied with defence. She hit back; and as her legions marched westward the Germans rose to join them. Castlereagh, the British Foreign Secretary, saw that the decisive hour had come. The princes of Germany were still as feeble and selfish as ever, but beneath them a spirit of liberty was surging up. Castlereagh, with a diplomacy unequalled since Marlborough's of a century before, welded all into the Fourth Coalition. It succeeded where its predecessors had failed, for it was a coalition of peoples. It had no easy task—1813 was a year of stubborn battles in which supreme generalship on the one side failed to overcome the common man's valour on the other. Leipsic in October finished the struggle in Germany, and the Napoleonic remnants streamed back to the Rhine. At the same time Wellington made his last march through Spain and routed Joseph Bonaparte at Vittoria. Before the end of the year the British were across the Pyrenees and the eastern allies across the Rhine.

Napoleon still fought on, but three more months saw the end. In the spring of 1814, with Paris lost, his marshals refused to continue. He retired to the Mediterranean isle of Elba, whilst the victors restored the Bourbons in the person of Louis XVIII.

In less than a year Napoleon was back. He landed in Provence and pushed northwards to Paris, joined by all his old soldiers, who were spoiling for another fight. Their eagerness is a mystery to the modern mind; they had long experience of war, and yet they wanted more of it. However, the fact is clear that Napoleon was never more enthusiastically served by his rank-and-file than in the campaign of 1815. With his marshals it was different. Some refused to rejoin him, and those who did were not optimistic. They knew that with only an exhausted France they had to face the whole of Europe. The great powers had formed the Fifth Coalition without delay and had bound themselves to fight on until Napoleon was hunted from his throne as an outlaw.

For three months neither side was ready. Then in June Napoleon advanced suddenly into Belgium, where Wellington and Blücher were slowly gathering British, Hanoverian, and Prussian forces. The Austrians were still far away, and the Russians had not issued from their own borders. Wellington and Blücher were surprised, but they pulled their scattered armies together. Blücher was beaten but not routed at Ligny, and retreated in a direction which kept him in touch with the British. They, attacked on the same day at Quatre Bras, likewise moved back to keep touch with the Prussians. It all ended at Waterloo on 18 June. There Napoleon, believing that Blücher was out of the game, attacked Wellington with superior numbers; but Wellington stood because he had Blücher's promise of support. The British and Hanoverian defence had broken all assaults when the Prussians arrived, but numbers were telling, and none can say what the issue would have been without Blücher. Wellington never encouraged discussion of the point.

'It was a damned near thing' was his only comment. With the
Prussians pressing on his flank Napoleon made a final great attack
on the British line before him. It failed, the British advanced
in counter-attack, and the last Napoleonic army dissolved in
such a rout as had not been seen since Jena. Blücher continued
the pursuit through the night, but failed to catch the Emperor,
whom he intended to shoot out of hand. The great fugitive
reached Paris, and thence Rochefort. British cruisers prevented
him from sailing to America, and he surrendered to the navy
which had ever stood between him and his desires.

The overthrow of Napoleon was the end for which Great
Britain had fought, and that end needed no treaty to confirm
it. The settlement of Europe at the Congress of Vienna in 1815
is thus the beginning of a new period rather than the closing of
an old. All its arrangements are important, more for their connexion with events that came after than with problems that
went before, and it is from that point of view that the Vienna
Treaties will be mentioned in subsequent pages as occasion may
arise. But their direct bearing upon English history is much
slighter than on that of the continental nations. Waterloo had
fulfilled Britain's policy; she had little to ask or to gain at
Vienna.

V. THE FACTORIES AND THE FIELDS

For a quarter of a century the rift in English life had widened,
and misery had increased. The war had been blamed for all,
and with peace men expected a new and happier time. They
did not get it. They had yet to learn that, apart from the bloodshed, the worst part of a long war is the peace that ends it. In
bloodshed, indeed, the British people had escaped lightly. There
was no conscription save that of the seamen by the press-gang,
and the regular army was small even at the height of its achievements. All Wellington's victories cost no more than 50,000
British lives, a much lower proportion to the population than
in Marlborough's great war of a century before. But on the
home front the suffering had been unexampled. Byron declared
in 1812 that after visiting the worst provinces of Turkey he had
never beheld such squalid wretchedness as in the heart of England. It is true that he was a romancer and a Radical, but he
was also no admirer of the Turk.

The long duration of the war had been good for the farmers

and landowners if for no one else. The price of corn was high, and even a bad harvest did not affect profits; it simply made prices higher. Those who gained by these artificial conditions did not look ahead. They acted as though high prices would last for ever. The farmer ploughed poor land which would never pay in normal times, and on the proceeds he adopted a style of living as luxurious as that of the squires of the eighteenth century. He bought blood horses, costly furniture, and costly wines. He wore fine clothes and patronized sport. He brought up his children to elegant accomplishments instead of to practical work. This went on for so long that his new status seemed to him his natural right. So also did the vast incomes gathered from inflated rents seem a natural right to the great landowners. To all this powerful landed interest any interference with war-won prosperity appeared unjust, a thing to be righteously resisted in the sacred name of Property.

The bubble was pricked some time before Waterloo. The expulsion of Napoleon from Germany in 1813 marked the end of the Continental System. In the next two years foreign corn from the North Sea coasts and the Baltic came in, and British prices collapsed. Thousands of farmers went bankrupt, and hundreds of great landlords found their incomes cut. It was computed that the total rents paid for land fell by nine million pounds. The first-fruit of victory was blank dismay. The remedy lay in Parliament, for there the landed interest was supreme. In 1815 the Corn Law was passed by substantial majorities. It enacted that no foreign corn should enter British ports until the home price stood at eighty shillings a quarter. The effect on the consumer was that the four-pound loaf rose from tenpence to one-and-twopence,[1] and this at a time when few mill-hands drew a pound a week and the farm labourer seldom more than eight shillings. To the latter the Speenhamland dole was supposed to make up the difference. But in most places the rates were already so high that they could not be raised any further without converting the ratepayers into paupers themselves. Thus starvation stared many a working family in the face, with crime as the only alternative.

One crime was tempting enough in the English countryside, and that was poaching, which few men believed in their hearts to

[1] Average prices of 1815 and 1817 respectively; but in places the prices were of course higher.

be a crime at all. Rabbits and hares, winged game and fish, were more abundant than they are to-day. They cost their legal owners nothing, and yet ownership was limited to a privileged few who would not have starved without them. The hungry man inevitably went poaching to fill his children's bellies. The answer was a new Game Law of 1816, which prescribed seven years' transportation beyond the seas for the man found in possession of so much as a net for taking rabbits. Such laws manufactured criminals. Few ever came home from the convict settlements, and the poacher grew as ready to kill gamekeepers as game in defence of his liberty. Often enough he was a brutal ruffian like Bill Sikes; but who made him one? Too often it was the sportsman who planted spring guns in his wood-land, loaded with buck-shot to blast the life out of any who tripped over the string, or man-traps with steel jaws that crushed bone and sinew and crippled their prey for ever. We know such things in our day as the horrors of modern war. For twelve years after Waterloo they were the legalized horrors of peace.

In the industrial towns things were no better. Manufacturers had accumulated stocks in the war, and with the opening of Europe there was a rush to sell. But war-ravaged Europe had no money to buy, and the stoppage of corn imports stopped the exports that would have paid for them. The momentary optimism gave place to panic. Millowners and merchant firms broke by the hundred, and their hands joined the unemployed. War-work ceased. Dockyards and gun-foundries turned off their men, to be joined in idleness by the homeless tramps who had blockaded Brest or broken the Old Guard at Waterloo. An ugly spirit of violence seethed through the land, and there were signs of combination about it that statesmen found ominous. Just as the villeins of old time had muttered passwords about Jack Trueman and John Amend-all, so now there were under-ground brotherhoods who committed outrages in the names of mysterious leaders. 'Captain Ludd' organized machine-break-ing in the midlands. 'Captain Swing' posted warnings to the village tyrant and set fire to his ricks at dead of night. To many it seemed that the Jacobin terror was nearer than ever before.

Two things were needful—firm discipline and an intelligent pursuit of remedies. The Tories were ready with the first but not the second. Their instinct was to sit tight and govern like martinets, but to change nothing; for them the headless ghost of

Louis XVI blocked the path to reform. The Liverpool ministry, which had taken office in 1812 and finished the war, remained in power. Lord Liverpool himself was its figurehead rather than its leader. The master spirit was Castlereagh, the Foreign Secretary. He and Wellington had brought about the fall of Napoleon, and he had worked at Vienna for a sane peace which should not be vindictive towards France. But he believed his own people to be on the verge of revolution, and blind repression was his only remedy. His views dominated the Home Secretary, Lord Sidmouth (the Dr. Addington of 1801), upon whom the task of repression chiefly fell. Another complete reactionary was Lord Eldon, the Lord Chancellor, whose opinions had great weight in the administration of justice. Finally, the Duke of Wellington came home from France in 1818 and took a seat in the cabinet. His influence was naturally repressive, for he had all his life been coping with wild characters and had not been accustomed to reason with them. The long years of strife had set their mark on all these men. They had won victory by hardening their hearts, and they could not soften them now. They who had looked Napoleon in the face could not truckle to rioters and Radicals.

The Whigs were unprepared as yet to stand forth as reformers. They numbered less than a quarter of the House of Commons. Most of them approved of the Corn Law, and only Lord John Russell and a few of their younger men were really in earnest for the abolition of the rotten boroughs. Fox would have been ready to ride the storm, but his successors were afraid of it. More constructive were some of the Tories who had not yet reached the front rank—Canning, Peel, Huskisson—who saw that mere repression would not cure the ills of the state. The reactionaries at present kept them down, but their turn was to come.

The great forces of reform worked outside Parliament, and therein lay the worst of the danger. Throughout a long life Jeremy Bentham had been teaching men to think about their institutions instead of taking them for granted. For him nothing was sacred that could not pass his question, 'What is the use of it?' He was no platform politician. He was quite respectable, and no one thought of putting him in prison; but he had become the brain of Radicalism. William Cobbett, a violent Radical although essentially a conservative, voiced the woes of the peasant. He denounced enclosures and game laws and the arrogant new breed of gentlemen-farmers, and for ever harked back to the days when the villager had his cow and his corn-strip and his common rights. As Bentham was all head, so Cobbett was all heart, a heart swelling with grief at the destruction of the old England of his boyhood. His fiery sorrow poured through his pen in the columns of his *Political Register*, which sold for twopence a copy, and week by week echoed the refrain that free Englishmen had been made slaves. Francis Place, the tailor of Charing Cross, was the political manager *par excellence*, one of those who stand in the background and pull the strings. He would have been a dangerous man but that he had little faith in violence. He indulged in no vain regrets for the past; indeed, as a Londoner born and bred, the past was not for him a golden age as it was for Cobbett. He accepted the new order and devoted himself to bettering the lot of the working man within it. His instinct was not to overthrow but to adapt, and for many a cool, shrewd stroke he deserved well of his country.

Platform Radicalism came out in force after the peace. In the industrial north it was the product of factory life and the new towns, which herded men of like interests in close association. The political meeting was their obvious outlet, to cheer their drab lives with a feast of oratory, the more of ginger in it the better to their taste. Dissenting chapels, where the common man might preach like the Ironsides of old, trained many a Radical speaker, between whom and the Anglican parson no love was lost. But the opposition of the clergy called forth orators of a different type, who pointed to the clergyman-magistrate as a 'black dragoon' and contemned all religion as a device of tyranny. This attitude estranged the god-fearing middle class who might otherwise have sympathized, and many a worthy man bracketed Radicals with atheists and took his stand against both.

Through all the hurly-burly of the post-war years one act became increasingly clear. The industrial workers had been bitten with the French idea of democracy. They believed that only with political power could they obtain better conditions of life. They were dissatisfied with Parliament and the constitution as it stood. The Radical demand was Parliamentary Reform, and for the reactionary Tory this was but another word for revolution.

So we have the forces ranged for the struggle; we have now

to notice some of its incidents. In 1816–17 there were Radical meetings all over the north, a so-called insurrection in Derbyshire, and serious riots in London. Cobbett was at the height of his influence, and the volunteer impulse showed itself in the new form of unlicensed assemblies to practise drill and the use of arms, not for the defence but for the overthrow of the state. Prosecutions generally failed, for juries, knowing the ferocious penalties, refused to convict. The government had to fall back on its last resource and suspend the Habeas Corpus Act. This enabled it to silence the agitators, and a brief calm ensued.

To suspend the Habeas Corpus Act, a pillar of the constitution the Tories were claiming to defend, was a confession of weakness, and the law was restored as soon as it seemed possible. The Radical speakers came out of gaol as eloquent as ever, and Cobbett, who had fled overseas, returned. In 1819 a great mass meeting was held in St. Peter's Fields at Manchester to listen to 'Orator' Hunt and other stars of the Radical platform. The local magistrates decided to arrest Hunt in the midst of the meeting. They sent troops to do it. To force dragoons and yeomanry through a close-packed multitude was to provoke a tragedy. The mob could not or would not clear a passage. The horsemen drew their swords and charged. There was a wild panic in which a large number were killed and injured—many more than some modern historians have admitted.[1] Four years earlier the country had rung with the exploit of Ponsonby's dragoons at Waterloo, smiting into a great French column and driving it like chaff before them. In bitter allusion the Manchester deed of prowess was christened the Charge of Peterloo. It lost nothing in the telling, in speeches, newsprints, and crude coloured cartoons showing 'the brave boys' mangling shrieking women with dripping swords. The Radicals grew savage, and the Whigs awoke from their lethargy. All but the extreme Tories were ashamed of their government. From that moment reaction began to lose the solid backing it had received from the sober elements of English opinion.

The ministry did not disown their magistrates. The prevention of future Peterloos was to consist not in the toleration but in the prohibition of speech-making. Castlereagh and Sidmouth passed the Six Acts of 1819. No gatherings for drill were to be

[1] For this matter see 'The Casualties at Peterloo', by Prof. G. M. Trevelyan, in *History*, vol. viii, No. 27 (1922).

allowed, no political meeting might be held without permission from the magistrates, a heavy stamp duty was placed on pamphlet literature with the object of making it too dear for circulation, and in disturbed districts the justices were empowered to search for arms. The Six Acts completely muzzled all open expression of Radical opinions.

Never since the 1680's had free speech been so effectively attacked, and for a parallel consequence we have to go back to the same period, when the Rye House plotters had sought to murder Charles II and his brother. In 1820 Arthur Thistlewood and a group of Radicals planned the Cato Street Conspiracy. They agreed to burst in upon a cabinet dinner-party and shoot the entire ministry as they sat at table. Of course there was a traitor in the gang, and authority was forewarned. The conspirators waited in their loft in Cato Street whilst their scouts reported that the party was duly assembling. But they were deceived, for the carriages were taking guests to an adjoining house, and the cabinet dinner had been cancelled. Then the constables burst in upon the gang. There was a scuffle in which Thistlewood killed a man and escaped. He was taken next morning, together with the others, and was executed a few weeks later.

Before the end of the year the cabinet lost all vestige of public support on a sentimental issue. George III died, and his son, who had been Prince Regent for the past ten years, became King as George IV. He at once began proceedings for the divorce of his wife, Caroline of Brunswick, and compelled his ministers to introduce a Bill in Parliament for that purpose. George IV's personal character was a byword, and for such a man to adopt a pose of outraged morality was nauseating. All classes united in championship of 'injured Queen Caroline' and in hooting down the unhappy ministers who were being made the instruments of her persecution. The Bill failed and left the ministry moribund. It had moreover given the Whigs a chance to assert themselves in a cause they really believed in; and Henry Brougham, their chief legal authority, had made the most of the opportunity.

Tory reaction now resembled an imposing façade with a ruinous building behind it. Its only prop was the vigorous character of Castlereagh. In 1822 his mind gave way, and he committed suicide. He had been a great diplomatist and a devoted public servant according to his lights; but Peterloo and the Six Acts were recorded against him. The London crowd turned out and gloated with hideous cheering as his funeral passed through the streets. Sidmouth, the Home Secretary, who had been his ally, resigned. Lord Liverpool remained premier, but at the head of a new ministry, to whose principal places he admitted the Tory reformers. Canning became Foreign Secretary, Peel Home Secretary, and Huskisson President of the Board of Trade.

By reason of these changes the year 1822 is more truly a turning-point in English life than the year of Waterloo. The rift had reached its greatest depth, and thenceforward the best efforts of statesmanship were bent on closing it. The process was destined to be a long one and full of clamours and dangerous phases. Once, perhaps twice, revolution was to appear imminent. But the difference was to be seen in the manner of meeting the threat—by reform, not by reaction.

A final word is necessary on the actual condition of the people at this time. Until a few years ago 'the miseries of the Industrial Revolution' was an accepted phrase, and its implication was that the great change had made the country uniformly wretched. Recent students have challenged this view, and their painstaking research entitles their opinions to respect. They show that some classes of the workers were better off than before the change, and that all the squalor and deadliness of the new towns had existed for centuries in the old ones. Their argument is that it was not the abuses that were new but the recognition of them, and that this awakening was itself a sign of improvement. Well, it is all a matter of proportion. It is quite true that the old town slums had been hotbeds of misery; but it is also true that only a very small proportion of the people had lived in them. The old population had been predominantly rural, but the proportion was changing. By 1820 one-third were town-dwellers; by 1850 one-half. Then again the statistics of wages for skilled workers may mislead. The majority were unskilled and could never hope for these wages. Moreover, the fluctuations of trade were more violent than in the past. In a bad year a whole town might be unemployed and starving, and the state had not yet learned that the new conditions must be met by new remedies.

But what has caused more error than anything else is the

fixing of attention on that unfortunate phrase 'the Industrial Revolution'. For the chief agent of misery was the Agricultural Revolution. No one suggests that the agricultural labourer was better off; and he formed the largest class in the community. In Walpole's time the village was the home of the normal free-born Englishman. It was a true unit of a well-balanced society. It had numerous grades of property, craftsmanship, and wealth, all closely knit together by common interests. A good harvest meant prosperity for all, a bad one that all tightened their belts together; and the by-industries, the cottage spinning and weaving, mitigated the worst of the misfortune. It was an article of faith in those days that the English villager was better nourished, more comfortable and self-respecting, than any continental peasant. In Castlereagh's time all that was changed. There were only two grades in the village, the owners and the labourers, and the latter were the great majority. Enclosures had abolished the little properties, factories the by-industries, the Speenhamland system had pushed wages below the limit of self-respect, and war and the Corn Law had raised the price of bread too high for the poor man's purse. There was sullen enmity between the farmer and the cottager. The harvest thanksgiving was a mockery to those who had no property in the kindly fruits of the earth. Rick-burning, which would have seemed a lunatic crime against the village in the old conditions, had become a sort of wild justice on the tyrant to the men whom he hunted for hunting rabbits.

No, the whitewashing of the eighteen-twenties can be carried too far. To the few they gave wealth and luxury hitherto unknown; to the many a misery equally unexampled. All was not well with a time which produced Peterloo and Cato Street and horrible cheers at a statesman's funeral.

IX

REFORM AND WEALTH

(*From 1822 to 1885*)

I. THE PROGRAMME OF REFORM

IT is instructive to compare the questions in which Englishmen were interested at two dates a hundred years apart: in 1721, when Sir Robert Walpole came into power, and in 1822, when Sir Robert Peel, George Canning, and William Huskisson took office. The contrast will be the measure of the changes which had taken place in British life and thought during that century.

In Walpole's time there was lively political strife, but it was on matters that had quite lost their prominence at the later period. The main question was whether the band of great men labelled Whigs should rule the country, or the other band labelled Tories; and the chief difference of principle between them was whether the Church of England should be allowed to persecute the nonconformists or not. A few of the Tories, joined by the Roman Catholic interest, thought they would do better under the Stuart Pretender than under the Hanoverian George I. There was thus a danger of revolution at both dates, but not the same kind of revolution: in 1721 it was a question of substituting one king for another; in 1822 of overthrowing monarchy altogether and setting up a republic. In 1721 there was no whisper of Radicalism, no suggestion that the mass of the people were unjustly treated in having no voice in government. The voteless multitude were quite content for the powerful few to represent them. This political contentment was based on social contentment. 'The rich man in his castle, the poor man at his gate, God made them high or lowly, and ordered their estate,' was a thesis accepted by all. The poor man had his rights, so well guarded by ancient custom that the rich man could not infringe them, and there was no disposition to question that happy state of affairs. Society, in a word, was static, poised in a sort of equilibrium. A century later it had become dynamic, unhappy, and restless.

Economic interests again show a great difference of emphasis. In 1721 commerce, the exchange of goods, was the prime topic of discussion. There was no serious demand for free trade;

protection was accepted by almost all. The favoured means of improving commerce were the expansion of colonies and the gaining of monopolies like the Asiento privilege of the South Sea Company. Existing monopolies were jealously guarded; and when the Austrian government in the Netherlands formed an Ostend Company to trade with India, the British people were quite ready to go to war to suppress it. By Huskisson's time monopolies were out of fashion, and *laissez-faire* was becoming the commercial ideal. But indeed the chief economic interest was not so much commerce as production, the constant improvement of all the new methods of manufacture which had so rapidly sprung up. In this sphere also the static had become dynamic.

Finally we must mention humanitarianism, which stands for the stirring of the public conscience to improve the lot of the unfortunate. In 1720 there was very little of it, none indeed as a government activity; charitable work was purely a private affair. A hundred years later humanitarianism was becoming one of the great forces of public life, and no statesman could afford to flout the humanitarian interest. *Laissez-faire* was an uneven leaven. In business relations the early nineteenth century believed in it, but in spiritual affairs not at all. It did not greatly matter if a man was unemployed and starving, but it was very important that his religious beliefs should be in a healthy state. In time, of course, the humanitarians did make it their business to relieve material woes among their fellow countrymen, but in the early stages they were much more sympathetic towards the heathen across the ocean than towards white unfortunates at home. It was this that caused Dickens, a tender-hearted and not a narrow-minded man, to gibe at the missionary humanitarians in so many passages of his novels.

We may sum up this contrast between our two periods by saying that in the early eighteenth century 'reform' was an idea almost unheard of, whilst in the early nineteenth it had become the most absorbing topic of the time.

The programme of reform was large and varied, and there were many competing bands of reformers, some of whom regarded others with great dislike. That was because some reforming movements sprang out of the French Revolution, which had been anti-religious, and others out of the fervid Christianity set on foot by John Wesley and carried forward by

William Wilberforce and his Evangelical school of thought. Between these two wings of the great impulse there was little common ground.

For the Radicals the greatest reform was that of Parliament, from which all else would follow. Parliamentary reform was to be twofold—the redistribution of the seats to accord with the shifting of population, and the granting of votes to the working classes. Redistribution was centuries overdue. It appealed to more than the working-class Radicals, for the new moneyed men of commerce and industry were beginning to feel jealous of the landowners' monopoly of Parliament. The aristocratic magnate might order his tenants to return his nominees for the pocket borough, but the captain of industry had no similar scope for his influence over his hands. Before 1832 the busy Birmingham described by Dickens sent no member to the House of Commons, nor did any of the new towns of the period. Reform in this particular had therefore a middle-class backing. Large extension of the franchise had not. Democracy was still a thing to be disavowed by the respectable; it called up too many memories of the Jacobins and the guillotine. For that very reason it was dear to the fiery orators of the mill and the mine, who had been in prison for sedition and blasphemy, and wished to get even with the squire and the parson who had sent them there.

In the ancient but still solid boroughs there was no less desire for reform. They might be 'rotten' enough to lose a member in the redistribution, but the loss would be that of the little clique who elected him, not of the townsmen at large. A more local reform appealed strongly to these places, that of the municipal governments themselves. With the new common needs of the age, the street lighting, paving, main drainage, and water-supply made possible by the new industrial science, it was intolerable that control should be in the hands of irresponsible corporations chosen by the influence of the few. The typical town council of the period was not elected by the votes of the householders. It was a permanent body whose members themselves selected the recruits to fill vacancies in their ranks. It had the right to levy rates on all, but it had not to account for the spending of the money. There was far more jobbery and incompetence in local than in national affairs—schools without scholars, streets left foul and dark, slums wallowing in sewage, their denizens poisoned by tainted air and water. All these were the 'jobs' that profited the few and caused growing resentment among the many. To the Benthamites who scoured the land with their perpetual question of 'What is the use of it? How do you justify it?' municipal abuses offered fine texts, and municipal reform was the substance of many a sermon. Municipal reform meant the free election of the corporation by all the ratepayers.

In Parliament there were few Radicals, and few Whig aristocrats who really interested themselves in the woes of the poor. High political society was much more concerned with a reform that cut across class distinctions and concerned the great as well as the small. This was Catholic Emancipation. The Test and Corporation Acts of Stuart days still remained in the statute-book. In theory they debarred all Catholics from public employment, but they had been whittled away by various Relief Acts until their oppression was much diminished. But it was still the law that no Catholic could sit in Parliament, or rather, that if he would he must first take an oath that would render him no true Catholic. The members of the Roman Church in England were by this time few, but in Ireland they were the majority of the population; and since Pitt's Act of Union of 1800 the representation of Ireland was at Westminster. Pitt had promised Catholic Emancipation, but George III had refused his consent. In the following generation Catholic resentment increased, and many Protestants grew convinced that the demand for emancipation was just. The Whigs as a body were in favour of it. Among the Tories resistance was strong, but not universal. Some of them inherited the ancient desire for Church of England ascendancy, some the ancient fear, once so well grounded, of a foreign jurisdiction claiming British allegiance; but some admitted that both privilege and fear were out of date, and were ready to agree to the reform. It was destined to be, in fact, the first of the disputed matters to be settled.

The question of free trade was twofold. It concerned the protection of the landed interest by the Corn Laws and also the maintenance of the general system of tariffs on all imported goods. There was no great opposition to the doctrine that heavy tariffs were harmful to trade. British manufacturers had such a decisive lead in the new industrial methods that they feared no foreign competition and desired no protection. They believed that in a free-trading world they could easily hold their own. The shipping interest, however, wished to retain the Navigation Acts in so far as they conferred a monopoly of the colonial trade. The chief obstacle to free trade in all articles but corn was therefore not one of principle but of expediency: the Exchequer had to levy taxes, and if it did not do so at the custom houses it would have to revive the income tax, which was very unpopular. This held back the cause of general free trade until the financial genius of Peel was able to solve the problem of revenue. In the matter of corn the position was different. The landed interest was determined to exclude foreign supplies. Against the Corn Laws were ranged the mass of the poor consumers, and also the manufacturers, who argued that cheaper bread would mean lower wages and a greater production of goods. But prior to the reform of Parliament the landowners were supreme, and the Corn Laws did not become a first-class political topic.

It was evident that the Poor Law needed a drastic overhaul. The Speenhamland system had produced its disastrous results in pauperism and high rates. The Benthamites were especially concerned with the problem, and the solution which was coming into favour was that of cutting down the outdoor relief and compelling the destitute to enter workhouses. It was a necessary change, but one that was bound to entail hardship in the period of transition. This was one of the reforms advocated by the intellectual few, and not demanded by the popular voice.

Another was that of the criminal law and the police. The chief causes of crime were lack of education, general misery, and the ease with which wrong-doers escaped justice. The eighteenth century had sought to check crime by enacting ferocious punishments. The death-penalty was imposed for a long list of offences, some of them quite trivial. The result was that juries often refused to convict, although they knew the prisoner was guilty. A necessary reform was therefore to make the punishment fit the crime, and then to exact it. Still more necessary was a proper police force. Hitherto the expense had been shirked. The towns maintained a few feeble watchmen, often appointed because they were unfit for hard work. In the countryside the parish beadle and the magistrates' private servants had been the only police, supplemented by special constables hastily sworn in at times of crisis. It was thus fairly easy for keen-witted offenders to escape arrest, and a huge criminal population existed. For putting down serious disorders the state still relied upon soldiers, with unhappy results. Had there been a police force in Manchester in 1819 there would have been no Massacre of Peterloo. Another necessary factor in the reduction of crime was the reform of the prisons themselves. They were undisciplined pest-houses, where multitudes died and where the old offenders associated freely with the comparatively innocent. Here a constant supply of new criminals was manufactured, and such crimes as that of coining base money were known to be carried on actually within the prison walls.

The Benthamite Radicals desired to go further than reforming the law. They discerned that ignorance lay at the root of many offences, and they advocated the spread of public education. The religious humanitarians went with them to a certain point; it was at least necessary that every child should learn to read the Bible. There was also a considerable popular demand for education, especially among the better sort of factory workers. Their keenness demanded a real sacrifice. Men who had worked the long hours then usual in the mills would gather eagerly for lectures at mechanics' institutes, and weary children would pick up their letters at night schools and Sunday schools. They were of course a small minority, but the leaven was destined to spread.

The great humanitarian movement was recruited more from the Tories and Whigs than from the Radicals. Its early interests were rather world-wide than national. In 1788 Burke and Fox, with Pitt's approval, prosecuted Warren Hastings for supposed tyranny in India. They had mistaken their man, who had really been a worthy ruler, but their motive was sincere. Hatred of oppression led the humanitarians to crusade against slavery and, having liberated the slaves, to form the Aborigines Protection Society to prevent ill-usage of native races by white colonists. On the purely religious side the closing years of the eighteenth century witnessed the formation of the great missionary societies. William Wilberforce was prominent in these activities. He was no Radical. He was indeed curiously blind to suffering at home. He introduced the Combination Acts and voted for the Corn Law, and was inclined to congratulate the poor upon their poverty because it saved them from temptation. The early humanitarians were often of the doctrinaire type which thought principles more important than facts. The man who did most to broaden their sympathies was the Tory Lord Shaftesbury of the next generation.

Parallel to the championship of black men by the humanitarians was that of oppressed white men overseas by broadminded statesmen. The Treaty of Vienna had neglected the rights of nationalities and had thought mainly of the interests of princes or of the balance of power. In consequence Greeks were left subject to Turks, Belgians to Dutchmen, Italians to Austrians, and Poles to a variety of tyrants. Even in the independent states of Europe absolute monarchy was the rule, and the Holy Alliance of the leading monarchs existed to maintain it. But everywhere there was a strong feeling that parliamentary government ought to be set up. British reformers of all parties sympathized with the struggle for liberty. Lord Byron, the Radical, died for Greek independence; Canning, the Tory, aided the Spaniards of the New World to the same end; and in later days Palmerston the Whig and Gladstone the Liberal were destined to do much for the liberation of Italy. Any exiled patriot was sure of a welcome in England, and notable oppressors heard some plain truths here. It is on record that the Austrian General Haynau, who had been guilty of atrocious cruelty in suppressing a Hungarian revolt, paid a visit to London some years afterwards. He had never crossed the path of any Englishman, but he was recognized and roughly handled by a party of London working-men. Most of them were probably unable to read, but they knew the reputation of 'General Hyena' and forcibly showed their opinion of it. With such a spirit animating all classes it was natural that a leading item in the programme of reform should be the furtherance of liberty in other lands.

II. THIRTY YEARS OF REFORM

The New Tories of the 1790's had become the Old Tories by 1822, and a younger generation of the party was pressing to be heard. These men realized that anti-Jacobin reaction had done its work and had its day. They drew their inspiration, not from the stern Pitt who had stemmed the tide of revolution, but from the happier Pitt who had sought to bring English institutions up to date after the War of American Independence. In 1822 they began again the reforming task which Pitt had laid aside in 1793.

Sir Robert Peel was distinctly the heir of Pitt. He had the same orderly mind and abhorrence of waste. He was a devoted servant of the public interest, although he did not admit that public opinion was always the best judge of that interest. Above all, he was no bigot; he was ready to change his views when reasonable evidence showed that they had been mistaken. He succeeded Sidmouth as Home Secretary and began at once to tackle the problem of crime and disorder.

William Huskisson became President of the Board of Trade in 1823. He was a convinced disciple of Pitt, bent upon freeing commerce from its shackles by careful reforms. He was no enthusiastic doctrinaire but a hard-headed student of detail. Solid work was to be expected from him, not a blind rush into free trade at a stroke.

George Canning, the most adventurous of the new-comers, took Castlereagh's place as Foreign Secretary. His outstanding quality was generosity, not the generosity of a prodigal giver but that of the man who can appreciate the point of view of others. He was prepared to act upon ideals, but always in practical fashion; for he had an unerring talent for discerning when time was ripe. He could handle fire without burning his fingers, and he could stimulate the popular imagination as Peel, with his colder nature, could not. It was largely owing to Canning that a breath of sweet air swept over the European world in the musty age of the Holy Alliance. His office of Foreign Secretary did not confine him to that single department of British affairs. He was in reality the head of the government, as Castlereagh had been, and the nominal premier, Lord Liverpool, filled a subordinate position. To all intents and purposes a new ministry took office in 1822–3.

Peel, although in most respects a rigid Tory, did not disdain the teachings of Jeremy Bentham and his philosophic Radicals in the matter of public order. He accepted the principle that if crime was rampant the law and its administration were to blame. His first years as Home Secretary were devoted to modifying the savage code of the eighteenth century. He reduced the number of offences punishable by death, and thus made juries more willing to convict offenders. By the same means he removed the positive incentive to murder which had

lurked in the older law; for when a man had been liable to be
hanged for robbery, he had often been tempted to murder his
victim in order to make good his escape. In such circumstances
there had been no punishment for the blacker crime, for the
felon could not be executed twice. Our present restriction of
the death penalty to murder (and, in time of war, to treason)
has made life much more secure. It was not until 1829, in his
second term of office, that Peel completed his work for order by
establishing the Metropolitan Police, an efficient force to supersede the watchmen and the Bow Street runners. The 'Peelers'
were an immediate success, chiefly because they made no pretence of being soldiers. Their top-hats and staves emphasized
their civilian character, and their discipline, unaided by steel
or gunpowder, was sufficient to break up riots which in other
countries still call for volleys and cavalry charges. The new
London force was gradually imitated by local authorities
throughout the country, and the problem of crime, which had
defied all governments since the Middle Ages, began to be
mastered.

No less important was the new government's attempt to
revive prosperity. The post-war depression had been long continued, and 1822 was a specially gloomy year for trade and
employment. Here Huskisson took the lead, in the earlier
tradition of Pitt. Huskisson's work was twofold. By his Reci-
procity of Duties Act (1823) he obtained power to bargain with
foreign countries for the removal of trade restrictions. The
Navigation Acts had provoked retaliation abroad by prohibit-
ing the import of many kinds of goods in foreign ships. Absurdity was reached when British vessels were forced to sail empty
to the United States to bring back cotton, whilst Americans had
to come empty to our ports to take our manufactures. This was
only one instance of many, and the result was general stagna-
tion. Huskisson's Act led to a general breaking of barriers. He
also threw open the colonies to foreign vessels sailing from their
own ports, but he still kept the trade between the mother-
country and the colonies (misleadingly called the coasting
trade) as a British monopoly. The other side of his policy was
the reduction or abolition of customs duties. He did not by any
means introduce free trade, but he moved towards it by cutting
down the vast array of imposts levied in the long war. In so
doing he was following the example of Walpole in 1721 and of

Pitt in 1785. Each in his generation had to clean up an unscientific mess of war-time finance.

In two years Huskisson substituted hope for despair in British trade, although he had prepared the success by twenty years' hard study of his problem. He left the colonial Empire on a new footing. Before his time the ideal had been that of a closed Empire, the mother-country and colonies trading exclusively with one another. Huskisson substituted the principle of imperial preference: the Empire admitted foreigners, but it gave favoured treatment to its own members. An instance was his modification of the Corn Law whereby Canadian grain was admitted at a much lower market price than the eighty shillings that marked the admission-point of foreign produce. In home enterprise there was an immediate improvement. A wave of prosperity swept the country in 1824, the first really happy year of the century. So bright was the prospect that speculators overdid it, gambled in unsound companies, and provoked a financial panic. Seventy banks broke, and thousands lost their money. But the disaster was superficial, as had been that of the South Sea Bubble a hundred years before, and the solid improvement of trade was not lost. The whole country was at length on the upward grade. The gain, however, was on a moderate scale. Times were not yet very good, although no longer at their worst. Twenty years were yet to elapse before the shadows should wholly pass away.

The new temper of toleration and goodwill infused by Canning bore fruit in the repeal of the Combination Acts in 1824. The cabinet was ready to listen to advice, even from Radicals. Francis Place seized the opportunity. He organized sober deputations of workmen to put the case before Parliament, mobilized the favourable members, and avoided exciting the alarm of the majority. Quietly, almost by stealth, a great reform was accomplished, and that by a man who kept a shop and could never in his own person aspire to a seat in the aristocratic House of Commons. In their new-found liberty the trade unions committed some indiscretions, and a cry soon arose for bringing back the restrictions. In 1825 a new Act limited certain powers of the unions, but in the main the reform was confirmed. It was nearly fifty years before the law was again seriously altered, and during that time the position of the working man improved out of all knowledge.

In foreign affairs Canning skilfully combined a regard for British interests with a championship of the oppressed. The Greeks revolted against Turkish misrule in 1821. English Radicalism and Russian despotism—a strange combination which in changing forms has persisted to our own day—alike favoured the Greek cause, the one moved by sentiment for freedom, the other by desire for power. Canning prevented the Czar from becoming the sole champion of the rebels and thus gaining a footing in the Mediterranean, and in the end the combined fleets of England, France, and Russia secured Greek independence at the Battle of Navarino (1827). This took place a few weeks after Canning's death, but it was the fruit of his work. Liberty had been served and British interests preserved.

The Treaty of Vienna had everywhere reinstated absolute monarchy. The people of Spain and its colonies revolted against their own tyrant Ferdinand VII as they had against Napoleon. Canning could not prevent the French Bourbon government from invading Spain and putting down the liberals, but he did intervene against a further plan for the French to reconquer the revolted Spanish colonies. He recognized the independence of the republics which now fill the map of Latin America, and he combined with President Monroe of the United States to declare that no expeditionary force from Europe would be permitted to cross the ocean. The Monroe Doctrine was enunciated at Washington, but it was the British navy that made it effective. Liberty and British interests had again gone hand-in-hand, for the success of the revolt meant the opening of the American ports to British trade. In the glow of achievement Canning declared that he had called a New World into existence to redress the balance of the Old, a world of freedom against a world of despotism. It was a short view, although in a sense a long one also, for many weary decades were to pass before the independence of South America should produce even a semblance of freedom for its downtrodden inhabitants. The immediate result was that local tyrants usurped the place of distant ones. Nevertheless the British impulse had been generous, and thousands of volunteers went out from England to spend their blood with Simon Bolivar the Liberator. Latin peoples have long memories for good and evil, and to this day the British are better liked in South America than in most regions of the world.

For five years the Tory reformers went from strength to
strength, but only because they were doing things that both
Whigs and Radicals desired. The reactionaries looked on in
sullen doubt, awaiting their opportunity. The true opposition,
it was said, sat on the government benches, and only the tact
of Lord Liverpool prevented a rupture. Early in 1827 he had
a paralytic stroke, and the ministry broke up. Canning became
prime minister with the open support of a section of the
Whigs, whilst Wellington and Peel and four other Tories resigned their posts. Within five months Canning was dead, and
the new coalition weakened in the feeble hands of his successor,
Lord Goderich, who resigned in tears in 1828. The three burning questions were now the mitigation of the Corn Law, Catholic
Emancipation, and Parliamentary Reform, beside which all
that had yet been done seemed mere tinkering with trifles.
Peel's reforming work had hitherto been in the direction of
stronger, because more efficient, rule; he was opposed to any
reforms which he thought would weaken the state. Peel therefore took office under Wellington to make a stand for the older
Toryism, which meant no Catholic Emancipation and no
Parliamentary Reform. They soon quarrelled with Huskisson
and got rid of him, but not before he had passed a measure of
vital importance. His Sliding Scale of 1828 took the worst
sting out of the Corn Law by substituting an import duty for an
absolute prohibition, and the duty was to vary inversely with
the market price—dear corn, low duty; cheap corn, high duty.
By this means prices were lowered and also kept more steady
than when they had depended solely on the chances of the
English harvest. Under that system the worst suffering had
been caused by a sudden dearness of bread without a corresponding rise of wages.

Wellington and Peel, now the Old Guard of Toryism, were
destined to lead it to disaster. They and their followers were
opposed to Catholic Emancipation, which the Canningites and
Whigs supported. The Irish, led by Daniel O'Connell, had
long demanded this reform. They held that they had been
cheated of it when the Union was passed in 1800, and they were
growing determined to be cheated no longer. O'Connell took
a leaf from the Radical book and organized monster meetings
at which his oratory inflamed the Celtic mind. In 1828 he
stood for election to Parliament. There was nothing illegal in

returning a Catholic; the barrier lay in the oath he must take before admittance to his seat. County Clare elected O'Connell by a huge majority, and the greater part of Ireland was ready to take up arms unless the oath was waived. The Old Tories were strong against concession—all but their leaders, Wellington and Peel. Neither of them wished to admit O'Connell, but they saw they must, or face a civil war. Wellington knew enough of war to desire no more of it. Peel's touchstone was the public welfare, to which his own views must give way. With heavy hearts (and Whig votes) they passed the Catholic Emancipation Act in 1829, and were reviled as traitors by their own followers.

It was the deathblow to the Tory ascendancy which had lasted since the French Revolution. Wellington and Peel had lost the loyalty of the Old Tories and had encouraged the Whigs to new efforts. They knew they had done the right thing, but their virtue had to be its own reward. They had no other, for events moved rapidly to their downfall. Clamour and the threat of violence had secured one concession, and were naturally applied to another. The Radicals redoubled the agitation for Parliamentary Reform, the whole Whig party was at length united for it, and the Canningite Tories prepared to go over to the same side. Wellington withstood the demand, but two things hastened the end of his ministry. In France the Bourbon Charles X was refusing all concession to popular demands; and in July 1830 a sudden rising in Paris drove him from the throne. Three days' rioting had sufficed to break a reactionary government, and the lesson was not lost upon England. It gave cause to the waverers to argue that reform was inevitable. Just as the Revolution of 1789 had created the Tories, that of 1830 overthrew them. At the same moment George IV, a whole-hearted Tory, died, and his brother William IV, a Whig, mounted the throne. Parliament was dissolved, and the general election returned an even balance of reformers and reactionaries. Wellington, without a working majority, had no option but to resign.

For the last time the Whig aristocrats took command of the state which they, more than any, had moulded. Theirs had been an eventful history. They had overthrown the Stuarts and remodelled the constitution in the Bill of Rights. They had ruled, magnificent and unquestioned, until George III had reasserted the power of the monarchy. No sooner had the royal experiment failed than Fox had blighted their prospects by his erratic leadership and had chained their remnant to the paradox of being nobles supporting Jacobins. They had stood aside whilst Tories had defended England, and they had been unable to play their part in the reconstruction after the war. Now at length the wheel had turned full circle, and England demanded the reform which their opponents refused to grant. Upon them it fell once more to remodel the constitution and to transfer political power to those lower classes from whom, as individuals, they were far more aloof than the Tories. For these men of long descent—Greys, Russells, Lambtons, and Stanleys—had no need to look up even to Wellington, and regarded Peel, the manufacturer's son, as an upstart. They took office to destroy the conditions from which they sprang, and they knew it. The King's government must be carried on.

The winter of 1830-1 was a troublous time. Trade was again bad and food scarce. The Paris revolution of July had been followed by another at Brussels, where the Belgians rose against their Dutch rulers and asserted their independence as a separate state. The success of these movements encouraged the English Radicals, who began to prepare for an armed rising if they could not get their own way. The industrial towns formed political societies, and there was a brisk demand for booklets on barricade fighting and the rest of the revolutionary technique. In the hitherto peaceful southern counties 'Captain Swing' began a campaign of rick burning, and the labourers struck for a living wage. It was the last peasant revolt, savagely put down with sentences of transportation and even with hangings. Wellington declared that the existing constitution was the best the wit of man could devise. No one took the Whig reformers very seriously. Their Canningite allies were known to be lukewarm, and it was expected that the cabinet would produce a sham measure amounting to no reform at all.

Under the shadow of disaster Lord Grey and his ministers devised their Reform Bill. If some of them, like Palmerston and Melbourne, had no heart for the task, there were others who had. Lord John Russell was an enthusiast, and so was the Earl of Durham ('Radical Jack'). These men were brave enough to face the facts. They knew that the old rustic England of their forbears was dead, and they saw that the new industrial England must be fitted with new institutions under which it could thrive.

On the first of March 1831 Russell read the Bill in the House of Commons. Its secret had been well kept, and was revealed with shattering effect. For the Bill was no sham, but the death sentence on the old political system—fifty-six rotten boroughs each with two members to be abolished altogether, thirty more to lose one member each, one hundred and forty-three seats to be transferred to the counties and the new towns, all payers of £10 rent to have the vote in the boroughs, all freeholders, all substantial leaseholders, and £50 tenants in the counties. The Tories and many of the Whigs listened in dismay, tempered only by flat disbelief that the thing could ever pass. But Grey was determined that it should pass. There should be no Jacobin Terror or battles in the streets if he could prevent it. A revolution there must be, but a revolution peacefully achieved by the natural leaders of the nation. Who can say that he was not a wise and courageous man? The easy course for men of the aristocrat tradition would have been to resist the *canaille* sword in hand and to die in the last ditch—and to ruin England in the process. The hard course was that of self-sacrifice for the public good. In only one other country of modern times have the ruling few taken that course with heroic grace—in romantic, feudalized Japan—and they also have had their reward.

The Bill passed its second reading by a majority of one, little better than a defeat, and Grey dissolved Parliament. The general election showed how the reform had captured the national mind. 'The Bill, the whole Bill, and nothing but the Bill' was the cry, and a substantial majority for it returned to Westminster. Public opinion had broken through the shackles of the rotten borough system, as it always could in a first-class crisis; and the fact that the last unreformed Parliament did represent the wish of the nation was actually an argument against the necessity for reform. However that might be, the public will was aroused, and the ministry pursued their course. The second Reform Bill passed the Commons, only to be thrown out by the Lords in October 1831. The only constitutional means of overcoming the Lords' veto was the creation of new reforming peers. That was in the King's prerogative, and William IV was disinclined to promise Grey the necessary number. The Third Reform Bill passed the Commons in 1832, and before the Lords had decided its fate Grey resigned. This threw upon Wellington and the Tories the onus of carrying on the government themselves. They tried to form a ministry, but had no chance of success unless they should undertake to pass the very measure they were resisting, for without that they could get no majority in the Commons. The whole country was against them, and Francis Place interpreted the opinion of London by a dramatic though unnecessary stroke. He posted placards which read: 'To stop the Duke go for gold', or in other words begin a run upon the banks and cause a financial crisis. The Duke confessed that he could not form a government, and Grey came back, on the King's promise to create peers. For the Tories the game was up. The Lords had no wish to see their House invaded by new-comers, and Wellington's men absented themselves whilst the Bill went through. Like Grey, they had seen the path of duty, although they took it tardily and with an ill grace.

So was passed the great Reform Act. The Tories abhorred it, many Whigs disliked it, the Radicals alone hailed it with delight. Yet it was no victory for democracy, and it did not give political power to the working masses. The £10 house-holders of the boroughs included few workmen; the qualification represented a class of property that would now be worth fifty pounds a year. Still less did the county franchise concern the labourers; the farm-hand then lived in a hovel rented at a shilling or two per week. The fruits of victory rested with the middle classes, the substantial farmers, tradesmen, and pro-fessional workers, and it was they who returned the Parliaments of the next forty years. Why then did the Radicals exult? Partly because they had a footing in the middle-class, who were jealous of aristocratic privilege (as in revolutionary France), and still more because they regarded the Act of 1832 as only a first instalment. The constitution, once reformed, could more easily be reformed again, and the path to democracy was opened. As the event showed, this was sound reasoning.

A dissolution followed the Act, and the new electorate re-turned a solid Whig majority. For three years the Benthamites and humanitarians laid lustily about them, hacking down abuses old and new—'reform in a flood'. In 1833 the ending of slavery under the British flag cheered the last hours of Wilber-force, who had devoted half a century of effort to the cause. 'Thank God,' he said, 'I have lived to witness the day in which England is willing to give twenty million pounds for the aboli-tion of slavery.' The compensation was indeed a large sum for an impoverished nation to pay, but it was less than half the value of the slaves, and the West Indian planters were ruined. The same year witnessed a humanitarian victory nearer home, the passing of Lord Ashley's Factory Act to better the lot of the child-workers. Children under nine were not to be employed, those under twelve were to work not more than eight hours a day, and young persons under eighteen not more than ten hours a day. David Livingstone was a factory boy of this period. He went to work in a cotton mill at the age of ten and educated himself by propping his tattered books on the machine he had to mind. Even under the old conditions the best could rise, and were the better for their difficulties. In 1833, however, the state recognized in a small way its responsibility for education and made a money grant to the poor schools founded by private enterprise. But there was as yet no general system, and no compulsion on parents to send their children to school. *Laissez-faire* was still the rule, and state action the exception.

A new Poor Law followed in 1834. It abolished the Speenhamland system of outdoor relief in supplement to wages, and compelled the destitute to enter workhouses. The ultimate effect was good, for the labourers regained their self-respect and made great efforts to avoid the stigma of the workhouse. But at first there were hard times, for wages did not rise at once to make up for the lost doles. The poorer workers were hungrier than ever and considered themselves betrayed by the more prosperous reformers. Hence arose two agitations, that of the Chartists for a new reform of Parliament, and that of the Anti-Corn Law League for free trade in corn. Both these movements were launched in 1838. Neither was countenanced by the Whigs, who by that time had lost their reforming zeal. Their last great measure was the Municipal Reform Act of 1835. It swept away the old corrupt corporations and placed the boroughs under councils elected by the ratepayers. Dark nests of jobbery and incompetence were thus exposed to public control, and it became possible to purify, if not to beautify, the town life which was rapidly embracing half the population.

The decline of the Whigs was mainly due to Lord Melbourne, who took the place of the aged Grey in 1834. His watchword, 'Why not let it alone?' was the negation of Benthamism and not at all to the taste of a generation greedy for change. The state of the country was better than it had been a dozen years before, and hopes were rising in quarters previously given over to despair. That fact increased the zest for reform, and a multitude of earnest minds were clamouring that the task was not half done. The Chartists saw the benefits derived by the middle class from political power, and concluded that the same medicine would be beneficial to the poorest. They demanded votes for every man, annually-elected Parliaments, and payment of members. Those things attained, they promised a working man's paradise. The programme was in advance of the time and staggered even the average Radical. Chartism was in fact a revolutionary creed, suited rather to the Continent than to England, and its supporters were more noisy than numerous. It really aided the return of the Tories by impressing the middle-class voter with the need for strong government. The agitation against the Corn Laws ultimately made a wider appeal, although not at the outset. At first it seemed to miss fire, and the general election of 1841 gave Sir Robert Peel a majority pledged to maintain the Corn Laws in the interest of English agriculture. The deciding factor had been the laziness of Melbourne contrasted with the vigour of Peel.

Peel had already renamed his party the Conservatives and had declared that whilst maintaining established rights they would be ready to correct proved abuses. He himself, he claimed, was 'no enemy of judicious reforms'. The reform he set before himself was to lower the cost of living by relieving taxation on all imported articles except corn. By this time the free-trade views of the Manchester School had converted most British manufacturers, and Peel, who sprang from their ranks, was sensitive to their opinions. In his budget of 1842 he reduced duties on imported goods to a maximum of 20 per cent. of their value, a lower scale than Huskisson had imposed. He made up the lost revenue by reviving the income tax which had been dropped after the Napoleonic wars. The effect of the lowered duties was an increase of trade, still further assisted by the railway development then in full career. In the budget of 1845 Peel took another step towards free trade by abolishing the duties on over four hundred articles. Harvests had been good for some years, and the corn taxes, more than once revised since Huskisson's time, were now of moderate amount. Altogether it seemed that a period of prosperity had dawned. In fact it had, but it was destined to be interrupted by an appalling disaster.

In 1845 the Irish potato crop failed completely. The Irish peasantry had been transformed since the eighteenth century from a nation of cattle-breeders into one of smallholders cultivating little potato plots. In the process their numbers had grown to more than eight millions, a desperately unsafe figure when compared with the resources of the land. Even in good times these people lived within sight of starvation, and a single bad year meant certain famine. The famine came with a vengeance in 1845, when a blight killed the potato plants. Thousands died of actual want, and thousands more from the epidemics which followed in its train. England could afford relief in money but not in food, for the same summer was abnormally wet and the English harvest was a failure. Men said afterwards that 'it rained away the Corn Laws'. On all hands there was a cry for free import of grain from overseas.

During all these years the Anti-Corn Law League had never ceased its efforts. The Manchester School were its inspirers, and particularly Richard Cobden and John Bright. These two men were idealists who worked unselfishly for their cause. They had convinced themselves that without free trade in corn the people could never be happy; and Cobden at least impoverished himself by neglecting his business to attend to his crusade. Attached to them were a host of pamphleteers and public speakers, who addressed all kinds of audiences with every grade of argument. Cobden reasoned so powerfully in the House of Commons that in the end he converted Peel himself. Bright could sway vast public meetings with a charm of oratory unequalled in his century. At the other end of the scale Ebenezer Elliott appealed to the simple with such balderdash as:

> Child, is thy father dead?
> Father is gone.
> Why did they tax his bread?
> God's will be done.[1]

[1] Elliott was a genuine poet, besides being a political rhymer. The following is from his *People's Anthem* :

> When wilt Thou save the people?
> O God of mercy, when?
> Not kings alone, but nations!
> Not thrones and crowns, but men!
> Flowers of Thy heart, O God, are they;
> Let them not pass, like weeds, away—
> God save the people!

The leaders of the Manchester School were men of the highest motive. But many of their followers were hard-headed business men for whom cheaper living spelt lower wages to their hands. They argued that in effect they were being taxed to support the landowners, and they advocated repeal without being moved by any special love for the poor. The Chartists were quick to see through them and denounced corn-taxers and free-traders impartially. The decision lay ultimately with the voters, the middle-classes of town and country whose interests were divided on the question. Sentiment, it seemed, could sway the balance, and to sentiment all the efforts of the League were directed. The horrible tragedy in Ireland clinched the business, and the whole country pronounced for free trade, oblivious of the fact that the tragedy would have happened in any event. For it was not the Corn Laws but their unsound social economy that slew the Irish.

Peel had long been convinced by Cobden's logic that the Corn Laws ought to go. The fact that his supporters were the landed interest had held his hand, but he decided that the time had come. At the close of 1845 he made it known that he would no longer defend protection, but he wished the Whigs to take office and strike the blow. Lord John Russell, hitherto a moderate corn-taxer, was also converted, but he failed to form a ministry; and Peel, with heavy heart, introduced the Bill. A few of the Conservatives, Gladstone among them, followed his lead; but the majority, headed by Benjamin Disraeli, denounced him as a traitor—and indeed an habitual traitor—for they remembered Catholic Emancipation. In the spring of 1846 the Corn Laws were repealed with the aid of Whig and Irish votes, and the prime minister was soon afterwards driven from office by Disraeli's Conservatives. He remained isolated and reviled until his death in 1850.

Peel deserved a better fate, for he had served his country well. His policy had set England on the way to the marvellous prosperity of the mid-Victorian age. 'The Hungry Forties' have become a legend; but the words are only a half-truth. The 'forties were hungry only by comparison with what came after; they were far more prosperous than the 'thirties or the 'twenties. And for that the credit is Peel's. The ending of the Corn Laws did not in fact cause any great decrease in the price of bread, since the Corn Laws of 1846 were moderate as compared with the measure of 1815. By the time they were repealed they were hardly worth fighting for, and English farmers continued to thrive until the advent of cheap corn in bulk from the American prairies a generation later. The true cause of the plenty that followed the repeal was that trade and employment had improved and the country had more money with which to buy its bread. The whole question of the Corn Laws has been obscured in a haze of sentimental assertions, and it is hard to find a general text-book of English history that gives the actual costs of corn in the years before and after 1846. They were as follows: for the five years 1841–5, the average price of wheat was 55 shillings a quarter; for the five years 1846–50, 52 shillings; and for the five years 1851–5, 56 shillings. Such was the basis of Ebenezer Elliott's tragic song.[1]

Peel was succeeded by Lord John Russell and the Whigs, who held office from 1846 to 1852. The Cobdenites had great influence in this administration, and the free-trade programme was virtually completed. Some import duties were of course retained, but they were for the purposes of revenue, not protection, and they were chiefly levied on articles not producible in this country. It was an age in which ideals tended to outweigh the sober examination of facts. Cobden and his friends were ardent lovers of peace and were convinced that they could secure the goodwill of foreign governments by making what our modern political jargon calls 'gestures'. Let England adopt absolute freedom of trade, they argued, and the world will follow suit. Colonial disputes, they said, have been in the past a cause of war; let us therefore attach no importance to the Empire, and connive at, even encourage, the separation of the colonies as independent republics. So the system of Empire preferences established by Huskisson was swept away in the free-trade flood. Statesmen were unmoved by the Canadian disappointment that led to talk of union with the United States, and were deaf to the despair and bitter words of the West Indian planters, whose sugar was exposed to the competition of slave-owning rivals in Cuba and Brazil and the French islands.

Laissez-faire reached its climax with the repeal of the Navigation Acts in 1849. British shipowners cried ruin, and indeed the Americans were pressing them hard. In fact British shipping

[1] Fuller statistics are in L. C. A. Knowles, *Industrial and Commercial Revolutions*, London, 1924, pp. 366–71.

was about to enter upon its most splendid period, and it is certainly true that free competition was a spur to enterprise. But the recovery was powerfully aided by two unforeseen factors, the change from wood to iron and steel construction, in which British shipbuilders had the advantage, and the destruction of much American tonnage in the Civil War of the 'sixties. In one respect the idealists of 1849 forgot the wise words of Adam Smith, that 'defence is of much more importance than opulence'. They repealed the provision that British ships must be manned by British seamen. Thenceforward it became common for the forecastles to be filled with foreigners, and even on occasion for an entire crew, from captain to cabin-boy, to be of alien blood. In spite of pacifist hopes a day was to come when nothing stood between England and surrender to a foreign conqueror but the valour of British sailors; and there were perilously few of them for their task.

One other series of reforms remains to be accounted for. Ashley's Factory Act of 1833 had bettered the condition of child workers in a limited number of trades, but it had left many abuses untouched. In 1842 the country was shocked by revelations of what was going on in the coal-mines. Accidents were common owing to the neglect of safety devices. Small children worked long hours in the dark, tending the ventilation shafts. Women toiled as beasts of burden, crawling on hands and knees harnessed to trucks, or climbing ladders with loads of coal on their backs. The Coal Mines Act was therefore passed, to prohibit the employment of women and children underground, and to enforce measures of safety for the men. Ashley (afterwards Earl of Shaftesbury) continued his work for the mill hands. The Factory Acts of 1844 and 1847 still further limited the employment of children and established ten hours as the normal day's work for men. By modern notions these were no very generous reforms, but they were bitterly contested by John Bright and the manufacturers, and were the utmost that could then be secured. The hostility between the Tory landowners and the Manchester captains of industry produced benefits for the dependants of both, for in one sense the Factory Acts were the squires' retaliation for the attack on the Corn Laws.

By the mid-nineteenth century the great rift that had divided the people since the middle years of George III showed signs of closing, although the work of reconciliation was by no means perfect. It was in the 'forties that Disraeli penned the famous definition of 'the two nations' which we have quoted on an earlier page. Karl Marx, a German resident in England, was in the same period working out his antithesis between 'the capitalist' and 'the proletariat', and predicting revolution as the outcome. Thomas Carlyle was diverted from his historical studies by the conviction that 'the condition of England' was the dominant question of the day. In *Past and Present* he contrasted the position of the masses under Queen Victoria with that in the Middle Ages, much to the advantage of the latter. Charles Kingsley, the sturdy patriot who extolled the Elizabethans in *Westward Ho!*, was moved by what he saw around him to write bitter Chartism in *Alton Locke*. When men of such different views and training could agree we cannot doubt that they spoke the truth. Yet they were writing in the 'forties of what they had seen from their youth up. What they were to see in the next twenty years was something different. Already the dawn was piercing the darkness.

III. THE MIDDLE-CLASS PARADISE

From 1846, when the Corn Laws battle was fought to its finish, there were twenty years of political tranquillity. It was a period chiefly of Whig ascendancy, for the Conservatives had been split by Disraeli's attack on Peel; and some of their best men, including Gladstone, had drifted off into separation as the 'Peelites', ultimately destined to join the Whigs. But the Whigs were no longer the party of 1830. They were becoming increasingly Liberal, and Liberalism was not the same thing as Whiggism. The distinction is hard to define but easy to illustrate. Lord Palmerston was the shining light of the Whigs in the 'fifties and 'sixties; Gladstone, who had never been a Whig, was to become the greatest of the Liberals. The difference between Gladstone and Palmerston is the difference between Liberalism and Whiggism. The Liberal element entered the party by way of Manchester. Cobden and Bright and their followers, although not regarded as eligible for cabinet rank, had an immense influence in these years. Gladstone and the Peelites, exiled from their own Conservative party for the Manchester cause, not only influenced but transformed the Whigs.

The governing fact of all this mid-century time was that trade was expanding. The long lean years were over, and the sun of

ENGLISH RAILWAYS IN 1850

By far the greater part of
the system was the work
of the decade 1840-50

Some branch lines are omitted

Miles

0   25   50   75   100

prosperity was up. Peel's free-trade policy, completed by his successors, came just in time to join with other favourable factors. The 'forties had seen the main railway lines laid down; the 'fifties saw them in full operation. England in relative proportion to the rest of the world became a great goods-yard where products in bulk were switched and shunted with unexampled speed to the spots where they could be most effectively handled. No other country at that date had so advanced a railway system. Sea-transport improved likewise. The wooden sailing-ship of 1850 was twice as large, as safe, and as swift as her forerunner of 1750; and ships were no longer exclusively of wood or driven solely by the winds. Iron and steel construction from the 'fifties onwards yielded vessels that would carry more goods with smaller crews. The iron ship leaked not a thimbleful whereas the hold of the wooden ship was never perfectly dry. The way was thus clear for the transport of cargoes like grain and guano in bulk instead of in bags—a saving in the cost of handling. Steam vessels had been used for short distances since the 'twenties. In the 'forties they regularly crossed the Atlantic. But all these were paddle-driven, and the paddles were delicate and cumbersome, unsuited for the rough-and-tumble of workaday trade. The vibration of the screw-propeller made wooden hulls leak, but the iron of the 'fifties enabled the screw steamer to come into its own. The following decade saw the introduction of the compound engine, with a great saving of fuel, and after that the surface-condenser, which obviated the necessity of carrying fresh water for the boilers. The country which took the lead in these inventions, and had cheap steel and skilled engineers, obtained an immense advantage in trade.

Peel's financial policy, carried forward by Gladstone, confirmed the position of London as the centre of the world's money movements at a time when powerful new factors began to operate. Hitherto the gold supplies had come in a scanty trickle from the sources known for centuries—a few rather poor mines in tropical America and West Africa. In 1849 there was an important find of gold in California, a region just conquered from Mexico by the United States. Two years later this was excelled by the opening of extremely rich goldfields in Australia, which poured out a stream of new currency to lubricate the expanding wheels of commerce. Industrial developments took a new lease of energy comparable with that of seventy years before. The reforms of the generation 1820–50 enabled this industrial revival to confer benefits upon the whole English people, to unite it instead of dividing it as in the earlier period.

Revolutionary discontent died rapidly down. In 1848 there were upheavals all over the continent, and the Chartists essayed to repeat them in England. The result was a fiasco. A monster meeting was announced on Kennington Common, to march on Westminster and overawe the government. Less than a fifth of the expected numbers attended, and these submitted tamely to police regulation which rendered them harmless. The great petition for the Charter was conveyed to the House of Commons in a cab instead of at the head of a tramping host. When examined, many of its signatures were found fictitious. They included the names of such prominent Chartists as Queen Victoria and the Duke of Wellington. Chartism was laughed out of existence, and England devoted itself to making money instead.

Cabinet ministers were still mainly drawn from the ranks of the old aristocracy, although there were, as there had always been, exceptions like Disraeli and Gladstone. Members of the Commons were still for the most part gentlemen of county families, although the business men were trickling in with Cobden and Bright. But the middle-classes ruled, for they were the voters who made Parliaments and ministries. They were classes, not a class as were the gentry or the workmen. Farmers, tradesmen, manufacturers, members of the professions, formed a multitude of grades distinguished by taboos and elaborate etiquette in a way which our generation would denounce as snobbish. What made the middle-classes a political entity was their common possession of the franchise based upon 'a stake in the country', or, in other words, the principle that a voter must be a man of substance with a sense of responsibility. The vote was a privilege to be exercised with deliberation. The voter studied political form as if he were staking his living on the issue. He read the speeches of Bright or Disraeli or Lord John Russell, which the newspapers reported in full as the most important items they had to purvey. The active citizen took an absorbing interest in every proceeding of the Parliament he helped to elect. 'The silly season' was the period in which Parliament was not sitting. The British Constitution, as a harmony of rulers and their constituents, was enjoying its period of highest prestige.

The Manchester School was an influence for international peace. Its members were happy in being able to square their ideals with their advantage. In the free-trade world honest profits and the brotherhood of man went hand in hand. The humanitarians also, never so powerful as in this period, had a hatred of violence. These were the great days of Exeter Hall, the chosen rallying-place for the advocates of missions to the heathen and of ragged schools in the slums, of total abstinence, and the reduction of armies and fleets. When Exeter Hall put forth its might it could mobilize a block of voters sufficient to make cabinets tremble.

Yet there was always a counter-current. It is never safe to label a whole nation as devotees of one opinion, however loudly that opinion may be voiced. The reading public laughed over the novels in which Dickens pilloried the types of humbug who clung to the precincts of Exeter Hall. There was a growing pride in the achievements of British soldiers and sailors against the hosts of Napoleon. As the decades passed the miseries of war grew fainter and its romance shone brighter. The Duke of Wellington, intensely unpopular in 1830, had become a demi-god by 1850. It was not he that had changed but the public taste; he was ever indifferent to jeers and cheers alike. It was an effect of the long peace and of the rise of a generation that had now known war and looked back to it as something exciting and pleasurable. There was moreover a cocksureness in the air of the early fifties, a feeling that the country was advancing as by some process of destiny and could not go wrong. So we find the Great Exhibition of 1851, deliberately staged as a festival of peace, followed by the Duke's funeral in 1852, an imposing military pageant adorned by Tennyson's *Ode*, which made much of the glories of the wars and little of their sufferings.

In 1853–4 it grew evident that the new generation was spoiling for a fight, and that the pacifism of the Manchester School had produced its reaction. In the midst of wire-pulling and cross-purposes the country gladly allowed itself to be muddled into the Crimean War. Our enemy was Russia under Nicholas I and our ally France under Napoleon III, who had revived the Bonaparte Empire by his *coup d'état* of 1851. All classes were keen for the adventure without understanding how it came about, and Bright was almost alone in denouncing it as a crime. But the war was fought in the old style by the regular army, with very little volunteering, and the non-military enthusiasts like Tennyson had to satisfy themselves with looking on. After the first months they had little joy of it. The siege of Sebastopol occupied the winter of 1854-5 and caused the death or disablement of most of the British troops who had sailed so cheerfully in the previous summer. The men died heroically, but the incompetence of the administration was terrible. Within a few miles of its sea base and a powerful fleet the army perished for lack of food and clothing. Jingoism changed to indignation, the greater because our French friends seemed to suffer less. War correspondents, then employed by the newspapers for the first time, revealed the truth to the public, and in the cry for scapegoats the Aberdeen ministry was overthrown. Lord Palmerston, who more than any man had caused the war, came into power to finish it. The neglect of the wounded had been especially shocking. Their care was taken in hand by Florence Nightingale. Backed by powerful friends at home, she went out to the Black Sea hospitals and reduced chaos to order—the first woman of her time to take the lead in the active affairs of men. Sebastopol fell in 1855, and the war ended in the following year. But British interests could have been substantially preserved without fighting at all.

The Crimean War, with its British death-roll of 25,000, was a small affair as compared with the efforts of later civilization. It did not cure the national propensity for jingoism, for the mass of the people had done their fighting by deputy and had not suffered in person. Other campaigns followed: the Indian Mutiny of 1857-8, for which the home statesmen were not responsible; and a war with China in 1857-60, which many thought indefensible. The political hero of all this period was Lord Palmerston, constantly in and out of office as the director of our foreign affairs. He was prime minister from 1855 to 1858, and again from 1859 to his death in 1865. He was active in asserting the rights of British subjects against oppression in foreign countries, and also in championing the cause of weak peoples bullied by strong ones. It has been said of him that 'whenever there was a despot to be insulted, he joyfully insulted him'. His sympathy with downtrodden Poland was a cause of his hostility to Russia, although at the close of the Crimean War he was able to do nothing for the Poles. More effective was his friendship for the Italians. In 1859 Napoleon III began the work of liberating

Italy from Austrian oppression, but stopped before it was half done. Thenceforward the Italians had to liberate themselves, which they did with wonderful courage and energy under the leadership of Garibaldi. Palmerston, backed by Gladstone and Lord John Russell, used British sea-power to keep the ring and give the patriots fair play. But for that they would have been crushed by outside interference.

Less fortunate were two other affairs which threatened to involve us in war. In 1864 Denmark was attacked by Prussia and Austria and deprived of certain disputed territories. English sympathy with the Danes was strong, and Palmerston gave them hopes of assistance, but ultimately withheld it. It was an inglorious but sensible decision, for the British army was too small to invade the continent against the great conscript forces of Prussia under the direction of Bismarck.

From 1861 to 1865 there raged the American Civil War. The sentiments of Palmerston, Gladstone, and the ruling class in England favoured the southern states, who claimed the liberty of withdrawing from the Union they had voluntarily entered. But the issue was complicated by the question of slavery. The southerners were slave-owners and the northerners abolitionists. John Bright sympathized actively with the North, and the British working class sided with him. Lancashire was hard hit by the stoppage of cotton supplies, but the mill hands cheerfully endured privation that slavery might be killed. There were disputes about the northern blockade of the southern coast and about the rights of neutral British ships on the high seas. Palmerston came near to war with the North, a misfortune that was averted by the wise counsels of the Prince Consort on the one side and of President Lincoln on the other. Ultimately the southern states were crushed and subdued without any British intervention on their behalf.

In our home politics the American Civil War had produced an effect. The voteless working man had asserted his opinions in a manner that really affected the issue. He had taken his stand, not on his own advantage, but on what he held to be a moral right. The argument for a further reform of Parliament was thus immensely strengthened. Already in 1859 a Reform Bill had been introduced but defeated. The question became more pressing as the 'sixties advanced. But Palmerston was opposed to change, and it was not until after his death that reform became a first-class topic. Gladstone was by this time the most important man in the party which had once been Whig but was now becoming Liberal. He was a convinced democrat whose watchword was 'Trust the people'; and he thought the time had come for a widening of the franchise. Meanwhile the country was showing interest in the question, but in a different manner from that of 1832. The reformers of the 'sixties were not desperately attacking a corrupt system and threatening revolution if they did not get their way. They were rather seeking to broaden the basis of an acknowledged good thing, the constitution as it stood. They contended that the progress of the country had rendered many more men fit to exercise the rights of citizenship, and that the extension of the franchise was but the continuation of a process already begun. There was thus very little heat and fury about the second reform contest. Bright and others addressed mass meetings and displayed their powers of oratory, and a London crowd broke down the railings of Hyde Park because they had been forbidden to assemble there. But the whole thing was good-humoured, and no one talked of barricades and battles.

In 1866 Gladstone and Lord John Russell introduced a Reform Bill, and resigned when it was defeated in the Commons. Disraeli and Lord Derby then took office. Most Conservatives were opposed to reform, but Disraeli led them towards it. It was now twenty years since he had driven Peel from the headship of the party, but he had gained little by his rebellion. In all that time the Conservatives had never been in office for more than a few months together. It seemed as though the middle-class franchise meant a permanent Whig ascendancy. Disraeli had always been imbued with the idea that working-class voters would be more Conservative, especially as he was prepared to study their interests. By this means the decaying fortunes of Conservatism would be revived. The party of authority would ally itself with the poor against the middle-classes and their *laissez-faire* liberty. At the same time middle-class support might be attracted by the appeal to patriotism such as Palmerston had always made—by a vigorous foreign policy, and by a care for the colonial empire which showed signs of coming into fashion again after long neglect.

Disraeli converted his party and passed the Second Reform Act in 1867. Although there was a redistribution of seats the extension of the franchise was the most important point. In the boroughs all male householders were given the vote, together with some lodgers. In the counties the middle-class qualification was extended to occupiers paying £12 a year. This still excluded the farm labourers, although the borough franchise became fairly democratic. It was a decision which fitted the facts. Education was still very backward in the villages, and most of their people were quite illiterate. The town workmen, on the other hand, although many of them had never been to school, were much more alive to political questions and had strong views about reforms that would be good for them. A clear picture of their character and conditions of life is given in Dickens's *Hard Times*, published in 1854, which describes the industrial midlands just as the age of prosperity was setting in. Thomas Gradgrind, the hard-headed manufacturer whose god was *laissez-faire*, who lived on cold facts and hated sentiment, but was at bottom a worthy man according to his lights; Josiah Bounderby, the bragging profiteer, a selfish bully risen from the ranks; Stephen Blackpool, the mill hand, uneducated but honest and industrious—these are living types of mid-Victorian England, the material that statesmanship had to work upon. Palmerston had ruled them by keeping them amused. Now he was gone there were two men with visions of mighty chess-play with these interesting pieces—Disraeli and Gladstone. They agreed that the pieces must be set free to move, and they agreed in nothing else. Hence the Second Reform Act.

Disraeli, it was said, had dished the Whigs and tempted his Conservatives to a leap in the dark. The immediate outcome was disastrous, for in the general election of 1868 the new voters gave Gladstone a thumping majority, and the first Liberal ministry entered upon a six-years' career.

In the sphere of religion the mid-nineteenth century produced some new phenomena. Ever since the Stuart days the English had reckoned themselves a Protestant people. The Revolution of 1688 and the rejection of the Pretender in 1714 had both been moved by the desire to secure a Protestant succession; and even the High Church of those times, whilst hating nonconformists, had shown no leanings to Catholicism. The religious revival begun by Wesley was ardently Protestant and ended by strengthening the nonconformists more than the Church. The humanitarians of the next generation were of the same faith.

Wilberforce and his group were known as the Clapham Sect—churchmen for the most part, not a distinct religious body, but much more akin to the Puritans of old than to any Church of England modelled on the doctrines of Laud. Exeter Hall carried on the same tradition, and the Protestant noncomformists were never so influential as in the period between the two Reform Acts.

When the tide flowed strongest there were signs of a reaction. Catholic Emancipation in 1829 was mainly of Irish importance. It made little practical difference to the Catholics of England, who were few in numbers and belonged chiefly to old families which had kept their faith since the Reformation changes. But in the succeeding years there was a considerable immigration of Irish labourers, who found employment in the construction of the railways and settled down in the industrial districts. From this source the proportion of Catholics in the population was greatly increased. At the same time there arose a new movement in the Church of England itself, a protest against the sleepy complacency of the bishops and the devotion of the clergy to worldly rather than spiritual interests. This Oxford Movement, as it was called, sought to emphasize the position of the clergy as a profession apart, and to assert their influence over the lay mind by an insistence upon the mysteries of ritual and ceremonial. Inevitably its exponents drifted away from Protestantism, for the Protestant Englishman was accustomed to respect his parson as a man and not as a priest. The Oxford reformers sought inspiration in history, and liked to think that the meaning of the Reformation had been misinterpreted, and that the English Church was no new beginning but of continuous descent from the primitive Church. The term 'Anglo-Catholic' expressed the conception, which made considerable headway as the nineteenth century advanced. The veiled schism that ensued was, however, much more an affair of the clergy than of the laity. The Englishman of the coming age tended to think more of works than of belief, and showed himself increasingly disinclined to take sides in matters of dogma. A practical effect of the Anglo-Catholic movement has been the strengthening of the Roman Catholic community by a steady trickle of conversions. Cardinal Newman and Cardinal Manning were both clergymen of the Church of England before they became Catholic priests.

A religious development that has affected a much greater numerical proportion of the population may be dated from 1859. In that year Charles Darwin published his *Origin of Species*, a book that has exercised a more powerful influence than any other since Adam Smith's *Wealth of Nations*. The *Origin of Species* was written as a work of natural science, but it had large religious implications. Before its appearance the general belief had been that the world was created in six days some four thousand years before the birth of Christ. Darwin's facts showed that an infinitely longer time had been occupied in the evolution of animals and mankind from simple life-forms. The literal authority of the Bible, attacked in one aspect, was questioned in others, and a flood of criticism was loosed, of a kind which in earlier ages would have earned its authors a speedy martyrdom at the stake. The churches at first condemned the new science and afterwards modified their doctrines to square with it. The outcome of this revolution in thought is highly important but hardly yet capable of definition. It is, however, true that the majority of Englishmen to-day, whilst they may be essentially religious, are not active members of any organized religion. That is one of the matters in which we differ profoundly from our forefathers.

IV. THE NEW EMPIRE

With the loss of the American colonies in 1783 there occurred a shifting of the basis of ideas about the colonial Empire. Men ceased to think very much about colonies as homes for the surplus population of the mother-country, because the American experiment had ended in a disastrous quarrel. On the other hand, the importance of oceanic trade was greater than ever, and so we find that in the fifty years after the American revolt statesmen thought of 'the Empire' chiefly as a system of tropical plantations and trading factories on the great trade routes of an expanding world. At the same time British subjects, over-crowded by the rise of population, were emigrating to new homes overseas. The emigration was not large until after Waterloo, and much of it went to the United States. But important streams of people did find their way to Canada and Australia and South Africa, and so there arose in the nineteenth century a new Empire of genuine colonies. Public interest in it was not great until the various reform struggles in England had been settled. Then the Empire gained a firm hold upon the popular imagination, and statesmen found themselves obliged to take careful account of their imperial policy. It is not possible to give a precise date to a change of sentiment, but the year 1867, that of the passing of the Second Reform Act, will serve approximately to indicate the re-entry of the Empire into British politics.

In spite of the fact that settlement colonies went out of favour with the American disaster, two of the fundamental steps in the making of a new colonial Empire were taken by the home government immediately after 1783. In the United States there were a number of loyalists who had fought on the British side in the War of Independence. When peace was made they were badly treated by their victorious fellow-countrymen, and were almost forced to leave their old homes. They moved down as refugees to New York and the other seaports, and the British authorities provided shipping to carry them away. They sailed, some to Nova Scotia and New Brunswick, and some into Canada by the St. Lawrence. Many more of these people trekked over the Canadian frontier by the inland routes. Altogether some 40,000–60,000 of them quitted the United States. They formed the entire population of New Brunswick, hitherto an empty region, and they were also the pioneer settlers of Ontario or Upper Canada, up-river from Quebec or Lower Canada, whose people were the French settlers planted before Wolfe's conquest in the Seven Years' War. George III granted these new Canadians the title of United Empire Loyalists, and Pitt's government assisted them in their pioneer days and conferred representative institutions by the Canada Constitutional Act of 1791. The Loyalist movement laid the foundation of Canada as a British dominion, for without it the population would have been mainly French.

The strengthening of British North America had been forced upon statesmen by the fact that they owed a debt of gratitude to loyal subjects. The foundation of another dominion proceeded much more from their own motion. In 1772 Captain Cook had come home to report his discovery of the eastern coast of Australia, which he named New South Wales. This great shore-line extended through nearly thirty degrees of latitude, with climates ranging from temperate to tropical. There were many who believed that it would be suitable for plantations of spices and other tropical products, and that a new 'West Indies' might be established in the South. That was quite in accordance with the ideas of statesmen who were eager to expand the long-distance trades. In addition there arose the problem of the host of criminals sentenced by the hard laws of the eighteenth century. They could no longer be sent to America, and they were too numerous to keep in prison at home. The humanitarians, led by Sir Joseph Banks, suggested that they should be started in a new life as colonists of New South Wales. Pitt agreed, and the first expedition arrived to found the settlement of Sydney in 1788. It was an entirely novel experiment, an undertaking to create a colony by means of convicts and their warders, without the presence of any free private individuals. In that state the experiment proceeded for some twenty years with fair results. The convicts served their sentences and remained as partially free settlers, locally called emancipists. The officers and soldiers of the guardian regiment, the New South Wales Corps, likewise quitted the service from time to time, and became freer settlers, with larger holdings of land than those allotted to the emancipists. Life in such a society was very rough, there was savage discipline and brutal crime, famine and drunkenness and hardship illimitable. All the early governors were naval officers, and the naval officer of those days was an expert in corporal punishment. But a colony emerged, the germ of greater things.

Apart from these foundations, Pitt and his successors thought more of sugar islands, trading factories, and naval bases. They captured them in great profusion in the Revolutionary and Napoleonic wars, but at the final settlement they gave back as much as they retained. This was partly due to Castlereagh's wide outlook on foreign affairs. In 1814–15 his was the deciding voice in British policy. He wished above all things to make a peace that would endure. He thought a strong Dutch kingdom would be a bulwark against French ambitions, and so he not only placed the Belgians under the Dutch but restored to the latter the rich island of Java, the gem of the Far East, and part of Guiana in the West. He wished to treat France generously and efface the memories of defeat. He therefore restored Martinique and Guadeloupe, the best sugar islands of the Caribbean, together with Pondicherry and the old French factories in India. But a whole chain of useful posts were nevertheless retained: St. Lucia and Tobago and the Spanish island of Trinidad in the West Indies; British Guiana in South America;

Ceylon and Mauritius in the Indian Ocean; the Cape of Good Hope on the way thither; and certain footholds in the Asiatic archipelago on its farther rim. The greatest acquisitions of the Empire during this warlike period were not, however, at the expense of European powers. They were the conquests of the Marquess Wellesley in India, which extended British rule from the coasts to the interior of that sub-continent. At the opening of the wars the East India Company had ruled but a fraction of the whole area; at their close the British Empire of India was in being.

By 1815, therefore, the Empire had become an affair of tropical possessions, held in the interests of trade and sea-power. The temperate regions suitable for colonists were thought of small account and scarcely mentioned in the public speeches of statesmen. The nineteenth century was to witness a drastic reversal of these values.

The old idea of trade monopoly began to weaken almost at once, for progressive men no longer believed in it. Java had been given up for reasons of foreign policy. Its British governor, Sir Stamford Raffles, sought another base for his countrymen's traffic and found it at Singapore. There, in 1819, he bought the derelict island from the local sultan and established a free port to attract the commerce of the Malay archipelago. The scheme prospered, and Singapore became what it is to-day, the focus of all the complicated trade-routes of the Far East, a triumph of open trade over the monopoly which the Dutch retained in Java. In the same way Castlereagh abandoned the West Indian monopoly by his treaty with the United States in 1814. American vessels were thenceforward allowed to trade with the islands, and the way was prepared for Huskisson's general opening of the Empire in 1823. In 1813 again the East India Company's charter came up for review, with the result that the Indian trade was thrown open to private British merchants. All this did not mean that statesmen no longer cared to promote trade. They cared more than ever, but they thought that the new free methods were better than the old restrictions. The leaven of Adam Smith was beginning to work.

Meanwhile emigration recommenced on a scale unknown since the days of Charles I. After 1815 the British Isles were overcrowded and a prey to unemployment and distress. Inevitably men cleared out to settle overseas, although for long they did so without much help from the government. Year after year the emigrant ships crossed the Atlantic. There were no Board of Trade regulations, and the vessels were closely packed and ill supplied. A prolonged passage in face of the westerly gales often caused a terrible death-roll from hunger and disease. Some made for New York or Philadelphia, and others entered the St. Lawrence, where their passengers built up the Canadian population on the foundation laid by the Loyalists. The people who went to North America were generally very poor, since the passage was cheap. They came from the industrial towns, and still more from the countryside, where there were more hands than employment. After the Irish famine of 1845 a new flow of emigrants poured out, and the population of Ireland was reduced to less than half its former figure. It was a good thing for Ireland, but very hard on the emigrants, who set forth starving and destitute and often arrived only to die. Quebec and Montreal had vast graveyards where the poor exiles were buried, dead for the most part of the typhus fever which broke out in the crowded 'tween-decks.

The longer voyage to the southern hemisphere attracted a less destitute class, for the fare was beyond the means of the very poor. Cape Colony had been captured during the wars on account of its value as a cruiser-base, and the region round Cape Town had a population of Dutch Boers. In 1820 a band of British emigrants founded the Albany Settlement in the eastern district, whose people are predominantly British to this day. Other settlers went out to New South Wales and Tasmania, attracted by the profits of sheep-farming. The English yeoman's son would scrape together a few pounds, take with him a stock of tools and the timbers of a hut, and obtain a grant of land in Australia. Sometimes he tried to acclimatize the plants and birds of the English landscape; and some misguided experimenters introduced the rabbit, which speedily bred in myriads, ravaged the crops, and became the worst pest in the country. By 1840, what with free settlers and freed convicts and the children of both, the character of New South Wales had changed. The convicts had become a minority, and the free men demanded that transportation should cease. It continued in certain other parts of Australia until 1868. During those eighty years 137,000 prisoners were transported. Most of them were real criminals, but many were not. Some were too ardent Radicals whose

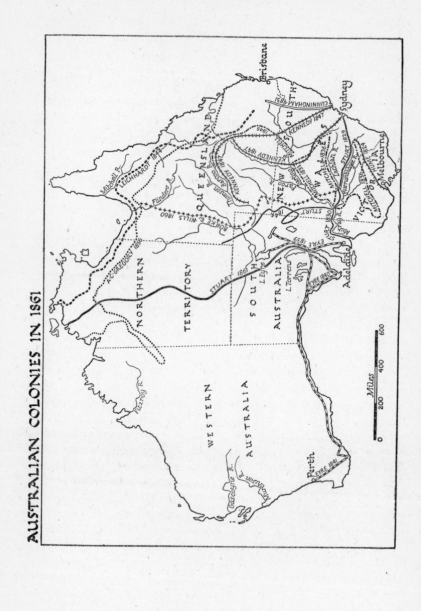

AUSTRALIAN COLONIES IN 1861

tongues had got them into trouble, some were poachers or
starving labourers who had ventured to riot for bread or break
machinery, some were mere children convicted of petty thefts.
There was no free passage home at the end of the sentence, and
most who survived it stayed in the colony. Charles Reade's
Foul Play gives a vivid story of transportation, and Rolf Boldre-
wood's *Robbery under Arms* is a great novel describing the life of
the bushrangers.

By the close of the 1820's influential men were taking up the
question of emigration on a large scale. One of them, Thomas
Peel, a cousin of Sir Robert, invested a fortune in the colonization of Western Australia. In 1829 he and his friends obtained
large grants of land on the Swan River, and took out some
thousands of labourers to develop the country. But the scheme
was badly thought out, and all the money was spent before the
emigrants could be set to profitable work. Peel was ruined, and
most of the men moved on to New South Wales. The few who
persevered did ultimately create a prosperous colony, but only
after long years of hardship.

Another projector, Gibbon Wakefield, evolved a plan of what
he called 'systematic colonization'. Colonial land, he said,
ought not to be granted free, but sold by government at a substantial price. Thus the leaders of the colony would be well-to-
do people, and the proceeds of the sales would provide a fund
for paying the passages of poorer emigrants. These, having no
land, would work for wages, and a complete English society
would be quickly established. Moreover, the landowners,
having to pay for every acre, would not take up more land than
they could use, and so the whole colony would be compact and
efficient. It was also part of Wakefield's doctrine that the
emigrants should be carefully chosen; no man should receive
a free passage unless his character was good.

The Wakefield plan was sound in principle. It was partially
applied in the new colony of South Australia, founded in 1836.
There, in spite of initial mismanagement and waste of money,
thousands of emigrants of a good type were successfully planted
in a few years. They were mostly English farmers who knew
their business, and South Australia never received any convicts.
A similar non-convict colony was Victoria, planted in New
South Wales territory in 1834, and separated under its present
name in 1851.

The energetic Wakefield was dissatisfied with the management of South Australia and severed his connexion with it. Then he entered upon his most ambitious scheme, the colonization of New Zealand. It was a beautiful country, revealed by Captain Cook, temperate and fertile, but inhabited by the warlike Maoris. The Whig government of the 'thirties viewed these new colonies with some distrust, arguing that they were a mere responsibility which would never yield the mother-country any profit. But the spirit of the age was too strong for cautious statesmen. The Wakefield party took their own line, formed the New Zealand Company in 1839, and sent out expeditions to take up land. Only then did the unwilling government consent to annex New Zealand—just in time, for the French had their eye upon it. The Company did its best work in selecting colonists and conveying them round the world with a minimum of suffering. It showed that the shocking hardships of the Canada voyage were unnecessary, for its own emigrants travelled seven times as far with very few casualties. On land the Company was less successful. It certainly looked after its settlers, but it did not treat the Maoris fairly, and there were long wars before the country became really secure. Gibbon Wakefield was a quarrelsome, unscrupulous man, but he had a spark of genius, and the Empire owes much to him.

So, in true British fashion, more by the enterprise of the people than of their rulers, the great dominions of to-day were founded. Few statesmen had any hope for their future. The Declaration of Independence seemed the final verdict on colonial empires. Whigs and Tories were alike doubters. Disraeli denounced the colonies as 'a millstone about our necks'. The Manchester School talked mere profit-and-loss. The colonies, they said, are costly to govern and defend, and are the cause of all wars. Let us cut them off, to sink or swim by themselves; if they prosper, we can trade with them as independent republics, just as we do with the United States. But in this matter Gradgrind and Bounderby mistook the spirit of their people, as did Melbourne and Disraeli. The true prophets were to be found among the Radicals. The Earl of Durham ('Radical Jack' of the Reform Bill) was won over by the teachings of Gibbon Wakefield. He knew the crowded miseries of industrial England, and he was fascinated by the fair empty lands waiting to be tilled across the sea. To take the landless labourer to the labourless land seemed to him a good work. He pictured the growing colonies peopled by the British stock, free but loyal, the equals and the brethren of those who stayed at home. He did not believe that the Declaration of Independence need repeat itself. Other Radicals worked with him, Charles Buller and Sir William Molesworth, whose names deserve to be remembered.

In 1838 Durham found the opportunity for his greatest work. Canada had been disturbed by two rebellions in the previous year—a French rising in Quebec, and a British in Ontario. The Melbourne ministry sent out Durham to investigate. He took with him Charles Buller and Gibbon Wakefield. He travelled through Canada, heard evidence of grievances, and drew up the Durham Report, a document that changed the course of the Empire's history. In this he expressed the faith of the Radical Imperialists: that British colonists were essentially loyal, but must be free. The means to freedom he described as responsible government. The colonies must no longer be ruled by officials sent out from England, but by cabinet ministers responsible to the colonial voters and removable by them. In other words, the British constitution, as it stood after 1832, must be applied to the colonies. The Durham Report was not immediately accepted; the Canada Act of 1840 embodied some of its less useful suggestions but omitted responsible government. The doubters argued that responsible government meant independence. So it did. But it was independence without separation from the Empire, which is the status enjoyed by the Dominions of to-day. Durham and his few friends were alone in foreseeing that the British race the world over would be all the stronger and more united for being completely free. It was not until after Durham's death that responsible government was applied to Canada—by his son-in-law, Lord Elgin. Thence it spread to New Zealand and the Australian colonies, to Newfoundland and South Africa. In our days enthusiasts talk of applying it to India. They may be right, but they may be wrong, for Asiatics are not Englishmen, and responsible government is a peculiarly British conception, needing cool heads, a sense of proportion, and generosity in allowing for the other man's point of view.

Through the tissue of the growing Empire ran the work of the humanitarians, and sometimes it was good, and sometimes bad. Wilberforce got slave-trading declared illegal in 1807, but a

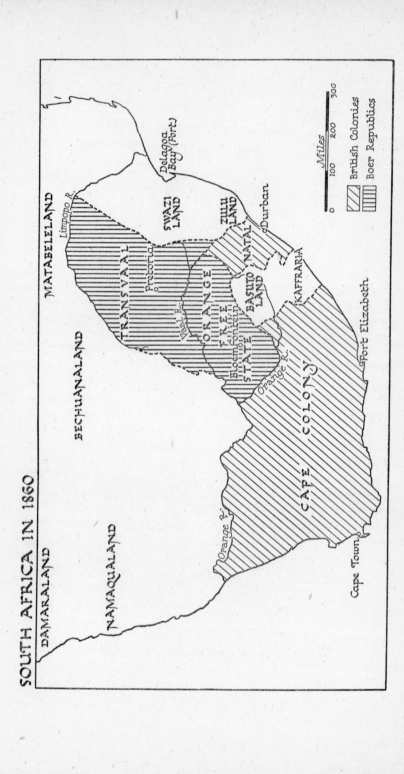

SOUTH AFRICA IN 1860

great deal of it nevertheless went on. The only cure, as the reformers saw, was to abolish slavery itself. For the British Empire this was done in 1833. It was a severe blow to West Indian prosperity, already attacked by competition in other parts of the world. The planters hoped at least that their sugar would be protected against that produced in slave-owning countries. But the Manchester School of the 'forties would have none of it, and the duties were equalized in the name of *laissez-faire*.

In South Africa the humanitarians pursued the same path of lofty ideals coupled with mean treatment of those who paid for the ideal. The Boer farmers lost their slaves in 1833 and were jobbed out of the partial compensation allowed by the law. The missionaries sang songs of exultation instead of exerting themselves to see the bargain carried out, and the Boers, with the long memories characteristic of unlettered men, never forgot it. The missionaries were certain that they could civilize the Kaffir tribes if only they had a free hand. They therefore demanded that white men must be forbidden to trek outside the existing Cape Colony. In 1834 the tribes invaded the eastern settlements and committed murder and rapine. Sir Benjamin D'Urban, the governor, called out the whites and drove back the blacks. He then annexed a strip of territory to form a buffer belt against future inroads. But the missionary interest was strong at home; Whitehall, in fact, was afraid of Exeter Hall. Lord Glenelg, Melbourne's Colonial Secretary, disallowed the annexation. D'Urban resigned in disgust, and the Boers of Cape Colony began the Great Trek which founded the Transvaal and the Orange Free State and divided South Africa between two jealous nationalities. Glenelg was a well-meaning man, but timid and sluggish. A wag declared that the South African affair cost him many sleepless days.

India was in some respects the most important part of the Empire before the new settlement colonies grew up. The Company desired to govern without interference, but Wilberforce secured a provision in its charter of 1813 compelling it to admit missionaries into the country. The next charter, in 1833, wound up the Company's trade and left it solely as a governing body. From this year dated the introduction of European education and the founding of Indian universities. Many have held that it was a mistake, and that the native literature of India should have been continued as the basis of culture. But the well-intentioned reformers of 1833 hardly knew that there was an Indian literature. To them nothing was knowledge that was not taught in England, and they made London University the model for their new foundations. The Company ruled for another twenty-five years and extended the frontier to its present line by annexing the Punjab in 1849. In 1857 the great Mutiny of the Bengal army broke out, and after its suppression the East India Company's powers were taken over by the Crown.

The missionary movement did its best work in New Zealand and the islands of the Pacific. The warlike and intelligent islanders were a race with many fine qualities, worthy to survive in the modern world. There is not much doubt, however, that they would have been wiped out if the missionaries had not intervened. At first the policy was that attempted in South Africa, to civilize the native tribes and train them in self-government whilst keeping white intruders at a distance. This could not succeed, for the Pacific was full of adventurers ready to take advantage of native simplicity. The New Zealand Company bought large blocks of land for trifling payments, and the Maori chiefs often did not own the property they were tempted to sell, or understand the documents to which they set their hands. In the other islands private speculators were playing the same game, getting valuable concessions for nothing, selling drink and muskets to the blacks, or carrying them off as 'indentured labourers', in reality slaves. The result was war and outrage, and it sometimes happened that the natives murdered a missionary in revenge for the villainies of a trader. The missionaries coped manfully with their task. They preached peace to the native, and they urged the government to protect him. Ultimately law and order took the place of crime and extermination, and the humanitarians had a solid achievement to their credit.

Perhaps the most fascinating aspect of the new Empire's story is the growth of trade and transport. The Cape passage to India had taken eight or nine months in Clive's time. The swifter vessels of the nineteenth century often did it in three. For mails and passengers a new overland route was opened—through the Mediterranean by steamer to Egypt, thence by land across the Isthmus of Suez, thence by another steamer to Bombay. The next improvement was to cut the Suez Canal, a work completed by the French in 1869. It shortened the passage to three weeks. From China the famous tea clippers, the fastest ships that ever sailed, raced each other to be first in London with the season's crop. After the 'fifties the emigrants to America went chiefly by steamer, but those to Australia still made the long voyage by sail. Hundreds of fine vessels made the passage round Cape Horn to the west coast of America. Some carried emigrants to California, where the gold-strike of 1849 soon collected a population. Some went to the coasts of Chile and Peru, where valuable goods were to be had—the nitrates from the desert shore-line and the guano from the adjacent islands. The wide Pacific attracted adventurers in thousands, whalers, pearl-seekers, traders in sandalwood and copra, 'blackbirders' who recruited native labour for the Queensland plantations. The Australian gold discoveries quadrupled the population of Victoria in a few years, and Melbourne harbour was choked with shipping whose crews had deserted to try their luck on the Ballarat field. A war with China in the 'forties opened the Chinese ports to trade, and those of Japan followed suit in the 'fifties. Even the deadly swamps of West Africa assumed a new importance. The stoppage of slaving had threatened to leave them derelict, but the spread of machinery caused a demand for their palm-oil for lubrication; the Oil Rivers were the mouths of the Niger, exploited by profit-hunters who died of fever in hundreds or made fortunes in dozens.

British enterprise and sea-talent, British coal and machinery and engineers, Peel's finance and Manchester's free trade, combined to make our islands the centre of all this pulsating industry. The docks of London and Liverpool extended by the mile, the blast-furnaces and collieries spread their blackness ever wider, the factory towns grew into cities, the population became denser; hard work and more money to spend were the national watchwords in that busy, striving generation between the two Reform Acts. The quiet England of young King George the Third had gone through whirlwind changes to become 'the workshop of the world' of Queen Victoria.

V. CONSERVATIVES AND LIBERALS

Gladstone was prime minister of a Liberal government from 1868 to 1874, Disraeli and the Conservatives were in office from 1874 to 1880, Gladstone reigned again from 1880 to 1885. These were the classic days of the contest between the two great leaders and the two great parties that emerged from the reconstructive period of the mid-nineteenth century. The Second Reform Act with its town-democracy had set the stage for their rivalry. The day of coalitions and composite cabinets was over. Each of three general elections returned a united party with a clear majority. Each ministry ran its full term with a definite programme of work and went down decisively as the pendulum of public approval swung in its opponents' favour. At the close of the sequence the country labourers were enfranchised, and democracy was made complete. It was democracy, that is to say, as understood by the early Radicals, of all settled, steady-going heads of families, not democracy as known to-day, of all adult men and women. That was to be the fruit of a later generation, whom war and the newer wage-earning have taught to regard the individual and not the household as the social unit.

Each of the two great statesmen was a master of men, head and shoulders above his colleagues. Each had a chequered past. Gladstone, of Lancashire business origin, had once been described as 'the rising hope of the stern unbending Tories'. The phrase has been often quoted, but it was singularly wide of the mark, for it implies an inflexibility that was never in Gladstone's nature. He was indeed unbending in pursuit of what he thought right at any given juncture, but he was not a man who formed his views when young and never afterwards revised them. Like Pitt and Peel, he was open to conviction by reasonable evidence, and his political principles changed rapidly as his country changed in the course of his long career. Truth is a jewel with many facets, and Gladstone was ever ready to reflect the one which shone most brightly at the moment. His detractors called it time-serving; it was really sincerity. That is now generally admitted by those who would nevertheless have voted against him at almost every crisis of his time. This sincerity of Gladstone had the defect of its quality. It so absorbed him that he could see nothing good in any who disagreed with him. To half the people of England his righteousness was that of a stern unbending Pharisee; and that good word 'righteousness', overworked by Liberal tongues, became nauseous to those whom he excluded from its scope. Every thinking man of his time either worshipped him or loathed him; there were no neutrals. That was a characteristic of Victorian politics which is hard to realize amid the tepid loyalties of our day.

Gladstone began as a Tory, became a Peelite Conservative, and ended as a Liberal. Disraeli began as a Radical, but failed to win his way into Parliament in that character. He first sat in the Commons as one of Peel's men, but he turned against his leader on the Corn Laws question. It was Disraeli who led the Conservatives in overthrowing Peel, and it was here that he parted company with Gladstone. Disraeli, however, like his great antagonist, was no adherent of lost causes, and a few years after the great split he was describing protection as 'not only dead, but damned'. He was a man of strange contradictions, a fop who worked hard, a drawing-room flatterer who thought deeply and revolved gigantic schemes, a Jew of undistinguished family who raised himself by sheer brain-power to the head of the Conservative party from which he had ejected Peel. His most amazing success was the ascendancy he gained in the favour of Queen Victoria. She had been nurtured in the aristocratic circle of the most exclusive Whigs. Her husband, whom she adored, disliked Disraeli. But after the Prince Consort's death she believed the Jew to be the one statesman who could be trusted, the only saviour of throne and altar amid the democratic whirlwinds evoked by the hated Gladstone.

Yet Disraeli, as his record shows, was as much a democrat as Gladstone. His policy was that the Conservatives should throw themselves upon the support of the working masses, should take the lead in reform instead of resisting it, and should set up new ideals for the people to worship in place of the too prominent 'righteousness' that jarred on so many minds. Under his lead the Conservatives competed with the Liberals in the reforming business, but in foreign and imperial affairs they took a new line of their own. Gladstone pursued peace unswervingly, even when it laid him open to the charge of betraying national interests. Disraeli took risks in order to appeal to that pride in the Empire and in British leadership which was ready to awaken in the national mind. Most people now agree that Gladstone was completely sincere. What the inner Disraeli was, no one knows. He is as much a mystery to our time as he was to his own.

Gladstone came in with a Liberal majority in 1868. In England there were few first-class abuses left to reform. In Ireland there were many. Disraeli had once defined them as 'an alien church, a starving peasantry, and an absentee aristocracy'. Gladstone at once tackled the first. In 1869 he disestablished the Anglican Church in Ireland; that is to say, he relieved the Catholic population from the obligation to support a religion they disapproved, and he converted part of the endowments to public purposes. The Protestant church continues to this day, but without any specially privileged position. In 1870 Gladstone passed the first Irish Land Act to better the condition of the peasants, but its practical effects were not great. It marks, however, the beginning of a huge reform, continued by Liberals and Conservatives alike, which in some forty years set right the wrongs of centuries and at length made the Irish people the owners of their soil.

In England the Liberals dealt with minor abuses. They abolished religious tests at Oxford and Cambridge, and so swept away the last vestige of that disfavour to nonconformists that had once bulked so large in the national institutions. They passed an Act in 1871 to extend the rights of the trade unions, unchanged since 1825. They modernized the army by creating a reserve and stopping the purchase of commissions. They passed the Ballot Act of 1872 to ensure the secrecy of voting and do away with bribery and intimidation. Their two greatest works were constructive. In 1873 they established the High Court of Justice to combine and make uniform the practice of the civil law. The King's Bench, the Common Pleas, the Exchequer, the Chancery, the High Court of Admiralty, and the ecclesiastical courts of Arches, Probate, and Divorce, were tribunals that had developed from origins far back in the Middle Ages. They had various special methods of their own, often cumbersome and dilatory and unintelligible to the ordinary citizen. The reform grouped them all as branches of one supreme court, and made their practice more speedy and uniform. It was one of the last great steps in providing the modern British state with a mechanism adjusted to the new conditions.

The remaining Liberal reform was a necessary consequence of the democratic vote. The chief argument against extending the franchise had been that many of the new voters were illiterate. After it had been passed one of its chief opponents insisted that 'we must educate our masters'. The state had made grants in aid of popular education since 1833, and a great deal had been done by religious bodies and private individuals in founding schools for the children of the poor. But there was no general system. Some districts were well provided for, and others not at all, neither was there any compulsion of parents to send their children to such schools as there were. The Education Act of 1870 supplied the deficiencies. In the English tradition it grafted the new upon the old. It absorbed into the general arrangements the existing schools, with provision for a standard of efficiency. Where schools did not exist, it enacted that the ratepayers should elect School Boards, which were to levy an education rate and establish schools, hence called the board schools. Until the Act had produced its schools it was not feasible to make attendance compulsory. That step was taken a few years later by the Conservatives in their Education Act of 1876. These measures were the beginning of a whole evolution of education as an affair of the state. One may appreciate its growth by comparing present conditions with those of a century ago. Then, it was not considered the business of the state at all; now, it is one of its prime activities.

In 1874 Disraeli was an old man of seventy. He was the acknowledged leader of the Conservatives, but he had never yet been prime minister save for a few months in 1868. The Gladstone government had shot its bolt and was losing popularity; Disraeli pointed scornfully to the ministerial bench and described its occupants as 'a row of extinct volcanoes'. The gibe was apt, as were most that fell from those lips. After a six years' career Parliament was dissolved, and the general election returned a large Conservative majority.

At last Disraeli reaped the harvest of his long belief in Tory democracy, and especially of his 'leap in the dark' in the Reform Act of 1867. He divined the ambitions of the new voters and had carefully prepared his ground. He realized that the great days of *laissez-faire* were over. It was essentially a middleclass doctrine, suitable to the pushing, successful man who was confident in his own abilities. It was not so attractive to the less fortunate, who looked to the state for help in the struggle of life. The Second Reform Act was in reality the death-warrant of *laissez-faire*, just as the First (of 1832) had been its charter. Gladstone had excelled in sweeping away disabilities. Disraeli was ready to come forward with aids. From the workman's point of view one was the complement of the other, and so he alternately supported both.

Disraeli, however, did not rely upon bribery of the electorate. Politics in his day were not at that depth. He had an ideal, and that was the Empire, so long neglected by the statesmen of both parties; and he appealed to the public to support it. In a great speech in 1872 he accused the Liberals of seeking to break up the Empire. It was to some extent true, although it had been true also of the Conservatives. Gladstone's Colonial Secretary had certainly been contemplating the cutting-off of Canada as a separate state, and in South Africa and New Zealand there had been an indecent haste to withdraw the regular troops and leave the settlers to defend themselves against native enemies. The pretext was that responsible government included responsibility for self-defence. But the colonists justly replied that their troubles were due to the policy of the home government, of which they themselves had always disapproved. It may be truly said that there had been a lack of tact and sympathy in dealing with the colonies, and that statesmen had too often regarded them as a nuisance: Disraeli himself had so regarded them twenty years before.

In the 'seventies, however, all that was changed. Disraeli now spoke of consolidating the Empire by an imperial tariff, a proper scheme of defence, and a central council of all the scattered units. He did not fill in the details, but the outline was attractive. It appealed especially to the sentiments of the poorer voters. The great emigration of the nineteenth century had been chiefly from their ranks. There was scarcely a working family that had not some friend or relation overseas; and cheap postage prevented distance from severing the bond. As we look at the faded old stamps of the 'sixties with the names engraved upon them—Queensland, Victoria, Nova Scotia, New Brunswick, the Cape of Good Hope, the scattered settlements swallowed now in mightier dominions—and at those other stamps that bear no country's name but simply the image of the Queen, we can imagine the news they carried, of hard times in

villages and mean streets, of luck at the diggings, of enterprise
in forest and prairie. This kinship of the Empire was a fact, and
its expression was a generous thing, an improvement indeed
upon the Manchester doctrine of fearing to acknowledge a kinsman lest you should be called upon to help him.

There were other things to touch the imagination. As Disraeli launched his policy, David Livingstone was finishing his
last journey in the darkness of tropical Africa. For six years he
had wandered, an old and failing man, collecting the knowledge
that was to let in the light of civilization among peoples given
over to the devilry of slave-raiding. Stanley went out to rescue
him, but he refused to be rescued, and died as he had lived, a
lonely servant of the black man's cause. The humanitarians
had long given up opposing the spread of British rule. They saw
that the world was entering on a competition for territory and
that worse things than British governance might befall the
weaker races. Their part was now to co-operate and not to
resist, and thus the imperial idea had its call for them also.

Disraeli himself was little touched by these sentiments. He
thought rather of dominance than of service. The Indian
Empire, its consolidation and defence, occupied much of his
thought. The Suez Canal had been cut by French enterprise,
but the greater part of its shares belonged to the Khedive of
Egypt. In 1875 extravagance forced the Khedive to sell, and
Disraeli bought the shares on behalf of the British government,
which thus acquired control of the Canal. It was a bold stroke,
for there were risks to be taken, and Gladstone even talked of
impeaching his rival for acting without the consent of Parliament. Two years later Disraeli passed a Bill creating the Queen
Empress of India, a step ridiculed at the time, but one which
is now agreed to have been wise. The remainder of his Indian
policy was not so fortunate and had much to do with his downfall; but first there are other matters to consider.

The Great Trek of 1836 had established two Boer republics
in South Africa, the Transvaal and the Orange Free State, side
by side with the two British colonies of the Cape and Natal. It
was the ambition of Lord Carnarvon, the Colonial Secretary,
to federate these four units into a Dominion like that of Canada,
which had been formed in 1867. Carnarvon forgot, however,
that the Canadians had made their Dominion of their own
accord, without urging from home. He tried to drive the South

Africans into the same course, and only set them against it.
The Transvaal Boers were especially unwilling, for they had no
intention of giving up their independence. But the Transvaal
was in a parlous state, its population weak and scattered, and
its borders threatened by the ferocious Zulus. It was generally
thought that the Zulus meant invasion, and no one believed
that the Boers could withstand them. Carnarvon therefore
ordered the annexation of the Transvaal for its own good, in
order that British troops might defend it. He meant well, but
his ambitions for a Dominion of South Africa were known, and
it seemed to many that the Boers had been deprived of independence on a poor pretext. Gladstone thought so, and made
great play with the matter in his speeches against the government. There followed the Zulu War of 1879. It was ill managed
and opened with a disaster in which a British column was wiped
out. Subsequent success did little to strengthen the government,
and men began to think the new imperialism a dangerous policy.
After the Zulus had been conquered there was no move to
restore the independence of the Boers, or even to grant the
responsible government that had been promised them.

Meanwhile a greater peril had arisen nearer home. The
Turks committed shocking massacres upon their Christian
subjects in Bulgaria. Russia declared war and invaded Turkey.
In 1878 her armies were victorious, and Constantinople seemed
certain to fall within their grasp. Russians in possession of
Constantinople and the Dardanelles meant a Russian sea-
power in the Mediterranean, a threat to cut the great artery
of the British Empire, which ran through Suez to the East.
Disraeli was ready to fight Russia on this matter. Among the
Conservatives there was an outburst of jingoism, a disposition
to defy the antagonist rather than negotiate with him. 'The
Russians shall not have Constantinople' was the refrain of a
bellicose song much in favour. Jingoism only discredited a
cause that was really sound enough, for the Empire was vitally
threatened. Gladstone took the high moral standpoint. The
Turks were stained with atrocious bloodshed. They ought to
be turned out 'bag and baggage' from the provinces they had
defiled. The Russians were doing a good work, and England
was wrong to object to it. Gladstone's sincerity and fiery speech
made a great impression. And he was quite right, if one looked
only at Turkey; there the issue was clear between God and the

devil, an issue such as Gladstone loved. But in human disputes the devil usually arranges to be represented on both sides, and it was so here. If the Russian crusaders were allowed to expel the Turk a day would come when they would roll southwards over the Empire's eastern road. Then, not only would England be hard hit, but all her work of peace and civilization in India would be brought to naught, a greater triumph for the devil than the massacre of the Bulgarians. Disraeli held to the long view and won his point. From the Congress of Berlin he brought back 'peace with honour', a settlement of Turkey that kept Russia far from the capital. London gave him a rapturous welcome, but in the industrial north Gladstone's words had sunk deep. Men shook their heads over imperialism. It seemed certain to lead to war.

It did lead to a war on the Indian frontier. The Amir of Afghanistan turned hostile to the British and friendly to the Russians. What if he should offer passage through his mountains to a Russian host? The British in India were greatly alarmed, and the Viceroy sent a force into Afghanistan to avert the peril. The expedition easily drove out the Amir and then sought to install a successor who would serve the British interest. But the Afghan tribesmen rose in revolt. There was wild fighting all over the country, and a disaster at Maiwand in 1880. It was retrieved by the famous march of Lord Roberts from Kabul to Kandahar, but the whole formed an unhappy record with which to face the electors in the general election of 1880.

In home affairs Disraeli had been more fortunate. A whole list of useful reforms marked his ministry—housing for workmen, fairer law for tenant farmers, the Education Act of 1876, increased liberty for trade unions, a revision of the Factory Acts. But the Liberals promised as much, and what was more they promised peace. 'Peace, retrenchment, and reform' was the cry that won them the election. They won it very thoroughly, and Disraeli could only resign. He died in the following year.[1]

Gladstone came in with high aims, but his ministry was a record of misfortune. The 'eighties were a gloomy period, in contrast with the long tide of prosperity which had flowed since the days of Peel. Cheap corn from Russia and America bit deep into the profits of the land, and an agricultural depression set in that has never lifted since. The farmer even lost his monopoly of

[1] He had been created Earl of Beaconsfield in 1876.

beef and mutton, for live cattle began to cross the Atlantic from the American prairies, and frozen carcasses to be shipped from far New Zealand. The industrial revolution was spreading into other countries, Europe was now covered with a network of railways, and from Germany in particular there came a challenge to the manufacturing supremacy which the Manchester School had believed to be ours for ever. Unemployment, strikes, and discontent caused almost a panic in a generation which had been accustomed only to the good things of life. In fact the whole world was entering on a new phase of energy, and England had need to adjust herself to it.

The first trouble came from South Africa. The Transvaal Boers had read Gladstone's speeches and expected that now he was in power he would restore their independence. He was virtually pledged to it, since he had described Disraeli's annexation as dishonourable. But the months passed, and he made no move. In fact he was beginning to see that there were two sides to the question. The independent Boers had been harsh to the natives, and Exeter Hall was still strong enough to insist that this kind of independence would not do. If it was 'unspeakable' for Mahometan Turks to massacre their subjects, still more was it for Christian white men. Gladstone therefore did nothing, and the Boers rose in revolt. In 1881 they routed a small British force at Majuba Hill. Gladstone dispatched reinforcements, but before their arrival he changed his mind and made peace. The Transvaal became the South African Republic under the presidency of Paul Kruger, another stage in the policy of 'doing and undoing' that has been so fatal to South Africa. Many people thought that Gladstone had betrayed the honour of his country. Many more thought that he had done the right thing in the wrong way.

Irish affairs entered on a dangerous stage. Charles Stewart Parnell, leader of the Home Rule party in Parliament, formed the Land League in Ireland. The Home Rulers were Irish members who worked for the repeal of the Union and the restoration of an Irish Parliament. The Land Leaguers sought by violence and intimidation to force the Irish landlords to resign the land to the peasantry. They were guilty of murders and a whole catalogue of lesser crimes, and witnesses were afraid to give the evidence that would have brought the offenders to justice. Gladstone followed the only possible course in passing a Coercion Act to allow of the imprisonment of agitators without trial. At the same time he attempted to remedy grievances by the new Land Act of 1881, designed to make rents fair and moderate. Early in 1882 Parnell and his colleagues were in prison. They were released on agreeing to moderate the violence of their followers and allow the reforms to take effect. Gladstone appointed a new Chief Secretary for Ireland, and it seemed as though a happier era was to dawn. The prospect of peace was wrecked by the extremists. No sooner had Lord Frederick Cavendish, the new Secretary, landed in Dublin than he was murdered in Phoenix Park, together with his colleague Burke. A dozen cowardly assassins had plunged their country again into chaos, and Irish history for the ensuing years was an alternation of brutal crime and harsh retribution.

Still the tale of misfortune mounted. Before the Liberals came in, the British and French governments had been obliged to interfere in Egypt to check the Khedive's wasteful tyranny. They had set up the Dual Control for the supervision of the country. In 1882 the Egyptian army under Arabi Pasha revolted against this foreign rule, and in June Arabi was in possession of Alexandria, where Europeans were massacred in the streets. France refused to take action, and the peace-loving British government was forced into war. The British fleet bombarded Alexandria, and a British army landed and routed the rebels. Gladstone wished only to establish a sound Egyptian government and then to withdraw. But once in, it was impossible to come out, for no native government could stand without British support unless it was prepared to follow an anti-European policy. Gladstone thus found himself committed to the occupation of Egypt, much to the disgust of some of his Liberals. John Bright, the veteran pacifist, quitted the ministry as a protest against the use of force.

The western Soudan, the vast region of the Upper Nile, was a possession of Egypt. For years the Egyptian pashas had oppressed it, plundering and slave-raiding to their hearts' content. In 1881 the Mahdi, a religious enthusiast, proclaimed himself the deliverer of his people. From small beginnings his rebellion grew. In 1883 General Hicks led a rabble of Egyptian troops to suppress it. The fierce Dervish warriors entrapped him in the desert and destroyed him and his army almost to a man. The Mahdi was master of the Soudan. Egypt was incapable of reconquest, and the Gladstone ministry decided that it was not a British obligation. The Mahdists proved themselves worse tyrants than those they had overthrown, but this was not yet realized: Gladstone described them as 'a people rightly struggling to be free'. He sent General Gordon to withdraw the remaining Egyptian garrisons and leave the country to its own devices. Gordon, once beyond the reach of authority, took upon himself to reverse the policy. He talked of 'smashing the Mahdi', and stayed on at Khartum. There he was besieged, and a new expedition became necessary to rescue him. The government was in a dilemma. It was utterly opposed to this war, and yet could not leave Gordon to perish. It sent a relief force, but only after a fatal delay. After fierce fighting the expedition drew near to Khartum, only to find that the city had fallen and Gordon had been killed. He was a crusader who had defied every one for what he thought the right, and the English people made him their hero. When the news came that he was dead the curses on Gladstone were loud and deep. 'Three days too late' was the end of the expedition, but there had been weeks of delay before it had started. It was useless for the cabinet to plead that Gordon had disobeyed orders: democracy had taken him to its heart.

At home the Gladstone government completed its programme by passing the Third Reform Act of 1884. The democratic franchise of the towns was extended to the counties, and the farm labourer received the vote. But the ministry was staggering to its fall, and in 1885 Gladstone resigned. The luck had run strongly against him from the outset.

X

THE LAST SIXTY YEARS

(*From 1885*)

I. HOME RULERS AND UNIONISTS

THE condition of Ireland in the years which followed the Phoenix Park murders furnished the greatest problem of the time. It was admitted on all sides that something needed to be done to render that country contented and law-abiding, for it was scandalous that crimes and outrages should go unpunished and that a mere semblance of order could be maintained only by frequent suspensions of the Habeas Corpus Act. Gladstone had promised to pacify Ireland, and to that end he had disestablished the Church and passed his Land Acts; but Ireland remained obstinately unpacified. Meanwhile the Irish Home Rulers in Parliament, led by Parnell, were awaiting their opportunity. It would come on the day which saw Liberals and Conservatives so nearly equal that the eighty Irish members could hold the balance. Then Parnell might be able to dictate his terms or make government impossible.

The day arrived with the general election held at the close of 1885. Its result was that neither Gladstone nor his Conservative opponent Lord Salisbury could count on a majority without the Irish votes. Parnell turned first to the Conservatives, and although some of them were disposed to accommodate him Salisbury decided against it and resigned the premiership, which he had held since Gladstone's resignation in the previous summer. At this juncture (February, 1886) Gladstone announced his conversion to Home Rule. One may believe that he was honestly convinced, but it was easy for his enemies to say that he was changing his principles for the sake of office. He became prime minister for the third time and introduced his Home Rule Bill without delay.

In the theory of Home Rule, that is, the re-establishment of an Irish Parliament at Dublin, there was nothing disloyal or discreditable, and if some of the circumstances had been different it would have been the best solution of the problem. Unhappily the Home Rulers and their new ally made the error of taking a name for a thing. Ireland was a geographical expression, not a nation. Within the island were two nations. The Ulstermen of the north-eastern province were mainly of Anglo-Saxon blood, descendants of the English and Scottish settlers who had gone in to fill the vacuum caused by the revolts and devastations of the late sixteenth century. In religion they were puritanically Protestant, and this added to their sense of racial difference from the people of the other provinces. They were content to be represented at Westminster and bitterly hostile to the idea of making them subject to a Parliament at Dublin. The inhabitants of the other three provinces, the Irishmen proper, were mainly of Celtic origin and of the Catholic religion. The elections from Parnell's time onwards showed a steady Home Rule majority, but it should not be forgotten that scattered through the constituencies there were a large number of supporters of the existing order. This minority had a special claim to consideration, because the cause of Home Rule was intertwined with that of the Land League and its criminal violence. If the majority should gain control of the country there was not the least doubt that the minority would suffer in person and estate—that they would, in fact, be subject to a tyranny. Celtic Ireland, through no fault of its own, had suffered a history that deprived it of the first qualification for democratic self-rule—the hatred of persecution and the desire to give fair play to all. The English historian cannot afford to point the finger of scorn on that account, but he is nevertheless obliged to record the fact. This was the reality which Gladstone refused to consider and which transformed the theoretical justice of Home Rule into a practical injustice.

The Home Rule Bill of 1886 proposed to place the whole of Ireland under a Dublin parliament. It seemed as if there would be a majority for it in the House of Commons, but here Gladstone's calculations proved faulty. In the early nineteenth century the Conservative party had been twice split—in 1828 by the revolt of the Canningites against Wellington, and in 1846 by the expulsion of the Peelites over the Corn Laws question. In each instance the minority had hovered between the lines for a time, but had ultimately gone over to the opposite side. That had been Gladstone's own history as a Peelite Tory. Now it was his fate to split the Liberals with his Home Rule plan. A section of them refused to vote for the measure. They clung to the maintenance of the Union of 1800, and therefore styled themselves the Liberal Unionists. Their most prominent leaders were Joseph Chamberlain and Lord Hartington, better known by his later title of Duke of Devonshire. The consequence was that the Commons defeated the Home Rule Bill. Gladstone dissolved Parliament, but the country ratified the adverse vote by returning a Unionist majority. Lord Salisbury took office and remained prime minister from 1886 to 1892. The Liberal Unionists supported him and ultimately merged with the Conservatives in the Unionist Party, a name which remained in common use until the close of the Great War.

The Conservatives, although hostile to an Irish Parliament, had a definite policy for the satisfaction of Ireland. It was that of successive Land Acts to better the condition of the peasantry, and ultimately to make them the owners of the soil. At the same time they intended, by a vigilant enforcement of the law, to put a stop to the oppression of the Unionist minority in the Home Rule provinces. In other words the Conservative policy was realistic, whilst the Liberal was idealistic. History was to show that neither the one nor the other was able to solve the problem in a way that should be fair and acceptable to all Irishmen.

The Salisbury ministry passed the Land Acts of 1887 and 1891 for the protection of Irish tenants against unfair treatment by their landlords. Then, in 1892, the general election returned a majority for Gladstone. In the following year he introduced the second Home Rule Bill. The Commons passed it, but the Lords threw it out. It was the first occasion since 1831 that the upper house had rejected a first-class measure sent up by the lower. But this time there was no sensational conflict. Gladstone's majority was precariously based on the adhesion of the Irish members, and in Great Britain the people were not prepared for a revolution on that matter. Some of his own followers were unwilling to go further, and the rejection was quietly accepted. Gladstone, well over eighty years of age, retired, and his ministry continued under Lord Rosebery.

In 1895 the Conservatives (or Unionists) came in again, and remained in power for ten years. Their Land Act of 1896 extended the scope of previous measures. In 1898 they passed the Irish Local Government Act, which created County Councils and so established popular control over local affairs. The culmination of their policy was reached in the Land Purchase

Act of 1903, which set aside a sum of £10,000,000 for the buying-out of landlords, the purchase-money being advanced to their tenants on very easy terms. Subsequent measures enlarged and quickened the operation of this plan. The Land Acts, begun by Gladstone and continued by his opponents, removed the greatest social grievance of Ireland. In the mid-nineteenth century the people had been abjectly poor, overcrowded on tiny holdings, and subject to unreasonable increases of rent or to eviction without compensation for the improvements they had made. Such conditions had promoted the laziness and improvidence of which the peasant was accused, for no man could be expected to put hard work and savings into a farm from which he could be turned out at any moment. From long years of misery and anarchy better times slowly emerged. The excessive population was cut down by the great emigration that followed the Famine. The extension of the railway system made it possible to market produce, an economic method much more secure than that of growing for mere subsistence. Gladstone was the first prime minister to understand the wrongs of the tenants. The early Land Acts removed those wrongs one by one. The later ones converted tenants into freeholders. After 1890 public order greatly improved. By the early twentieth century Ireland was what it had never been before, a community with no material reason for not being prosperous and happy.

But the material was not everything; the ideal remained unsatisfied. During all these years the constituencies, save in Ulster, never ceased to return a solid block of Home Rulers, pledged to secure the Irish Parliament of patriotic dreams. These Nationalist members, as they came to be called, were for the most part not revolutionaries, but they were determined to extort a Home Rule measure whenever the opportunity should arise. That opportunity would come when a general election should again leave English parties equally balanced. It was long deferred. The election of 1895 gave the Conservatives a clear majority, and so did that of 1900. That of 1906 revealed a great swing of the pendulum and returned the Liberals with the largest majority of modern times. But the Liberals since Gladstone's time had dropped the disastrous item of Home Rule from the forefront of their programme, and so for four years to come the Nationalists could not achieve their purpose. Then, in 1910, the day arrived. The general election held in January produced a Parliament in which the eighty Nationalists held the balance, and at once Home Rule became practical politics. The outcome must be left to a subsequent page, for it is closely bound up with the English politics of those feverish years before the Great War.

II. THE DOMINIONS AND THE DEPENDENCIES

The formation of the Dominion of Canada in 1867 has already been mentioned. It was not the Dominion of to-day. It consisted of the four provinces of Quebec, Ontario, Nova Scotia, and New Brunswick, the first two lying inland on the St. Lawrence and the Great Lakes, the last two on the Atlantic coast-line, with a seafaring population. A third maritime province, Prince Edward Island, joined the Dominion a few years later. The oldest and largest, Newfoundland, has always preferred to remain a separate unit with complete self-government of its own. The great expansion of Canada took place to the westward, where the territory of the Hudson's Bay Company stretched right across the continent. In 1869 the Company made over its political rights to the Dominion. It was many years before the prairies could be peopled, but they became in time the provinces of Manitoba, Saskatchewan, and Alberta, stretching from Ontario to the Rocky Mountains. Beyond the mountains, British Columbia and Vancouver Island had been colonized in the 'fifties, and in 1871 they entered the Dominion.

Such was the framework as drawn upon the map. The effective occupation was done by emigration from the British Isles and by expansion of the older Canadian stock, all assisted by railways. Without the railways to link the Atlantic with the Pacific the Dominion could not have grown, for none but hunters and traders could have reached the prairies, and no farmers could have sent their produce to market. The Canadian Pacific Railway was completed in 1886, and others followed. By 1901 the population was over five millions. In the next thirty years this figure was doubled, and by 1941 the Canadian total had grown to nearly twelve millions.

The Australian colonies, planted on the sea-coasts of a country whose interior was less attractive, had more communication with the outer world than with one another. Partly for this reason their move to form themselves into a dominion came later, when the ambitions of foreign powers in the Pacific seemed to threaten the security of Australia. In 1901 the six colonies of New South Wales, Tasmania, Western Australia, South Australia, Victoria, and Queensland were federated under a dominion government. The new state took the title of the Commonwealth of Australia. New Zealand, a thousand miles away to the south-east, did not join the Commonwealth. It has been styled a Dominion since 1907. These two southern dominions contain between them a population of about eight millions, almost entirely of British origin.

Since 1815 the soil of Canada, Australia, and New Zealand has not seen any serious warfare between white men. The history of South Africa has been less happy. After the war of 1881, in which the Transvaal obtained its independence, a period of rapid expansion set in. In the Transvaal itself the discovery of a rich goldfield on the Witwatersrand caused an influx of new settlers. These people, called Outlanders by the Boers, built Johannesburg and worked the mines with expensive machinery owned by powerful companies. Within a few years their numbers equalled those of the Boer farmers spread over the veldt, and President Kruger was faced with a difficult problem of government. At the same time British pioneers were pushing northwards into the untapped regions on either side of the Zambezi. They found fertile, healthy country and valuable metals, including gold. The gold-mines had been exploited in very remote times, but no one knows certainly by whom; all that can be said is that the ancient workings and the ruins of large buildings still exist to testify to the fact. Cecil Rhodes, prime minister of Cape Colony, was active in this northern enterprise, and the country was named Rhodesia. In 1889 he formed the British South Africa Company ('The Chartered Company') to exploit it.

Rhodes made no secret of his ambition to unify South Africa. The Boers grew alarmed at the threat to their independence, and Kruger was accused of planning to expel the British, and thus unify South Africa in a different manner. The bone of contention was the treatment of the Outlanders. They complained of oppression, to which the Boers replied that they were uninvited guests in the Transvaal and could go away if they did not like their welcome. The trouble was in essence the conflict of two kinds of civilization, the rural and the industrial, made keener by differences of language and race. In 1896 the Chartered Company's men from Rhodesia made a raid into the Transvaal under Dr. Jameson. They were surrounded and captured by the Boers, having placed their country in an awkward position; for they had invaded in time of peace and without any commission from the British government. Respectable powers do not countenance this in modern times, however usual it may have been in Drake's day, and Kruger had a just grievance. The quarrel was patched up for the time, but war broke out in 1899 over the Outlander question. Kruger certainly provoked it at the last moment, but he seems to have been convinced that the British meant to subjugate his people when the time should be ripe.

The South African War of 1899–1902 was a tedious business in which the Boers put up a great resistance against superior numbers. Ultimately the numbers won, and the Transvaal and Orange Free State ceased to be separate republics. In 1907, however, they were granted responsible government. In 1910 they combined with Cape Colony and Natal in the Union of South Africa, the fourth of the modern dominions. The Boer and British elements in the white population (about 1½ millions strong) are supposed to be about equal. The peace of 1902 and the terms of the Union prescribed equality for both races, and the Boers have exerted themselves to secure that position, and perhaps rather more. South Africa, in fact, has never quite settled down since the conflict, race bitterness has never died out, and a considerable feeling for separation from the Empire has persisted. But the wisest leaders disclaim it, for they have no wish to plunge their country again into disorder.

The decade of the 'eighties witnessed an outbreak of empire-building by the great European powers. It showed itself chiefly in the tropical regions of the world, and it was largely due to the spread of the industrial revolution. Modern industry requires supplies of raw material and markets for its finished products, and the more backward races were expected to provide both. At the Berlin Conference of 1884–5 most of tropical Africa was parcelled out. In Asia the British were already established in India and were completing the conquest of Burma. France built up a great dependency in Indo-China. Germany, an Empire since 1871, obtained valuable shares of Africa, and competed keenly for possessions in the Pacific Islands. It was the German occupation of New Guinea which awoke the Australians to the need for combining into a dominion to protect their interests. Great Britain revived a method of the past, that of expansion by chartered companies. That of British South Africa was the fourth of a series founded in the space of eight years; the others were the British North Borneo Company (1881), the Royal Niger Company (1886), and the British East Africa Company (1888). The Borneo Company still exists, as does the British South Africa Company. The other two resigned their rights after some years, but their spheres of operation became respectively the dependencies of Nigeria and Kenya Colony. In 1896 British and Egyptian forces began the reconquest of the Soudan, the region of the Upper Nile which had been abandoned on Gordon's death eleven years before. Sir Herbert Kitchener completed the work by his victory at Omdurman in 1898. The Soudan then became a joint Anglo-Egyptian dependency governed by British officers.

The new imperialism which became a force after the Reform Act of 1867 continued to make progress. The unfortunate wars with the Zulus and Afghans occasioned a check to it in the general election of 1880. But the set-back was only temporary, and the leaven spread. Gladstone's backwardness in dealing with the Transvaal in 1881 and with the relief of Gordon in 1884–5 did more than anything else to increase his unpopularity and ensure his failure in the Home Rule policy. During his ministry of the 'eighties the public showed great interest in colonial problems, and a movement for imperial federation took shape. The proposal was that since the colonies had become self-governing by virtue of responsible government, they should voluntarily combine with Great Britain in surrendering some of their powers to a supreme Empire authority, which should deal with questions of common interest. Imperial federation has never been more than an idea, and the problem of unity has been attacked in a different way. But the desire for unity has always been strong, and has in fact grown stronger with the progress of the dominions to complete self-government. The two things appear contradictory, but they nevertheless exist side by side.

In 1895 the Empire found a statesman of greater weight than any since the days of Huskisson. The Colonial Secretary of the new Salisbury ministry was Joseph Chamberlain. He boldly threw over the doctrine of *laissez-faire*, which had been a paralysing influence in the past. He proclaimed, on the contrary, that the Empire was an undeveloped estate, and that the government's duty was to develop it. The British West Indies had been in a languishing condition ever since the abolition of slavery and the adoption of free trade. Chamberlain arranged loans for making railways, established colleges for the study of tropical agriculture, and compelled foreign powers to abandon the sugar bounties whereby they had artificially encouraged beet-sugar to the detriment of the West Indian planters. Within a few years there was a dawn of new prosperity after half a century of depression. Elsewhere Chamberlain granted loans for railway- and port-construction, and promoted schools of agriculture and tropical medicine. By these means the African and Far Eastern dependencies were given a new lease of life. West Africa, notorious as 'the white man's grave', became comparatively healthy, and enterprise equipped with modern transport was able to spread inland from the coast. The new imperialism paid respect to native interests, and time has shown that railways and trade have been the strongest factors in putting down slavery, human sacrifices, and tribal wars. The Chamberlain policy did not die with its author, and flourishes in full vigour to this day. Its results were not limited to Africa and the West Indies. They have nowhere shown to greater advantage than in the colonies and protectorates of the Malay Peninsula, where peace and industry have taken the place of oppression and constant warfare.

The South African War of 1899 was the first in which the Empire as a whole took part. The free democratic dominions agreed that the British government was in the right and Kruger in the wrong. South Africans fought in large numbers on the British side, and they were backed by little armies from Canada, Australia, and New Zealand. In fact the most hopeful part of the whole business was its demonstration that the virtually independent dominions believed in imperial unity and were willing to make the greatest sacrifice for it. So at length was Lord Durham justified of his famous *Report*.

When the South African struggle ended, Chamberlain believed that the war-time unity should be continued under the normal conditions of peace. He did not advocate imperial federation, which would have obtained no great support in the dominions. His plan was that of preferential trade between the units of the Empire. It was the system which Huskisson had established, but which had been swept away by the *laissez-faire* of the 'forties and 'fifties. The essence of a preferential system is that there must be protective tariffs. The dominions had such tariffs, and they were willing to modify them so as to impose higher rates upon foreign than upon British goods. Great Britain on her side had no duties upon the products that mattered most—the bulky foodstuffs and raw materials which the Empire could supply. Unless she levied duties on these articles when of foreign origin she had no means of granting a preference to the dominions. But the free-traders argued that to tax food and raw materials would be fatal to British industry, since it would raise the cost of producing manufactures and render Great Britain incapable of competing with rivals. The argument was hard to answer. Imperial preference indeed seemed feasible only on condition that the greater part of our trade should lie within the Empire. In that case we could afford to neglect the foreign markets. In Chamberlain's day the populations of the Empire were not large enough to furnish the necessary markets, and the verdict of his fellow-countrymen was against his plans. But in the succeeding generation the relative importance of the dominions greatly increased. From time to time there were revivals of the doctrine of imperial preference, and at length it won acceptance in circumstances to be noted on a later page.

Imperial federation would mean the creation of a great parliament of the whole Empire, to which all the local parliaments, including that of Great Britain, would be subordinate. That is why the plan has never been carried out, for the sacrifice of local liberty would be too serious. Nevertheless there has come into being a central council in which the whole Empire is represented. It has no legal authority, but its influence has grown great. It is called the Imperial Conference. It began (as the Colonial Conference) in 1887, when many Empire statesmen were assembled in London to celebrate the Jubilee of Queen Victoria. Since that date the meetings have been frequent, and the general rule now is that an Imperial Conference shall be held every four years. The prime ministers of the dominions meet the premier of Great Britain and the

Secretary of State for India, whilst the Colonial Secretary attends to represent the minor units of the Empire. Important questions of law, defence, trade, and transport are discussed. Resolutions are passed to recommend the carrying out of improvements. These resolutions are not laws, and no one is legally bound by them. But the premiers represent the public opinion of their different units, and if they agree to a course of action they can usually get it translated into law when they return to lay it before their several parliaments. In this way complete local liberty is preserved, whilst unity of action often results from these personal meetings of the Empire's leading men. The Imperial Conference is an example of the evolution of an organ of the state to meet a new need. It was not deliberately created; it has grown from small beginnings. Its growth continues, and its greatest days may be still to come.

At the time of the first great war in 1914 the English nationality had become merged in the British, and its habitation was no longer insular but world-wide. The different units already showed variations of type—the Australian, for instance, as compared with the Canadian—but there was a substantial agreement on great issues that was the stronger for the absence of any central domination. This was not an empire in the usual meaning of the word, and during the war a new title for it became current, namely, the British Commonwealth of Nations.

III. THE NEW REFORMERS

We return now to the progress of English affairs in the latest age. In the closing years of the nineteenth century the condition of the English people was better than it had ever been before. Public health had greatly improved by reason mainly of the century's work in sanitary measures—the sewerage systems, the pure water supplies, and the street cleaning which had at length rendered the towns as wholesome as the countryside. The public education established in the 'seventies was bearing fruit in thrift and soberness and more sensible habits of life. The trade unions were strong enough to protect the interests of their members, and they had developed methods of self-help in the shape of sickness and unemployment funds, subscribed and administered by the workers themselves. Agriculture was indeed depressed, although it was the landowners rather than the labourers who were worse off. The cause of the depression, the import of cheap foodstuffs from distant parts of the earth, was a benefit to the town population, which was by this time a decided majority of the whole. Manufactures and all the employments that depended on them—railway and shipping work and the like—had taken a new lease of energy with the rapid opening-up of the less civilized parts of the world. British machinery and textiles were in ever-increasing demand, and the mercantile marine enjoyed a scarcely challenged supremacy on every sea. There had been no great war for a long period. The national debt was low in proportion to the national wealth. Taxation, even of the wealthy, was light. The workman was barely taxed at all. Prices of the necessaries of life were lower in the 'nineties than they have ever been before or since.

In many ways it seems, as we look back on those golden days, that democracy and the earthly paradise had been inaugurated together. Yet there is another side to the picture, and we find it if we dip into the social and economic writings of the period. The prosperity was for the county magnate and the captain of industry, the established professional man, the tradesman, and the workman with a steady job. These did not comprise the whole people. They were a large number—estimated by some as one-third of the whole population—who had not shared in the general betterment. For various reasons—ill luck, inferior talents, idleness—these unfortunates hovered on the line of extreme poverty. They were often out of work or living by sweated employment, unskilled and mistrusted, unable to belong to a trade union, the last to be taken on and the first to be turned off when times were good or bad. The poor-law might save them from outright starvation, although they often went hungry rather than submit to the hard discipline of the workhouse, which many looked upon as worse than prison. Their children were ill clad and underfed; without a decent home life, the schools could do little for them, and they grew up as inferior as their parents. This submerged class showed no signs of ceasing to be recruited. It was a product of *laissez-faire*, which allots the prizes to the fit and has no mercy on the unfit. *Laissez-faire* had indeed been challenged by many reforming achievements since the middle of the century, but over large areas of the national life it still prevailed. In effect the social system of the 'eighties and 'nineties said to the citizen: You have a fair chance in the struggle for existence, and the advantages offered you are free to all and greater than you ever had before. But you must exert yourself. If you do not or cannot, you must go under.

The Radicals of the early days, of Tom Paine and Francis Place, would have asked nothing better. Freedom for a man to work out his own salvation had been their battle-cry, and they were ready to stand or fall by the result. But in this later time the doctrine failed to satisfy a great many thinkers. The problem of poverty, they declared, must be actively tackled, not left unsolved; if the unfortunate and the shiftless cannot help themselves they must be helped at the expense of the fit and the fortunate.

Hence arose the modern programme of reform. It is best described as 'social reform', in contrast with the political reforms of the earlier period. The programme was launched in an age of prosperity, when it seemed that the community could well afford it. It was a mighty innovation in the methods of civilization. Every social system of the modern world had hitherto been based on individual effort—the race to the swift, and the devil take the hindmost, whether his failing were laziness or ill luck. Now the leaders of democracy undertook to create a system in which every person should enjoy the good things of life, irrespective of his industry and ability. After thirty years they do not claim to have completed it, neither have they proved that their work when done can permanently stand. This is the design underlying the political work of all parties in England since the twentieth century set in.

As with all English developments, the new grew out of the old without any violent break in procedure. The Reform Act of 1884 had completed the parliamentary representation of heads of households (except women) throughout the nation. In 1888 the Local Government Act created elective County Councils for the control of local affairs and taxation. This extended to the whole country the system provided for the boroughs alone by the Municipal Reform Act of 1835. The County Councils have steadily extended their prestige and the scope of their work, and have become an indispensable part of government. Especially is this true of the London County Council, which has ever proved itself an enlightened body and can claim much of the credit for improving the dingy, sordid

London of the poorer quarters, which was typical of the mid-Victorian era. Two factors may be held to account for the success of the L.C.C. From the outset public servants of first-class reputation and ability have worked for it (Lord Rosebery was one of its early Chairmen); and the L.C.C. alone undergoes a complete general election every three years, whereas the other County Councils never have a general election but renew one-third of their members every year. The London method undoubtedly keeps the popular interest more active and infuses life into the elected body.

With this extended mechanism of democratic control there came an increased democratic interest in government. Before 1890 the trade unions had viewed their functions in a narrow sense, each looking after the affairs of its own members and showing little interest in labour problems as a whole. At that time, as has been noted, the trade unions included only the pick of the working men, and the very poor were unorganized and without spokesmen in public affairs. In 1892, in fact, the unions had 1½ million members, or only 4 per cent. of the population. Thenceforward the union leaders widened their views and gradually made their object that of improving the conditions of the working class as a whole. In 1892–3 Keir Hardie, a Socialist, was elected to Parliament, and formed the Independent Labour Party to secure the special representation of the manual workers in the House of Commons. The rank-and-file, however, still thought of politics on the old lines of Liberal versus Conservative, and were slow to support the new movement. In the general election of 1895 every one of the twenty-eight Independent Labour candidates was defeated. Then and in 1900 there were working-men's members returned, but they allied themselves with the Liberals instead of forming a separate party. In the general election of 1906 there was a new departure. A distinct Labour Party of fifty-four members was elected,[1] and since that date it has continued with increasing weight until in 1929 it grew to be the largest party in the Commons.

Laissez-faire had long been attacked by such measures as Factory Acts and Education Acts. In the 'nineties statesmen of all colours united to put it to death. Democracy showed itself far more favourable to state interference than to abstract doc-

[1] Not all of the I.L.P. connexion.

trines of liberty. Chamberlain's Empire policy meant an increase in government activities. Education also became a
special care of the Conservatives. In 1899 they established the
Board of Education to concentrate a good deal of scattered work
and act as a supreme authority. Next year the age of compulsory attendance at school was raised to fourteen, a measure
which served as an indirect Factory Act by preventing the
full-time employment of children under that age. Educational
reform appealed to social workers and also to those who
were concerned for England's place among the nations.
German competition in industry was being severely felt,
and the German success was set down to superior methods
of education. It was generally agreed that England was
behindhand in the matter. In 1902 an Education Act of
great importance was passed. It made the County Councils
(or the Borough Councils of populous places) the authorities for
controlling education, and empowered them to create secon-
dary schools and technical schools where none existed. The
School Boards of 1870 ceased to exist, and the term 'board-
school' became obsolete. It was a change from small units to
large, and it produced more efficient schools. It has produced
also a system of scholarships which make it possible for talented
children to obtain a university education without expense to
their parents. The new order imposed responsibility on the
local authorities for schools hitherto operated by religious
bodies without aid from the rates, and this led to much unseemly squabbling over the religious instruction given in such
schools; but in the main the Act of 1902 was a great reform.

The more ardent social reformers accused the Conservatives
of backwardness in dealing with the problems of poverty. When
the general election of 1906 gave a Liberal government a great
majority, and returned also the first strong group of Labour
members, a whole series of new measures was introduced.
School medical services were established to detect and treat the
infirmities of children in elementary schools, and funds were
provided for giving free meals to underfed scholars. Expenditure on these matters and on scholarships steadily increased.
The trade unions had had a grievance since 1901, when the
judges in the Taff Vale case decided that the funds of a union
were liable for damage committed by its members in the course
of a strike. In 1906 the new Parliament passed the Trade

Disputes Act, which made the union funds immune in this respect. In the same year also, a Workmen's Compensation Act greatly extended the liability of employers to pay for injuries suffered by their servants in the course of their work. The aged poor were relieved by the Old Age Pensions Act of 1908, whilst the Coal Mines Act limited the hours of work of miners to eight per day. Labour exchanges were established in 1909 to assist in finding work for the unemployed.

From 1906 onwards the Liberal government's measures were strongly criticized by the House of Lords, and several of them were thrown out. The trouble was that social reform cost money, which the more fortunate had to find for the benefit of the less. Charitable obligations have always been well recognized in modern England, but here it seemed that a new principle of compulsory charity was being introduced. Advanced politicians, in fact, were arguing that all wealth is created by the community, and that the community has therefore a right to dispose of it. The climax came with the budget of 1909, in which Mr. Lloyd George, as Chancellor of the Exchequer, proposed a variety of new taxes, most of them directly levied on the more wealthy. Of this 'People's Budget' it was avowed that 'Superfluous wealth has been taxed . . . to improve the lot of the poor and to bring into being social reforms'. Its importance was the greater because it was meant to be only a beginning of a much wider programme of such reform, described in the metaphor of its author as 'rare and refreshing fruit for the parched lips of the multitude'.

The Lords took the strong course of throwing out the 1909 budget. Legally they had a right to do so, but constitutional usage was against any interference with a money bill by the upper house. There is no doubt that they believed they would have the support of the country, in which a number of by-elections had gone against the government. Mr. Asquith, the prime minister, took up the challenge and dissolved Parliament. The general election of January 1910 returned the Liberals in a majority of two as against the Conservatives, but the Labour party, which supported the government, came back forty strong. It was therefore true that the electors had endorsed the 'People's Budget', although in no very enthusiastic manner, for the great majority of 1906 was heavily reduced. Above all this the election yielded a momentous result, namely, that the

Irish Home Rulers once again held the balance of power. There were seventy-five of them, elected, not on the merits of the budget, but solely to carry a Home Rule Bill. If they should vote against the government not even the Labour alliance could save it. It was certain, therefore, that Home Rule would once more become a prime object of Liberal policy.

The Lords bowed to the country's verdict and passed the disputed budget in the spring of 1910. But it was well known that they would reject a Home Rule Bill, as they had done in 1893, and their opponents determined not to let the matter rest there. It is unfair to the Liberals to say that the Irish position alone pushed them to further action, for they had sufficient grievances of their own in the rejection of several of their bills to warrant them in an attack upon the Lords' veto. They had never officially disowned Home Rule as a part of their policy, although they had let it sleep for many years. Now they set about a reform of the constitution which they could carry with Irish support, and the price of that support was well understood to be that Home Rule should follow.

In 1910 the government introduced its Parliament Bill. It provided that the Lords should have no power to reject a money bill. They might still reject or amend other bills, but if the same measure should be passed by the Commons in three consecutive sessions of the same Parliament, spread over two years, it might then receive the assent of the Crown and become law without the approval of the Lords. The Lords, therefore, still preserved a practical veto on legislation passed by an expiring House of Commons which might have lost the confidence of the country. This was rendered still more effective by a reduction of the duration of Parliament from seven to five years. The duty of deciding what was or was not a money bill was laid on the Speaker of the House of Commons, a high compliment to the impartiality with which that office has always been exercised in the modern British Parliament.

The Lords determined not to pass the Parliament Bill without a further appeal to the country, and Mr. Asquith, having received a promise from the King to create peers if it should be necessary, again dissolved Parliament before the end of the year. The general election of December 1910 was known as 'the no-change election', for it returned the four parties with numbers almost exactly the same as in January. The result was, therefore, that Great Britain gave a mild approval to the Parliament Bill, whilst Ireland was heavily in favour of it. After a temporary stilling of party strife in the coronation festivities of King George V, the Lords yielded to the inevitable, and the Bill became law in August 1911. The Parliament Act was a democratic advance, for it confirmed the position of the elected Commons as the predominant power in the constitution. It left, however, a considerable moderating influence to the Lords, since they are able to reject or amend any measure put forward by ministers without the clear approval of the country. A further recommendation in the preamble of the Act, that the Lords themselves should be reconstituted to embody more fully the collective wisdom of the nation, has never been proceeded with by any party, Liberal, Conservative, or Labour, which has since been in office.

The national verdicts of 1910 were primarily in favour of further social reform, and secondarily, of Home Rule. It is true that ostensibly the elector had given his voice for or against a change in the constitution, but political theory for its own sake excites little interest, and the consequence of the change was what every one had in mind. Further reform ensued at once in the shape of the National Insurance Act of 1911, whereby provision was made against sickness, and, in certain trades, unemployment, from a fund contributed by workers, their employers, and the state. The divergence between democracy and liberty was well illustrated by this measure, for all persons whose wages were below a certain figure were compelled to subscribe to this insurance scheme, whether they wished to or not. The Conservatives raised an impassioned resistance; but in subsequent days the Conservative party has approved and extended the scope of the measure it then denounced. Two other Acts of this Parliament may be mentioned: that for the payment of members of the Commons (1911), a fulfilment of an old Chartist demand; and that for the disestablishment of the Anglican Church in Wales (1913–14), comparable to the Irish disestablishment of 1869.

Leaving the question of Home Rule to separate consideration, the above completes the list of the more important political matters of the period prior to the Great War. By 1914 a great deal had been done to remedy the social sufferings endured for the most part in silence during the 'nineties. As a result, the condition of the very poor had improved, and all manual workers were better protected against the accidents of life. But this had been partly at the expense of the more fortunate kind of workman who had prospered in the days of cheapness and light taxation. He was now not so prosperous. His living cost more, and his wages had not gone up in proportion. As for persons living on salaries and incomes from investment, they were considerably worse off. The income tax had grown from a trifling to a serious amount, and other taxes, direct and indirect, had increased. Moreover, there was a feeling of unrest and uncertainty in the air. The old *laissez-faire* governments of mid-Victorian times had aimed chiefly at preserving order and giving fair play to all by the removal of injustices. The new reformers acted on the principle of 'doing something' for some part of the community at the expense of some other part. The process did not produce contentment, even amongst the gainers. The years 1911–14 were marked by a succession of strikes and disputes, some of them with an element of underlying revolution. The sight of armed soldiers guarding the stations during the railway strike of 1911 was a new portent to that generation, who had never beheld the like in England before. They were unhappily destined to see it again. In another respect public order decayed. From 1906 onwards women's political organizations proclaimed that democracy was incomplete and that women must have the vote on the same terms as men. Some women used reasoned argument and others unreasoning violence. They interrupted public meetings and even the debates of Parliament, fought the police in the streets, and destroyed a great amount of property. To slash a priceless picture, to pour corrosive chemicals into a letter-box, or to break an unoffending tradesman's windows was to demonstrate the qualities of citizenship. The whole age was a little mad, with the madness of those whom the gods mean to destroy.

The Irish question added to the turmoil, and ended by dominating it. The Parliament Act having been passed, the Asquith ministry introduced a Home Rule Bill in 1912. It provided for an Irish Parliament with limited powers and for the continued presence of forty-two Irish members at Westminster. Preceding events deprived the measure of cool consideration by its opponents. The 'People's Budget' and the Parliament Act had made Conservative tempers raw and rabid, and the

Bill was contested less on its own merits than as a ground of attack upon the government. A strong debating point was that the Liberals themselves were insincere, since they had never promoted Home Rule except when at the mercy of the Irish vote. But to demand a higher standard of conduct than this was to demand more than politicians of any party have commonly displayed. A more solid ground of objection was that the Bill, whilst recognizing the nationalism of Celtic Ireland, trampled on the nationalism of Ulster. Ulster declared vehemently for maintaining the Union, but was nevertheless to be subjected to Dublin. All the arguments for liberty advanced by the three provinces were equally valid for the fourth, and they were dismissed without concession.

The Lords rejected the 1912 Bill, as they were empowered to do, but its passage under the Parliament Act was only a matter of time. To anticipate the inevitable, Ulster prepared to fight. In 1913 its people made a Covenant to oppose Home Rule, and 100,000 volunteers enrolled to resist Dublin governance by force of arms. To counter the Ulster Volunteers the other party immediately formed the Irish Volunteers. Both sides smuggled in weapons from abroad, and serious war was in prospect as soon as the Bill should become law. It was at this time that the Sinn Fein movement became dominant in Ireland. It had been founded some years earlier to work for self-government by constitutional means. It now became revolutionary and demanded independence, The Irish Volunteers were its armed force. Sinn Fein despised the political Home Rulers in Parliament, and denounced them as timid and treacherous.

Meanwhile, what was the British government to do? To drop the Home Rule Bill would mean a cry of betrayal in Celtic Ireland and most probably a formidable rebellion there. It would mean also the collapse of the government and all the policies it stood for. To pass the Bill meant a rebellion in Ulster, a rebellion supported by half of England, and one that there was no certainty of putting down. For the armed forces of the Crown were not to be counted upon to shoot down men who stood in arms under the British flag and protested their loyalty to the Crown. So much was testified by the action of regular officers who resigned their commissions rather than proceed against the Ulster Volunteers. The only solution seemed to be to exclude Ulster from the scope of Home Rule. A Bill for that purpose was introduced in the summer of 1914. It was necessary to discuss how large an area should be excluded, for the division of nationality did not coincide with the political boundary of Ulster. The King summoned a conference of party leaders on July 21. They could not agree. Civil war, it seemed, must decide the issue.

A month earlier a murderer had fired a shot in distant Bosnia, and had killed a man whose name was scarcely known in England. From that day all the madness of the European world had mounted in an inky thunder-cloud of hatred and suspicion. The cloud spread westwards unnoticed by brawling English and Irish, and at the close of July it was nearly overhead. A flash and a roar and a chill shadow made them pause and look eastwards together.

IV. THE FIRST WORLD WAR

For many years before 1914 there were factors in European affairs threatening to produce war, and the threatening elements grew stronger as time went on. It did not, however, appear completely certain that they would provoke a conflict. To some it seemed that they were well within the control of Europe's statesmen and were paraded from time to time as bluff or bogy to help in achieving a diplomatic success, but not with any real intention of their being unleashed. In those years the 'international crisis' became of more frequent occurrence. Some cautious encroachment by a great power or some rebellious movement by a subject people would create a diplomatic contest, with inflammatory speeches and press articles, decently veiled threats from official quarters, military and naval activity, and increasing alarm and apprehension. After causing scare headlines for a week all this would end in a conference of the powers resulting in some minor transference of territory or insincere scheme of reform, and the fleets would return to port and the armies to barracks to continue their training for the next display. It was the method of conducting international relationships which had been evident since 1870. It was a dangerous method, but in skilled diplomatic hands the danger was repeatedly averted. The skill was great. The foreign offices of those times knew their trade. For forty-four years they staved off the catastrophe to civilization. But by 1914 the war-making factors had grown strong beyond control, and diplomacy broke down. The occasion was the old Eastern Question which had festered through the nineteenth century. But the occasion was not the cause.

The fundamental causes of the outbreak of 1914 lay in the minds and thoughts of the peoples of Europe. Although most men, in theory, would have declared that they disliked war and hoped there would be none in their time, they undoubtedly did not feel that passionate abhorrence of the whole business which only experience could engender. History, .modern European history, seemed to teach that in certain circumstances war could be made to pay, and still more, that national preparedness for war, used as a threat in the recurrent crises, could be made very profitable to the country that employed it. National preparedness involved the maintenance of a large number of professional soldiers who grew weary of the make-believe of peace-time exercises and longed to test their work in 'the real thing'. They and the writers associated with them hoped and said that war was certain to come. There were able soldiers indeed who viewed war not as a call to duty but as an opening for personal ambition. The career of Napoleon had a corrupting influence through all the century that followed, and not least at its latter end. Ambitious dreamers thought only of his meteoric rise. They forgot that his success was fugitive and that he was beaten by men who were true to their salt and had no thought of subverting the governments which they served. The number of miniature Napoleons and would-be Napoleons was large, and they and their literature glorified war.

Changing conditions caused the recurrent crises and necessitated the bargains that concluded them. From 1870 to 1914 Europe and the whole world were changing more rapidly than ever before. The nationalism that had produced the German empire and the Italian kingdom, Belgium and Greece and the undying hopes of the Poles, was spreading among the subject-peoples of the Turkish Empire and creating desires that refused to be stilled. The consolidated major states of Europe were recognizing that power depended on industry, that agriculture might produce soldiers but could not equip them, that modern military strength rested upon wealth, wealth upon trade, and trade upon footholds in the outer world. Hence came the partition of Africa, the sharing-out of the Pacific islands, the ambitions and jealousies of Europe in southern Asia, the gathering of the prospective inheritors around the death-bed of imperial China. Mechanical transport opened up new roads to power. The previous generation had established national railway systems, but after 1870 railways became continental. Half a dozen lines raced across the United States and Canada to link the oceans and transplant the surplus population of Europe, but they were no threat to peace. European railway building set up economic stresses and had often a military motive behind it. Trunk lines through Europe, such as that provided by the piercing of the Alps by the St. Gothard tunnel in 1882, favoured the industries of Germany and Austria as against those of the sea-carrying peoples of the west. The great main line through Germany and the Austrian Empire and the Balkans to Constantinople was in operation before the nineteenth century ended. Its successor was the plan of 1904 to extend the line, by German enterprise, through Asia Minor to the Euphrates and so to the Persian Gulf and the Indian Ocean— the Baghdad Railway whereby ambitious Middle Europe was to 'march to the East', to a destiny of wealth and power achievable only at the expense of the British and everyone else. Russia also was a railway builder. Her internal lines carried raw materials to industry and fed her town-workers with the grain of the south. Her trans-Siberian railway was in the continental style and made her a power in China and the north Pacific.

These were some among the many convergent factors that produced the generation of armed peace, in which there was a widespread expectation of a great European war, a general anxiety over national preparedness, but not, among men of the highest responsibility, any intention of precipitating a conflict so long as they could gain advantages without it. In that last condition lay the seeds of disaster, since the advantages were to be gained by threat of force, in other words by bluff. If diplomatic skill and psychology should once be at fault and produce an error of judgement, the bluff would be called and the diplomatic contest of wits break down into the long-expected resort to force.

There was a war in 1877–8 in the Balkan Peninsula, and the Treaty of Berlin provided a settlement. Part of European Turkey was made independent as the states of Bulgaria, Serbia, and Montenegro, and Greece had already been liberated fifty years before. But the Turks were left in possession of a wide strip from the Black Sea to the Adriatic, and this strip contained Serbs, Bulgars, and Greeks, all subject to oppressive rule, and all eager to unite with their independent fellow countrymen. The Berlin Treaty was a good one at the time, since it averted a war between the great powers (Disraeli's 'Peace with honour'); but it could not last for ever, because the subject peoples were growing stronger and their Turkish masters weaker. There were reasons why it was dangerous to interfere with the Treaty. For two centuries the Russians had believed that it was their destiny to drive the Turk out of Europe and take Constantinople, the mother-city of the Greek Church and yet subject to Mahometan rule. Russia regarded herself as the natural champion of her kinsmen, the Southern Slavs of the Balkan Peninsula. Against the Russian ambition stood the Austrian. The Austrian Empire was a combination of two ruling minorities, the Austrians (Germans) and the Magyars of Hungary, and under them were a majority of subject-peoples, mostly Slavs. The Slavs of Austria grew increasingly restive as the nineteenth century gave place to the twentieth. They hoped to get free and unite with their kinsmen in Serbia to the southward. Austrian statesmen believed that if they did not tackle this Slav problem, it would destroy their Empire. Their solution was that Austria should expand southwards, grasp all the Southern Slavs, and so keep them all in order. Russia would never permit it, and here lay the seeds of tragedy. There was only one Balkan Peninsula and only one Constantinople, and two competitors had their eyes upon them.

For thirty years Austrians and Russians watched each other like duellists preparing to lunge. In 1908 Austria took advantage of the fact that the Russian army was in confusion, and annexed Bosnia, a Slav province of which she had hitherto been a temporary occupant. Russia was for the moment powerless and did not take up the challenge. The independent Slavs of Serbia, adjoining Bosnia, believed that they would be the next victims. Then, in 1912, the Southern Slavs moved on their own account and tore up the Treaty of Berlin. Greeks, Serbs, and Bulgars invaded European Turkey and easily conquered it. They quarrelled over the spoil and fought one another. The result was that Bulgaria gained a little, and the others a great deal. Serbia emerged doubled in area and strength, much to

the disgust of the Austrians. As for the Turks, they kept Constantinople and little else. The violent revision of the Berlin
Treaty left hatred and suspicion all round. The losers were
bent on further change. The gainers feared to be attacked by
them. For the first time the minor characters on the European
stage had made an important move in defiance of the great
powers. The responsible statesmen of Europe had seen the
situation slip from their grasp. The possibility of a general war
was greatly increased.

Western Europe had its own anxieties. Bismarck had unified
Germany and made it an empire by three short, bloody, and
successful wars. The last and worst was that against France in
1870. It ended with the siege and surrender of Paris and the
proclamation of the Prussian King as German Emperor in the
Hall of Mirrors at Versailles. The symbolism was dramatic.
Louis XIV had built Versailles and reigned there in splendour,
bullying his neighbours, the Germans included. After two
centuries the Germans came there to consummate their triumph.
Yet another half-century, and they were to come there again,
to acknowledge defeat, and again after twenty years in a surge
of triumph greater than any of the past. Victorious Germany
in 1871 annexed the two provinces of Alsace and Lorraine,
themselves snatched from the feeble Germany of the days of
French greatness.

She had won by the might of conscript armies, by training
every man in peace for his function in war. The outcome was
obvious. To guard what she had won, Germany trained harder
than ever. To avert further losses, France trained also. Russians, Austrians, and Italians applied the moral. 'The nation
in arms' became the rule of European life. Every young man
did his three years' training and passed into the reserve, to
remain on the books until he was fifty. Long-service officers
and sergeants put them through it, instilling into every man's
mind that one day he would inevitably fight. Conscript life was
hard, and the discipline was brutal. But to most men it had its
attraction. There was food and clothing and freedom from all
but military restraint. The conditions were better than many
a peasant or slum-dweller could look for in civil life. The
conscript army was the poor man's university, and public
opinion held it to be a good thing. And so it went on for forty
years, all Europe preparing for the day of wrath and fearful

that it would one day come. Great guns grinned over the frontiers from armoured forts, railways were laid to concentrate millions of men, the kit was all ready in the depots for the reservists, the general staffs planned their invasions and worked out their time-tables for the assembly of so many men at such a place at a given minute. This was the science that Germany taught the world.

France never forgot the lost provinces, and Germany knew that France never forgot. Bismarck had gained his ends and wanted no more war. But he feared his victim and dreaded her recovery. So quick was that recovery that in 1875 Bismarck was tempted to pick another quarrel and destroy the new French army before it could grow stronger—the typically German doctrine of 'the preventive war'. But England and Russia intervened, and he stayed his hand. In later years he sought to insure his gains by alliances, and so was formed the Triple Alliance of Germany, Austria, and Italy, pledged to come to one another's aid if attacked. Russia was at odds with Austria, and therefore France and Russia drew together in the Dual Alliance with a similar purpose. The aim of these alliances was peace, and they had a steadying influence; but on the other hand they made it certain that if once the peace was broken the whole continent would be involved. Statesmen were growing desperate and staking every life in Europe on their perilous diplomacy.

In the eighties the competition for possessions in the tropics grew keen. It was the consequence of the industrial revolution and the desire for monopoly in markets and raw materials. Bismarck did not think that Germany had much interest in colonies, but he skilfully encouraged the French efforts, for he saw that colonial questions were likely to raise disputes between France and Great Britain and so keep them apart. The reasoning was correct, and a period of bad feeling set in between ourselves and the French. In 1898 the Fashoda quarrel nearly provoked a war. In spite of Bismarck the younger generation of Germans insisted upon entering the colonial competition. Germany secured large shares of Africa and valuable Pacific islands, and at the same time developed her mercantile marine to carry on the new ocean trades.

To guard colonies and trade required a fighting navy; that was the teaching of history. Germany followed the tradition and spent large sums on battleships and cruisers. The German

fleet was the creation of the young Kaiser Wilhelm II, who came
to the throne in 1888 and dismissed Bismarck two years later.
He steadily built ships with the avowed object of making his
navy the equal of the British. He had a right to do so, and yet
it was a menace to peace. The German colonies were a smaller
interest than the British, and sea-borne imports were not a necessity of German life. Moreover, the British fleet has never in the
past century been used to gain unfair advantages; in the
colonial scramble of the eighties we could have insisted upon
much larger shares had we chosen to parade our sea-power.
For Great Britain, on the other hand, the sea-routes were the
arteries of life—once cut, the nation would perish. By building
a great navy the German Empire was placing itself in a position
to deal a mortal blow at a country which had always been its
friend; and the German record proved that force would be
used without scruple if the occasion arose. From about the year
1900 the German navy-plans began to excite British fears, and
the possibilities of a German invasion were frequently discussed.
Great Britain alone possessed no conscript army, and her small
forces would be overwhelmed by a mere fraction of the German
hosts if they could effect a landing. Novelists wrote imaginative
tales of the disaster in store, and writers in newspapers and
reviews were never weary of contrasting naval strengths and
counting up the rising totals of the battle-fleets. The German
navy increased at a faster rate than the British, and much of
the political rancour of the period 1906–14 was due to the fear
that money was being spent on social reform when it was needed
for the national defence.

The conditions of the age had produced this constant threat
of war. No single man or group of men was responsible. It was
the whole world's enterprise, more powerful and feverish than
ever before, constantly creating new problems and altogether
lacking any mechanism to solve them. The world's leaders
wished for peace, but the world was getting out of their control.
Some public men imitated the ostrich and refused to face the
peril that appalled them. War has become impossible, they
said; modern weapons will wipe out every man who faces them;
international finance has become so intricate that no country
can fight another with any prospect of advantage; the working
men of the nations are so permeated with socialism that if a
government declares war its people will not follow it. Arguments

of this sort poured from the press. They were mere doctrinaire dope, for the facts were otherwise.

Steadier minds sought to do something while yet there was time. King Edward VII, always popular in France for his personal qualities, used his influence to restore Anglo-French good humour. He made a state visit to Paris, and President Loubet made one to London. The Foreign Offices got to work and achieved the Entente Cordiale of 1904. All the irritating colonial disputes were settled by give and take, and the two democracies buried the hatchet amid toasts and compliments. In 1907 there followed a still more difficult achievement, an Entente with Russia on similar terms. But the Ententes did not ensure peace. They had dealt with the outer continents, the fringes of the problem. The affairs of Europe took a worse turn than ever. Germans saw their rivals drawing together. 'We are being encircled!' they cried, and they thoroughly believed it. They had the power of self-deception developed to a pitch that enabled them to view every situation in terms of their own innocent righteousness. A legend grew up, repeated to this day, that King Edward deliberately planned the destruction of Germany. In reality no man worked harder for peace than he. But it would have been criminal to ignore the German fleet and army, growing ever stronger as the years went by. France was outnumbered and needed black troops from Africa if the worst should come. The French fleet was stationed in the Mediterranean to cover their passage. The British fleet was concentrated in the North Sea or German Ocean. By 1914 peace was so balanced on a razor edge that the hand of one puny man could overthrow it.

A man did it. On June 28 a Serbian gunman shot the Archduke Francis Ferdinand, the heir to the Austrian throne. The Austrian government decided that now or never was the time to deal with the Southern Slavs, and particularly with these Serbians who had grown so strong in the Balkan War of 1912. It sent an ultimatum to Belgrade, in terms which would render Serbia a vassal state under Austrian domination. Serbia behaved meekly and accepted most of the terms but not quite all. Austria resorted to force, and mobilized her army.

Then it was seen that these great armies were an automatic mechanism which no statesman could control. Mobilization meant calling up the millions of reservists, serving out their kit and weapons, and entraining them to the frontier strongholds whence they could invade the enemy. It was a matter of two or three weeks, more or less, according to the railways available. At the end of that period the move across the frontier could begin, and if the enemy were not also mobilized, woe to him! Once a great power began to mobilize, its rivals must do the like—to neglect it might be swift ruin. Moreover, the quicker power had an advantage, two or three days or a week or even more. Once ready, it could not stand still for the rival to catch up. Invasion must begin the instant the army stood ranked on the border, or all the fruit of superior organization was thrown away. To give the order for mobilization was therefore the same thing as declaring war. It is clear that the statesmen only half realized this. They mobilized as a threat or a precaution, and then found that their generals were out of hand. The military machine of Europe bolted like a mad horse at the first touch of the spur, and none could stop it.

Austria began to mobilize on July 28, and Russia, Germany, and France all followed suit. As soon as they were in contact the covering forces began fighting on the frontiers, to seize favourable positions in readiness for the main armies to come up. Within five days of the Austrian move against Serbia, French and German patrols were exchanging shots in the Vosges. Behind them all Europe was getting into uniform. For the second time, and in utter disaster, diplomatic control had broken down.

The British government strove earnestly to keep the peace. The Foreign Secretary, Sir Edward Grey, sent note after note to the various powers, urging them to stay action and meet in conference. They could not do it. No country could trust any other country not to go on with military preparations during the discussions. Once war was in the air, the soldiers were everywhere stronger than their nominal masters the statesmen. When fighting began between France and Germany the French looked to England. What were we going to do? The Entente was not an alliance, merely an informal understanding. We were not bound in plain words to do anything. Yet the French said with truth that they had transferred their fleet to the Mediterranean with our approval, and on the understanding that the British navy would guard the northern coasts. If we stood aside, the Germans might sail down the Channel and land in France with none to stop them. The soldiers also had been making plans whose full meaning was not understood by some at least of the British ministers, and the French scheme of mobilization was based on the co-operation of the British army in northern France. To refuse it would be to throw the whole delicate combination out of gear. Without consciously intending it, the British people were bound in honour to play their part in the tragedy.

Grey warned the Germans that if their fleet came through the Straits of Dover it would be resisted. To persuade his colleagues and Parliament to a land campaign was a different matter. Here, however, Germany ensured a decision. The German armies were directed to march through Belgium in order to attack the French on their northern flank. Belgium refused consent, and her little forces stood up to a hopeless fight with the giant invader. In 1839—seventy-five years before—the governments of Great Britain, France, Prussia, Austria, and Russia had signed a treaty wherein they solemnly bound themselves to protect the neutrality of Belgium. The German Empire was the inheritor of the Prussian pledge, and could not honourably send a man across the Belgian frontier. The British ambassador protested, and the German Chancellor retorted that the treaty was only 'a scrap of paper' which could not stand in the way of military plans. To uphold a pledged word the British ministry, Parliament, and people almost unanimously went to war on 4 August 1914.

The war was not made by the men of 1914; it was made by the whole 'century of hope' that had gone before. It cost the British Empire a million lives lost outright and a million others permanently injured. It showed the inherent strength of the Empire by calling forth the loyal co-operation of all but a small minority of its peoples. It shattered the financial position of Great Britain by leaving us with a public debt greater than that of any other nation. It destroyed many illusions. The Germans had cherished the notion that the British were an unmilitary people who could never fight seriously on land; whereas by the closing year the British army was the strongest on the continent and did the hardest fighting in the final stages which broke the German power. The British on their side had been prone to believe that their navy had some God-given monopoly of talent on the sea; whilst in fact the Germans displayed good material and training and inflicted damaging loss on the victors in the Battle of Jutland, the only fight between the main fleets on either side.

At the end, after four years and three months of the most intensive devilry the world had seen, the Europe of 1914 had been destroyed, and in the fragments something different was taking shape. The German Empire became a republic. It lost Alsace and Lorraine, its share of Poland, and part of Silesia, But the real Germans held together. With poor allies they had put up a magnificent fight against numbers and had only broken in the end after sufferings greater than those of their opponents. Their spirit had been that of the Prussians of the eighteenth century. It is well described in Carlyle's *Life of Frederick the Great*. Carlyle's account of the Battle of Kunersdorf typifies the German record in the Great War—a triumphant attack, a long-drawn agony, and a collapse after the limit of resistance had been passed. The difference lay in the head. Wilhelm II was no Frederick, to seek death on the field when all was lost. He skipped over the frontier into neutral territory, and by so doing destroyed the hold of his dynasty upon the most monarchist people of the modern world. The Austrian Empire no longer existed. In its place stood a patchwork of states, amid which the Southern Slavs came into their own. The new national name Jugoslavia, and the large area it covered, illustrated the problem that had hurried the Austrian statesmen into war in 1914. The Russian czardom had also gone. Nicholas II and his family were obscurely done to death in a cellar in 1918—a contrast to the ceremonious guillotining of Louis XVI in 1793—and the Bolshevists ruled Russia with a terrible new version of the Rights of Man. Between Bolshevist Russia and mutilated Germany a whole series of new republics were struggling into life, the largest being that of Poland, whose fragments were reunited after more than a century of separate bondage.

Two motives governed the great settlement made at Versailles in 1919. The first was the victors' belief that the guilt of causing the war lay solely upon the Germans and their Austrian allies. The Treaty contained an explicit statement of that war-guilt, and the vanquished had to sign it. On that moral basis central Europe was remodelled, and Germany sentenced to pay the costs of all the combatants. The second motive was a determination that there should be no more war. The League of Nations was founded to deal peacefully with future disputes, and its covenant was embodied in the Treaty. The League was never joined by the United States, whose President had been its begetter. Russia in her militantly Communist phase declined to associate with non-Communist powers, but after Stalin's rule had succeeded that of Lenin she changed her decision and joined. The German Republic, after what was judged to be a sufficient term of moral quarantine, was admitted in 1926. All the other important powers had joined at the outset.

V. THE NEW BRITISH WORLD

In 1918, whilst the war was yet undecided, Parliament passed the Representation of the People Act, proposed by a ministry which contained members of all three parties, Conservative, Liberal, and Labour. The Act gave the vote to virtually all men over twenty-one and to women over thirty. Another measure of the same year enabled women to be elected members of the House of Commons. In 1928 the restriction on the women's franchise was removed, and they became entitled to the vote on the same terms as men. Democracy was thus made coincident with the whole adult population. Conditions had indeed changed since the last revision of the franchise in 1884. The war had called upon all fit members of both sexes to render service in some form to the national effort. Apart from war work, the family, with its womenfolk supported by the wage-earning male, was no longer the ordinary economic unit. The newer industry relied increasingly upon women workers, and they were more independent besides being more numerous than in the nineteenth century. For many purposes the family was split into its constituent individuals, and they were the units of the new society. The extension of the franchise was a recognition of the fact.

The outbreak of the war interrupted the hot dispute over the Irish question. John Redmond, the leader of the Irish Home Rulers in Parliament, supported the British cause, and his brother Colonel William Redmond was killed in action in Flanders in 1917. A few of the Irish Volunteers and nearly all the Ulster Volunteers joined the British armies, but the Sinn Feiners as a party stood aloof and worked for an independent Irish republic. The Home Rule Bill was passed by consent, but its operation was suspended until the claims of Ulster should be satisfied. At the outset no one expected the war to last as long as it did, and it seemed better to postpone a final settlement of Ireland until the coming of peace. The anti-British elements took advantage of the delay. In the spring of 1916 they concerted a rebellion, with money supplied from America and the promise of aid from Germany. Sir Roger Casement, a man who had served the state and accepted knighthood from the King, was landed from a German submarine. He was taken and executed, but the revolt broke out in Dublin. It lasted a week and cost a thousand casualties. Some of the ringleaders were executed, but the government acted both feebly and foolishly, and failed to inspire respect by its handling of the matter. The result was that Sinn Fein was greatly strengthened in the estimation of the Irish people.

In the closing year of the war Ireland was in a state of anarchy, a state which continued through 1919 and 1920. The Sinn Feiners described it as a war and themselves as a sovereign power. But their methods were those of assassins, and they never obtained the recognition of other nations. The British government on its side (a coalition of Conservatives and Liberals) displayed an entire lack of faith and principle. It denounced the Sinn Fein leaders as murderers, and ended by negotiating with them. In 1921 it offered to recognize the three provinces as a self-governing dominion of the Empire under the style of the Irish Free State. The terms were accepted and the new constitution was passed as an Act of Parliament in 1922. Two years previously Ulster had been placed under its own Parliament at Belfast. The long contest thus ended with the partition of Ireland into two units. The decision to grant a greater measure of Home Rule than ever Gladstone had proposed, and one without any safeguards for the unhappy loyalists of the southern provinces, was taken without reference to the electorate. It was followed by a further outbreak of violence in Ireland, where the new Free State government had to put down the republicans who still strove for complete separation.

Great Britain emerged from the war with a national debt of £8,000,000,000 or more than ten times as much as in 1914, and a further debt to the United States of £1,000,000,000, which in the main represented munitions supplied to the continental allies on British security. There was little hope of anything like full payment from France and Italy, and the British government would have been glad of an all-round cancellation of debts and credits. The United States was unwilling, and the British continued for ten years to pay interest on this vast sum until the world collapse of finance and currency in 1931 made continuance impossible.

For a year and more after the armistice a trade boom prevailed, with a brisk demand for goods at high prices. It was a temporary phenomenon caused by the resettlement of millions of people, many of them having money to spend in the shape of war profits or gratuities. Export trade was not brisk, and soon it appeared that industry was not absorbing the whole of the demobilized soldiers and war-workers. By 1920 unemployment had reached a high figure, and in that year a slump supervened on the short-lived boom. The trade slump became less acute but was not overcome during the rest of the decade, although by 1929 the position was so far improved that men imagined the bad times to be behind them and an age of prosperity ahead. Interest on debt, doles in relief of unemployment, increased expenditure on education, pensions, and other social objects maintained taxation permanently at a height undreamed of before the war.

The post-war period was one of social tension, not caused by class prejudice or privilege but by economic inequity. Men with long service in the forces had no wealth to show for it and had become, to the short view, disqualified for many civilian jobs. Others had gained high wages at home and had entrenched themselves in the best jobs. Others again had made huge profits in war-time business. The word 'profiteer' was coined to denote the latter class. Although perhaps his numbers and iniquities were exaggerated, the profiteer was nevertheless a reality. The finance of the first world war was fairly reckless. To pour out money was thought the best way to get things done, and there were opportunities for many to amass fortunes out of the common woe. After the war the profiteers were intensely unpopular, but nothing was done to make them disgorge; probably nothing could have been done without inflicting injustice on the innocent. The frustration of any possible attempt was largely due to the holding of a general election a month after the armistice, when the forces were not yet demobilized and were very thinly represented among the candidates. This election confirmed in power Mr. Lloyd George and the ministry which had presided over the winning of the war. The element of big business was strong in this ministry, and its newly returned supporters of 1918 were notably businesslike, described in an oft-quoted phrase as 'the Parliament of hard-faced men who looked as if they had done well out of the war'. The next election took place four years later, by which time the profiteers had successfully melted into the social mass.

These jealousies were added to the grievances of inflation. High profits and wages caused a demand for many goods that was greater than the supply. Prices rose steeply. Wages climbed after them, with strikes and threats of strikes and a widespread impression that the economic system was rotten and in danger of collapse. Society was split into warring factions striving not for ideals but for more spending-money and the things it would buy. The post-war tone was low, partly because many of the nation's best had been killed, partly because the governments of the period were headed by men whose method was rather to pander to the impulses of their constituents than to give a lead towards something better.

Three years of inflation having produced growing confusion, a reaction towards deflation set in. The government restored the British pound to the gold standard from which the war had forced it, while the great employers sought to diminish wages. Prices began to fall, which to many of the poor and the war-impoverished was a needed reparation; but the monetary change cut some of the demand for export goods and so increased the prevailing unemployment. Strikes continued, and the culmination came with the General Strike of 1926. The coal miners had stopped work in resistance to a cut in wages, and there was a good deal of public sympathy with them. The transport and distributive workers decided to strike in unison, not for any cause arising out of their own employment but to exert pressure upon the public to intervene on behalf of the miners. This was a general strike for a political object, something new in British affairs. After holding up transport and food supplies for nine days, the strike was broken by volunteer labour under the protection of armed force. In other words, the public, which supplied a sufficiency of volunteers, was against the strikers. It was the manifestation of a sound constitutional instinct. Most of the trade union leaders were not revolutionaries, but they had unwisely adopted a policy which forced them into that guise. They used phrases implying that they considered themselves a governing authority; and had they succeeded in overcoming the King's ministers a revolution would in fact have taken place. That would have meant the defeat of democratically elected government and a blow to the constitutional liberties slowly built up through the centuries. Many people, who were for the miners and considered them hardly treated, were against the general strike. Next year a new Act declared such strikes illegal.

The party politics and party leaders of the 1920's do not yield an inspiring record. The Lloyd George coalition which had gained a fresh lease of life by the election of 1918 broke up in 1922. It had shown itself lacking in principle in its handling of Ireland, and it had come within danger of a new war with Turkey. In other matters the strong business interest closely connected with it aroused suspicion that it was serving sectional before public interests; and this suspicion put an end to Mr. Lloyd George's political supremacy and ruined the Liberal party which in the main had followed his lead. The Conservatives withdrew in 1922 and gained a majority at the consequent general election. Bonar Law, a dying man, became prime minister for a few months, and was succeeded by Mr. Stanley Baldwin, who was Conservative prime minister in 1923 and again from 1924 to 1929. The Labour party at this time formally declared itself socialist and took a wide view of what the individual could expect the community to do for him. It was a criticism of Mr. Baldwin that though conservative in label he was socialist in practice, and that the creation of a socialist state went on whether he or his Labour opponents were in office. It was a belief among politicians that no party could remain in power without devising ever new programmes of benefits to successive sections of the electors. The crisis of 1931 was to prove that this cynical estimate was undeserved by the British people. Meanwhile it played some part in inciting Germany, Italy, and Japan to dreams of conquest by proclaiming to the world that in the opinion of its own leaders England was decadent. The Labour party was under the guidance of J. Ramsay MacDonald, a man more able as a political leader than as an administrator. He was prime minister with an insecure majority dependent on the support of the Liberals in 1924, and again took office in 1929 with a majority in which he was obliged to count the fifty-nine Liberals who were all that remained of that once dominating party.

After ten years of peace unemployment was still excessive, and there appeared no prospect that the great northern industries which had been the backbone of Victorian England would revive. Steel, coal, shipbuilding, and cotton were all depressed, and agriculture, which had come forward during the last war, was losing heart and withering away in the struggle against cheap imports. At the same time there was something approaching a boom in a variety of new manufactures such as artificial silk, gramophones and wireless sets, electrical goods and household appliances of many kinds, and, above all, motor vehicles, now cheap enough for mass sales. The new manufactures did not for the most part site themselves in the unemployed north, where rates were high and labour embittered, but in southern England, where the tone was more cheerful and the workers more amenable. The 'southward shift of industry', much noted at this time, was an effect of the long depression. The investing public, which had grown used to its losses in the heavy industries, was cheered by the new developments. About 1928–9 there was a rush of new capital issues, while at the same time the United States was experiencing a boom without any precedent. To many in England it seemed that prosperity was at hand. To many more, however, the gloom was unrelieved, and in the general election of 1929 the country half-heartedly decided that it had had enough of sham conservatism and would give avowed socialism a trial.

Five months after the return of Labour to office the American boom suddenly collapsed in a panic to which the South Sea Bubble of 1720 offers a historical parallel. Holders of stocks and shares were smitten with a contagious fear and rushed with one accord to sell. In a few hours speculators, small savers, and wealthy men became penniless. There followed a fall in the demand for goods, which deepened to an unprecedented depression, with unemployment on a scale never known before.

The British depression was slower in its onset and never as profound as the American, but it was easily the worst since that of the period after the Napoleonic War. It followed the American crash, but was not caused solely by it. The fundamental cause was extravagant national living in the ten years after the peace of Versailles. The war had entailed enormous expenditure of the capital which represented the saved-up energy and industry of the previous century of peace. Yet after the war the nation took things easily, worked less hard and enjoyed more luxuries, kept the unemployed quiet with substantial doles, and year by year spent unnecessarily instead of tightening its belt and wiping off debt. It was all done by an apparent enormous growth of capital, with larger incomes all round than before the war, and larger proportions of them taken in taxation for public purposes. But this capital was not, like that of 1914, the fruit of industry. It was mainly fool's gold produced by paper transactions rather than hard work. The whole world, which had really been impoverished by that first world war, was living dishonestly, spending beyond its means, juggling with currency, using principal to pay interest, looking forward to the right moment for repudiation. Germany was doing it, and Italy and France, the succession states of the Austrian Empire, the republics of Latin America. The British and the North Americans were not guiltless. The Wall Street slump was merely the lever that overturned structures already unsound. Every man knows that if he has spent all he had, and more, he cannot go on in as good a style, much less expect a higher standard of living. The British nation knew it in its heart, but was beguiled from facing the facts by its political leaders, Labour-socialist and Conservative-socialist, who would be popular at all costs.

The great depression came as a corrective, a stern instructor in economics. At first its seriousness was not realized. The American slump, it was hoped, would be temporary, and there seemed no reason why the British economic system should be deeply involved. The Labour ministers were not men of great experience in state affairs, and most of them were too old to be ready to grasp new conditions and form new plans. MacDonald believed in his ideals, but was poor in command of detail and management of colleagues. It was said of him that he would rather make a speech to a great audience than sit down to tackle an administrative problem. Philip Snowden, his Chancellor of the Exchequer, was probably the ablest man in the cabinet, but he was growing old and ill. The others were for the most part men of fixed opinions and short vision. They had come in to operate the policy on which their hearts were set, and they could not understand that all its props were falling as they pored over elaborations of its familiar theme. By the summer of 1931 the crisis arrived. Trade was falling off, hundreds of idle ships encumbered the ports, unemployment was increasing, expenditure going up, incomings to the Treasury going down. The budget was unbalanced, the Bank of England without sufficient reserves to support the currency, a run on the other banks distinctly possible, and all set for a collapse that would deprive taxpayers of the means to pay and the state of the means to disburse. Reform was urgent, or bankruptcy imminent.

Ramsay MacDonald showed himself a man of principle who thought first of the national safety. With a minority of his ministers and supporters he decided for a drastic reduction in expenditure on projects dear to his party. The majority refused to admit the necessity, cried out upon him as a traitor, and were ready to plunge together down to chaos. MacDonald formed a coalition with the Conservatives and the Liberal remnant, and there emerged a National Government with himself as prime minister and Baldwin as second-in-command. These two, who between them were largely accountable for the disaster, now took measures to retrieve it. They reduced expenditure on salaries to state and local government employees and on doles to the unemployed. They converted the interest on the great War Loan of over £2,000,000,000 from 5 per cent. to $3\frac{1}{2}$ per cent. They reversed ninety years of free trade by imposing protective duties on foreign goods in order to revive home employment. They abandoned the gold standard and thus stimulated exports by increasing the purchasing power of foreign currencies in terms of British goods. These measures restored first confidence and then by slow degrees prosperity, using that word in its comparative, post-1914 sense, not to be confused with the broad-based Victorian reality.

The cuts in doles and wages directly hit the greatest number of persons, and it was not until some weeks after they had been effected that Parliament was renewed. At the general election democracy gave an emphatic approval of the sacrifice by returning an enormous majority for the National Government. The protective duties and the currency measures caused some rise of prices, but unemployment began to diminish. The unemployment figures would have shown a still greater improvement but for the progress of industrial rationalization, which meant the overhauling of staffs and reduction of redundant employees by a more efficient allocation of duties. The reduction of interest on the War Loan, or, more strictly speaking, the paying-off of the 5 per cent. loan and its replacement by a new one at 3½ per cent., was in no sense a repudiation, being clearly permitted by the original terms of issue. On the whole, the country submitted with a good grace to a reducing treatment which it might profitably have undertaken ten years earlier.

In 1935 Ramsay MacDonald retired owing to failing health, and not long afterwards died. Mr. Baldwin became prime minister and dissolved Parliament before the end of the year. The general election confirmed the National Government in power. The country was substantially agreed on the domestic policy in progress, and the ministry had avoided giving prominence to the foreign affairs that were becoming increasingly threatening. It was time to look to the national defences, which had almost perished during the social extravagance and misguided optimism of the twenties. The Baldwin ministry knew this, or if it did not was culpably ignorant; but nothing was said about rearmament at the general election, which provided no mandate for that necessity to survival. Owing to lack of armed force and of a government which would resolutely create it, England cut a poor figure in her feeble attempt to divert the Italians from their conquest of Abyssinia in 1935–6, and was jeered at as decadent by the corrupt and hysterical rabble that constituted Mussolini's following. For two years, 1935 and 1936, nothing was done to arm the country against the growing peril of Germany's preparations for conquest. Those two lost years, courageously used, might have averted the war of 1939; at least it can be positively said that they would have shortened it. It is perfectly true that rearmament at that juncture would have been unpopular and that the country did not want to be told of its danger. Is that an excuse for a prime minister, whose high responsibility demands unflinching acceptance of facts? But before pursuing foreign affairs to their catastrophe this sketch requires some notice of events in the British Empire and Commonwealth.

The national distinctness of the dominions grew into nationhood by the sacrifices that they made in the first great war. Although they had long had undisputed control of their internal affairs, their foreign relations up to 1914 conformed with those of Great Britain and were directed, as a unity, by the King's ministers in London. This meant, among other things, that the dominions were bound by the British declaration of war. They all agreed in 1914 that war was just and necessary, but they desired in future to keep so momentous a decision in their own hands. The dominion share in the control of foreign policy was agreed in principle at the Imperial Conference of 1917 and established in the Treaty of Versailles at the close of the war. Canada, Australia, South Africa, and New Zealand all signed the treaty as distinct states and became individual members of the League of Nations. Their national independence was thus established. Their desire for joint and co-operative action was no less evident, and was satisfied by periodical meetings of the Imperial Conference and by free consultation on matters of general concern. No formal rules for such consultation came into existence.

Although the dominions were self-governing and in control of their own destinies, this was a matter of practice and was not explicitly stated in constitutional documents. British thought regards established practice as on a higher plane than that of a written constitution. But in the Commonwealth, notably in South Africa, there were holders of the contrary view, and to meet their wishes a formal statement was made, first by a resolution in Imperial Conference, and then by a parliamentary enactment. The Imperial Conference of 1926 resolved that 'Great Britain and the Dominions are autonomous communities within the British Empire, equal in status, in no way subordinate to one another in any aspect of their external or domestic affairs, though united by a common allegiance to the Crown, and freely associated as members of the British Commonwealth of Nations'. The Imperial Conference expresses desires and opinions, but has no legislative power. Legislation followed upon further work in the same direction by the Imperial Conference of 1930. In the following year Parliament passed the Statute of Westminster, whereby Great Britain divested herself of any powers to override dominion legislation or to make law for the dominions without their own consent. The Statute of Westminster did not create a new constitutional position. It gave formal definition to one that had been developing for half a century and had been complete since 1919.

The record of India during the same period was so full of incident and development that only its salient features can be noted here. Broadly speaking, the educated classes desired what they called self-government, which did not and could not mean what it means in a western democracy. It meant rather the government of the illiterate masses by the small minority of the educated. The British (again, broadly speaking) were willing to concede this power, but were anxious to delay the handing-over until there should appear some stable body of Indian political men with their position well rooted in the constructive activities of the country. Such men could be produced only by taking part in the administration and learning gradually to control it. To this end the British devised first the representative institutions of the reforms of 1909, then the dyarchy or mixed representative and responsible government of the Act of 1919, followed by the full responsible government in the provinces but reserved controls at the centre as set up by the Act of 1935. The progressive extension of self-government was possible because there was always a sufficient number of Indians ready to take office and learn the art of government, an art different from that of platform oratory. It was also due to the pressure brought to bear by the extremists who refused to take office and co-operate, but demanded full self-rule at once. They, notably under the inspiration of Mr. M. K. Gandhi, organized successive phases of passive resistance, rioting, and even terrorism, and in a sense hastened the movement towards dominion status. In another sense they retarded it, for there can be no doubt that if they had devoted their energies to more constructive ends both they and India would have been in a fitter state for them to exercise control in a shorter time. By 1940 a further extension to complete responsible government was in contemplation but had to await the solution of the problem of safeguarding the Indian minorities. These, of whom the largest were the Moslems, were not eager to be merged in a common democracy in which the caste Hindus would enjoy a permanent majority and might be expected to use it without much generosity.

The non-dominion and non-Indian parts of the Empire are generally classed nowadays as the colonies, although the word is completely misapplied to the majority of them. The true colonies of the modern Empire have become the dominions, and the present so-called colonies (with certain exceptions) contain few or no colonists, but are peopled by non-European races. Government is partly by British officials, who are not permanent residents, and partly by native authorities under British guidance. But there is no uniformity, and in some communities, such as Ceylon, Burma, and the British West Indies, the British type of electoral institutions prevails, with varying degrees of representative or responsible government. Some units are formally styled colonies, some protectorates, some mandates. Collectively they might best be described as dependencies. In the present century the clue to their history lies in the word trusteeship. Lord Lugard, one of the greatest of their administrators, has defined the purpose of rule in tropical colonies as the promotion of the benefit of mankind at large and also of the material and moral rights of the natives. Criticism in detail has been many-sided and well founded, although often the most experienced and accurately informed critics have displayed little sense of proportion in exposing defects. Criticism in principle is that control of one people by another, to however good an end, cannot be justified. The answer to that is a simple contradiction, that it can be and is justified in this imperfect twentieth-century world, where the weak cannot prosper without protection against political and economic marauders. Neither would international control be anything but a greater disadvantage. It would be a greater infringement of liberty yielding a less efficient administration. To control the controllers would be nobody's business, whereas under the British system the Colonial Office is under the vigilant eye of a Parliament that always contains unsparing critics. To place any aspiring people, with a capacity for progress, under international control would be to condemn them to an appalling hopelessness. British trusteeship is only a phase, and will probably merge gradually into some other relationship.

VI. THE END OF A HOPE

The League of Nations had been designed as a means to preserve peace, and its covenant was a part of the Treaty of Versailles. The use of the biblical word covenant was characteristic of a sanctimonious flavour that clung to the League's manifestations, at any rate in the British world, throughout its active existence. There was a tendency among its ardent supporters to exact unconditional adherence and to regard any questioning as heresy. The voting power behind this attitude impressed politicians and impelled them, as Lord Cecil has recorded, to pay the League lip-service while not really believing in it.[1] There was very little public study or understanding of the League's responsibilities, powers, or difficulties. Leading men of all parties combined to uphold it with speeches that were laudatory rather than instructive. The same quality was evident in many of the lectures sponsored by the League of Nations Union, an influential organization that was encouraged by the Board of Education to establish branches in the majority of the country's schools. In a war-weary England the promise of no more war was a gift-horse that few wished to scrutinize too directly; and so press and platform united in acceptance, critical voices obtained no hearing, and an agreed, non-political, semi-religious mantle was thrown over one of the most difficult of political undertakings, which called for cool study and unsentimental assessment of its every detail. 'We all say so, so it must be true' was the attitude of the writers and lecturers, and anyone who harboured doubts was suspect of ill will to peace. The deadly peril in all this was that public opinion was drugged and national defence failed to compete with more attractive claims upon expenditure. When, in the 1930's, armed aggression was rampant as never before, the British Commonwealth was not only physically disarmed but morally had lost its nerve, and was unable to take the lead for enforcement of order which the other well-intentioned peoples awaited.

In the 1920's the war-god slept the sleep of recuperation, from which on a not distant day he was to awake a giant refreshed. The interval was the League's opportunity, and the League lost it. It intervened successfully in disputes between some of the minor powers such as Sweden and Finland, but it did not solve the major problems left outstanding by the Treaty of Versailles. As time elapsed such a treaty was bound to need

[1] 'All or almost all the House professed support of the League; very, very few knew anything about it. Some of the Conservatives in their hearts disliked it, many disbelieved in it. Even the Labour members were at that time doubtful. The Liberals in the opposition were its best friends.'—A Great Experiment, by Viscount Cecil, London, 1941, p. 101, speaking of the year 1920.

revision for two main reasons, that it had been framed when
men's minds were not in a normal state, and that new developments in Europe resulting from the war had not been evident
in 1919 but were unfolding themselves in the succeeding period.
But the League did little. It failed miserably in its effort to
carry out one undertaking that was prescribed in the treaty,
that of all-round disarmament. Its deliberations at Geneva on
that subject were fruitlessly protracted and, while the world was
already ringing to the renewed clangour of Vulcan's forges,
died out in such futilities as discussing the calibre which entitled
a gun to be classed as an offensive or a defensive weapon. As
the new decade opened, Japan, a member of the League, committed with impunity a naked aggression on China, another
member, in the seizure of Manchuria. It was then evident that
the Geneva mechanism, not being backed by force and a
determination to use it, was no more effective than the old
pre-1914 diplomatic system. On the Manchurian question the
thorough-going British supporters of the League declared that
we should resort to force, although having none, and expect a
miracle to follow. Such a proposition, from those who had
consistently opposed national preparedness for war, evoked
little assent.

Meanwhile Germany was recovering. After a period of confusion and currency inflation, carried so far as to destroy all
old economic contracts, she stabilized her position and rede-
veloped her industries with the aid of loans from her former
enemies. With part of these loans she paid a small proportion
of the reparations for war damage due from her under the
Treaty of Versailles. Germany went through a liberal period
in the 20's, with a democratic republic that failed to produce a
strong administration. The economic blight smote it in 1930.
Markets and confidence withered together, unemployment
grew colossal, and there were no more loans to be had. In
three years these things killed the republic and carried Hitler
and his Nazis into power with a programme of efficiency,
rearmament, employment, and discipline. German self-esteem,
low in the 20's, was reconstructed by two main propaganda
assertions, that Germany had been the victim of aggression in
1914 and that the German army had not been defeated in
1918, but had been sold by traitors in the rear. The Germany
of the 30's was militarist and aggressive, teaching its people that

war was their trade, and getting ready for a war with a moral and material preparation so thorough that this time there should be no chance of defeat.

Of the former allies Great Britain and France refused to face the new peril. The French would not purge their politics of dishonest men, balance their budget by paying adequate taxes, or sink party differences in a national effort; instead of a resolute call to arms there was heard the voice of defeatism saying, 'We are no longer a first-class power: it is no use pretending that we can defend ourselves.' With the British it was not so much a shrinking from the menace as a refusal to acknowledge its existence. 'The Germans know what war means', we said. 'They can't be such fools as to want more of it.' British opinion did not believe the new Germany to be nearly so powerful as it was, and did not believe that the Germans really wanted war; and from this idle dream there was an awakening when it was almost too late. Italy, while fearing Germany, took occasion to gratify her own ambitions and to round off an African empire with bombs and poison gas. Russia looked doubtfully at the western powers and decided to rely on her own strength. The United States, enjoying a remoteness that was more apparent than real, sought isolation from European difficulties whilst commenting on European sins. Such was the attitude of the civilized powers to a resurgence of the beast which they could easily have crushed in its initial stage.

England followed the lead of Stanley Baldwin in preoccupation with domestic affairs, in a slothful optimism about the continent, and in resentful anger against men like Winston Churchill, who told the truth however unpopular it might make them. Nazi propaganda denounced them as 'warmongers', and more than half of England agreed with its enemy in crying down its own best men.

The League of Nations was moribund, for statesmen who had never had more than a half-belief in it had ceased to have any, and there was no prospect of the world co-operation against aggressors which was the essence of its being. The League of Nations Union in Great Britain was more active and influential than ever. In its 'Peace Ballot' of 1935 it secured several million affirmatives to a policy of continued support to the League, international limitation of armaments, and combined sanctions against aggressors. This was unexceptionable in the absolute,

but completely detached from reality. The United States had
never been in the League. Russia had just joined (in 1934)
after years of abstention, and there was no trust or friendli-
ness between her and the western powers. Japan, Italy, and
Germany were the actual or intending aggressors, although at
the moment still nominal members. The League thus consisted
for active purposes of Great Britain and France, both out of
condition and unfit for a struggle. To talk of further disarmament (in which the aggressors would naturally not be included),
and at the same time to propose provocative acts (sanctions)
against them was the depth of futility. The Peace Ballot was
organized by persons whose intentions were in the highest
degree pure and it was carried out by thousands of volunteer
workers who sought only the public good. It was interpreted
by disturbers of the peace to mean that the British public
shirked the issue, and while willing to wound was afraid to
strike; for no wrong-doer was by this date in any fear of what
the League might do. These and other manifestations of a
distaste for facing the hard problems of self-defence were
reported through the world as proofs of British decadence. And
such, to tell the truth, they were. The decadence was real, but
it had not gone too far for recovery. Its manifestations exaggerated its extent. They may have done some good in helping
to hasten the reaction, but they did incalculable harm in
encouraging the blackguards of Europe and Asia to believe that
they would meet with no opposition.

In 1937 Mr. Baldwin retired with an earldom, and Neville
Chamberlain became prime minister. His ministry covered the
period of transition from national flabbiness to a new self-respect
that was to produce great things under his successor. It recognized that the country's defences had been neglected and pushed
on with a programme of rearmament, although not on the
necessary scale. It accustomed the public to study the facts
of the European situation. It did not handle that situation
with firmness, and could not for lack of military power.
Chamberlain's Munich agreement with Hitler averted war for
the moment in 1938 and gained a year for rearmament. Some
measure of its value may be seen in Hitler's obvious chagrin
that the British had agreed to his terms. But whether Great
Britain or Germany made the better use of that year is doubtful.
Amid all the peril and preparation Chamberlain committed

one inexplicable error. In 1938, by an agreement with the Irish Free State, he surrendered the Navy's right to use the southern Irish ports, which had been of immense strategical value in the previous war. One may hope that the history of that transaction will some day be laid bare for the future guidance of public servants; and that the responsibility of the persons concerned will be placed on record.

From 1936 onwards aggression followed aggression: Italy against Abyssinia; Japan against China again; a civil war in Spain converted into a disguised international war, with Germany and Italy supporting one side and France and Russia the other; then the mutual adherence of Germany and Italy in the so-called Axis, and the final crescendo of armed seizures, of Austria, Czecho-Slovakia, and Albania. Italy alone could have been stopped without a great war even in the later stage; for her people, although well armed, were essentially unapt for military undertakings. Germany was different. A large part of her people were subject to a craving for war and to a belief that its evils could be made to afflict others but not themselves. They were eager to swallow any lie that fed their self-esteem, such as the denial of defeat in 1918 and the fable[1] of their Nordic blood and its superiority to all other. Unlike the Italians they possessed the military qualities, and they had a large class of officers born of officer-families who had done nothing but study war for generations. Of military training and battle-tactics these men had an inherited knowledge that had become an instinct and was not exhibited in so high a degree by any other military caste in the world. Added to this was a body of master-manufacturers capable of a vast industrial output and ready to place themselves at the service of a bid for world-domination; and, above all, in Hitler and his associates, a band of political leaders with a genius for dominating all men and for administration of great energies with speed and decision.

The new Germany developed swiftly after 1933, so swiftly that the civilized peoples, hating war, could hardly believe that the threat was serious before it was upon them. Civilization

---

[1] The features of the Nordic type described by anthropologists included a long and narrow skull. Observers who had never heard of the Nordic legend noticed a precisely contrary characteristic in the Germans: long before the days of enmity British merchant seamen were accustomed to refer to German shipmates as 'squareheads'.

was surprised by a gang of arch-criminals in command of a mainly criminal nation. However the responsibility for war in 1914 may have been divided—and there is no doubt that much more than fifty per cent. of it was Germany's—the guilt in 1939 was entirely German, and the mass of the German people supported their leading scoundrel with acclamation. They had caught their neighbours unprepared and were confident of great spoils easily gained.

INDEX

PRINTED IN
GREAT BRITAIN
AT THE
UNIVERSITY PRESS
OXFORD